The Bare Essentials Plus

SECOND EDITION

Sarah Norton
Brian Green
Nell Waldman

NELSON

THOMSON LEARNING ™

Australia • Canada • Mexico • Singapore • Spain • United Kingdom • United States

NELSON

THOMSON LEARNING

The Bare Essentials Plus
Second Edition

by Sarah Norton, Brian Green, and
Nell Waldman

Editorial Director and Publisher:
Evelyn Veitch

Acquisitions Editor:
Anne Williams

Marketing Manager:
Cara Yarzab

Developmental Editor:
Liz Radojkovic

Production Editor:
Sheila Barry

Production Coordinator:
Hedy Sellers

Copy Editor/Proofreader:
Susan Harrison

Creative Director:
Angela Cluer

Cover and Interior Design:
Sonya V. Thursby,
Opus House Incorporated

Cover Image:
Woodblock Type provided by
Dreadnaught Press

Illustrations:
Kathryn Adams

Compositor:
Bookman Typesetting Co.

Printer:
Transcontinental Printing Inc.

**National Library of Canada
Cataloguing in Publication Data**

Main entry under title:

Norton, Sarah,
    The bare essentials plus

2nd ed.
ISBN 0-7747-3752-2

1. English language—Composition
and exercises. 2. English
language—Textbooks for second
language learners. I. Green, Brian
II. Waldman, Nell III. Title.

PE1128.N67 2001   808'.042
C2001-901207-1

Preface

In the tradition of Harcourt's Essentials series of writing skills texts, *Bare Essentials Plus*, Second Edition, is designed for Canadian college students who want to learn how to write clearly and correctly, both for their college courses and for their professional lives. The Essentials series has been used by more than 400,000 Canadian college students since the first edition of *Bare Essentials* was published in 1980. This edition of *Bare Essentials Plus* builds on that experience, focussing on the skill-building needs of all college students, while addressing the special needs of second-language learners. We had three primary audiences in mind while developing this text: post-secondary students in classes comprised of both native speakers and second-language learners; advanced students in ESL writing classes; and students enrolled in individualized, self-paced learning programs.

This second edition of *Bare Essentials Plus* is a major revision of the first edition. Most of the examples, exercises, and tests have been revised and updated, and both text and exercises have been simplified to reach college students who are not quite prepared for a traditional first-year composition course. Despite these modifications, the book still contains everything a student needs to know to pass a typical first-year course, including how to write a college paper. There is also a new chapter that covers stylistic matters such as levels of language, pretentious language, slang, wordiness, and usage.

Bare Essentials Plus adds a new feature to the Essentials series: a diagnostic preview quiz at the beginning of each unit, (with the exception of Unit 5). The quizzes consist of short essays on topics of interest such as names or movie "bloopers." Students edit the "quick quiz" for errors that are dealt with in the unit. The answer key not only provides the correct answer, but also informs students which chapter they need to focus on if they miss an item. The addition of these quick quizzes makes *Bare Essentials Plus* an even more effective text for self-directed learning.

New to this edition is a Web site designed to support both teachers and learners (**http://www.essentialsplus.2e.nelson.com**). Students who need more practice than is provided in the text will find additional exercises and self-scoring practice tests, as well as additional readings, a write-in "Ask the Authors" feature, links to reference sites, and much more. The teachers' site offers teaching tips, sample syllabuses, answers to mastery tests in the text, and supplementary mastery tests for each chapter. The site also features

PowerPoint slides and transparency masters, reading and reference links, *The Essentials Test Manual* with comprehensive diagnostic tests and pre- and post-tests for each chapter and unit, as well as a writers' forum that is a direct link to the authors.

Bare Essentials Plus, Second Edition, takes the same basic approach as *The Bare Essentials Form A* and *Form B* in teaching writing skills, but adds instruction and exercises for advanced ESL students. Unit 6, "For ESL Learners: A Review of the Basics," completely revised from the previous edition, covers troublesome aspects for those coming to English from another language: verbs, plurals, articles, and prepositions. In Units 1 through 4, we have included instructions and exercises on points that ESL students find challenging, and have marked these sections with a special icon.

Like its predecessors, *Bare Essentials Plus*, Second Edition, covers the skills that are indispensable to effective written communication: organization, syntax, grammar, spelling, and punctuation. Each "essential" is presented as a discrete unit, and the units may be covered in any order (with the ESL-specific Unit 6 as a ready reference at all times). The chapters within the units, however, should be presented in the order in which they appear since the exercises within a unit are cumulative: those in later chapters often include questions that assume mastery of skills covered in earlier chapters.

Most of the exercises can be completed in the text, and the answers in the back of the book are easy to find. Students are instructed to check their answers immediately after completing an exercise. If they follow this instruction, they get immediate feedback on their understanding and can review the explanation, if necessary, before proceeding. **We urge instructors to emphasize the importance of this procedure.** If students complete an entire set of exercises before checking their answers, they run the risk of reinforcing rather than eliminating the error the exercises are designed to correct.

Bare Essentials Plus, Second Edition, is based on our experience that students learn to write clear, error-free prose if they understand the principles involved, master the principles through practice, and apply the principles in their own writing. We acknowledge that students will not learn unless they want to learn. We've tried to motivate them by beginning most chapters with a few words about the practical significance of what they are about to tackle. Complex material is presented in easy-to-follow steps. Most of each chapter is devoted to practice exercises; students are encouraged to do as many as they need to master the rule. We've tried to forestall boredom by appealing to the interests of Canadian students, by introducing a little humour, and by incorporating in each chapter exercises for which there is no one "right" answer. We believe that tests should be teaching instruments as well as measures of knowledge, and we hope instructors will use our "suggested answers" as the basis for classroom discussion.

Inside the front cover is a "Quick Revision Guide." Students can use it as a checklist to help them revise and edit their work. Instructors can duplicate the guide, attach a copy to each student's paper, and mark ✔ or ✗ beside each point in the guide to identify the paper's strengths and weaknesses. We strongly recommend this strategy. It saves hours of marking time and provides students with point-by-point feedback in a consistent format. On the back cover is a fold-out page presenting The Time Line: a diagram and a chart illustrating the correct use of English verb tenses. Students can see at a glance which tense is appropriate in a particular context.

Finally, we thank the hundreds of thousands of Canadian students and teachers who, for more than 20 years, have been our sharpest critics and staunchest supporters. This edition is a product of their suggestions, praise, criticism, and experience.

Acknowledgements

We would like to thank our reviewers: Rosemary Coupe, Capilano College; Nola Clarke, Mount Saint Vincent University; Marianne Glofcheski, Algonquin College; Philip Lanthier, Champlain College (Lennoxville); Jane Merivale, Centennial College; Joan Page, York University; and John Parkes, Centennial College, whose comments, criticisms, and suggestions helped to make this a more useful book.

Sarah Norton
Brian Green
Nell Waldman

A Note from the Publisher

Thank you for selecting *Bare Essentials Plus*, Second Edition, by Sarah Norton, Brian Green, and Nell Waldman. The authors and publisher have devoted considerable time and care to the development of this book. We appreciate your recognition of this effort and accomplishment.

Introduction

Why You Need This Book

Here's what a manager with IBM Canada had to say recently about the kind of employee they were looking for:

At the entry level, we're looking for people with excellent communication skills: reading, listening, speaking, and—above all—writing. It's much more efficient for us to teach a good communicator how to code than it is to try to teach a good coder how to communicate.

To an employer, any employee is more valuable if he or she is able to write well. No one can advance very far in a career without the ability to communicate clearly. It's that simple. Fairly or unfairly, no matter what field you are in, employers and others will judge your ability largely on the basis of your communication skills. If you want to communicate effectively and earn respect both on and off the job, you need to be able to write well.

That's the bad news. The good news is that you can improve your writing skills with time, care, and attention to the details of written language. If putting your ideas down in writing frustrates or intimidates you—for whatever reason—you need to work hard to master the conventions and the structures of standard written English. This book is intended to help you do just that. It provides simple, accessible explanations and plenty of practice to help you develop and improve your writing skills.

How to Use This Book

In each chapter, we do three things: explain a point, illustrate it with examples, and provide exercises to help you master it. The exercises are arranged in sets that get more difficult as you go along. After some of the exercises, you will find a symbol directing you to the *Bare Essentials Plus* Web site (**http://www.essentialsplus.2e.nelson.com**), where we have provided additional exercises for students who need extra practice. By the time you've completed the last set of exercises in a chapter, you should have a good grasp of the skill.

Here's how to proceed.

1. Read the explanation. Do this even if you think you understand the point being discussed.
2. Study the highlighted rules and the examples that follow them.
3. Now turn to the exercises. If you've found an explanation easy and think you have no problems with the skill, try an exercise near the end of the set that follows the explanation. Check your answers. If you get all the sentences right, skip the rest and go on to the next point. Skip ahead only if you're really confident, though.

   If you don't feel confident, don't skip anything. Start with the first set and work through all the exercises, including those on the Web site, until you're certain you understand the point. As a general rule, getting three sets in a row entirely correct demonstrates understanding and competence.
4. **Always check your answers to one set of exercises before you go on to the next.** If you ignore this instruction, this book can't help you. Only if you check your results after every set can you avoid repeating mistakes and possibly reinforcing your errors.[1] The answers to the exercises in the text are in Appendix C at the back of the book. The exercises on the Web site are self-scoring.
5. When you find a mistake, go back to the explanation and examples and study them again. Try making up some examples of your own to illustrate the rule. If you are truly stuck, check with your instructor. Continue with the exercises only when you are *sure* you understand. You can reinforce your understanding—and prepare for in-class tests— by doing the practice tests that you will find in the Study Guide on the Student Home Page of the *Bare Essentials Plus* Web site.

---

[1] You can cheat, of course. You can check out the answer for a question before doing it, or you can even look up all the answers before starting an exercise. If you do, you will waste your time (because you won't learn anything) and your money (because you will prevent the book you've paid for from helping you). If, however, you use *Bare Essentials Plus* as it has been designed to be used, we guarantee that you will improve your writing skills.

What the Symbols Mean

Occasionally, an exercise in the text will be followed by a Web icon and directions to go to specific supplementary exercises on the *Bare Essentials Plus* Web site. Once you've logged on to the Web site, click on the button that says "Study Guide," then click on "Exercises." The exercises are listed by chapter, so to get to the exercises for Chapter 2, for example, click on "Chapter 2" in the list and go to the numbered exercises identified for you underneath the icon. Your answers are marked automatically, so you will know instantly whether or not you have understood the material.

When this symbol appears in the margin beside an exercise, it means the exercise is a mastery test—an exercise designed to check your level of understanding of the principles covered in the chapter you've just completed. The answers to these tests are not in the back of the book; your instructor will provide them.

We've used this symbol to highlight writing tips, helpful hints, hard-to-remember points, and information that you should apply whenever you write, not just when you're dealing with the specific principles covered in the chapter containing the icon.

When this symbol appears in the margin beside a paragraph or an exercise, it means that the material is specifically designed to help ESL students master a point that many second-language learners find troublesome.

A Final Suggestion

On the inside of the front cover, you'll find the "Quick Revision Guide." Use it to help you revise your papers before handing them in. This book is meant to be a practical tool, not a theoretical reference. Apply the lessons in all the writing you do. Explanations can identify writing problems and show you how to solve them; exercises can give you practice in eliminating errors; but only writing and revising can bring real and lasting improvement.

Contents

UNIT 1

Spelling

Spelling

The following quick quiz will let you see at a glance which chapters of Unit 1 you need to focus on. The paragraph below contains 20 errors: spelling, capital letters, and apostrophes. When you've made your corrections, turn to page 421 and compare your version with ours. For each error you miss, the answer key directs you to the chapter you need to work on.

The Atacama Desert in the Northern part of Chile (which is in south America) is the driest place on Earth. It gets about one centimetre of rain each year. Amazingly, parts of the Atacama recieve no recorded rainfall at all—ever. Yet the dessert, in spite of it's dryness, is truely beautiful. The Atacamas landscape looks allot like the landscape of the moon, with craters, lose rocks, strange rock formations, and no vegetation. In fact, one of the uses of the Atacama is as a testing ground for the robot vehicles that explore the moon or Mars. If moon rover's in the remote Atacama can be controled from Houston or Cape Canaveral, chances are good that they can be equiped to maneuver on the moon. Most of the Atacama is uninhabited, but their are a few village's scattered here and there. The area has become

a popular tourist destination because of its dramatic desert landscape that
includes volcanoes; thermal geysers at a ~~hieght~~ *height* of 4500 metres in the Andes
Mountains; and unusual forms of wildlife such as pink flamingoes, vicunas,
and llamas. The Atacama Desert is a ~~lonly~~ *lonely* place that most of us ~~here~~ *hear* about
only in ~~Geography~~ *geography.* class. Travellers who venture as far as northern Chile,
however, are ~~completly~~ *completely* captivated by the ~~deserts~~ *desert's* unearthly beauty.

1

Three Suggestions for Quick Improvement

Of all the errors you might make in writing, spelling is the one that is noticed by everyone, not just English teachers. Misspellings can cause misunderstandings, as when an English teacher promised his students a course with "a strong *vacational* emphasis." (Those students who weren't misled wondered what he was doing teaching English.)

They can also cause confusion. Take this sentence, for example:

Mouse is a desert with a base of wiped cream.

It takes a few seconds to "translate" the sentence into a definition of *mousse,* a *dessert* made with *whipped* cream.

Most often, though, misspellings are misleading; they spoil the image you want to present. You want to be seen as intelligent, careful, and conscientious. But if your writing is riddled with spelling errors, your reader will think you are careless, uneducated, or even stupid. It is not true, by the way, that intelligence and the ability to spell go hand in hand. It is true, however, that most people think they do. So, to prevent misunderstanding, confusion, and embarrassment, it is essential that you spell correctly.

There are three things you can do to improve your spelling almost instantly.

1. Buy and use a good dictionary.

A dictionary is a writer's best friend. You will need to use it every time you write, so if you don't already own a good dictionary, you need to buy one. For Canadian writers, a good dictionary is one that is Canadian, current, comprehensive (contains at least 75,000 entries), and reliable (published by an established, well-known firm).

A convenient reference is the *Gage Canadian Dictionary*, available in an inexpensive paperback edition. It is the dictionary on which we have based the examples and exercises in this chapter. Also recommended are the *Canadian Dictionary of the English Language* (Nelson, 1997) and, for those whose native language is not English, the *Cobuild English Dictionary* (HarperCollins, 1995). Unfortunately, no comprehensive Canadian dictionary is available on the Internet.

A good dictionary packs a lot of information in a small space. Take a look at the *Gage Canadian Dictionary* entry for the word *graduate*, for example. The circled numbers correspond to the numbers in the list of information dictionary entries provide, which follows the entry.

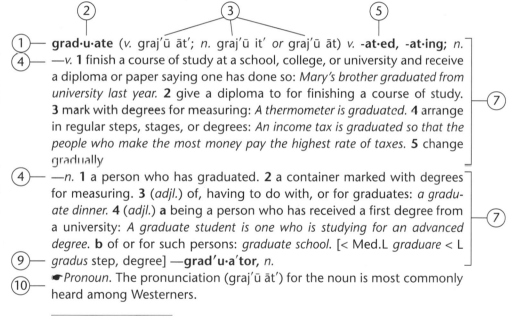

Source: *Gage Canadian Dictionary*. Toronto: Gage Educational Publishing Company, 1983. 508.

In a dictionary entry, you will find some or all of the following information.

1. **Spelling:** if there are two or more acceptable spellings, the most common one is normally given first
2. **Syllables:** to show you where hyphens can go, if you need to break a word at the end of a line

3. **Pronunciation:** if there is more than one acceptable pronunciation, the most common one is listed first
4. **Grammatical form(s):** e.g., noun *(n.)*, verb *(v.)*, adjective *(adj.)*
5. Any **irregular forms** of the word, such as the plural form of a noun, or the past tense and past participle of a verb
6. **Usage restrictions:** e.g., slang, informal, archaic, offensive
7. **Definition(s):** the most common meanings are given first, followed by the technical or specialized meanings, together with phrases or sentences illustrating how the word is used
8. **Idioms** using the word
9. **Origins** of the word (etymology)
10. **Other helpful information:** e.g., homonyms (words that sound the same as the entry word); synonyms (words that are similar in meaning to the entry word); antonyms (words opposite in meaning); and special variations in grammar, spelling, pronunciation, and usage

Unless you have already done so (and most people haven't) begin by reading the "Guide to the Dictionary." The information in the Guide may not be very entertaining, but it is essential if you want to understand how to read your dictionary accurately. No two dictionaries are alike. Each sets out its information a little differently from its competitors. Only if you are familiar with your dictionary's symbols, abbreviations, and the format of its entries, will you be able to use it efficiently.

Knowing what is in the Guide will also save you time. For example, you may not need to memorize long lists of irregular plurals. Good dictionaries include irregular plurals in their entries. They also include irregular forms of verbs, adjectives, and adverbs. And if you've forgotten how regular plurals, verbs, adjectives, and adverbs are formed, you'll find that information in the Guide as well.

Take half an hour to read the Guide in your dictionary; then do the following exercises. Be sure to check your answers to each set before you go on to the next. Answers for exercises in this chapter begin on page 421.

Exercise 1.1

1. What is another spelling of the word *humour*? Which spelling must you use when you add an ending such as *-ous* or *-ist* to the root word?
2. Is *harrassment* spelled correctly? Which syllable do you stress when you pronounce this word?
3. Is *tatoo* spelled correctly? Is the word a noun or a verb?

4. Are people who live in Saskatchewan more likely to experience a *tornado*, a *typhoon*, or a *tsunami*? Explain why.
5. Find alternative spellings for the words *programme*, *centre*, *skillful*, *traveler*, and *judgement*. In each case, indicate the spelling most commonly used in Canada.

Exercise 1.2

Write the plural form of each word.

1. ratio	6. data
2. criterion	7. mother-in-law
3. analysis	8. nucleus
4. personnel	9. appendix
5. crisis	10. formula

Exercise 1.3

Combine each root word with the ending given.

1. delay + ed	6. lonely + ness
2. journey + s	7. policy + s
3. play + er	8. easy + er
4. destroy + ing	9. lazy + ness
5. repay + ment	10. necessary + ly

After you have checked your answers to this exercise, go back and look closely at the questions. What do the root words in questions 1 to 5 have in common? What do the root words in questions 6 to 10 have in common? How do these similarities affect the way they are spelled when an ending is added?

Exercise 1.4

Using hyphens, show where each word could be divided at the end of a line. (Some words can be divided in two or more places: *po-li-tics*, for example.)

1. discuss	4. distribute
2. management	5. through
3. accommodate	6. chaos

7. solution

8. algorithm

9. conscience

10. business

Exercise 1.5

The following words are tricky to spell because they are not pronounced the way you might expect if you've had no previous experience with them. Look them up in your dictionary and, in the space beside each word, write out its pronunciation (the information given immediately after it in parentheses). Using your dictionary's pronunciation key to help you, practise sounding out each word, one syllable at a time. No answers are given for this exercise.

1. preferable

2. epitome

3. impotent

4. comparable

5. subtle

6. eulogy

7. indict

8. irreparable

9. corps

10. chassis

2. Get help!

In addition to your dictionary, there are three other resources you can use to help you turn a misspelled mess into a perfectly spelled document.

- The spell-checker in your word processing program. While far from fool-proof, online spellers are a reliable way to catch most typos and many misspelled words. Get into the habit of spell-checking every document before you print it.
- A hand held electronic spell-checker. Conveniently pocket-sized and not expensive, these devices contain a large bank of words and can provide the correct spelling if the guess you type in is not too far off. Some checkers even pronounce the word for you. Ask your instructor if you can use this device (with the sound turned off, please) when you are writing in class and during exams.
- A good speller. Some people seem to have been born with the ability to spell. They're usually proud of their talent and pleased to demonstrate it, so don't be afraid to ask. The time to seek their help is at step 3 of the revision process (see pages 304 and 305).

3. Learn three basic spelling rules.

If you *never* write except with a word processor, and if you *always* use its spell-check function, you can skip this step and go on to Chapter 2. If, however, like most of us, your job requires you to fill out forms and occasionally to write memos, notes, and messages in longhand, you'd be wise to review these three simple rules.

Ninety percent of English words are spelled the way they sound. Unfortunately, many of the words we use most frequently have irregular spellings, and no rule holds true in all cases. The three rules that follow do hold for most words, however. Mastering them will help you to avoid many common and potentially embarrassing errors.

Before learning the three rules, you need to know the difference between **vowels** and **consonants**. The vowels are **a**, **e**, **i**, **o**, and **u** (and sometimes **y**). All the other letters are consonants.

Rule 1
Dropping the Final *e*

The first spelling rule tells you when to drop the final, silent *e* when adding an ending to a word.

Drop the final, silent *e* when adding an ending that begins with a vowel.
Keep the final, silent *e* when adding an ending that begins with a consonant.

Keeping the rule in mind, look at these examples.

Endings Beginning with a Vowel	**Endings Beginning with a Consonant**
-ing: amuse + ing = amusing	*-ment:* amuse + ment = amusement
-ed: live + ed = lived	*-ly:* live + ly = lively
-able: like + able = likable	*-ness:* like + ness = likeness
-ible: force + ible = forcible	*-ful:* force + ful = forceful
-er: use + er = user	*-less:* use + less = useless

Exercise 1.6

In this exercise, combine each word with the ending to form a new word. When you have finished the exercise, check your answers.

1. safe + ly =

2. argue + ing =

3. love + able =

4. accelerate + ing =

5. extreme + ly =

6. improve + ment =

7. reduce + ing =

8. use + able =

9. immediate + ly =

10. require + ing =

GO TO WEB

EXERCISES 1.1, 1.2

Exercise 1.7

In the following exercise, add *e* in the blank space wherever it's needed to complete the spelling. If no *e* is needed, leave the space blank.

1. bor____ing

2. mov____ment

3. scarc____ly

4. unus____able

5. car____ful

6. advertis____ment

7. excus____able

8. provid____ing

9. sens____ible

10. improv____ment

GO TO WEB

EXERCISES 1.3, 1.4

Exercise 1.8

Make up sentences using the words you got wrong in Exercises 1.6 and 1.7.

EXCEPTIONS TO RULE 1

Three common words do not follow the rule.

argue + ment = argument
nine + th = ninth
true + ly = truly

There is one more exception to rule 1: after soft *c* (as in *notice*) and soft *g* (as in *change*), keep the final, silent *e* when adding an ending beginning with *a* or *o*. Here are two examples.

notice + able = noticeable
outrage + ous = outrageous

Rule 2
Doubling the Final Consonant

The second spelling rule tells you when you need to double the final consonant before adding an ending to a word.

When adding an ending that begins with a vowel (e.g., *-able*, *-ing*, *-ed*, or *-er*), double the final consonant of the root word if the word
  1. ends with a single consonant preceded by a single vowel
          and
  2. is stressed on the last syllable.

Notice that a word must have *both* characteristics for the rule to apply. Let's look at a few examples.

begin + er	ends with a single consonant *(n)* preceded by a single vowel *(i)* and is stressed on the last syllable *(begín)*, so the rule applies, and we double the final consonant:	**beginner**
control + ed	ends with a single consonant *(l)* preceded by a single vowel *(o)* and is stressed on the last syllable *(contról)*, so the rule applies:	**controlled**
drop + ing	ends with a single consonant *(p)* preceded by a single vowel *(o)* and is stressed on the last syllable (there is only one: *dróp*), so the rule applies:	**dropping**

appear + **ing**	ends with a single consonant *(r)* preceded by two vowels *(ea)*, so the rule does not apply, and we do not double the final consonant: **appearing**
turn + **ed**	ends with two consonants *(rn)*, so the rule does not apply: **turned**
open + **er**	ends with a single consonant *(n)* preceded by a single vowel *(e)* but is not stressed on the last syllable *(ópen)*, so the rule does not apply: **opener**

In words such as *equip*, *quit*, and *quiz*, the *u* should be considered part of the *q* and not a vowel. These words then follow the rule: *equipping*, *quitter*, and *quizzed*.

Note: There are a few common words ending in *l*, *s*, or *t* that, according to the rule, do not need a double consonant before the ending. Some examples are *cancel*, *counsel*, *focus*, *format*, *level*, and *travel*. In Canadian spelling, however, the final consonant is usually doubled: for example, *cancelled*, *counsellor*, and *focussing*.

The following exercises require you to combine each word with the ending to form a new word. Check your answers to each set before going on. If you make no mistakes in the first two sets, skip ahead to Exercise 1.11.

Exercise 1.9

1. plan + ing =

2. stop + ing =

3. admit + ed =

4. nail + ing =

5. stir + ed =

6. suffer + ing =

7. allot + ed =

8. write + ing =

9. map + ing =

10. interrupt + ed =

GO TO WEB

EXERCISES 1.5, 1.6

Exercise 1.10

1. prefer + ing =

2. omit + ed =

3. acquit + ed =

4. develop + ing =

5. control + er =

6. occur + ed =

7. equip + ing =

8. forgot + en =

9. replace + ing =

10. quiz + ed =

GO TO WEB

EXERCISES 1.7, 1.8

Exercise 1.11

1. defer + ed =

2. rebel + ious =

3. refer + ing =

4. concur + ed =

5. trim + ed =

6. subsist + ence =

7. differ + ence =

8. depend + ence =

9. recur + ence =

10. insist + ence =

When it comes to adding -ence, three words are especially troublesome. *Prefer*, *refer*, and *confer* all appear to require a doubled final consonant. But they don't because, when you add -ence, the stress shifts to the first syllable of the word.

prefér	preférring	*but*	préference
refér	reférring	*but*	réference
confér	conférring	*but*	cónference

Exercise 1.12

Find and correct the eight spelling errors in this paragraph.

Although I am just a beginer, I am finding cooking to be a compeling new

skill. For many years, I have sufered from eating frozen dinners that look delicious in the pictures on the packages, but look and taste disgusting when transfered from freezer to plate. Now I am rebeling against packaged slop, and making truely delicious meals from scratch. If you have a preferrence for nutritious, tasty, and attractive meals, I suggest you stop paying outragous amounts for pre-packaged food, and start cooking.

Exercise 1.13

Make up sentences using the words you got wrong in Exercises 1.9 through 1.12.

Rule 3
Words Containing *ie* or *ei*

There are almost a thousand common English words containing *ie* or *ei*, so remembering the rule that governs them is worthwhile. It helps to keep in mind that *ie* occurs approximately twice as often as *ei*.

The old rhyme tells you most of what you need to know to spell these words.

> Write *i* before *e*, except after *c*,
> or when sounded like *a*, as in *neighbour* and *weigh*.

If you remember this rhyme, you'll have no difficulty in spelling words such as *belief, piece, ceiling, receive,* and *freight*.

Unfortunately, the rhyme covers only two of the cases in which we write *e* before *i*: after *c*, and when the syllable is pronounced with a long *ā* sound. So we need an addition to the rule.

> If short *ĕ* or long *ī* is the sound that is right,
> write *e* before *i*, as in *their* or in *height*.

This rule covers words such as *Fahrenheit, seismic, heir,* and *leisure* (pronounce it to rhyme with *pleasure*). *Either* and *neither* can be pronounced "eye-ther" and "nye-ther," so they too require *ei*.

There are, of course, exceptions. This silly sentence contains the most common ones.

A *weird species* of *sheik seized caffeine, codeine,* and *protein.*

These exercises will help you to master *ie* versus *ei*. Fill in the blanks with *ie* or *ei*. After you finish each set, check your answers.

Exercise 1.14

1. br____f

2. cash____r

3. rec____ve

4. p____rce

5. rel____f

6. retr____ve

7. c____ling

8. misch____vous

9. dec____tful

10. hyg____ne

GO TO WEB

EXERCISE 1.9

Exercise 1.15

1. I'd give you a p__ce of my mind, but I don't have enough to spare.

2. N__ther of us seems able to keep e-mail messages br__f.

3. With his new l__sure time, my father hopes to travel to for__gn countries.

4. That spec__s was __ther unknown or wrongly identified.

5. If I drink any more caff__ne, you'll have to help me down from the c__ling.

6. She has a w__rd and misch__vous sense of humour.

7. "S__ze the day" is a saying that I bel__ve in.

8. My new d__t consists mostly of prot__n, with a little starch for rel__f.

9. You're dec__ving yourself if you think you'll lose w__ght on that menu.

10. Occasionally my n__ghbour and I get together over a couple of st__ns of beer.

Exercise 1.16

Find and correct the ten spelling errors in the following paragraph.

My freind Sunil and I decided to go south for the spring break. At the last minute, our roommate, Wierd Wayne, decided to join us. We all beleived that a week's vacation would do us far more good than staying at home and studying. Unfortunately, our holiday experience was not quiet the liesurely getaway we had planned. Our first near disaster occured at the airport, where the police threatened to sieze Yvonne's luggage because her high-tech hair dryer looked on the x-ray machine like a bomb. In Florida we all got sick from eating tainted weiners at a hot dog stand, and we all got sunburned lying on the beach. Niether Sunil nor Wayne can beleive me when I say I'm going again next year.

GO TO WEB

EXERCISE 1.10

There are three or four more spelling rules we could explain here, but we won't—for two reasons. First, there are many exceptions to the remaining rules for English spelling. And second, you don't need to memorize more rules if you use your dictionary and a spell-checker.

Exercise 1.17

This exercise, which contains 20 errors, will test your mastery of the spelling rules you've worked through in this chapter. It would be a good idea to review the three rules before attempting this exercise. You won't find the answers to this or the other mastery tests in the back of the book. Please ask your instructor to provide them to you.

There can be no arguement that television has led to many improvments in our society. The movment away from smokeing is a good example because, when characters on TV stoped useing cigarettes, the habit became noticably less acceptable to veiwers. Given the impact of television on our opinions and behaviour, it is concievable that now is the time to use television to influence our managment of democracy. Now that "reality-based" shows are using voteing to determine a group's preferrence for who stays in a group and who goes, why don't we begin transfering this idea to the workplace or even the family? Far from being a wierd or outragous suggestion, this is truely an idea that should recieve consideration for the Nobel peace prize. By permitting the members of a group—for example, a classroom—to vote to have certain individuals bared from attending, we would be actively demonstrating our beleif in the principles of democracy!

2

Sound-Alikes,
Look-Alikes,
and Spoilers

Using a dictionary and a spell-checker, asking for help, and applying the three spelling rules will make an immediate improvement in your writing. Two additional suggestions will further increase your spelling accuracy, but the skills involved take longer to master. First, learn to tell apart words that are often confused because they look or sound alike. Second, learn the correct spellings of the words most people find troublesome—words we have called spelling spoilers. A word processor won't help you with the first task, but it will with the second—so long as you remember *always* to spell check your document before printing it.

Sound-Alikes and Look-Alikes

There's a poem that was widely circulated on the Web not so long ago. It begins like this:

> Eye halve a spelling chequer
> It came wit my pea sea
> It plainly marques four my revue
> Miss steaks eye kin knot sea.

The point of this epic rhyme (it goes on for about 40 lines) is that spell-checkers can't correct spelling mistakes they can't find. All the words in the poem are correctly spelled; they're just the wrong words for the context. To a reader, these words might as well be misspelled because they have the same effects: difficulty in understanding, confusion about meaning, and a very unfavourable impression of the writer!

Below you will find a list of the sound-alikes and look-alikes that writers most commonly misuse. Careful pronunciation sometimes helps to correct this problem. For example, if you pronounce the words *accept* and *except* differently, you'll be less likely to confuse them in your writing. It's also useful to make up memory aids to help yourself remember the difference in meaning between words that sound or look alike.

Only some of the words from the list below will cause you trouble. Make your own list of problem pairs and keep it where you can refer to it whenever you write. For example, tape it inside your dictionary, or post it over your computer. Get into the habit of checking your document against this list every time you write.

accept
except

Accept means "take." It is always a verb. *Except* means "excluding."

> I **acc**epted the spelling award, and no one **ex**cept my mother knew I cheated.

advice
advise

The difference in pronunciation makes the difference in meaning clear. *Advise* (rhymes with *wise*) is a verb. *Advice* (rhymes with *nice*) is a noun.

> I *advise* you not to listen to free *advice*.

affect
effect

Affect as a verb means "change." Try substituting *change* for the word you've chosen in your sentence. If it makes sense, then *affect* is the word you want. As a noun, it means "a strong feeling." *Effect* is a noun meaning "result." If you can substitute *result*, then *effect* is the word you need. Occasionally, *effect* is used as a verb meaning "to bring about."

> Learning about the *effects* (results) of caffeine *affected* (changed) my coffee-drinking habits.
> Depressed people often display inappropriate *affect* (feelings).
> Antidepressant medications can *effect* (bring about) profound changes in mood.

a lot
allot

A lot (often misspelled *alot*) should be avoided in writing. Use *many* or *much* instead. *Allot* means "distribute" or "assign."

>   *many*   *much*
> He still has ~~a lot of~~ problems, but he's coping ~~a lot~~ better.
> The teacher will *allot* the marks according to the difficulty of the questions.

allusion
illusion

An *allusion* is an implied or indirect reference. An *illusion* is something that appears to be real or true but it is not what it seems. It can be a false impression, idea, or belief.

> Many literary *allusions* can be traced to the Bible or to Shakespeare.
> A good movie creates an *illusion* of reality.

are
our

Are is a verb. *Our* shows ownership. Confusion of these two words often results from careless pronunciation.

> Where *are our* leaders?

beside
besides

Beside is a preposition meaning "by the side of" or "next to." *Besides* means "also," or "in addition to."

> One evening with Mario was more than enough. *Besides* expecting me to buy the tickets, the popcorn, and the drinks, he insisted on sitting *beside* Lisa rather than me.

choose
chose

Pronunciation gives the clue here. *Choose* rhymes with *booze*, is a present tense verb, and means "select." *Chose* rhymes with *rose*, is a past tense verb, and means "selected."

> Please *choose* a topic.
> I *chose* to design my own Web page.

cite
sight
site

To *cite* means "to quote from" or "to refer to."

> A lawyer *cites* precedents; writers *cite* their sources in articles or research papers; and my friends *cite* my essays as examples of brilliant writing.

Sight is the ability to see, or something that is visible or worth seeing.

> She lost her *sight* as the result of an accident.
> With his tattoos and piercings, Izzy was a *sight* to behold.

A *site* is the location of something: a building, a town, or an historic event.

> The *site* of the battle was the Plains of Abraham, which lies west of Quebec City.

coarse **course**	*Coarse* means "rough, unrefined." (Remember: the slang word ***arse*** is co**arse**.) For all other meanings, use *course*.

> That sandpaper is too *coarse* to use on a lacquer finish.
> *Coarse* language only weakens your argument.
> Of *course* you'll do well in a *course* on the history of pop music.

complement **compliment**	A *complement* completes something. A *compliment* is a gift of praise.

> A glass of wine would be the perfect *complement* to the meal.
> Some people are embarrassed by *compliments*.

conscience **conscious**	Your *conscience* is your sense of right and wrong. *Conscious* means "aware" or "awake"—able to feel and think.

> After Ann cheated on the test, her *conscience* bothered her.
> Ann was *conscious* of having done wrong.
> The injured man was *unconscious*.

consul **council** **counsel**	A *consul* is a government official stationed in another country. A *council* is an assembly or official group. Members of a *council* are *councillors*. *Counsel* can be used to mean both "advice" and "to advise."

> The Canadian *consul* in Venice was very helpful.
> The Women's Advisory *Council* meets next month.
> Maria gave me good *counsel*.
> She *counselled* me to hire a lawyer.

desert **dessert**	A *désert* is a dry, barren place. As a verb, *desért* means "to abandon" or "to leave behind." *Dessért* is the part of a meal you'd probably like an extra helping of, so give it an extra *s*.

> The tundra is Canada's only *desert* region.
> If you *desert* me, I'll be all alone.
> I can't resist any *dessert* made with chocolate.

dining
dinning

You'll spell *dining* correctly if you remember the phrase "wining and dining." You'll probably never use *dinning*. It means "making a loud noise."

> The dog is not supposed to be in the *dining* room.
> We are *dining* out tonight.
> The sounds from the karaoke bar were *dinning* in my ears.

does
dose

Pronunciation provides the clue. *Does* rhymes with *buzz* and is a verb. *Dose* rhymes with *gross* and refers to a quantity of medicine.

> Josef *does* drive fast, *doesn't* he?
> My grandmother used to give me a *dose* of cod liver oil every spring.

forth
fourth

Forth means "for**th**ward." *Fourth* contains the number **four**, which gives it its meaning.

> Please stop pacing back and *forth*.
> The Raptors lost their *fourth* game in a row.

hear
here

Hear is what you do with your **ear**s. *Here* is used for all other meanings.

> Now *hear* this!
> Ranjan isn't *here*.
> *Here* is your assignment.

imply
infer

A speaker or writer *implies*; a listener or reader *infers*. To *imply* is to hint or say something indirectly. To *infer* is to draw a conclusion from what is stated or hinted at.

> Our instructor *implied* that we should have done better on the test.
> We *inferred* that he was disappointed with us.

it's
its

It's is a shortened form of *it is*. The apostrophe takes the place of the *i* in *is*. If you can substitute *it is,* then *it's* is the form you need. If you can't substitute *it is,* then *its* is the correct word.

> *It's* really not difficult. (*It is* really not difficult.)
> The book has lost *its* cover. ("The book has lost *it is* cover" makes no sense, so you need *its*.)

It's is also commonly used as the shortened form of *it has*. In this case, the apostrophe takes the place of the *h* and the *a*.

> *It's* been a bad month for software sales.

later
latter

Later refers to time and has the word **late** in it. *Latter* means "the second of two" and has two *t*'s. It is the opposite of *former*.

> It is *later* than you think.
> You take the former, and I'll take the *latter*.

lead
led

Lead is pronounced to rhyme with *speed* and is the present tense of the verb *to lead*. (*Led* is the past tense of the same verb.) The only time you pronounce *lead* as "led" is when you are referring to the soft, heavy, grey metal used to make bullets or leaded windows.

> You *lead,* and I'll decide whether to follow.
> Your suitcase is so heavy it must be filled with either gold or *lead*.

loose
lose

Pronunciation is the key to these words. *Loose* rhymes with *goose* and means "not tight" or "unrestricted." *Lose* rhymes with *ooze* and means "misplace" or "be defeated."

There's a screw *loose* somewhere.
The graduates are about to be turned *loose* on the job market.
Some are born to win, some to *lose*.
You can't *lose* on this deal.

miner
minor

A *miner* works in a **mine**. *Minor* means "lesser" or "not important." For example, a *minor* is a person of less than legal age.

Liquor can be served to *miners*, but not if they are *minors*.
For some people, spelling is a *minor* problem.

moral
morale

Again, pronunciation provides the clue you need. *Móral* refers to the understanding of what is right and wrong. *Morále* refers to the spirit or mental condition of a person or group.

Most religions are based on a *moral* code of behaviour.
Despite his shortcomings, he is basically a *moral* man.
Low *morale* is the reason for our employee's absenteeism.

peace
piece

Peace is what we want on **Earth**. *Piece* means a part or portion of something, as in "a **pie**ce of **pie**."

Everyone hopes for *peace* on Earth.
A *piece* of the puzzle is missing.

personal
personnel

Personal means "private." *Personnel* refers to the group of people working for a particular employer or to the office responsible for maintaining employees' records.

The letter was marked "*Personal* and Confidential."
We are fortunate in having highly qualified *personnel*.
Yasmin works in the *Personnel* Office.

principal **principle**	*Principal* means "main." A *principle* is a rule. A *principal* is the main administrator of a school. The federal government is Summerside's *principal* employer. The *principal* and the interest totalled more than I could pay. (In this case, the principal is the main amount of money.) One of our instructor's *principles* is to refuse to accept late assignments.
quiet **quite**	If you pronounce these words carefully, you won't confuse them. *Quiet* has two syllables; *quite* has only one. The chairperson asked us to be *quiet*. We had not *quite* finished our assignment.
stationary **stationery**	*Stationary* means "fixed in place." *Stationery* is writing paper. Did you want a laptop or *stationary* computer? Please order a new supply of *stationery*.
than **then**	*Than* is used in comparisons: bigger than, better than, slower than, etc. Pronounce it to rhyme with *can*. *Then* refers to time and rhymes with *when*. Karim is a better speller *than* I. I'd rather be here *than* there. Once you have paid, *then* you can have my notes.
their **there** **they're**	*Their* indicates ownership. **There** points out something or indicates place. It includes the word **here**, which also indicates place. *They're* is a shortened form of *they are*. (The apostrophe replaces the *a* in *are*.) It was *their* fault. *There* are two weeks left in the term. Let's walk over *there*. *They're* late, as usual.

too **two** **to**	The *too* with an extra *o* in it means "more than enough" or "also." *Two* is the number after one. For all other meanings, use *to*.

> It's *too* hot, and I'm *too* tired *to* go for another hike.
> There are *two* sides *to* every argument.
> The *two* women knew *too* much about each other *to* be friends.

were **where** **we're**	If you pronounce these three carefully, you won't confuse them. *Were* rhymes with *fur* and is a verb. *Where* is pronounced "hwear," includes the word **here**, and indicates place. *We're* is a shortened form of *we are* and is pronounced "weer."

> You *were* joking, *weren't* you?
> *Where* did you want to meet?
> *We're* on our way.

who's **whose**	*Who's* is a shortened form of *who is* or *who has*. If you can substitute *who is* or *who has* for the *who's* in your sentence, then you have the right spelling. Otherwise, use *whose*.

> *Who's* coming to dinner? (*Who is* coming to dinner?)
> *Who's* been sleeping in my bed? (*Who has* been sleeping in my bed?)
> *Whose* paper is this? ("*Who is paper*" makes no sense, so you need *whose*.)

woman **women**	Confusing these two is guaranteed to irritate your women readers. *Woman* is the singular form; compare **man**. *Women* is the plural form; compare ***men***.

> One *woman* responded to our ad.
> The affirmative action policy promotes equality between *women* and men.

you're **your**	*You're* is a shortened form of *you are*. If you can substitute *you are* for the *you're* in your sentence, then you're using the correct form. If you can't substitute *you are,* use *your*.

> *You're* welcome. (*You are* welcome.)
> Unfortunately, *your* hamburger got burned. ("*You are* hamburger" makes no sense, so *your* is the word you want.)

In the exercises that follow, choose the correct word in each pair. There are ten corrections in each of the first five exercises. If you don't know an answer, go back and reread the explanation. Check your answers after each set. Answers for exercises in this chapter begin on page 423.

Exercise 2.1

1. This is a (coarse course) that I should be able to pass easily.
2. My sister is a (woman women) who (hears heres) everything and remembers even more.
3. We need (piece peace) in order to concentrate.
4. Do you suppose (they're their) still sick from eating (to too) much?
5. It certainly is (quiet quite) once (your you're) roommates leave for school.
6. I'd like to (lose loose) four kilos by New Year's, but I can't resist (deserts desserts).

Exercise 2.2

1. (Its It's) the wrong (sight site) for a house, but it might work for a barn.
2. If you submit your assignment any (later latter), the professor won't (except accept) it.
3. Our (moral morale) is so low, we wouldn't recognize a (compliment complement) if someone gave us one.
4. It is in (their they're) best interest to recognize the (affects effects) of bad eating habits.
5. It was the (fourth forth) quarter of the game, and we (led lead) by 20 points.

GO TO WEB

EXERCISES 2.1, 2.2

Exercise 2.3

1. Is there anyone (who's whose) (advise advice) you would listen to?
2. (You're Your) confidence in your own superiority is an (allusion illusion).
3. Occasionally, my (conscience conscious) bothers me when I send (personal personnel) e-mails on the office computer.
4. (A lot Allot Much) of the time, we decide (whose who's) going first by flipping a coin.
5. Are the political party's (principles principals) more important (than then) its desire to get elected?

Exercise 2.4

1. We (lead led) them to the (site sight) of the old mine.
2. She (sited cited) my essay when she spoke about the (affects effects) of poor grammar.
3. I will (except accept) your (council counsel) if you can provide me with proof of what you say.

4. Were you still (conscious conscience) after falling off your (stationery stationary) bicycle?
5. We were (lead led) into the (dining dinning) room by the maitre d'.

GO TO WEB

EXERCISES 2.3, 2.4

Exercise 2.5

1. No (women woman) is going to be impressed by your insincere (complements compliments).
2. "Buy low, sell high" is one of my (principals principles); (beside besides), it makes money.
3. Are you (implying inferring) that I should (choose chose) another career goal?
4. I would rather have my shirt collar too (lose loose) (than then) too tight.
5. As a (minor miner) she isn't allowed to have icewine with her (dessert desert).

GO TO WEB

EXERCISE 2.5

Exercise 2.6

Find and correct the 16 errors in the following sentences.

1. Most people's ability to learn is effected by they're personnel well-being.
2. I'd much rather write a 2,000 word essay then do an oral report in front of our class.
3. During my six month review, my supervisor inferred that I would do better to chose another line of work.
4. Their will be no piece in are office until moral improves.
5. The principle causes of the moral problem are to much overtime and too few "perks."
6. The advise given us by the personnel firm we hired was to appoint a women whose only qualifications were a huge ego and shoes that complimented her every outfit.

Find and correct the ten errors in this paragraph.

I had a hard time chosing between two colleges, both of which offered the coarses I wanted. Both had good placement records, and I just couldn't make up my mind. I asked my friends for advise, but they were no help. Several were surprised that any college would even except me. Their negative view of my academic ability did nothing to improve my moral; in fact, it lead me to re-evaluate my selection of friends. My school councillor, a women who's opinion I respect, didn't think one college was better then the other, so she suggested that I choose the school that was located where I preferred to live. I followed her advice, and I haven't regretted it.

Find and correct the 15 errors in this paragraph.

Many people today are chosing a quieter way of life, hoping to live longer and more happily by following the "slower is better" principal. Some, on the advise of they're doctors, have been forced to slow down. One heart surgeon, for example, tells his patients to drive only in the slow lane rather then use the passing lane. They may arrive a few minutes later, but their blood pressure will not be effected. Others don't need to be prompted by their doctors. They except that living at a slower pace doesn't mean loosing out in any way. In fact, the opposite is true: choosing a healthy lifestyle benefits everyone. The affect of increased piece and quite in your person-

nel life leads to increased productivity, higher moral, and greater job satis-

faction. Sometimes the improvements are miner, but as anyone who has

consciencely tried to slow the pace of life can tell you, the slow lane is the

fast lane to longevity.

Exercise 2.9

Below is a list of word pairs that are often confused. Use each word in a sentence that clearly differentiates the word from its sound-alike or look-alike. Use
your dictionary to help you. When you are finished, exchange papers with
another student and check each other's work.

1. altar, alter
2. breath, breathe
3. capital, capitol
4. stake, steak
5. waist, waste

6. cite, site
7. cloths, clothes
8. emigrate, immigrate
9. hoard, horde
10. precede, proceed

Exercise 2.10

This exercise is more challenging. All the words in the following paragraph are
correctly spelled. The problem is that 20 of them are the wrong words—they
don't mean what the writer intended. Can you solve the puzzle by supplying
the right words?

Its latter than you think! As miners, we imagine that time goes on for-

ever, and are options are unlimited. Than, as we get older and begin taking

postsecondary coarses, we learn that its necessary to chose, and that their

are some things in life we will never experience. We are confronted with

decisions—some personnel, some professional—that will effect were our

lives led us. Often the council and advise of others can help us make good decisions, but these decisions are still difficult. When were young, its hard to except that we can't do everything we want to do. Now, however, is the time to set our sites on realistic goals, ones that will carry us through the rest of are lives.

Spelling Spoilers

Here is a list of words that are frequently misspelled. Have someone dictate the list to you. Circle the ones you misspell and memorize them, a few at a time. Try to learn ten each week. Review your list often, until you have mastered every word. Making up memory aids for especially troublesome words will help you to conquer them. Here are some examples to get you started.

accommodate	It means "make room for," and the word itself makes room for two *c*'s and two *m*'s.
business	*Business* is no **sin**.
environment	The word *environment*, like the earth, has **iron** in it.
friend	He is a *friend* to the **end**.
grammar	Poor *grammar* will **mar** your writing.

absence	category	eighth
accommodate	clothes	embarrassed
achievement	committee	environment
acknowledge	conscious	exercise
acquire	convenience	existence
across	criticism	explanation
address	definitely	extremely
adolescence	dependent	familiar
among	desperate	February
answer	development	finally
apparent	disappear	forty
argument	disappoint	friend
beginning	discipline	gauge
business	dissatisfied	government
careful	doesn't	grammar

guarantee
guidance
height
hoping
hypocrisy

immediately
independent
indispensable
laboratory
library

license (or licence)
likely
loneliness
lonely
maintenance

marriage
mentally
necessary
ninety
ninth

occasion
occasionally

omission
opinion
opportunity

paid
parallel
perform
planned
possess

prejudice
privilege
procedure
proceed
professor

psychology
recommend
relevant
repetition
restaurant

rhythm
ridiculous
safety

schedule
secretary

separate
shining
similar
somewhat
speech

studying
succeed
surprise
technique
thorough

tragedy
truly
unnecessary
until
unusual

usually
vacuum
Wednesday
writing
written

We'd like to make one last suggestion about spelling. Despite all your efforts, you may find there are a few words that you simply cannot remember how to spell correctly. The best solution is to write out a list of these pesky words and tape it on the inside cover of your dictionary or post it close to your computer.

A less satisfactory solution is to try to avoid these words. You could check your dictionary or a thesaurus to find synonyms (different words with the same meanings) for the words you can't spell and use the synonyms instead. The main problem with this solution is that it is even more time-consuming than learning the correct spellings in the first place!

There are, however, occasions when using a synonym will help you convey more accurately the meaning you intend. Two thesauruses are available in inexpensive paperback editions: *Roget's Thesaurus* (buy the one in dictionary form, not the one organized by subject) and the *Collins Paperback Thesaurus in A–Z Form*, which, as its title suggests, is organized alphabetically. Your word processor probably has a built-in thesaurus you can consult, but be careful. You can't just choose any word from the list that pops up when you ask for a synonym for a word you've used too frequently or for one you don't quite feel confident is the word you need.

The information provided by a thesaurus must be used with caution. Inexperienced writers sometimes assume that long, obscure words are sure to impress their readers. In fact, the opposite is usually true. Most readers are irritated, if not confused, by unnecessarily "fancy" language. Why write "The children were enthralled by the antics of the prestidigitator" when what you mean is "The children loved the magician's act"? (For more information on this subject, see Chapter 11.)

Finally, there is the possibility that some words on the list your word processor provides in response to your request for a synonym are simply wrong. Here's an example of how far off the mark your word processor can be in "assisting" you. (This is a true story. We couldn't make it up.) A student wasn't sure how to spell "synagogue," so he typed the word into his word processor's thesaurus. He chose the first word on the list provided and incorporated it into his paper, as follows: "Worship is what matters, not where it takes place. One may worship in church, in temple, or in Senegal." Only when his instructor read his sentence aloud did she realize he intended to say "synagogue."

3

Capital Letters

Capital letters should be used in a few specific places and nowhere else. Some writers suffer from "capitalitis": they put capital letters on words randomly, regardless of where the words occur in a sentence or whether the words are nouns, verbs, or adjectives.

Not many people have this problem. If you are in the majority who generally use capitals correctly, skip this chapter and go on to something else. If you are puzzled about capital letters, though, or have readers who are puzzled by your use of them, read on.

Capitalize the first letter of a word that fits into one of the six categories listed below:

1. The first word in a sentence, in a direct quotation, or in a sentence from a quoted source.

Are you illiterate? Write to us today for free help.
Supermodel Tyra Banks cooed, "I love the confidence makeup gives me."
Writer and broadcaster Lister Sinclair claims that the only thing Canadians have in common is that "We all hate Toronto."

Exercise 3.1

Add the seven missing capital letters to the following sentences. Answers for exercises in this chapter begin on page 424.

1. time is nature's way of keeping everything from happening at once.

2. Brad sang, "there's a light in the Frankenstein house."

3. my parents have a bumper sticker that reads, "money isn't everything, but it sure keeps the kids in touch."

4. Richard Harkness, writing in *The New York Times*, said "a committee is a group of the unwilling, picked from the unfit, to do the unnecessary."

5. in conclusion, I want you to consider the words of Wendell Johnson: "*always* and *never* are two words you should always remember never to use."

---

2. The names of specific people, places, and things.

Names of people (and their titles):

Shania Twain, Prime Minister Jean Chrétien, the Rev. Henry Jones, the Hon. Eugene Forsey, Lieutenant-General Linda Geoffreon

Names of places, regions, and astronomical bodies (but not general geographic directions):

Stanley Park, Lake Superior, Cape Breton Island; Nunavut, the Prairie Provinces, the Badlands; Saturn, Earth, the Moon, the Asteroid Belt; south, north

Names of buildings, institutions, organizations, companies, departments, products, etc.:

the Empress Hotel; McGill University, Red Deer College; the Liberal Party, the Kiwanis Club; Petro-Canada, Radio Shack; the Department of English, the Human Resources Department; Kleenex, Volvo, Labatt's

---

Exercise 3.2

Add capital letters where necessary in the following sentences. There are 30 errors in this exercise.

1. After a brief stay in the maritimes, captain tallman and his crew sailed west up the st. lawrence.

2. The broadcast department of niagara college has ordered six sony cameras for their studios in welland, ontario.

3. Do you find that visa is more popular than American express when you travel to far away places such as mexico, france, or jupiter?

4. Our stay at the seaview hotel overlooking the pacific ocean certainly beat our last vacation at the bates motel, where we faced west, overlooking the city dump.

5. As a member of the alumni association I am trying to raise funds from companies like disney, general motors, corel, and the cbc, where our graduates have positions.

3. Names of major historical events, historical periods, religions, holy texts, and holy days.

World War II, the Depression, the Renaissance; Islam, Judaism, Christianity, Buddhism, Hinduism; the Torah, the Koran, the Bible, the Upanishads; Ramadan, Yom Kippur, Easter

Exercise 3.3

Add the 20 capital letters that are missing from the following sentences.

1. The crusades, which were religious wars between muslims and christians, raged through the middle ages.

2. The hindu religion recognizes and honours many gods; islam recognizes one god, allah; buddhism recognizes none.

3. The koran, the bible, and the torah agree on many principles.

4. The jewish festival of hanukkah often occurs near the same time that christians are celebrating christmas.

5. After world war I, many jews began to emigrate to Palestine, where they and the muslim population soon came into conflict.

GO TO WEB

EXERCISE 3.1

4. The days of the week, months of the year, and specific holidays (but not the seasons).

Wednesday; January; Remembrance Day, Canada Day; spring, autumn

Exercise 3.4

The following sentences contain both missing and unnecessary capitals. Find and correct the 15 errors.

1. My favourite months are january and february because I love all Winter sports.

2. This monday is valentine's day, when messages of love are exchanged.

3. In the summer, big meals seem too much trouble; however, after thanksgiving, we need lots of food to survive the winter cold.

4. A National Holiday named flag day was once proposed, but it was never officially approved.

5. By thursday, I'll have finished my st. patrick's day costume.

5. The major words in titles of published works (books, magazines, films; essays, poems, songs; works of art; etc.). Do not capitalize minor words (articles, prepositions, conjunctions) in titles unless the word is the first word in the title.

The Colony of Unrequited Dreams
Of Mice and Men
Maclean's
A Room with a View

The Thinker
"An Immigrant's Split Personality"
"In Flanders Fields"
"If I Had a Million Dollars"

Exercise 3.5

Add the 30 capital letters that are missing from the following sentences.

1. The review of my book, *the life and times of a chocoholic,* published in *the globe and mail,* was not favourable.

2. Clint eastwood fans will be delighted that the two early movies that made him internationally famous, *a fistful of dollars* and *for a few dollars more,* are now available on DVD.

3. Joseph Conrad's short novel *heart of darkness* became the blockbuster movie *apocalypse now.*

4. Her poem, "a bright and silent place" was published in the april issue of *landscapes* magazine.

5. Botticelli's famous painting, "birth of venus," inspired my poem "woman on the half shell."

 Pay special attention to this next category. It is one that causes everybody trouble.

6. The names of school courses.

Marketing 101, Psychology 100, Mathematics 220, English 110,

but

a) not the names of school subjects:

marketing, sociology, mathematics

b) *unless* the subjects are languages:

English, Spanish, Greek, the study of Chinese history, modern French literature

(The names of languages, like the names of countries, are always capitalized.)

Exercise 3.6

Add capital letters where necessary in the following sentences. There are ten errors in this exercise.

1. After studying geography for two years, I began taking courses in ancient greek and modern history.

2. We began our study of sociology with the concept of relationships.

3. By taking Professor Subden's non-credit course, introduction to wine, I qualified to register for oenology 120 the next semester.

4. While math is her strong subject, Laurie has trouble with accounting, english, and conversational french.

5. The prerequisite for theology 210 is introduction to world religions, taught by Professor Singh.

GO TO WEB

EXERCISE 3.2

Exercise 3.7

In the two exercises that follow, correct the spelling by adding or deleting capital letters as necessary. There are 25 errors in each exercise.

1. There will be a fundraising spaghetti dinner in the anglican church on birch avenue next thursday evening.

2. You must take some Science courses, or you'll never get into the program you want at malaspina college in the Fall.

3. It should come as no surprise that Gore Vidal, author of *the best man*, once said, "it is not enough to succeed; others must fail."

4. After the Game, we went to the burger palace for a late snack and then went home to watch *this Hour Has 22 minutes* on television.

5. In our english course at caribou college, we studied *the englishman's boy*, a novel about life among the settlers of the american and canadian west.

Exercise 3.8

1. Marg Delahunty's campaign to be elected mayor of our fair city ran into trouble on friday when she was quoted as saying, "our political system is nothing but mob rule with taxes."

2. I wonder how our College gets away with requiring students to take english and Mathematics courses in addition to our Major subjects.

3. Leonard Cohen first became famous as a novelist when he published *the favourite game* and *beautiful losers*.

4. Years later, cohen's career was spectacularly revived with the release of albums such as *I'm your man* in 1988 and *the future* in 1992.

5. I was raised a baptist, but since taking professor Chan's course, introduction to world religions, I've been interested in hinduism and buddhism.

6. I plan to travel to asia next Summer to learn more about these religions.

Exercise 3.9

The following exercise is the mastery test. It would be a good idea to review the six capitalization rules before you attempt this exercise. There are 30 errors in this exercise.

1. my fear of flying is best expressed in the famous saying, "if god had meant us to fly, he would have given us wings."

2. *The lion king*, which is based on the disney animated movie, is a musical with a gorgeous african setting and spectacular costumes.

3. We travelled North to nunavut, where we boarded skidoos for the trek up to rankin inlet on hudson's bay.

4. No canadian History course would be complete without mentioning general sir Isaac Brock, who defended Canada against the american invasion in the war of 1812.

5. My Biology course is boring, Trigonometry is tedious, and Botany is bland. The only two courses I like this term are sociology 210, urban society, and psychology 301, the study of stress.

4

The Apostrophe

Can you spot why this job applicant's letter revealed his poor writing skills? Here's a sentence from his application:

I would like to be an active participant in you're companies success as it enters it's second decade of outstanding service to customer's.

Misused apostrophes display a writer's ignorance or carelessness. They also confuse, amuse, and sometimes annoy readers. The example above contains four apostrophe errors, which irritated the reader so much that the applicant didn't even make it to the interview stage.

Sometimes you need an apostrophe so that your reader can understand what you mean. For example, there's a world of difference between these two sentences:

The instructor began class by calling the students' names.
The instructor began class by calling the students names.

In most cases, however, misused apostrophes just amuse or irritate an alert reader:

The movie had it's moments.
He does a days work every week.
The Lion's thank you for your contribution.

It isn't difficult to avoid such mistakes. Correctly used, the apostrophe indicates either **contraction** or **possession**. It never makes a singular word plural. Learn the simple rules that govern these uses and you'll have no further trouble with apostrophes.

The instructor began the class by calling the students names.

Contraction

Contraction is the combining of two words into one, as in *they're* or *can't*. Contractions are common in conversational, informal English; however, unless you are quoting someone else's words, you should avoid them in the writing you do for college or work.

The rule about where to put an apostrophe in a contraction is one of those rare rules that has no exception. It *always* holds.

> When two words are combined into one, and one or more letters are left out, the apostrophe goes in the place of the missing letter(s).

Here are some examples.

I am	→ I'm	they are	→ they're
we will	→ we'll	it is	→ it's
she is	→ she's	it has	→ it's
do not	→ don't	who has	→ who's

Exercise 4.1

Place apostrophes correctly in these words, which are intended to be contractions. Notice that when the apostrophe is missing, the word often has a different meaning. Answers for exercises in this chapter begin on page 426.

1. cant
2. shed
3. hell
4. wed
5. lets

6. hasnt
7. youre
8. wont
9. shell
10. well

Exercise 4.2

Make these sets of words into contractions.

1. they are
2. I will
3. it has
4. can not
5. everyone is

6. could not
7. who has
8. you are
9. we would
10. will not

GO TO WEB

EXERCISES 4.1, 4.2

Exercise 4.3

Correct these sentences by placing apostrophes where they are needed.

1. Wed help if theyd ask us.

2. There wont be any problem if youve got an invitation.

3. Im sure that contractions shouldnt be used in formal writing.

4. You cant leave until the shows over.

5. Dont worry about your heart; itll last as long as you do.

6. Your sisters very nice, but I think your brothers a nutbar.

7. Its certain that hell be late.

8. Its best to begin your paper well before the deadline unless youre confident about getting an extension.

9. Wouldnt it be wonderful if everyone whos celebrating a birthday today could get together for a party?

10. Id support the idea only if the party wasnt held anywhere near my apartment.

Exercise 4.4

In some formal kinds of writing—academic, legal, and technical, for example—contractions are not acceptable. A good writer is able not only to contract two words into one, but also to expand any contraction into its original form: a two-word phrase. In the following paragraph, find and expand the contractions into their original form.

I'm writing to apply for the position of Web Master for BrilloVision.com that you've advertised in the *Daily News*. I've got the talent and background you're looking for. Currently, I work as a Web designer for an online publication, Vexed.com, where they're very pleased with my work. If you click on their Web site; I think you'll like what you see. There's little in the way of Web design and application that I haven't been involved in during the past two years. But it's time for me to move on to a new challenge, and BrilloVision.com promises the kind of opportunity I'm looking for. I guarantee you won't be disappointed if I join your team!

Possession

The apostrophe is also used to show ownership or possession. Here's the rule that applies in most cases.

> Add 's to the word that indicates the *owner*.
> If the resulting word ends in a double or triple s, delete the last s, leaving the apostrophe in place.[1]

Here are some examples that illustrate the rule.

singer + 's = singer's voice women + 's = women's voices
band + 's = band's instruments student + 's = student's report card
players + 's = players's uniforms students + 's = students's report cards
ships + 's = ships's crews colleges + 's = colleges's teams

To form a possessive correctly, you must first identify the word in the sentence that indicates possession and determine whether it is singular or plural. For example, "the managers duties" can have two meanings, depending on where you put the apostrophe:

the manager's duties (the duties belong to one *manager*)
the managers' duties (the duties belong to two or more *managers*)

> To solve an apostrophe problem, follow this two-step process:
> 1. Find the owner word.
> 2. Apply the possession rule.

Problem: Gretas hair is a mess.
Solution: 1. The word that indicates possession is *Greta* (singular).
    2. Add 's to *Greta*.

Greta's hair is a mess.

---

[1] Many writers today prefer to keep the final s when it represents a sound that is pronounced, as it is in one-syllable words such as *boss* and *class*, and in some names such as *Harris* and *Brutus*.

Problem: The technicians strike halted the production.

Solution: 1. The word that indicates possession is *technicians* (plural).

2. Add *'s* to *technicians*, then delete the second *s*, leaving the apostrophe.

The *technicians'* strike halted the production.

Sometimes the meaning of your sentence is determined by where you put the apostrophe.

Problem: The writer was delighted by the critics response to her book.

Now you have two possibilities to choose from, depending on your meaning.

Solution A: 1. The owner word is *critic* (singular).

2. Add *'s* to *critic*.

The writer was delighted by the *critic's* response to her book.

Solution B: 1. The owner word is *critics* (plural).

2. Add *'s* to *critics*, then drop the second *s*, leaving the apostrophe.

The writer was delighted by the *critics'* response to her book.

Both solutions are correct, depending on whether the book was reviewed by one critic (A) or by more than one critic (B).

Possession does not have to be literal. It can be used to express the notion of "belonging to" or "associated with." That is, the owner word need not refer to a person or group of people. Ideas or concepts (abstract nouns) can be "owners" too.

a month's vacation = a vacation of one month
a year's salary = the salary of one year
"A Hard Day's Night" = the night that follows (belongs to) a hard day

Exercise 4.5

In each of the following phrases, make the owner word possessive.

1. woman beauty

2. heaven gate

3. families budgets

4. crew mutiny

5. armed forces uniforms

6. everyone choice

7. the Gulf Islands weather

8. the Simpsons daughters

9. the oldest child responsibility

10. our country flag

GO TO WEB

EXERCISES 4.3, 4.4

Note that a few words, called **possessive pronouns**, are already possessive in form, so they don't have apostrophes.[2]

your/yours
her/hers
his, its

our/ours
their/theirs
whose

His music is not like *yours.*
Whose lyrics do you prefer, *theirs* or *ours*?
The dog lost *its* bone.

Four of these possessive pronouns are often confused with the contractions that sound like them. It's worth taking a moment to learn how to avoid this confusion. When you are trying to decide which spelling to use, expand the contraction into its original two words and substitute those words for the contraction in your sentence. If the sentence still makes sense, use the contraction. If it doesn't, use the spelling that indicates possession.

Possessive

its   = *It* owns something
their   = *They* own something
whose = *Who* owns something
your   = *You* own something

Contraction

it's   = it is/it has
they're = they are
who's = who is/who has
you're = you are

Error: They're (they are) going to sing they're (they are) latest song.
Revision: They're going to sing *their* latest song.

---

[2] If you add an apostrophe to any of these words, you create an error. There are no such words as *your's, her's, their's,* or *our's.*

Error: It's (it is) you're (you are) favourite song.
Revision: It's *your* favourite song.

Error: Who's (who is) CD are you listening to?
Revision: *Whose* CD are you listening to?

Error: I think it's (it is) price is too high.
Revision: I think *its* price is too high.

Exercise 4.6

Make the words in parentheses possessive. This exercise will help you discover how well you understand the difference between possessive pronouns and their sound-alike contractions.

1. (Stanley) greatest fear is his (mother) disapproval.

2. (Bikers) equipment is on sale this week at (Leather Larry) Boutique.

3. My parents would like to know (who) yogurt was left in (they) fridge for three months.

4. After only a (month) wear, my (sons) new jacket fell apart.

5. Unfortunately, the (book) cover was much more interesting than (it) contents.

6. Our (team) biggest win came at the same time as our rival (teams) most serious losses.

7. Virtue may be (it) own reward, but I won't refuse (you) offer of cash.

8. (Texas) record of executing people is one of the (United States) most notorious statistics.

9. This year, our (family) Thanksgiving celebration will be a quiet one, as we think of other (families) poverty.

10. This weeks *Fashion* magazine devotes four pages to (men) clothing and twelve pages to women's.

In the two exercises that follow, correct the sentences by placing apostrophes where they are needed in contractions and possessive constructions. Delete any misused apostrophes. There are ten errors in each exercise.

Exercise 4.7

1. Theres a rumour that youre going to quit smoking.

2. Its true. My family doctors concerns about my health finally convinced me to quit.

3. Whos perfect? I am, in my mothers opinion, at least.

4. Its a fact that most mothers opinions about their children are unrealistically positive.

5. Most fathers opinions are highly negative when they first meet their daughters boyfriends.

Exercise 4.8

1. The candidates debate was deadly boring until the fans started fighting in their seats.

2. Todays styles and tomorrows trends will be featured in our display window.

3. Hockeys playoff schedule puts the final's into the middle of June.

4. My in-laws home is about four hours drive north of Red Lake.

5. Todays paper features a short article entitled "Its Clear the Apostrophes Days Are Numbered."

GO TO WEB

EXERCISE 4.5

Plurals

The third apostrophe rule is very simple. Memorize it, apply it, and you will instantly correct many of your apostrophe errors.

Never use an apostrophe to make a word plural.

The plural of most English words is formed by adding *s* to the root word, not *'s*. The *s* alone tells the reader that the word is plural: e.g., *memos, letters, files, broadcasts, newspapers, journalists*. If you add an apostrophe + *s*, you are telling your reader that the word is either a contraction or a possessive.

Incorrect: Never use apostrophe's to make word's plural.
Correct: Never use apostrophes to make words plural.

Exercise 4.9

Correct the misused and missing apostrophes in the following sentences. There are ten errors in this exercise.

1. When you feel like a snack, you can choose between apples or Timbit's.

2. Annas career took off when she discovered its easy to sell childrens toys.

3. Golfing requires the use of different club's: woods for long shots, irons for short ones.

4. Poker's an easy game to play if you are dealt ace's more often than your opponent's are.

5. Nobodies perfect, but must the prime minister of our country display so many more fault's than virtue's?

GO TO WEB

EXERCISES 4.6, 4.7

Correct the misused and missing apostrophes in the two exercises that follow. There are ten errors in each exercise.

Exercise 4.10

1. Ive posted a sign on my front lawn: "Salespersons visits are always welcome. Dog foods expensive."

2. A dog always knows it's owners mealtimes.

3. Do you really think your employee's will be disappointed when they hear that you've cancelled the companies annual picnic?

4. In Canada, when it's warm enough to expose you're skin to the sun, the insects feeding season is at it's height.

Exercise 4.11

1. Candy is dandy, but liquors quicker. (Ogden Nash)

2. The storm devastated the two small town's in it's path.

3. Thank you for the flower's you sent us on the occasion of the twins graduation.

4. Somebodys going to be very disappointed when the panel releases its decision.

5. Four months work was wasted by a few minutes carelessness.

6. We will need everybodies maximum effort if we're going to meet tomorrows deadline.

Before you do the final exercise in this chapter, you may want to review what you've learned about using apostrophes correctly.

Summary

- When contracting two words into one, put an apostrophe in the place of the missing letters.
- Watch for owner words: they need apostrophes.
- To indicate possession, add *'s* to the owner word. (If the owner word already ends in *s*, just add the apostrophe.)
- Possessive pronouns (e.g., *their, its, ours*) do not take apostrophes.
- Never use an apostrophe to form the plural of a word.

Exercise 4.12

This exercise will test your mastery of the apostrophe. There are 20 errors in the following sentences. Find and correct them.

1. In just a weeks time, womens' fashion's will go on sale in our downtown store.

2. Our year-end sale is you're opportunity to stock up on some of the seasons most exciting suit's, coat's, and casual wear.

3. While you browse through our impressive womens wear collections, the man in you're life will be happy to head to the fifth floors year-end sale of tools for his home workshop.

4. Its the perfect opportunity for woodworker's and auto enthusiast's to update their tool collection's.

5. We also offer a childrens' program that let's you drop off your kid's in a professional daycare for only $5.00 an hour.

6. If your husband is the problem, you can drop him off at the Mens' Lounge on the fifth floor, where he can while away the time playing dart's and pinball, thus allowing you to get in a whole days guilt-free shopping.

UNIT 2

Sentence Structure

11 Choosing the Right Words
Levels of Language
Wordiness
Slang
Pretentious Language
Abusages

Sentence Structure

The following quick quiz will let you see at a glance which chapters of Unit 2 you need to focus on. The paragraphs below contain 20 errors: fragments, run-ons, modifier problems, lack of parallelism, and inappropriate diction (slang, wordiness, pretentious language, etc.). When you've made your corrections, turn to page 428 and compare your version with ours. For each error you miss, the answer key directs you to the chapter you need to work on.

1   You know that the heart pumps blood through our bodies, but did you also know that the word "heart" pumps through the English language in interesting ways? Let's look at some of the idioms using the word "heart." An idiom being a group of words whose meaning is difficult to figure out from the meaning of its individual words, such as "heart of gold" and "heart of stone." The word "heart" is found in many idioms. Some have positive connotations, negative connotations cling to others, and some are neutral. Some have to do with love and loss others have nothing at all to do with romance.

2   For starters, there are heart idioms that apply to romance. You "lose your heart" to someone you're hot for; in other words, you fall in love. As the relationship develops, you have many "heart to heart talks," you love each other "from the bottom of your hearts." There are also tons of positive heart idioms

that don't refer to love, such as "to have your heart in the right place," which means to be sincere and kind. To be "good hearted" means to be a good person; a "heart-warming" story causes you to feel real warm and happy.

3   Once the love affair has been terminated, heart idioms can also be called upon to describe the pain. For example, you "cry your heart out" about your lover's "change of heart" your "heart sinks" whenever you hear his or her name you are "heartbroken" you believe that your lover is a "heartless" rogue. Other idioms with a negative connotation include "to lose heart," which means to become discouraged, and "to be sick at heart," an expression meaning feeling fear or grief.

4   Then there are the myriad, almost innumerable heart idioms that express a variety of meanings with neither positive nor negative connotations. For instance, to learn something "by heart" is to memorize it; to "have your heart set" on something is to want it badly. Scared out of your wits, the "heart-stopping" movie you are watching is tense and exciting. The "heartland" being the most important part of a country. If you ask someone to "have a heart." You're asking her to be sympathetic. When you describe people as "young at heart," it's meant to be a compliment it still means they are old.

5   To conclude, I personally think that English idioms using the word "heart" have a bewildering number of meanings that only we learn through experience. Experience teaches us not to say that those spicy Buffalo wings gave us "heartache," or that an ex-lover effectuated our "heartburn." Anyways, my "heart goes out to" the many language learners who are confused by the difference.

5

Cracking the Sentence Code

A baby's first word is a big step, one that all parents mark as a significant stage of development. Not all parents recognize that an even more significant step in a baby's progress is the first time she puts together the two elements of a complete sentence: a subject and a verb. This is sophisticated communication, even if it's just "Me go!" *Words* enable us to communicate images; *sentences* are the tools with which we communicate ideas.

There is nothing really mysterious or difficult about sentences. You've been speaking them successfully since you were two years old. The difficulty arises when you come to write—not sentences, oddly enough, but paragraphs. Most college students, if asked to write ten sentences on ten different topics, could do so without errors. But when those same students write paragraphs, then fragments, run-ons, and other sentence faults appear. Sometimes these errors cause a failure of communication; at other times, they simply give the reader a poor impression of the writer.

The solution to sentence-structure problems has two parts.

Be sure every sentence you write
  1. sounds correct
          and
  2. has both a subject and a verb.

Your ear may be the best instrument with which to test your sentences. If you read your sentences aloud, you may be able to tell by the sound whether they are complete and clear. Sometimes, however, your ear may mislead you, so this chapter will show you, step by step, how to decode your sentences to find their subjects and verbs. When you know how to decode sentences, you can make sure that every sentence you write is complete.

Read these sentences aloud.

Snowboarding is one of the world's newest sports.
Although snowboarding is still a young sport.

The second "sentence" doesn't sound right, does it? It does not make sense on its own and is in fact a sentence fragment.

Testing your sentences by reading them aloud won't work if you read your paragraphs straight through from beginning to end. The trick is to read from end to beginning. That is, read your last sentence aloud and *listen* to it. If it sounds all right, then read aloud the next-to-last sentence, and so on, until you have worked your way back to the first sentence you wrote.

Now, what do you do with the ones that don't sound correct? Before you can fix them, you need to decode each sentence to find out if it has both a subject and a verb. The subject and the verb are the bare essentials of a sentence. Every sentence you write must contain both. There is one exception:

In a **command**, the subject is suggested rather than stated.

Consider these examples.

Sign here. = [You] sign here. (The subject you is implied or understood.)
Charge it. = [You] charge it.
Play ball! = [You] play ball!

Finding Subjects and Verbs

A sentence is about *someone* or *something*. That someone or something is the **subject**. The word (or words) that tells what the subject *is* or *does* is the **verb**. In the following sentences, the subject is underlined once and the verb twice.

Snow falls.
Meiling dislikes winter.
We love snowboarding.
Mt. Whistler offers excellent opportunities for winter sports.
In Canada, winter is six months long.
Some people feel the cold severely.

The subject of a sentence is always a **noun** (the name of a person, place, thing, or concept) or a **pronoun** (a word such as *I, you, he, she, it, we,* or *they* used in place of a noun). In the examples above, the subjects include persons (*Meiling, we, people*); a place (*Mt. Whistler*); a thing (*snow*); and a concept (*winter*). In one sentence, a pronoun (*we*) is the subject.

One way to find the **verb** in a sentence is to ask what the sentence says about the subject. There are two kinds of verbs:

- **action verbs**, which tell you what the subject is doing.
  In the examples above, *falls, dislikes, love,* and *offers* are action verbs.
- **linking verbs**, which link or connect a subject to a noun or adjective describing that subject. In the examples above, *is* and *feel* are linking verbs. Linking verbs tell you the subject's condition or state of being. (For example, "Tadpoles *become* frogs," "Frogs *feel* slimy.") The most common linking verbs are forms of *to be* (*am, is, are, was, were, have been,* etc.) and verbs such as *look, taste, feel, sound, appear, remain, seem,* and *become.*

Another way to find the verb in a sentence is to put a pronoun (*I, you, he, she, it,* or *they*) in front of the word you think is the verb. If the result makes sense, it is a verb. For example, you could put *she* in front of *falls* in the first sentence listed above: "she falls" makes sense, so you know *falls* is the verb in this sentence. Try this test with the other five example sentences.

Keep this guideline in mind as you work through the exercises below.

Ask <u>who</u> or <u>what</u> the sentence is about to find the subject.
Then ask what the subject <u>is</u> or <u>is doing</u> to find the verb.

In each of the following sentences, underline the <u>subject</u> with one line and the <u>verb</u> with two. Answers for exercises in this chapter begin on page 429. If you make even one mistake, go to the Web site and do the exercises listed beside the Web icon that follows this exercise. Be sure you understand this material thoroughly before you go on.

Exercise 5.1

1. Canadians love donuts.

2. They eat more donuts than any other nation.

3. Most malls contain a donut shop.

4. Donuts taste sweet.

5. Glazed donuts are my favourite.

6. Hot chocolate is good with donuts.

7. Try a bran donut for breakfast.

8. It is good for your health.

9. Donut jokes are common on television.

10. Dentists like donuts too, but for different reasons.

GO TO WEB

EXERCISES 5.1, 5.2

Exercise 5.2

Underline the subject with one line and the verb with two.

1. My computer is usually reliable.

2. Today, however, it keeps crashing.

3. Turn it off.

4. Maybe the processor is tired.

5. Perhaps the operator needs a vacation.

6. Computing is a necessary part of my life.

7. My work depends on it.

8. Without a functioning computer, I feel frustrated and angry.

9. Eventually, I decided to hit it with a hammer.

10. The computer booted right up!

GO TO WEB

EXERCISE 5.3

Usually, but not always, the subject comes before the verb in a sentence.

Occasionally, we find the subject after the verb:

- In sentences beginning with *Here* + some form of *to be* or with *There* + some form of *to be*

  Here and *there* are never the subject of a sentence.

  Here <u>are</u> the test <u>results</u>. (Who or what <u>are</u>? <u>Results</u>.)
  There <u>is</u> a <u>fly</u> in my soup. (Who or what <u>is</u>? A <u>fly</u>.)

- In sentences that are deliberately inverted for emphasis

  Finally, at the end of the long, boring joke <u>came</u> the pathetic <u>punch line</u>.
  Out of the stadium and into the pouring rain <u>marched</u> the <u>parade</u>.

- In questions

  <u>Are</u> <u>we</u> there yet?
  <u>Is</u> <u>she</u> the one?

  But notice that in questions beginning with *who, whose, what, where,* or *which,* the subject and verb are in "normal" order: subject followed by verb.

  <u>Who</u> <u>ate</u> my sandwich?   Whose <u>horse</u> <u>came</u> first?
  <u>What</u> <u>caused</u> the accident?   Which <u>car</u> <u>runs</u> best?

Exercise 5.3

Underline the subject with one line and the verb with two. Watch out for inverted order sentences. If you made even one mistake, do the Web exercises that follow this exercise.

1. Is Tomas still on the team?

2. Consider it done.

3. Here are the answers to tomorrow's quiz.

4. Is winter warmer this year than last?

5. Into the pool leaped the terrified cat.

6. Where are the children?

7. There are two new students in class today.

8. Which elective is easier?

9. Are you happy with your choice?

10. Who let the dogs out?

GO TO WEB

EXERCISES 5.4, 5.5

More about Verbs

The verb in a sentence may be a single word, as in the exercises you've just done, or it may be a group of words. When you are considering whether or not a word group is a verb, there are two points you should remember.

1. No verb preceded by *to* is ever the verb of a sentence.[1]
2. **Helping verbs**[2] are often added to main verbs.

The list below contains the most common helping verbs.

be (all forms of to *be* can act as helping verbs: e.g., *am, are, is, was, were, will be, have/had been*, etc.)	can could/could have do/did have/had may/may have might/might have	must/must have ought shall/shall have should/should have will/will have would/would have

The complete verb in a sentence consists of the main verb together with any helping verbs.

Below are a few of the forms of the verb *to take*. Study this list carefully, and note that when the sentence is in question form, the subject comes between the helping verb and the main verb.

We <u>are taking</u> a required English course.
You <u>can take</u> it with you.
<u>Could</u> Ravi <u>have taken</u> it?

We <u>might have taken</u> your advice.
You <u>must take</u> the bus.
Lucy <u>ought to have taken</u> a course in stress management.

---

[1] The form *to* + verb—e.g., *to speak, to write, to help*—is an infinitive. Infinitives can act as subjects or objects, but they are never verbs.
[2] If you are familiar with technical grammatical terms, you will know these verbs as **auxiliary verbs**. They also include modal auxiliaries (see Chapter 29).

<u>Did</u> you <u>take</u> your turn? The money <u>has been taken</u>. We <u>have taken</u> too much time. You <u>may take</u> a break now.

<u>Shall</u> we <u>take</u> his offer? I <u>should take</u> more time. We <u>will take</u> the championship. We <u>should have taken</u> the gold medal.

One verb form ALWAYS requires a helping verb. Here's the rule.

A verb ending in *-ing* MUST have a helping verb (or verbs) before it.

Here are a few of the forms a verb ending in *-ing* can take.

Ralph <u>is taking</u> the test.
<u>Am</u> I <u>taking</u> your place?
You <u>are taking</u> an awfully long time.
Our new computer <u>will be taking</u> over your job.
<u>Have</u> you <u>been taking</u> French lessons?

Exercise 5.4

Underline the complete verb with a double line.

1. My brother Ted is calling from Mexico.

2. His wife will arrive on Tuesday.

3. Have you arranged for a party to celebrate the election results?

4. The president could have fixed the election.

5. The party in power might have won again.

6. Xue should have completed her diploma by now.

7. Do you know anything about Linux?

8. We have played in the rain before.

9. I will be looking for verbs in my sleep.

10. We must have practised enough by now.

GO TO WEB

EXERCISES 5.6, 5.7

Beware of certain words that are often confused with helping verbs.

Words such as *always*, *ever*, *just*, *never*, *not*, *often*, *only*, and *sometimes* are NOT part of the verb.

These words usually appear in the middle of a complete verb, but they are modifiers, not verbs. Do not underline them.

Sofia <u>is</u> always <u>chosen</u> first.
They <u>have</u> just <u>got</u> married.
The question <u>has</u> not often
   <u>been asked</u>.

<u>Do</u> you ever <u>have</u> doubts about
  your ability?
<u>Will</u> you never <u>learn</u>?
I <u>have</u> often <u>wondered</u> about that.

In the following exercises, underline the subject with one line and the verb with two. Check your answers to the first set before going on to the next.

Exercise 5.5

1. I am making a nutritious breakfast.

2. It does not include Coca Cola.

3. You can add fresh fruit to the cereal.

4. The toast should be almost ready now.

5. My doctor has often recommended yogurt for breakfast.

6. I could never eat yogurt without fruit.

7. With breakfast, I will drink at least two cups of coffee.

8. I don't like tea.

9. I simply cannot begin my day without coffee.

10. I should probably switch to decaf.

Exercise 5.6

1. Winners are always watching for opportunities.

2. Losers are usually looking for lucky breaks.

3. I should be riding my bicycle to work.

4. My bike has been broken for nearly two years.

5. I cannot ride a broken bike.

6. My broken bike is really just an excuse.

7. Given the opportunity, I will always drive.

8. Also, I have been waiting for the bicycle fairy to fix it.

9. Wouldn't that be a lucky break?

10. Maybe I should simply start working on it myself.

GO TO WEB

EXERCISES 5.8, 5.9

More about Subjects

Groups of words called **prepositional phrases** often come before the subject in a sentence or between the subject and the verb. When you're looking for the subject in a sentence, prepositional phrases can trip you up unless you know the following rule.

The subject of a sentence is NEVER in a prepositional phrase.

You must be able to identify prepositional phrases so that you will know where *not* to look for the subject. A prepositional phrase is a group of words that begins with a preposition and ends with a noun or pronoun that answers the question *what* or *when*. This noun or pronoun is called the object of the preposition, and it is this word that, if you're not careful, you might think is the subject of the sentence.

Below is a list of prepositional phrases. The italicized words are prepositions; the words in regular type are their objects.

about your message	*around* the office	*concerning* your request
above the door	*before* lunch	*despite* the shortfall
according to the book	*behind* my back	*down* the corridor
after the meeting	*below* the window	*except* the contract
against the wall	*beside* my computer	workers
along the hall	*between* them	*for* the manager
among the staff	*by* the way	*from* the office

(continued on next page)

in the filing cabinet	*on* the desk	*under* the table
inside the office	*onto* the floor	*until* the meeting
into the elevator	*over* the page	*up* the corridor
near the wall	*through* the window	*with* permission
of the memo	*to* the staff	*without* the software

Before you look for the subject in a sentence, cross out all prepositional phrases.

A bird ~~in the hand~~ <u>is</u> messy.	(What <u>is</u> messy? The <u>bird</u>, not the hand.)
This deck ~~of cards~~ <u>is</u> unlucky.	(What <u>is</u> unlucky? The <u>deck</u>, not the cards.)
Many houses ~~in our neighbourhood~~ <u>need</u> painting.	(What <u>need</u> painting? The <u>houses</u>, not the neighbourhood.)

In the following exercises, first cross out the prepositional phrase(s) in each sentence. Then underline the subject with one line and the verb with two. Check your answers on page 431, and if you make even one error, do the Web exercises before going on to Exercise 5.8.

Exercise 5.7

1. Many people in the crowd were confused.

2. Fifty of her friends gave her a surprise party.

3. The official opening of the new city hall will be held tomorrow.

4. In the movies, the collision of two cars always results in a fire.

5. A couple of burgers should be enough for each of us.

6. Please decide on dessert before dinnertime.

7. Only a few of us have finished our homework.

8. After the rain, the flowers in the garden began to bloom.

9. There is a show about laser surgery on television tonight.

10. In the land of the blind, the one-eyed man is king. (Erasmus)

GO TO WEB

EXERCISES 5.10, 5.11

Exercise 5.8

1. A party in our neighbours' apartment kept us awake until dawn.

2. The meeting of all students in our class solved nothing.

3. In front of the mirror stood the wicked stepmother.

4. According to the news, the temperature in Yellowknife fell 20°C overnight.

5. My invention of a phoneless cord was designed for untalkative people.

6. Nothing in this world travels faster than a bad cheque.

7. For many students, lack of money is probably their most serious problem.

8. The plural of "choose" should be "cheese."

9. Despite her doubts about my condition, the nurse on duty at the hospital admitted me.

10. My guarantee of an A in this course is valid only under certain conditions.

Exercise 5.9

1. In my opinion, the fear of flying is entirely justifiable.

2. In our basement are stacks of magazines dating from the 1950s.

3. The rats in our building have written letters of complaint to the Board of Health.

4. When did the president of your company decide on this policy?

5. For reasons of privacy, I am listed in the telephone book under my dog's name.

6. Into the classroom and up to the front marched a tall woman with a determined look in her eyes.

7. Most of the students in the class instantly decided not to argue with her.

8. In future, be sure to read through your notes before the exam.

9. In your brochure, you advertise a "semi-annual after-Christmas sale" of quality items.

10. According to my dictionary, the word "semi-annual" means twice a year.

GO TO WEB

EXERCISES 5.12, 5.13

Multiple Subjects and Verbs

Up to now, you have been decoding sentences containing a single subject and a single verb, even though the verb may have consisted of more than one word. Sentences can, however, have a multiple (or **compound**) subject and/or a multiple (or compound) verb.

Here is a sentence with a multiple subject.

French fries and onion rings are Brian's idea of a balanced diet.

This sentence has a multiple verb.

Selena walks and dresses like a super model.

And this sentence contains both a multiple subject and a multiple verb.

Alan and Vijay drove to the mall and shopped for hours.

The parts of a multiple subject are usually joined by *and* or *or*; sometimes by *but* or *nor*. A multiple subject or a multiple verb may contain more than two elements. Look at the following examples.

Clarity, brevity, and simplicity are the basic qualities of good writing.
Raj deleted his work, shut down the computer, unplugged it, and dropped it out the window.

Identify the subjects and verbs in the three exercises that follow. First, cross out any prepositional phrases. Then underline the subjects with one line and the verbs with two. Be sure to underline all elements of a multiple subject or verb (there may be more than two). Check your answers to each set, and if you you've made any errors, do the Web exercises before you go on to the next exercise.

Exercise 5.10

1. My mother and father support me in college.

2. I can save or spend the money.

3. My parents and the rest of my family are expecting me to do well in school.

4. Entertainment and clothing are not included in my budget.

5. Tuition, books, lab fees, and rent take all my money.

6. A student's life can be sad and lonely.

7. In my letters home, I whine and moan at every opportunity about my lack of money.

8. Unfortunately for me, my mother and father were students too and had the same experience.

9. They laugh and shake their heads and tell me about their college days.

10. According to my parents, they ate only Kraft Dinner, lived in a shack, wore hand-me-down clothes, and walked ten kilometres to school.

GO TO WEB

EXERCISES 5.14, 5.15

Exercise 5.11

1. Verbs and subjects are sometimes hard to find.

2. Farmers, loggers, and fishers need and deserve the support of consumers.

3. Open the bottle, pour carefully, taste, and enjoy.

4. When can the salesperson and her clients visit your home?

5. Werner, Italo, and Pierre discussed and debated recipes all night.

6. During the following week, each one chose and prepared a meal for the other two.

7. Werner's sauerbraten and Black Forest cake amazed and delighted his friends.

8. Italo chopped, sliced, simmered, and baked a magnificent Italian meal.

9. Pierre and his sister worked in the kitchen for two days and prepared a delicious cassoulet.

10. By the end of the week, Pierre, Italo, and Werner were ready for a diet.

GO TO WEB

EXERCISE 5.16

Exercise 5.12

1. A fool and his money are soon parted.

2. I dream of success and worry about failure.

3. Nur and Aman paddled and portaged for ten days.

4. From under an oak leaf stepped a tiny elf and his equally tiny companion.

5. In the mist of early morning, a Brontosaurus and a Tyrannosaurus Rex sniffed the moist air and hunted for food.

6. Study my methods, use my research, but do not copy my work.

7. Why are goalies in hockey and kickers in football so superstitious?

8. In my dreams, the maid, butler, housekeeper, and chef wash the dishes, vacuum the floors, do the laundry, and make the meals.

9. According to the official course outline, students in this English course must take notes during every class and submit their notes to their instructor for evaluation.

10. In the opinion of many Canadians, the word *politician* means "idiot."

GO TO WEB

EXERCISE 5.17

Here's a summary of what you've learned in this chapter. Keep it in front of you as you write the mastery test.

Summary

- The subject is *who* or *what* the sentence is about.
- The verb tells what the subject *is* or *does*.
- The subject normally comes before the verb (exceptions are questions, sentences that begin with *here* or *there*, and sentences that begin with a series of prepositional phrases and are inverted for effect.)
- An infinitive (a phrase consisting of *to* + verb) is never the verb of a sentence.
- The complete verb consists of a main verb + any helping verbs.
- A word ending in *-ing* is not, by itself, a verb.
- The subject of a sentence is never in a prepositional phrase.
- A sentence can have more than one subject and verb.

Exercise 5.13

This exercise will test your ability to identify subjects and verbs in different kinds of sentences. First, cross out any prepositional phrases. Next, underline the subject(s) with one line and the verb(s) with two. Be sure to underline all elements in a multiple subject or verb.

1. "Take only pictures. Leave only footprints." (A sign posted in Banff National Park)

2. Ming and Asha have never worked so hard in their lives.

3. We took the bus from Montreal to Toronto, then went by train to Lake Louise.

4. Many nineteenth century immigrants to Canada worked and saved all their lives and died miserable and alone.

5. Our politicians sometimes try to change the world but seldom try to change themselves.

6. Among the many kinds of cheese made in Canada are Camembert, fontina, and Oka.

7. In the tidal pool were two starfish, several sand dollars, and dozens of tiny crabs.

8. Shoe companies, exercise equipment manufacturers, and video producers are all profiting from Canadians' desire for physical fitness.

9. Everybody except me is going to camp or spending a few weeks at a cottage this summer.

10. According to their campaign promises, the new government will provide jobs for all Canadians, pay down the national debt, eliminate the lineups in hospital emergency rooms, and lower taxes, all in its first year of office.

6

Solving Sentence-Fragment Problems

Every complete sentence has two characteristics. It contains a subject and a verb, and it expresses a complete thought. Any group of words that is punctuated as a sentence but lacks one of these characteristics is a **sentence fragment**. Fragments are appropriate in conversation and in some kinds of writing, but normally they are not acceptable in college, technical, or business writing.

There are two kinds of fragments you should watch out for: the "missing piece" fragment and the dependent clause fragment.

"Missing Piece" Fragments

Sometimes a group of words is punctuated as a sentence but is missing one or more of the essential parts of a sentence, the subject and verb. Consider these examples.

Found it under the pile of dirty clothes on your floor.

(Who or what <u>found</u> it? The sentence doesn't tell you. The subject is missing.)

Their arguments about housework.

(The sentence doesn't tell you what the arguments <u>were</u> or <u>did</u>. The verb is missing.)

During my favourite TV show.

(<u>Who</u> or <u>what</u> <u>was</u> or <u>did</u> something? Both subject and verb are missing.)

The programmers working around the clock to trace the hacker.

(Part of the verb is missing. Remember that a verb ending in -*ing* needs a helping verb to be complete.)

Finding fragments like these in your work when you are revising is the hard part. Fixing them is easy. There are two ways to correct sentence fragments. Here's the first one.

To change a "missing piece" fragment into a complete sentence, add whatever is missing: a subject, a verb, or both.

You may need to add a subject:

Your <u>sister</u> found it under the pile of dirty clothes on your floor.

You may need to add a verb:

Their arguments <u>were</u> about housework. (linking verb)
Their arguments about housework eventually <u>destroyed</u> their relationship. (action verb)

You may need to add both a subject and a verb:

My <u>mother</u> always <u>calls</u> during my favourite TV show.

Or you may need to add a helping verb:

The programmers <u>have been</u> working around the clock to trace the hacker.

Don't let the length of a fragment fool you. Students sometimes think that if a string of words is long, it must be a sentence. Not so. No matter how long the string of words, if it doesn't contain both a subject and a verb, it is not a sentence. For example, here's a description of children going from door to door for "treats" on Halloween:

In twos and threes, dressed in the fashionable Disney costumes of the year, as their parents tarried behind, grownups following after, grownups bantering about the schools, or about movies, about local sports, about their marriages, about the difficulties of long marriages, kids sprinting up the next driveway, kids decked out as demons or superheroes or dinosaurs . . . beating back the restless souls of the dead, in search of sweets.

Source: Moody, Rick. *Demonology* New York: Little, Brown, 2001. 291.

At 68 words, this "sentence" is long, but it is a fragment. It lacks both a subject and a verb. If you add "The <u>children</u> <u>came</u>" at the beginning of the fragment, you would have a complete sentence.

Exercise 6.1

In the following exercise, decide whether each group of words is a complete sentence or a "missing piece" fragment. Put S before each complete sentence and F before each fragment. Make each fragment into a complete sentence by adding whatever is missing: the subject, the verb, or both. Then compare your answers with our suggestions. Answers for exercises in this chapter begin on page 432.

1. _____ About sentence fragments.

2. _____ Glad to be able to help you.

3. _____ Hoping to hear from you soon.

4. _____ Saved by the bell.

5. _____ To prevent a similar tragedy from happening again.

6. _____ Not a good idea.

7. _____ Watching television a cheap form of entertainment.

8. _____ Close the door quietly on your way out.

9. _____ A computer with true artificial intelligence and full control of the vehicle.

10. _____ Working as a server, for example, can be exhausting.

GO TO WEB

EXERCISES 6.1, 6.2

Most of us have little difficulty identifying a fragment when it stands alone. But when we write, of course, we write in paragraphs, not in single sentences. Fragments are harder to identify when they occur in a context, as you'll see in the next exercise.

Exercise 6.2

Read the following selections carefully and decide whether each question contains only complete sentences or whether it contains one or more sentence fragments. Put S beside the questions that contain only sentences. Put F beside those that contain fragments. Then check your answers.

1. _____ This apartment suits me in every way. Except for the price. I can't afford it.

2. _____ In track and field, this college is very well respected. Our team won the championship last year. Setting three new provincial records.

3. _____ Whenever I go fishing, the fish aren't biting, but the mosquitoes are. Maybe I should give up fishing. And start collecting insects as a hobby instead.

4. _____ My son is a genius. On his last birthday, he was given a toy that was guaranteed to be unbreakable. Used it to break all his other toys.

5. _____ We weren't lost, but we were certainly confused. I realized this when we passed City Hall. For the third time.

6. _____ I've had bad luck with cars. I wrecked two in three years. Perhaps this is why my parents don't let me borrow their car.

7. _____ My husband and I often go to the hockey arena. Not to watch sports, but to hear the concerts of our favourite local bands. These concerts give new meaning to the word "cool."

8. _____ According to the weather reporter at our local radio station, a storm with high winds and heavy rains is approaching our region. Yesterday, when the temperature hit 0°C, she predicted light snow.

9. _____ I enjoy reading travel books. About far-away, exotic places that I have never visited and will probably never get to see. The fun is in the dreaming, not the doing.

10. _____ Spending my remaining days skiing and the nights dining and dancing. That's how I picture my retirement. Unfortunately, by then I'll be too old to enjoy it.

Once you have learned to identify fragments that occur within a paragraph, it's time to consider the best way to correct them. You could fix all of them the way we've identified above, by adding the missing piece or pieces to each one, and in some cases, that is your only choice. However, there is another, shorter, way that can often be used to correct fragments in context. You need to be familiar with this "fragment fixer."

> You can sometimes correct a "missing piece" fragment by attaching it to a complete sentence that comes before or after it—whichever one makes sense.

Sometimes you need to put a comma between a missing piece fragment and the complete sentence to which you attach it. (See Chapter 18, "The Comma," Rule 2, page 211 and Rule 4, page 213.)

Exercise 6.3

Now go back to the sentences in Exercise 6.2 and correct the fragments. As you go through the exercise, try to use both techniques we've identified for fixing fragments:

- add the missing piece(s)
- join the fragment to a complete sentence next to it

When you've finished, compare your answers with ours on page 433.

Exercise 6.4

Read through the following paragraph, and put S before each complete sentence and F before each fragment. Then check your answers.

(1) _____ I decided to take swimming lessons for several reasons. (2) _____ First, knowing that swimming is one of the best activities for physical fitness. (3) _____ Second, safety. (4) _____ You never know when the ability to

swim might save your life. (5) _____ Or the life of someone you're with. (6) _____ Third, being able to enjoy water sports such as diving and snorkeling instead of being stuck on shore watching others have fun. (7) _____ By summer, I hope to be a confident swimmer. (8) _____ Able to enjoy myself in and on the water. (9) _____ I can hardly wait!

Exercise 6.5

Now correct the fragments you identified in the paragraph above. Use both fragment-fixing techniques we've highlighted for you on pages 74 and 77. Then compare your answers with ours on page 433.

Dependent Clause Fragments

Any group of words containing a subject and a verb is a clause. There are two kinds of clauses. An **independent clause** is one that makes complete sense. It can stand alone as a sentence. A **dependent clause**, as its name suggests, cannot stand alone as a sentence. It depends on another clause to make complete sense. Dependent clauses (also known as **subordinate clauses**) begin with words such as these:

Dependent Clause Cues

after	that
although	though
as, as if	unless
as long as	until
as soon as	what, whatever
because	when, whenever
before	where, wherever
even if, even though	whether
if	which, whichever
since	while
so that	who, whose

Whenever a clause begins with one of these words or phrases, it is dependent.

A dependent clause must be attached to an independent clause. If it stands alone, it is a sentence fragment.

Here is an independent clause:

I am a hopeless speller.

If we put one of the dependent clause cues in front of it, it can no longer stand alone:

Because I am a hopeless speller

We can correct this kind of fragment by attaching it to an independent clause:

Because I am a hopeless speller, I have chained my dictionary to my wrist.

Exercise 6.6

Let's start with an easy exercise. Put an S before each clause that is independent and therefore a sentence. Put an F before each clause that is dependent and therefore a sentence fragment. Circle the dependent clause cue in each fragment. Then check your answers on page 433.

1. _____ After class is over.

2. _____ When you wish upon a star.

3. _____ Because of her, I am here.

4. _____ As soon as the fog lifts.

5. _____ Who encouraged us to keep trying until we succeeded.

6. _____ Close the door before you leave.

7. _____ Even if there is an earthquake.

Most sentence fragments are dependent clauses punctuated as sentences. Fortunately, this is the easiest kind of fragment to fix.

> To correct a dependent clause fragment, attach it to a sentence that comes before it or one that comes after it, depending on which linkage makes better sense.

Problem: Learning a new language is difficult. When you are an adult. It can be done, though.

The second "sentence" is incomplete; the dependent clause cue *when* is the clue you need to identify it as a sentence fragment. You could join the fragment to the sentence that follows it, but then you would get " Learning a new language is difficult. When you are an adult, it can be done, though," which doesn't make sense. The fragment should be linked to the sentence before it.

Revision: Learning a new language can be difficult when you are an adult. It can be done, though.

 If, as in the example above, your revised sentence *ends* with the dependent clause, you do not need to use a comma before it. If, however, your revised sentence *begins* with the dependent clause, put a comma between it and the independent clause that follows.

Although it is difficult to learn a new language when you're an adult, it can be done. (See Chapter 18, "The Comma," Rule 4, on page 213.)

Exercise 6.7

Correct the fragments in Exercise 6.6 by attaching each one to an independent clause that you have made up. Then compare your answers with our suggestions. Be sure to put a comma after a dependent clause that comes at the beginning of a sentence.

Like "missing piece" fragments, dependent clause fragments are harder to identify when they appear in the middle of a paragraph.

Check your fragment-finding skills by trying the following exercises. The items in these exercises each contain three clauses, one of which is dependent, and therefore a fragment. Highlight the dependent clause in each item.

Exercise 6.8

1. Walking is probably the best form of exercise there is. Unless you're in the water. Then swimming is preferable.

2. Rain doesn't bother me. I love staying inside with a good book. When the weather is miserable.

3. Try this curry. After you've tasted it. I am sure it will be your favourite.

4. The report identifies a serious problem that we need to consider. Whenever our Web site is revised or updated. It is vulnerable to hackers.

5. Sanir and Jade asked us what we thought about their recent engagement. Since they want to go to Canada's Wonderland for their honeymoon. We concluded they were probably too young to get married.

GO TO WEB

EXERCISE 6.3

Exercise 6.9

1. You keep the temperature in your apartment very low. In order to save money. I have to wear a sweater every time I visit.

2. Your idea that we should ask for directions was a good one. If we had relied on the hand-drawn map we were given. We would still be lost right now.

3. Home decoration isn't all that difficult. When you don't have enough money for furniture, carpets, or curtains. You have no choice but to be creative.

4. I believe that honesty is the best policy. If I found a million dollars in the street and discovered that it belonged to a poor homeless person. I'd give it right back.

5. The names of many Canadian landmarks have been changed over the years. The Oldman River, for example, which runs through Lethbridge, used to be called the Belly River. Until local residents petitioned for a change to a more dignified name.

GO TO WEB

EXERCISE 6.4

Exercise 6.10

Correct the sentence fragments you highlighted in Exercises 6.8 and 6.9 above. Make each fragment into a complete sentence by attaching it to the independent clause that precedes or follows it, whichever makes better sense. Remember to punctuate correctly: if a dependent clause comes at the beginning of your sentence, put a comma after it. Check your answers after each exercise.

Exercise 6.11

In the following paragraph, you'll find a mixture of "missing piece" fragments and dependent clause fragments. Revise the six fragments any way you choose: either by adding the missing piece(s), or by joining fragments to appropriate independent clauses. Check your punctuation carefully.

Because the chances of winning are so small. Lotteries have been called a tax on people with poor math skills. Buying a lottery ticket will gain you about as much as betting that the next U.S. president will come from Moose Jaw. Or that the parrot in the pet store speaks Inuktitut. While winning a lottery is not impossible. It is so unlikely that you'd do better to use your money to light a nice warm fire. Though the winners are highly publicized. No one hears about the huge numbers of losers. Whose money has gone to pay the winners. In order for the lottery corporation to make its enormous profits. Millions of dollars must be lost whenever a lucky winner is declared.

GO TO WEB

EXERCISES 6.5, 6.6

Exercise 6.12

Find and fix the ten fragment errors in this paragraph.

Shopping on the Internet is convenient and efficient, but there are a few disadvantages. That cause me to shop "offline." From time to time. When I'm looking for something for myself, I like to talk with a person who can help me select the right item. And show me how to use it. Most of the time, I don't know what questions to ask. About using or maintaining whatever it is I am buying. Unless I actually see the item. Furthermore, when I go shopping, I enjoy the contact with people in the store or mall. Which is where I do most of my socializing. I would feel isolated and lonely. If I did all my shopping online. On the other hand. Maybe I should listen to my mother. Who disapproves of my spending so many hours on the Net. And often tells me to "get a life."

7

Solving Run-On Sentence Problems

Does the following sentence sound like something you might write?

> I was sitting on my bed listening to the radio when my roommate came in and complained about the noise which she said was disturbing her because she was trying to work and I just stared at her because the radio was on low and besides, she has her TV on so loud all the time that I can't sleep but I don't complain about it because I'm trying to get along with her so she'll stay in the house with me and continue to share the rent because I can't afford to live here by myself.

If this sentence sounds fine to you, read on. Help is at hand.

A sentence with too many ideas in it or with inadequate punctuation between clauses is a **run-on**. Run-ons tend to occur when you write in a hurry without taking time to organize your thoughts first. By thinking about what you want to say before you say it and by punctuating carefully, you can solve any problems you may have had in the past with run-ons.

There are three kinds of run-on sentences that, unless you're careful, you might write: the comma splice, the fused sentence, and the "monster" run-on.

Comma Splices and Fused Sentences

As its name suggests, the **comma splice** occurs when two complete sentences (independent clauses) are joined together with only a comma between them. Here's an example:

> This film is boring, it has no plot.

A **fused sentence** occurs when two complete sentences are joined together with no punctuation between them. For example:

This film is boring it has no plot.

There are three ways you can fix a comma splice or a fused sentence.

1. Use a semicolon to separate the independent clauses.

This film is boring; it has no plot.

(If you are not sure how to use semicolons, see Chapter 19.)

2. Add an appropriate linking word between the two clauses.

Two types of linking words will work.

1. You can add one of these words: *and, but, or, nor, for, so,* or *yet.*[1]

These words should be preceded by a comma. Here is an example:

This film is boring, for it has no plot.

2. You can change one of the independent clauses into a subordinate clause by adding one of the dependent clause cues listed on page 78. For example:

This film is boring because it has no plot.

3. Make the independent clauses into two separate sentences.

This film is boring. It has no plot.

Note: All three solutions to comma splices and fused sentences require you to use a word or punctuation mark strong enough to join two independent clauses. A comma by itself is too weak, and so is a dash.

---

[1] These words are called **coordinating conjunctions** because they are used to join two equal (or coordinating) clauses. If you are not sure how to handle coordinating conjunctions or which one to use in a particular sentence, see Chapter 18, "The Comma," Rule 3, on page 212.

The sentences in the following exercises will give you practice in correcting comma splices and fused sentences. Revise the sentences where necessary (note that there is one correct sentence in each set), and then check your answers. Answers for exercises in this chapter begin on page 435. Since there are three ways to fix each incorrect sentence, your answers may differ from our suggestions. If you are unsure about when to use a semicolon and when to use a period, be sure to read pages 219 and 220 before going on.

Exercise 7.1

1. She's late again; she's always at least 15 minutes late.
2. Our manager works hard, *and* she is efficient.
3. It's getting dark; we'd better hurry.   *It's getting dark, so we'd better hurry.*
4. I think I have some change, it's in my pocket.
5. Here's my number; give me a call.
6. We're going to Kim's; it's not very far.
7. Leo needs your help; his homework is too hard for him.
8. Press on the wound; *that* will stop the bleeding.
9. I'm busy right now, *so* you'll have to wait.   ;
10. I wish my computer would do what I want it to do, not what I tell it to do.

Exercise 7.2

1. I hate computers they're always making mistakes.
2. I'm trying to stop playing computer games, they take up too much of my time.
3. This pie is delicious, I must have the recipe.
4. I'm innocent, this is a case of mistaken identity.
5. This desk is made of pine with maple veneer the other is solid oak.
6. I'm going to stay up all night tonight I don't want to miss my 8:30 class.
7. It's too bad you don't like hockey because I have two tickets to tomorrow's game, it'll be a good one.

8. You can't take your money with you, it's not a good idea to give it away too soon.

9. There are two kinds of people in the world: the good and the bad.

10. The good may sleep better at night, the bad seem to enjoy their waking hours more.

GO TO WEB

EXERCISE 7.1

Exercise 7.3

1. His favourite music is the Blues, it complements his personality and temperament.

2. This restaurant is terribly slow, it will be supper time when we finally get our lunch.

3. I'm investing all my money in this week's lottery the jackpot is over ten million dollars.

4. Computers make it easier to do many things most of the time these things don't need to be done.

5. Canadians are people who will travel to the United States to buy cheap cigarettes, then return home for cancer treatment paid for by Canadian taxpayers.

6. If I never again see a fast-food breakfast, it will be too soon, the last one I ate nearly put me in the hospital.

7. The fine art of whacking an electronic device to get it to work again is called "percussive maintenance," nine times out of ten, it works.

8. The English language makes no sense, why do people recite at a play and play at a recital?

9. I write in my journal every day when I'm ninety, I want to read about all the important events in my life.

10. We have not inherited the Earth from our ancestors we are borrowing it from our children.

GO TO WEB

EXERCISE 7.2

"Monster" Run-Ons

In a monster run-on, so many clauses are crowded together in a single sentence that the reader becomes confused. The opening sentence of this chapter is a good example of a monster that needs taming. While there is no hard-and-fast rule about how many independent clauses you can include in one sentence without confusing your readers, the general rule is that more than three clauses can result in a sentence that is hard to read. Consider this problem sentence:

> The party didn't turn out to be much fun, we decided to leave and we collected our coats, we said our goodbyes and we drove home very slowly, the snow was falling heavily, then we sat up drinking coffee until three o'clock, gossiping about our friends.

To turn a monster sentence into a correct and civilized one, follow these three steps:

1. Find and number all the independent clauses in the sentence.

(1) The <u>party</u> <u>didn't</u> <u>turn</u> out to be much fun (2) <u>we</u> <u>decided</u> to leave (3) <u>we</u> <u>collected</u> our coats (4) <u>we</u> <u>said</u> our goodbyes (5) <u>we</u> <u>drove</u> home very slowly (6) the <u>snow</u> <u>was falling</u> heavily (7) then <u>we</u> <u>sat up</u> drinking coffee until three o'clock, gossiping about our friends.

2. Decide which independent clauses are closely linked in meaning and could be smoothly joined together.

- The party didn't turn out to be much fun + we decided to leave.
- We collected our coats + we said our goodbyes.
- We drove home very slowly + the snow was falling heavily.
- Then we sat up drinking coffee until three o'clock, gossiping about our friends.

Your original seven separate clauses are now clustered into four potential sentences that will be much easier for your reader to understand. The third and last step requires you to decide how to combine your clause clusters into four clear sentences.

3. Choose the links between clauses that will convey your meaning most effectively:

- which clauses are so closely connected in meaning that they could be joined by a semicolon?
- which clauses would benefit from a coordinate or subordinate conjunction to clarify the relationship between them?
- which clauses should stand alone, punctuated as two separate sentences?

The party didn't turn out to be much fun, *so* we decided to leave. *After* we had collected our coats, we said our goodbyes. *We* drove home very slowly; the snow was falling heavily. *Then* we sat up drinking coffee until three o'clock, gossiping about our friends.

Exercise 7.4

Correct the five monster run-on sentences below by following the three-step process outlined above. This exercise works best if you tackle it with a partner or in a small group. Try to use all three solutions to run-on sentence problems: semicolons, linking words, and sentence breaks. Then compare your solutions with our suggestions on page 435.

1. Many parents will agree, the first sign of adulthood is the discovery that volume can be turned down as well as up, this realization does not happen overnight for some people, the process takes years.

2. There are two students in this class named Xan, one is from China, the other is from Russia, the latter's name is a nickname, a short form of Alexandra.

3. I'm reading a collection of unintentionally funny newspaper headlines they are hilarious, the book contains hundreds of examples of headlines that did not say what their writers intended and my favourite is from the sports pages, it reads, "Grandmother of Eight Makes Hole in One."

4. Some of my other favourites include examples of the remarkable talent of headline writers for stating the obvious, such as "Smokers are Productive, but Death Cuts Efficiency," another is "Man is Fatally Slain," is the reader really supposed to think these headlines are news?

5. If you have trouble getting your child's attention, all you have to do is sit down and get comfortable, pick up a book, turn on the TV, or just relax, your child will be all over you in no time and this is why, when children are out of school for summer holidays, parents begin to understand why primary school teachers deserve twice the salary they currently earn.

Grandmother of eight makes hole in one.

Exercise 7.5

In the following exercise, correct the ten run-on errors any way you choose. This would be a good time to review the three ways of fixing these errors. Your goal is to produce a paragraph in which the sentences are both correct and effective. (Our answers, on page 436, are only suggestions.)

Once upon a time, three travellers came upon a raging river, it prevented them from continuing their journey, luckily, however, they got to the river just in time to rescue a magic elf from the rushing water, she was so grateful to them for saving her life that she told them she would grant each of them one wish so the first man wished for the strength to be able to cross the river and instantly his arms and legs developed powerful muscles that enabled him to swim easily to the other side and the second man wished for a boat that would carry him across and his wish was granted in the form of a sturdy rowboat and strong oars, it allowed him to make his way safely to the other side. The third man, having observed the success of his two companions, wanted to show that he could outsmart them, he asked for the intelligence that would enable him to cross the water with the least possible effort and he was immediately transformed into a woman who realized there was a bridge a few metres downstream and walked across it to the other shore.

The following exercise will provide you with a double challenge of your sentence structure expertise. In this exercise, you will find both fragments and run-ons. Work through it slowly and carefully, and check your results with our suggestions on page 436.

1. That joke isn't the least bit funny it's sexist and I'm surprised you told it.

2. The snow continues to fall, hasn't let up for three days.

3. I've always driven a small car, I think the huge boats driven by many North Americans are ridiculous. Though I agree they are comfortable.

4. Mike has given up meat and become a vegetarian, counting today and the day he started his new diet, he hasn't had a hamburger in two days.

5. I need a cup of coffee, a caffeine lift in the middle of a difficult day helps keep me alert.

6. CRNC is the home of the million dollar guarantee, you give us a million dollars, we guarantee to play any song you want.

7. Tamara plays violin in a professional orchestra, it's unlikely she'll be impressed by my skill on the one instrument I can play. The tambourine.

8. The cat is attacking the curtains again since yesterday, when you put up the bird feeder outside the window, she's been climbing the curtains all day long. To get at the birds.

9. Television is a mass medium, comedians since the 1950s have suggested that it's called a mass medium because things on it are rarely well done. A joke that was funny once but now is old and tired.

10. It's far too hot, no one feels like working. Not even people who claim to like summer temperatures.

GO TO WEB

EXERCISE 7.3

Exercise 7.7

The following exercise contains ten errors: comma splices, fused sentences, and "monsters." We suggest you review the three ways of correcting these errors before you tackle this exercise. Your goal is to produce paragraphs in which all sentences are correct and effective.

An acquaintance of mine recently became a Canadian citizen, when she told me about her citizenship hearing, I couldn't bring myself to offer the congratulations she expected. Before her hearing, she was given a small book containing basic facts about Canada, she was told that the judge who interviewed her would question her on the information in that book, she didn't study the book, she never even opened it.

At the hearing, the judge asked her a few simple questions, such as the name of the governor general, some advantages of being a Canadian citizen, and whether health care was a federal or a provincial responsibility but since she couldn't answer any of these questions, my friend just shrugged and waited for the judge to give her the answers. She expected to be told to come back when she had learned more about her adopted country, she was astonished when the judge congratulated her for successfully completing the interview and set a date to confirm her citizenship.

I find the judge's decision appalling for several reasons first, my friend's refusal to read the book suggests she doesn't have much respect for

Canadian citizenship, second, her low opinion of our country's citizenship process was confirmed when the judge approved her application. Third, I can't help but feel she was passed because she is an attractive blonde teacher who speaks with a slight English accent, if she had been a man or woman of colour, or spoken little or no English, I can't help but think her application would have been rejected, it deserved to be.

8

Solving Modifier Problems

Having been underwater for more than 150 years, Dr. Philbrick found the warship in excellent condition.

Both students were expelled as a result of cheating *by the college registrar.*

Peng visited his family, who live in China *during the summer.*

How could Dr. Philbrick stay underwater for 150 years? Was the college registrar cheating? Does Peng's family live in China during the summer, or did Peng visit them during the summer? As you can see, the meaning in these examples is not clear. The confusion comes from problems with modifiers.

A **modifier** is a word or word group that adds information about another word in a sentence. In the examples above, the italicized words are modifiers. Used correctly, modifiers describe or explain or limit another word, making its meaning more precise. Used carelessly, modifiers cause confusion or, even worse, amusement. Few experiences are more embarrassing than being laughed at when you didn't mean to be funny.

You need to be able to recognize and solve two kinds of modifier problems: **misplaced modifiers** and **dangling modifiers**.

Misplaced Modifiers

Modifiers must be as close as possible to the words they apply to. Readers usually assume that a modifier modifies whatever it's next to. It's important to remember this because, as the following examples show, changing the position of a modifier can change the meaning of your sentence.

(Only) I love you. (No one else loves you.)

I (only) love you. (I have no other feelings for you.)

I love (only) you. (You are the only one I love.)

To make sure a modifier is in the right place, ask yourself "What does it apply to?" and put it beside that word.

When a modifier is not close enough to the word it refers to, it is said to be misplaced. A **misplaced modifier** can be *a single word in the wrong place*:

My boss told me that the payroll department needed someone who could use a word processor (badly).

Is some company really hiring people to do poor work? Or does the company urgently need someone familiar with word processing? The modifier *badly* belongs next to the word it applies to, *needed*:

My boss told me that the payroll department (badly) needed someone who could use a word processor.

Be especially careful with these words: *almost, nearly, just, only, even, hardly, merely, scarcely*. Put them right before the words they modify.

Misplaced: I (nearly) passed every course I took in college.

Correct: I passed (nearly) | every course | I took in college.

Misplaced: George W. Bush was (almost) elected by 50% of the U.S. voters.

Correct: George W. Bush was elected by (almost) 50% of the U.S. voters.

Misplaced: Sondra (only) writes with her left hand.

Correct: Sondra writes (only) | with her left hand |.

A misplaced modifier can also be *a group of words in the wrong place*:

(Babbling contentedly), |the new mother| watched her baby.

The modifier, *babbling contentedly*, is too far away from the word it applies to: *baby*. It seems to modify *mother*, making the sentence ridiculous. We need to revise the sentence.

The new mother watched her baby (babbling contentedly).

Look at this example:

I worked for my aunt, who owns a variety store (during the summer.)

During the summer applies to *worked* and should be closer to it:

(During the summer,) I worked for my aunt, who owns a variety store.

Notice that a modifier need not always go right next to what it modifies. It should, however, be as close as possible to it.

Occasionally, as in the examples above, the modifier is obviously out of place. The writer's intention is often clear, and the sentence is easy to correct. Sometimes, however, modifiers are misplaced in such a way that the meaning is not clear, as in this example:

My boss told me (on Friday) |I was being let go|.

Did the boss speak to the employee on Friday? Or did she tell the employee that Friday would be his last day? To avoid confusion, we must move the modifier and, depending on the meaning we want, write

(On Friday), my boss told me I was being let go.

Or

My boss told me |I was being let go| (on Friday).

Rewrite the following sentences, placing the modifiers correctly. Check your answers to each set before going on. Answers for this chapter begin on page 437.

Exercise 8.1

1. The president only fired those who had failed to meet their sales quotas.
2. We were run over by nearly every car that passed.
3. The flag was just raised at sunrise.
4. She was exhausted after merely walking 300 metres.
5. After the fire, she took her clothes to the cleaners with the most smoke damage.
6. The French almost drink wine with every meal, including lunch.
7. The suspect scarcely gave the police any information.
8. He was nearly underwater for two minutes before surfacing.
9. We camped in a national park with lots of wild life during August.
10. A huge tree can be cut by any idiot with a chainsaw, even one more than 300 years old.

Exercise 8.2

1. They just closed before five.
2. I have been fired nearly every week that I have worked here.
3. A computer that crashes needs to be replaced frequently.
4. Braying loudly, Matti couldn't force the donkey to take a single step.
5. We have computers for all office staff with little memory and constant breakdowns.
6. Canadians almost enjoy the highest standard of living in the world.
7. We bought gifts for the children with batteries included.
8. Kevin only bought three lottery tickets this week.

9. This is a book for avid readers with real weight and depth.

10. Trevor crouched behind a tree and watched the rabbit with binoculars.

EXERCISES 8.1, 8.2

Dangling Modifiers

A **dangling modifier** occurs when there is no appropriate word in the sentence for the modifier to apply to. That is, there is no *specific word* or *idea* to which the modifier can sensibly refer. With no appropriate word to refer to, the modifier seems to apply to whatever it's next to, often with ridiculous results:

After a good night's sleep, my teachers were impressed by my alertness.

(This sentence seems to say that the teachers had a good night's sleep.)

While paying for our purchases, a security guard watched closely.

(The security guard paid for our purchases?)

Dangling modifiers are harder to fix than misplaced ones. You can't simply move danglers to another spot in the sentence. There are two ways to correct them. One way requires that you remember the following guideline.

When a modifier comes at the beginning of the sentence, it modifies the subject of the sentence.

This means that you can avoid dangling modifiers by choosing the subjects of your sentences carefully. The subject must be an appropriate one for the modifier to apply to. With the guideline in mind, we can correct both examples simply by changing the subjects.

After a good night's sleep, I impressed my teachers with my alertness.

(While paying for our purchases), we were closely watched by a security guard.

Another way to correct a dangling modifier is to change it into a dependent clause.

After I had a good night's sleep, I impressed my teachers with my alertness. While we paid for our purchases, a security guard watched us closely.

Sometimes a dangling modifier comes at the end of a sentence.

A bear blocked our path, (skiing through the national park).

Can you correct this sentence? Try it; then look at the suggestions we've given at the bottom of the page.[1]

Summary

1. Ask "What does the modifier refer to?"
2. Be sure there is a word or word group in the sentence for the modifier to apply to.
3. Put the modifier as close as possible to the word or word group it refers to.

The sentences in Exercises 8.3 and 8.4 contain dangling modifiers. Correct them by changing the subject of each sentence to one the modifier can appropriately apply to. There is no one right way to correct these sentences. Our answers on page 437 are only suggestions.

Exercise 8.3

1. When running competitively, a thorough warm-up is necessary.

2. As a college teacher, dangling modifiers are annoying.

---

[1] Here are two suggested corrections:

1. Add a subject: (Skiing through the national park), we came across a bear blocking our path.
2. Change the dangler to a dependent clause: When we were skiing through the national park, a bear blocked our path.

3. After revising her résumé, filling out the application, and going through the interview, the position was taken by someone else.

4. Getting to the meeting room 20 minutes late, everyone had left.

5. After cooking all day long, the gourmet meal was worth the effort.

6. Having arrived so late, the meal was cold.

7. Driving recklessly, the police stopped André at a road block.

8. Dressed in a new miniskirt, her boyfriend thought she looked terrific.

9. After waiting for 20 minutes, the server finally came to our table.

10. Having been convicted of breaking and entering, the judge sentenced Bambi to two years in prison.

Exercise 8.4

1. Travelling in Quebec, a knowledge of French is useful.

2. Her saddle firmly cinched, Marie led the mare out of the barn.

3. After playing for the crowd all night, the applause was welcome.

4. Being terribly shy, the family gave her a quiet birthday party.

5. Badly banged up in the collision, Kathy slowly brought the boat into dock.

6. Standing in the cold water for more than an hour, the cold numbed him to the bone.

7. Being very weak in math, the job was out of my reach.

8. Looking for a job, a good résumé is vital to success.

9. Living kilometres away from anything, a car is a necessity.

10. Having had the same roommate for three years, my parents suggested

    that I look for another.

Exercise 8.5

Correct the dangling modifiers in Exercise 8.3 by changing them into dependent clauses.

Exercise 8.6

Correct the dangling modifiers in Exercise 8.4 by changing them into dependent clauses.

Correct the misplaced and dangling modifiers in Exercises 8.7 and 8.8 in any way you choose. Our answers on pages 438 and 439 are only suggestions.

Exercise 8.7

1. The sign said that students were only admitted to the pub.

2. While sleeping, the blankets were kicked off the bed.

3. The lion was recaptured before anyone was mauled or bitten by the

    trainer.

4. Swimming isn't a good idea if polluted.

5. Gnawing on a bone, Joseph found his dog.

6. Employees who are late often are dismissed without notice.

7. After waiting for you for more than an hour, the evening was ruined.

8. Driving through the desert, our mouths became drier and drier.

9. We hired the first designer who applied because of her experience.

10. The president spoke glowingly of the retiring workers who had worked

    long and loyally for 20 minutes.

Exercise 8.8

1. Everyone stared as she rode through town on a horse in a bikini.

2. Though drunk daily, many residents don't trust city water.

3. Being an introvert who disliked crowds, a dog became Paul's chief companion.

4. Although Jan lives more than 50 km away, he nearly manages to come to every class.

5. Before beginning to write the exam, prayer is a recommended strategy.

6. After giving birth to a litter of twelve, my sister had her Dachshund neutered.

7. I heard about the team's star player being hurt on a sports phone-in show.

8. Canadians learned that a new government had been elected in a news flash.

9. Before buying a used car, the police recommend checking the owner-ship records.

10. We were shot almost the first time we went into the forest during hunting season.

GO TO WEB

EXERCISES 8.3, 8.4

Exercise 8.9

Now test your mastery of modifiers. Correct the errors in this final exercise.

1. Having been torn to shreds and lost a sleeve, Nina realized she could never repair her jacket.

2. It is very annoying when papers are handed out to students with no holes punched in them.

3. It's so cold today that my neighbour is walking her dog wearing earmuffs.

4. Now that he's agreed to take over the cooking, my husband often says he will make chicken vindaloo.

5. In going over your marks, you have an intellect comparable to that of an unwatered plant.

6. Having a college education, a large accounting firm offered Sue a management position with a generous salary.

7. When roasted, you will see how delicious beets can taste.

8. Gary was informed that his application had been rejected by a secretary, who kindly offered him a handkerchief.

9. Being completely prepared for the morning's presentation, a few drinks with friends could not do any harm.

10. Having finally decided which computer to lease, a salesman was summoned to complete the deal.

9

The Parallelism Principle

Brevity, clarity, and force: these are three characteristics of good writing style. **Parallelism** will reinforce these characteristics in everything you write.

When your sentence contains a series of two or more items, they must be grammatically parallel. That is, they must be written in the same grammatical form. Consider this example:

Shefali likes *dancing, skiing,* and *to travel.*

The three items in this series are not parallel. Two end in *-ing*, but the third, *to travel*, is the infinitive form of the verb. To correct the sentence, you must put all the items in the same grammatical form. You have two choices. You can write

Shefali likes *dancing, skiing,* and *travelling.*

Or you can write

Shefali likes *to dance, to ski,* and *to travel.*

Now look at an example with two nonparallel elements:

Most people seek happiness in *long-term relationships* and *work that provides them with satisfaction.*

Again, you could correct this sentence in two ways. You could write "Most people seek happiness *in relationships that are long-term* and *in work that provides them with satisfaction*," but that solution produces a long and clumsy sentence. The shorter version works better: "Most people seek happiness in *long-term relationships* and *satisfying work.*" This version is concise, clear, and forceful.

> Correct faulty parallelism by writing all items in a series in the same grammatical form; that is, all words, or all phrases, or all clauses.

One way to tell whether the items in a series are parallel is to write them out in list form, one below the other. That way, you can see at a glance if all the elements are in the same grammatical form.

Not Parallel	**Parallel**
My ex-boyfriend is *messy, rude,* and *an obnoxious person.*	My ex-boyfriend is *messy, rude,* and *obnoxious.*
(This list has two adjectives and a noun phrase.)	(This list has three adjectives.)
I support myself by *delivering pizza, poker,* and *shooting pool.*	I support myself by *delivering pizza, playing poker,* and *shooting pool.*
(This list has two phrases and one single word as objects of the preposition *by.*)	(This list has three phrases as objects of the preposition *by.*)
Jules wants a job that *will interest him, will challenge him,* and *pays well.*	Jules wants a job that *will interest him, (will) challenge him,* and *(will) pay him well.*
(This series of clauses contains two future tense verbs and one present tense verb.)	(All three subordinate clauses contain future tense verbs.)

As you can see, achieving parallelism is partly a matter of developing an ear for the sound of a correct list. A parallel sentence has a smooth, unbroken rhythm. Practice and the exercises in this chapter will help. Once you have mastered parallelism in your sentences, you will be ready to develop ideas in parallel sequence—in thesis statements, for example—and thus to write clear, well-organized prose. Far from being a frill, parallelism is a fundamental characteristic of good writing.

Correct the sentences where necessary in the following exercises. As you work through these sentences, try to spot parallelism errors from the change in rhythm that the faulty element produces. Then revise the sentence to bring the faulty element into line with the other elements in the series. Check your answers to each set of ten before going on. Answers for this chapter begin on page 439.

Exercise 9.1

1. This is a book to read, enjoy, and keep in your memory.

2. The new brochure on career opportunities is attractive and contains lots of information.

3. Except that it was too long, too much violence, and too expensive, it was a great movie.

4. He ate his supper, did the dishes, watched television, and bedtime.

5. Barking dogs and children who never stop screaming keep me from enjoying the park.

6. In this clinic, we care for the sick, the injured, and also those who are disabled.

7. If she wasn't constantly eating chips, playing bingo, and cigarette smoking, she'd have plenty of money for groceries.

8. Despite the good salary, stimulating environment, and the benefits package that is very generous, I won't be taking the job.

9. So far, the countries I have enjoyed most are China for its people, France for its food, and the beaches of Brazil.

10. She was discouraged by the low pay, being forced to work long hours, and the office politics.

GO TO WEB

EXERCISES 9.1, 9.2

Exercise 9.2

1. During her presentation, she appeared professional, sounded knowledgeable, but was feeling foolish. *[felt]*

2. They are a good team, hard hitting, fast skating, and thinking quickly. *[quick thinking]*

3. I hold a baseball bat right-handed but play hockey left-handed. *[a stick]*

4. A good student attends all classes and projects are always finished on time. *[finishes projects on time]*

5. A good teacher motivates with enthusiasm, informs with sensitivity, and is a compassionate counsellor. *[counsels with compassion]*

6. A good college president has the judgement of Solomon, Plato's wisdom, and the wit of Rick Mercer. *[Th wisdom of Plato]*

7. All his life, Churchill was a walking advertisement for Cuban cigars, the wines of Portugal, and English hats. *[Portugals wine]*

8. Our staff development budget must be increased if we are to provide upgrading and supply training, as well as the encouragement of personal development for 40 new employees. *[and encourage]*

9. Canadians must register the cars they drive, the businesses they own, the contracts they make, the houses they buy, and now gun possession. *[the guns they possess.]*

10. Winter for its cozy fires, summer for its outdoor sports, the flowering trees of spring, and the spectacular colours of autumn: each season has its special appeal. *[spring for; its flowering trees; autumn for its spectacular]*

GO TO WEB

EXERCISES 9.3, 9.4

Exercise 9.3

Revise the following lists by changing the last element to make it parallel with the first two.

Example: mechanically   ~~by using your hands~~   manually

1. happily	joyfully	with sadness
2. see the sky	feel the warmth	wine could be tasted
3. read	learn	have understanding
4. tighten	adjust	make looser
5. broadcasting	nursing	being an engineer
6. insight	intelligence	being knowledgeable
7. highly motivated	fully trained	having lots of education
8. evaluating carefully	waiting patiently	fully exploring

Exercise 9.4

Create a sentence for each of the parallel lists you developed in Exercise 9.3. Example: Our butcher sells chicken that has been manually rather than mechanically deboned.

Exercise 9.5

Here's a more challenging exercise for you to try. The following paragraphs contain errors in fragments, run-ons, and modifiers as well as parallelism. There are ten errors in total. When you've finished your revision, compare your answers with our suggestions.

Photography is a hobby that is educational, provides enjoyment, and practical. Anyone can be successful as a beginning photographer because entry level cameras are now well made, almost foolproof, and they don't cost very much. The pictures they take, however, are of excellent quality. Which encourages the beginner to learn more. The next step might be a

35 mm camera with interchangeable lenses that permit the photographer to enlarge an image and special effects can be created. While these are expensive toys, they provide a great range of possibilities, the "point and press" cameras, no matter how expensive, just don't measure up.

An alternative to 35 mm is digital photography. Compared to 35 mm, digital cameras are less flexible and the price is higher. These cameras are evolving so rapidly, however, that within a few years, digital will over-take 35 mm in price, quality, and it will be more popular. Even now, digital photography has significant advantages. Pictures are loaded on computer disks, so the images can be stored, re-recorded, and manipula-tion is possible. By downloading the pictures into a computer with imag-ing software, the images can be enhanced, re-sized, and changes can be made. Digital photography is the latest stage in the evolution of this intriguing hobby.

Exercise 9.6

As a test of your ability to correct faulty parallelism, revise the following sen-tences.

1. Liza has a daily workout, a weekly lesson, and a massage once a month.

2. The fear of losing is forgotten in the winning joyfulness.

3. Our company hires locally, advertises nationally, and has global sales.

4. They are an odd couple: Suniti is calm and placid, while Ranjan exhibits nervousness and tension.

5. Travel teaches us to be tolerant, resourceful, patience, and independence.

6. After I go to the bank for money, I'll go to the hardware store for nails, and I'll also get paint there.

7. When setting goals, choosing strategies, or policy application, always watch the bottom line.

8. She is addicted to watching the soaps on television, eating junk food in bed, and while at school she plays computer games.

9. A good nurse is knowledgeable, kind, and has sensitivity and skill.

10. She is talkative and aggressive but also has enthusiasm and works hard.

10

Refining by Combining

Sentence Combining

To reinforce what you've learned so far about sentence structure, try your hand at sentence combining. Even though you've eliminated fragments, run-ons, modifier problems, and parallelism problems, you may still find that your sentences don't flow smoothly. Although technically correct, they may be choppy or repetitious. You may also be bored with conveying your ideas in the same old way. If you are not bored, you can be pretty sure your reader is. A paper made up of nothing but short, one-clause sentences is enough to put even the most conscientious reader to sleep. Sentence combining accomplishes three things: it reinforces your understanding of sentence structure; it helps you to refine and polish your writing; and it results in a style that will keep your reader alert and interested in what you have to say.

Sentence combining is a technique that enables you to avoid a monotonous style while at the same time producing correct sentences.

Let's look at two short, technically correct sentences that could be combined:

My boss always arrives late.
She is cranky in the morning.

There are several ways of combining these two statements into a single sentence.

1. You can connect them with an appropriate linking word, such as *and, but, or, nor, for, so,* and *yet.*

My boss always arrives late *and* is cranky in the morning.
My boss is cranky in the morning, *so* she always arrives late.

2. You can change one of the sentences into a subordinate clause.

My boss, *who* is cranky in the morning, always arrives late.
Because my boss is cranky in the morning, she always arrives late.

3. You can change one of the sentences into a modifying phrase.

Being late, my boss is always cranky in the morning.
My boss, *always late,* is cranky in the morning.

4. Sometimes you can reduce one of your sentences to a single-word modifier.

My *cranky* boss always arrives late in the morning.

In sentence combining, you are free to move parts of the sentence around, change words, add or delete words, or make whatever other changes you think necessary. Anything goes, so long as you don't drastically alter the meaning of the base sentences. Remember that your aim in combining sentences is to create effective sentences—not long ones. Clarity is essential and brevity has force. Here's another example to consider.
Correct but choppy sentences conveying an idea:

Water is vital to life.
It is an important Canadian resource.
It must be protected.

Correct and smooth sentences conveying the same idea:

Water, which is vital to life, is an important Canadian resource that must be protected.
An important Canadian resource, water is vital to life and must be protected.
Water is an important Canadian resource that must be protected because it is vital to life.

The skills that you learn by combining sentences develop your understanding of the connections between ideas. They are useful not only in writing and speaking, but also in reading, listening, and problem-solving.

REVIEW OF CONJUNCTIONS AND RELATIVE PRONOUNS

Two of the most common methods of combining sentences are by using conjunctions and relative pronouns, both of which often cause problems for students whose native language is not standard English. So we will review the rule governing these two linking techniques first, before moving to the creative writing aspect of sentence combining. Those who do not need this review should turn now to Exercise 10.3.

A. USING CONJUNCTIONS TO COMBINE CLAUSES

Use only one connecting word between two clauses.

This rule holds whether you intend to create a sentence consisting of two coordinating independent clauses or one consisting of a main clause and a subordinate clause. For example, let's suppose you want to combine "I enjoy school" with "I also like my part-time job."

Incorrect: *Although* I enjoy school, *and* I also like my part-time job.
Correct: I enjoy school, *and* I also like my part-time job.
Also correct: *Although* I enjoy school, I also like my part-time job.

Now test your understanding of this important point by doing the following exercise.

Exercise 10.1

Read through the sentences below and decide whether each one is correct or incorrect. For the incorrect sentences, cross out the unnecessary conjunction. Be sure your revised sentences are correctly capitalized and punctuated. Answers to exercises in this chapter begin on page 440.

1. Although the test was difficult, so I passed it.

2. After eating our lunch, then we continued working.

3. When December is over, winter continues for two or three months.

4. Since our essay is due tomorrow, so we must stay up late tonight.

5. Even though the pictures are good, yet I hate seeing myself.

6. Before the party, she cooked food for 12 people.

7. Though having a car would be convenient, but I need the money for other things.

8. If this book will help me, so I will buy it.

9. Where a mistake has been found, so it must be corrected.

10. Although many are cold, few are frozen.

GO TO WEB

EXERCISE 10.1

B. USING RELATIVE PRONOUNS TO COMBINE CLAUSES

You can often combine two clauses by using a relative pronoun (*who, whom, whose, that, which*) to join them. (If you are not sure when to use *that/which* or *who/whom*, see Chapter 16, page 186). Below are some examples of the different ways you can use a relative pronoun to join two clauses.

Separate Sentences	**Combined Sentence**
The man is waiting in the car. He is my father.	The man *who* is waiting in the car is my father. (NOT "The man who is waiting in the car he is my father.")
Yesterday Gina met Raffi. His family lives in Beirut.	Yesterday, Gina met Raffi *whose* family lives in Beirut.
I need a copy of *Frankenstein*. Ms. Lee assigned this book last week.	I need a copy of *Frankenstein*, *which* Ms. Lee assigned last week.
Frankenstein is a novel. It was written in 1818 by Mary Shelley.	*Frankenstein* is a novel *that* was written in 1818 by Mary Shelley.

Exercise 10.2

Combine the following sentences, using the relative pronoun given in parentheses as the link. Then check your answers on page 440.

1. I have a teacher. The teacher always wears a tie. (who)

2. Here is the car. This car is always breaking down. (that)

3. I am enrolled in an art class. The class meets Wednesday evenings. (that)

4. That singer just won a Grammy. I always forget her name. (whose)

5. The pen is broken. It is the pen you gave me. (that)

6. My plant is dead. You never watered it. (which)

7. The cell phone is ringing. You always carry it. (that)

8. Lisa babysits for a man. The man's wife speaks only Japanese. (whose)

9. The taxi driver took me to the airport. He drove 20 km over the speed limit all the way. (who)

10. My roommate is finally moving out. His snoring keeps me awake. (whose)

GO TO WEB

EXERCISE 10.2

In the following exercises, try your answers aloud before you write them down. (You may want to scan the punctuation information in Chapters 18 and 19 before you tackle these exercises.)

Exercise 10.3

1. There is bad weather.
   The wind blows from the east. (when)

   When the wind blows from the east, there is bad weather.

2. These shoes fit well.
   These shoes weren't very expensive. (yet)

   These shoes fit well, yet they weren't very expensive

3. High marks in college are a matter of luck.
   Some college students believe this. (that)

   _____

   _____

4. She has both oars in the water.
   The oars are on the same side of the boat. (but)

   _____

   _____

5. Rail travel is declining.
   Rail travel is economical. (even though)

   Even though _____

   _____

6. Shelagh Rogers is an announcer for the CBC.
   Shelagh Rogers has an unforgettable giggle. (who)

   _____

   _____

7. They won the lottery.
   They ran out of money. (just when)

   _____

   _____

8. Newfoundland's economy cannot rely on unlimited fish stocks.
   Newfoundlanders are beginning to realize this. (that)

   _____

   _____

9. Our department needs an increase in its budget.
   The company's accountants want to reduce our department's budget.
   (but)

   _____

   _____

10. Strong coffee keeps me awake.
    I love the taste of strong coffee.
    I like my coffee hot. (although)

    _____

    _____

    _____

In the two exercises that follow, use all four sentence combining techniques to combine each set of statements into longer, more interesting units.
(*Hint*: Read each set of statements through from beginning to end before you begin to combine them. Try out several variations aloud or in your head before writing down your preferred solution.) There are many ways to combine these short statements to make smooth, effective sentences. Our answers are only suggestions.

Exercise 10.4

1. The cursor is blinking.
   There is no response.

   _____

   _____

   _____

2. The village is very small.
   I grew up in the village.

   _____

   _____

   _____

3. My car is in the repair shop.
   It needs a new alternator.

   _____

   _____

   _____

4. The textbook contains information.
   The information will be on the exam.
   The exam is tomorrow.

   _____

   _____

   _____

5. I'm not in favour of apathy.
   I'm not against apathy, either.

   _____

   _____

   _____

6. Banging your head against a wall uses calories.
   Doing this uses 150 calories an hour.

   _____

   _____

   _____

7. The movie was terrible.
   Our car broke down.
   We had a good time anyway.

   _____

   _____

   _____

8. Many of my friends send me pictures with their e-mail.
   My computer doesn't have much memory.
   It doesn't have enough to receive the pictures.

   _____

   _____

   _____

9. This restaurant is very expensive.
The food is good.
The service is excellent.
I don't mind paying the price.

_____

_____

_____

10. Some people enjoy hockey.
Others prefer soccer.
Soccer is the world's most popular spectator sport.

_____

_____

_____

Exercise 10.5

1. A good manager must have many skills.
The most important skill is the ability to delegate.

_____

_____

_____

2. The stapler is missing.
The stapler was clearly labelled.
It had my name labelled on it.

_____

_____

_____

3. Saskatchewan is where I was born.
I was born in Weyburn.
I have not lived there since I was a baby.

_____

_____

_____

4. A sauna provides no proven health benefits.
   I find a sauna very refreshing.
   A sauna is refreshing when the weather is cold.

   _____

   _____

   _____

5. English muffins were not invented in England.
   French fries were not invented in France.

   _____

   _____

   _____

6. "Irritainment" is a word used to describe media spectacles.
   These are spectacles that are annoying.
   These are spectacles that are strangely addictive.

   _____

   _____

   _____

7. An example of "irritainment" was the Monica Lewinsky scandal.
   An example of "irritainment" was *Survivor*.

   _____

   _____

   _____

8. Our college has a Continuing Education Department.
   The Continuing Education Department offers courses at night.
   Some of the courses are for credit.
   Others are for interest.

   _____

   _____

   _____

9. Tisa is a Canadian citizen.
   She was born in Halifax.
   She has lived most of her life in Texas.
   She has American citizenship, too.

   _____

   _____

   _____

10. My roommate is not too bright.
    He watches *60 Minutes* on television.
    It takes him an hour and a half.

    _____

    _____

    _____

GO TO WEB

EXERCISES 10.3, 10.4

Exercise 10.6

Combine each set of statements below into a single concise, smooth, and interesting sentence.

1. The train was late.
   We missed our connection.
   We didn't arrive until 4:00 a.m.

   _____

   _____

   _____

2. Your address has changed.
   Our delivery person could not find your location.
   She was unable to deliver your parcel.

   _____

   _____

   _____

3. It is important to choose unfamiliar passwords.
   It is important to change passwords frequently.
   Hackers can do serious damage if they break into our system.

   _____

   _____

   _____

4. Bonita won a silver medal.
   She won it at the 1998 Winter Games.
   Last year, she gave it to her parents.
   She gave it to them for their 25th anniversary.

   _____

   _____

   _____

5. A consultant is a jobless person.
   A consultant is given huge sums of money.
   A consultant shows executives how to work.

   _____

   _____

   _____

6. My eight-year-old sister bought a giant poster.
   The poster was of Britney Spears.
   She hung the poster on her bedroom wall.

   _____

   _____

   _____

7. He finished high school.
   He worked for six months.
   He worked at a telemarketing company.
   He travelled in Spain for three months.

   _____

   _____

   _____

8. Our computer system is down.
   All orders must be taken by hand.
   Orders can be transferred to the computer later.

   _____

   _____

   _____

9. There is a flight leaving in half an hour.
   It will get you to Winnipeg.
   You will have to change planes in Lethbridge.

   _____

   _____

   _____

10. Our community has a recycling program.
    Cardboard, glass, aluminum, and newspapers are recycled.
    Recycling is less expensive than dumping.
    It is better for the environment.

    _____

    _____

    _____

11

Choosing the Right Words

It is of absolutely essential importance that, irregardless of his or her level of education, the writer make every effort to eschew a lot of linguistic constructions that are inappropriate to the subject matter of the composition or that the average dude doesn't get.

What's wrong with this sentence? It contains no errors in spelling, punctuation, grammar, or sentence structure, but it doesn't communicate well. It is a mixture of wordiness, slang, and inappropriate language—all of which are confusing and annoying to readers, who are not going to take the time to "translate" such a message into plain English. Writers are responsible for communicating in standard English, and readers expect them to do so.

Error-free writing should be your goal, and the focus of this book is to help you achieve that goal. However, there are some considerations beyond correctness that you should address if you are to be a competent communicator. These considerations include, first, choosing an appropriate level of language; and second, avoiding wordiness, slang, pretentious language, and non-standard expressions (the words and phrases we call "abusages").

The key to successful communication is consideration of your "receiver," the person who is going to read your words. Readers do two things at once: they look for meaning, and they form an impression (often unconsciously) of the writer. In this chapter, we will give you some tips to help you ensure that your writing is easy to understand and makes a good impression on the reader.

Levels of Language

Communication can occur at many levels, from grunts and mumbles to inspiring speeches; from unintelligible graffiti to moving poetry. Different levels of language are appropriate for different messages and different audiences. In academic and professional writing, you will be expected to use what is called standard written English. Anything less than that will be thought inappropriate by your readers.

Levels of language are defined by vocabulary, by the length and complexity of the sentences and paragraphs, and by tone (how the writing "sounds"). Most of the communication you will encounter or be required to write will be at the **general level**, which is the level used in college and business. Outside of school and off the job, it is appropriate for you to communicate at the **informal level**, which is used in personal writing and in conversation.

The following chart outlines the characteristics of general and informal English.

	Informal	General
Vocabulary	Casual, everyday; some slang and colloquial expressions; contractions commonly used	The language of educated persons; non-technical; readily understood by most readers; few if any colloquial expressions; no slang, few contractions
Sentences and paragraphs	Short, simple sentences; some sentence fragments; dashes used; short paragraphs	Complete sentences of varying lengths; paragraphs vary in length, but are often short
Tone	Casual, conversational; sounds like ordinary speech	Varies to suit message and purpose of writer
Typical uses	E-mail between friends; some fiction; some newspaper columns; often used in advertising	Most of what we read, including newspapers, magazines, most textbooks, business correspondence

Examples:

Informal: I'm dying to take these cool wheels for a spin.
General: I'd like to test drive this sports car.

Informal: She's not going to go for the job.
General: She will not be applying for the position.

Informal: We're fed up with you people, so we're getting somebody else.

General: We are not satisfied with your service, so we have decided on another supplier.

From the chart and these examples, you can see why the general level is preferred for written communication. It's more precise, and it's clear to a wide audience of readers. Informal English is best reserved for conversation or other communication between friends.

Exercise 11.1

Write two reports explaining how you are doing in your program at mid-term. One is an e-mail to a good friend; the other is a report required by the director of your program. Adapt your level of language so that it is appropriate to each situation.

Wordiness

One of the barriers to clear communication is **wordiness**. This problem is caused by using two or more words where one would do. As a matter of courtesy to your reader, you should make your writing as concise as possible.

Here's an example of what we mean. Read through the following passage. Then read it a second time and cross out the unnecessary words and phrases. Finally, compare your revision to the original to see how much shorter and clearer you have made the message.

Recycling, it seems to me, is, in fact, an idea that is so timely and current that it ought to be enforced by the laws of the land. If people in this country, no matter where or who, were required by legislation from our political leaders to recycle wherever, whenever, and whatever possible, then and only then would recycling take on the importance and significance it so rightly deserves.

By eliminating the redundant phrases, you probably came up with a sentence similar to this one: "Recycling is so important that it should be enforced by law." This sentence is concise, clear, and forceful. And it has the added advantage of not irritating readers.

Careless writers fall into the bad habit of using phrases that they think sound important but are actually redundant—that is, they say the same thing twice. The following is a list of some common examples.

Wordy	Concise
a large number of	many
absolutely nothing/everything/ complete	nothing/everything/complete
actual (*or* true) fact	fact
almost always	usually
at that point in time	then
at the present time	now
continue on	continue
could possibly (*or* may possibly, might possibly)	could (*or* may, might)
due to the fact that	because
equally as good	as good
few and far between	rare
final conclusion	conclusion
for the reason that	because
I myself (*or* you yourself, etc.)	I (*or* you, etc.)
I personally think/feel	I think/feel
in every instance	always
in my opinion, I think	I think
in the near future	soon
in today's society/in this day and age	now (*or* today)
is able to	can
personal friend	friend
real, genuine leather (*or* real antique, etc.)	leather (*or* antique, etc.)
red in colour (*or* large in size, etc.)	red (*or* large, etc.)
repeat again	repeat
really, very	These words add nothing to your meaning. Leave them out.
8:00 a.m. in the morning	8:00 a.m.
such as, for example	such as
take active steps	take steps
totally destroyed	destroyed
very (most, quite, almost, rather) unique	unique

By studying these examples, you can see how these and many other phrases add words without adding any meaning to your message. Teachers and editors call these phrases "fill" or "padding," and they urge students to eliminate them from their writing if they want to build a good relationship with their readers.

Exercise 11.2

Revise these sentences to make them shorter and clearer. Answers for exercises in this chapter begin on page 441.

1. Several of my close personal friends and I myself have discussed it among ourselves and decided to go to the gym.

2. We were amazed and surprised to learn that the art painting hanging in our residence was a real, genuine work by a really famous and well known artist.

3. Though small in size and light in weight, in actual fact she is the best forward on our team.

4. There is absolutely no way that we can ever be completely free of the violence that seems to surround us on all sides in today's society.

5. The professor at that point in time totally destroyed my concentration by announcing and saying that we had only five minutes left, no more.

Slang

Rad, wicked, chewy, dude: are these slang expressions familiar to you? **Slang** is "street talk": non-standard language used in conversation among people belonging to the same social group. Because slang words go out of date quickly and are understood by a limited group of people, you should avoid them in all but your most informal conversations and personal e-mails.

If you are in doubt about a word, check a dictionary. If the word you want is a slang term, it will have *sl.* beside it. Some words—for example, *cool, neat, bombed*—have both a standard meaning and a slang meaning. By taking the time to choose words and expressions that are appropriate to written English, you will increase your chances of communicating clearly and gaining your readers' respect.

Exercise 11.3

Write a list of ten slang expressions in current use. If you aren't familiar with that many slang terms, consult with others to develop your list. "Translate" these words or phrases into general level English that would be appropriate in writing.

Here are some examples to get you started:

phat	that's dope
that's cas	he's money
shot not!	bling bling

Pretentious Language

If slang is language that is too casual for informal writing, its opposite is **pretentious language**: words that are too formal for general writing. Never use a long, difficult, or obscure word when a simpler word will do. Your writing will be easier to read and your message clearer and more convincing if you write to inform rather than to impress.

You can recognize pretentious language easily: the words are long, unfamiliar, and sound unnatural. If the average reader needs a dictionary to "translate" your words into general English, then your writing is inflated and inappropriate. Consider these examples:

Before we embark on our journey, we must refuel our vehicle.

The refrigerator is bare of comestibles, so it is time to repair to the local emporium and purchase victuals.

With your dictionary in hand, you can translate these pompous sentences into plain English.

Before we leave, we need to put gas in the car.

The refrigerator is empty, so it's time to go to the store and buy some food.

But why should you? It's the writer's job to communicate, and a pretentious writer makes the reader do too much work. Here is a list of the most common offenders, together with their general level equivalents.

Pretentious	**Clear**
ascertain	find out
commence	begin
endeavour	try
facilitate	help
finalize	finish
manifest	show
reside	live
transmit	send
utilize	use

The cure for pretentious language is simple: be considerate of your readers. If you want your readers to understand and respect you, write in a simple, straightforward style.

Exercise 11.4

Revise the following sentences to eliminate pretentious language in favour of plain English. You may need to use your dictionary to complete this exercise. Compare your answers with our suggestions.

1. You should exercise diligence when utilizing an axe.

2. We reside at the conjunction of Elm and Trasker Streets.

3. After we had surveyed the task, we opted to request assistance.

4. His supervisor is conscious of that male juvenile's aversion to physical exertion.

5. We are all endeavouring diligently to finalize this project so that we can transmit it coincident with the deadline.

Abusages

Some words and expressions that occasionally appear in writing are ALWAYS incorrect. Using these expressions tells your reader that you lack basic knowledge of standard English. It's true that you will hear these words and expressions in everyday speech, but wherever they appear, they are non-standard, and they give the listener the impression that the speaker is uneducated.

The list below includes some of the worst offenders. Be sure none of these words or expressions EVER appears in your writing.

alot	There is no such word. Use *much* or *many*. (*A lot* is acceptable in informal usage.)
anyways (anywheres)	There is no *s* on these words.
between you and I	A commonly misused expression for *between you and me.*
can't hardly **couldn't hardly**	Use *can hardly* or *could hardly*.
could of (would of, should of)	The helping verb needed is *have*, not *of*. Write *could have, would have, should have*.
didn't do nothing	All double negatives ("couldn't see nothing," "couldn't get nowhere," "wouldn't talk to nobody") are wrong. Write *didn't do anything, couldn't see anything, couldn't get anywhere, wouldn't talk to anyone*.
I/you/he be	Non-standard verb forms. Use *I am, you are, he is*.
I/you has; he have	Non-standard verb forms. Use *I/you have; he has*.
irregardless	There is no such word. *Regardless* is the word you want.
***media* used as singular**	The word *media* is plural. The singular is *medium*. Newspapers and television are mass *media*. Radio is an electronic *medium*.
off of	Use *off* alone: "I fell *off* the wagon."
***prejudice* used as an adjective**	It is wrong to write "She is *prejudice* against blondes." Use *prejudiced*.
prejudism	There is no such word. Use *prejudice*. "A judge should show no *prejudice* to either side."
***real* used as an adverb**	"Real good," "real bad," and "real nice" are wrong. You could use *really* or *very*, but such filler words add nothing to your meaning.

reason is because	Use *the reason is that*: "The reason is that my printer blew up."
suppose to	This expression, like *"use to,"* is non-standard. Use *supposed to* and *used to*.
themself	Also "theirself," "ourselfs," "yourselfs," and "themselfs." These are all non-standard words. The plural of *self* is *selves*: *themselves, ourselves,* and so on. Don't use "theirselves"; it's another non-standard word.
youse	There is no such word. *You* is the singular and plural form of the pronoun. This word is often heard in restaurants: "Are youse ready to order?" and labels the server as a speaker of non-standard English.

Exercise 11.5

Revise the following sentences to eliminate all abusages. Then compare your answers with our suggestions.

1. Prakash is real talented, so he could of chosen alot of different careers.

2. Irregardless of your opinion, I think the media is fairly reliable.

3. Between you and I, Karol didn't perform real well in this afternoon's practice.

4. The reason I be home now is because I couldn't do nothing to help at the hospital.

5. The reason youse are failing is because you don't do no homework.

6. We were real sure of ourselfs going into the race, but once we fell off of our bikes, we couldn't hardly hope to win.

7. Isa's father is not prejudice; he hates all her boyfriends, irregardless of their backgrounds.

8. There has been alot of investigations into charges that our police department demonstrates prejudism against minority groups.

9. I'm real grateful to you for helping me the way you use to so long ago.

10. We drove Karia home because, after the police took her licence off of her, she wasn't suppose to be driving anywheres.

Exercise 11.6

Revise the following sentences to eliminate all instances of wordiness, slang, pretentious language, and abusages. There are 20 errors. You may need your dictionary for this exercise.

1. Absolutely no one should be allowed or permitted to manifest prejudice and get away with it.

2. Despite the irrefutable fact that exams commenced on your birthday, we wouldn't of bombed if we had studied more and partied less.

3. Get real. I wouldn't copy an essay off of nobody who is failing English.

4. Your suggestion is equally as good as hers; nevertheless, I cannot choose yours for the simple reason that you are a good personal buddy of mine.

5. The old antique car elicited a wicked price at the auction due to the fact that it was in real excellent condition.

Now that you have completed Unit 2, you are ready to begin revising whatever you write. Read your work aloud. How your sentences sound is important. Test your writing against the six characteristics of successful sentences:

Summary

1. **Meaning**: Have you said what you mean?
2. **Clarity**: Is each sentence clear? Can it be understood on the first reading?
3. **Coherence**: Do the parts of your sentences fit together logically and smoothly?
4. **Emphasis**: Are the most important ideas either at the end or at the beginning of each sentence?
5. **Conciseness**: Is every sentence direct and to the point? Have you cut out all redundant or repetitious words?
6. **Rhythm**: Do your sentences flow smoothly? Are there any interruptions in the development of the key idea(s)? If there are, do the interruptions help to emphasize certain points, or do they distract the reader?

If your sentences pass all six tests of successful sentence style, you may be confident that they are both technically correct and pleasing to the ear. No reader could ask for more.

Grammar

Grammar

The following quick quiz will let you see at a glance which chapters of Unit 3 you need to focus on. The paragraphs below contain 20 errors in grammar: verb forms, subject-verb agreement, verb tense consistency, pronoun form, pronoun-antecedent agreement, and pronoun consistency. When you've made your corrections, turn to page 442 and compare your version with ours. For each error you miss, the answer key directs you to the chapter you need to work on.

1   "What's in a name?" Shakespeare asked. The answer is, "a lot." For instance, the decade in which you were born may be indicated by your name. Like skirt length and tie width, names will go in and out of fashion. If your grandparents was born in North America, it wouldn't be surprising if their names be John and Mary because those names were very popular in the early part of the 20th century. Other favourites of the era was William, James, George, Helen, Margaret, and Mildred.

2   If your father and mother were born in the 1940s or 1950s, him and her might very well be named Robert, Mark, or Richard, and Linda, Barbara, or Patricia. Interestingly, the name Michael first appeared on the top ten list

in the 1950s and then tops the charts as the most popular male name for the next 40 years. Men's names seem to change fashion more slowly than women's names.

3   In the 1960s, the name Lisa become the most popular female name. Other favourites included Kimberley, Donna, and Michelle. If you was born in North America in the 1970s, there is a good chance that one's parents named you Jennifer, Amy, or Jessica; or Christopher, Matthew, or Justin. In the 1980s, baby boys were likely to be named Joshua, Daniel, or Jason. Those little boys probably go to kindergarten with a lot of little girls named Amanda, Ashley, and Tiffany. In the 1990s, the most popular names were Jacob, Nicholas, and Tyler for boys; Emily, Brittany, and Megan for girls.

4   What about the future? A Web site called Babyzone.com offers advice for soon-to-be parents. It tells you that "power names" for the new century includes one-syllable names such as Grace, Cole, and Claire. Place names are also high on the list: Dakota, Dallas, Phoenix, and India. For new parents that are curious about unusual names celebrities have gave their children, Babyzone advises that musician Bob Geldof and his wife names his three daughters Peaches, Pixie, and Fifi-Trixibelle.

5   If you are interested in tradition, a list of Shakespearean names are also provided by Babyzone. The works of Shakespeare are full of beautiful names (e.g., Miranda, Olivia, Ariel), but if you're tempted to choose a

Shakespearean name for your baby, the play should be read by you first. It would be a real burden for a child to go through their life as Malvolio, Goneril, or Caliban.

12

Choosing the Correct Verb Form

Errors in grammar are like flies in soup. Most of the time, they don't affect meaning any more than flies affect flavour, but they are distracting and irritating. You must eliminate grammar errors from your writing if you want your readers to pay attention to what you say rather than to how you say it.

The verb is the most complex and essential part of a sentence. In fact, a verb is to a sentence what an engine is to a car: the source of power and a frequent cause of trouble.[1]

This chapter will look at two verb problems that occur in many people's writing: incorrect use of irregular verbs and difficulties with the passive voice.

The Principal Parts of Verbs

All verb formations are based on one of the verb's **principal parts**. Technically, the principal parts are not the **tenses** (time indicators) of the verb; they are the elements that are used to construct the various tenses.

Every verb has four forms, called its principal parts.
1. The **base** (or **infinitive**) form: the form used with *to*
2. The **simple past** (also called the **past** form)
3. The **present participle** (the *-ing*) form
4. The **past participle**: used with *has* or *have*

[1] Verb tenses are reviewed in Chapter 28. Negatives, modals, and participial adjectives (e.g., *confused* vs. *confusing*) are reviewed in Chapter 29.

Errors in grammar are like flies in soup: distracting and irritating.

Here are some examples:

Base	Simple Past	Present Participle	Past Participle
A. (to) call	called	calling	(has) called
(to) dance	danced	dancing	(has) danced
(to) work	worked	working	(has) worked
B. (to) do	did	doing	(has) done
(to) eat	ate	eating	(has) eaten
(to) say	said	saying	(has) said

If you study the list above, you will notice an important feature of principal parts. In the first group of three verbs (A), the simple past and the past participle are identical: they are both formed by adding -ed (or simply -d if the verb ends in *-e*, as *dance* does). When both the simple past and the past participle of a verb are formed with *-ed*, the verb is called a **regular verb**. Fortunately, most of the many thousands of English verbs are regular.

In the second group (B), the verbs are called **irregular verbs** because the simple past and past participle are not formed by adding *-ed*. With *do* and *eat*, the simple past and the past participle are different words: *did/done, ate/eaten*. The simple past and past participle of *say* are the same, *said*, but they are not formed with the regular *-ed* ending.

Unfortunately, although there are only a few hundred irregular verbs in English, they are some of the most common verbs in the language; for example, *begin, come, do, go, see,* and *write* are all irregular. Consider the following sentences, all of which are grammatically incorrect:

I begun classes yesterday.

He come to see me last week.

I done it before.

She has went away on vacation.

He seen his girlfriend with another man.

I have wrote you an e-mail answering your questions.

These sentences probably sound wrong to your ear, but if you look at the list of irregular verbs that follows, you will understand *why* they are incorrect. What are the correct forms of the verbs in the sentences above? Write them in above the incorrect forms.

If you are not sure of the principal parts of a verb, check your dictionary. If the verb is regular, you will find the principal parts listed after the entry for the base form. For instance, if you look up *sing* in your dictionary, you will find *sang* (simple past), *sung* (past participle), and *singing* (present participle). If no principal parts are listed after the verb you are checking, it is regular and forms its simple past and past participle by adding *-ed*.

The verbs in the list below are used so frequently that it is worth your while to learn their principal parts. We have not included the present participle (the *-ing* form) because it rarely causes difficulty. Problems with it are usually spelling problems. Do you drop the final *-e* when you add *-ing*? What happens to the *-y* in the verb *study*? (The simple past and past participle are *studied*.) Use your dictionary and your spell-checker to be sure you have spelled the forms correctly.

The Principal Parts of Irregular Verbs

Base (Use with *to* and with helping/auxiliary verbs)	Simple Past	Past Participle (Use with *has, have, had*)
be (am, is)	was/were	been
bear	bore	borne
beat	beat	beaten
become	became	become
begin	began	begun
bend	bent	bent
bind	bound	bound
bite	bit	bitten
bleed	bled	bled
blow	blew	blown
break	broke	broken
bring	brought (*not* brang)	brought (*not* brung)
broadcast	broadcast	broadcast
build	built	built
burst	burst	burst
buy	bought	bought
catch	caught	caught
choose	chose	chosen
cling	clung	clung
come	came	come
cost	cost	cost
cut	cut	cut
deal	dealt	dealt
dig	dug	dug
dive	dived/dove	dived
do	did (*not* done)	done
draw	drew	drawn
dream	dreamed/dreamt	dreamed/dreamt
drink	drank (*not* drunk)	drunk
eat	ate	eaten
fall	fell	fallen
feed	fed	fed
feel	felt	felt
fight	fought	fought
find	found	found

Base (Use with *to* and with helping/auxiliary verbs)	Simple Past	Past Participle (Use with *has, have, had*)
flee	fled	fled
fling	flung	flung
fly	flew	flown
forbid	forbade	forbidden
forget	forgot	forgotten/forgot
forgive	forgave	forgiven
freeze	froze	frozen
get	got	got/gotten
give	gave	given
go	went	gone (*not* went)
grow	grew	grown
have	had	had
hear	heard	heard
hide	hid	hidden
hit	hit	hit
hold	held	held
hurt	hurt	hurt
keep	kept	kept
know	knew	known
lay (to put or place)	laid	laid
lead	led	led
leave	left	left
lie (to recline)	lay	lain (*not* layed)
light	lit/lighted	lit/lighted
lose	lost	lost
make	made	made
mean	meant	meant
meet	met	met
mistake	mistook	mistaken
pay	paid	paid
raise	raised	raised
ride	rode	ridden
ring	rang	rung
rise	rose	risen
run	ran	run
say	said	said
see	saw (*not* seen)	seen
seek	sought	sought
sell	sold	sold

Base (Use with *to* and with helping/auxiliary verbs)	Simple Past	Past Participle (Use with *has*, *have*, *had*)
set	set	set
shake	shook	shaken (*not* shook)
shine	shone	shone
shoot	shot	shot
show	showed	shown
shrink	shrank	shrunk
sing	sang	sung
sink	sank	sunk
sit	sat	sat
sleep	slept	slept
slide	slid	slid
speak	spoke	spoken
speed	sped	sped
spend	spent	spent
spin	spun	spun
stand	stood	stood
sting	stung	stung
strive	strove	striven
steal	stole	stolen
stick	stuck	stuck
strike (hit)	struck	struck
strike (affect)	struck	stricken
swear	swore	sworn
swim	swam	swum
swing	swung (*not* swang)	swung
take	took	taken
teach	taught	taught
tear	tore	torn
tell	told	told
think	thought	thought
throw	threw	thrown
understand	understood	understood
wear	wore	worn
weave	wove	woven
win	won	won
wind	wound	wound
withdraw	withdrew	withdrawn
write	wrote	written

The sentences in the exercises below require both the simple past and the past participle of the verb shown at the left. Write the required form in each blank. Do not add or remove helping verbs. Be sure to check your answers after each set. Answers for this chapter begin on page 444.

Exercise 12.1

1. wear   You _____ your good hiking boots only once, but after you have _____ them several times, you won't want to take them off.

2. give   The tourists _____ Terry a tip after she had _____ them directions to the hotel.

3. begin   After the project had _____ , the members of the team soon _____ to disagree on how to proceed.

4. eat   I _____ as though I had not _____ in a month.

5. cost   The vacation in Cuba _____ less than last year's trip to Jamaica had _____ and was much more fun.

6. bring   If you have _____ your children with you, I hope you also _____ a play pen to keep them out of trouble during your stay.

7. grow   The noise from the party next door _____ louder by the hour, but by midnight I had _____ used to it, and went to sleep.

8. sit   Marc _____ in front of the TV all morning; by evening he will have _____ there for eight hours—a full working day!

9. write   After she had _____ the essay that was due last week, she _____ e-mails to all her friends.

10. pay   I _____ off my credit cards, so I have not _____ this month's rent.

Exercise 12.2

1. ride   I had never _____ in a stretch limo until I _____ in one at Jerry's wedding.

2. sing   She _____ a silly little song that her father had _____ when she
was a baby.

3. teach   Harold had been _____ to play by a loving father, and that was
the way he _____ his daughter.

4. find   He _____ the solution that hundreds of mathematicians over
three centuries had not _____ .

5. fly   Suzhu had once _____ to Whitehorse, so when she _____ north
to Tuktoyaktuk, she knew what to expect.

6. feel   At first, they had _____ silly in the new uniforms, but after winning three games in a row, they _____ much better.

7. lie   The cat _____ right where the dog had _____ all morning.

8. go   We _____ to our new home to find that the movers had _____
to the wrong address to deliver our furniture.

9. lose   The reason you _____ those customers is that you have _____
confidence in your sales technique.

10. steal   I _____ two customers away from the sales representative who
earlier had _____ my best account.

GO TO WEB

EXERCISE 12.1

Exercise 12.3

1. think   I had _____ that you were right, but when I _____ more about
your answer, I realized you were wrong.

2. buy   If we had _____ this stock 20 years ago, the shares we _____
would now be worth a fortune.

3. do   They _____ what was asked, but their competitors, who had
_____ a better job, got the contract.

4. show   Today our agent _____ us a house that was much better suited

to our needs than anything she had _____ us previously.

5. hurt   Budget cuts had _____ the project, but today's decision to lay

off two of our workers _____ it even more.

6. throw   The rope had not been _____ far enough to reach those in the

water, so Mia pulled it in and _____ it again.

7. lay   Elzbieta _____ her passport on the official's desk where the

other tourists had _____ theirs.

8. put   I have _____ your notebook in the mail, but your pen and

glasses I will _____ away until I see you again.

9. fight   My parents _____ again today, the way they have _____ almost

every day for the last 20 years.

10. break   She _____ the Canadian record only six months after she had

_____ her arm in training.

GO TO WEB

EXERCISE 12.2

Exercise 12.4

Correct the 20 verb errors in the following sentences.

1. We have chose to stay, but we could have went if we wanted to.

2. I have not forgave Tran for taking the essay that had took me three

weeks to write.

3. After our long walk to school we were froze, but we quickly recovered

once we had drank some hot chocolate.

4. Sneaking in to class late, Vic lay the essay on the desk with the others;

he had wrote it during his lunch.

5. The twins had dove into the pool before they realized that they had never swam in water over their heads before.

6. Once they had ate all the salad and pasta they wanted, they seen the dessert table.

7. A storm had blew the old tree over; it had grew there for over a hundred years.

8. They had ran all the way to school, while their boyfriends had rode in an air conditioned car.

9. We brung a suitcase full of souvenirs when we come home from Taiwan.

10. They insist they done nothing wrong, but she says that she has forgave them anyway.

Choosing between Active and Passive Voice

Verbs have another quality besides tense (or time). Verbs also have what is called "voice," which means the quality of being either active or passive. In sentences with **active voice** verbs, the "doer" of the action is the grammatical subject of the sentence.

> Active voice: Good parents <u>support</u> their children.
> A car <u>crushed</u> the cat.
> Someone <u>will show</u> a movie in class.

In sentences with **passive voice** verbs, the grammatical subject of the sentence is the "receiver" of the action (that is, the subject is "passively" acted upon), and the "doer" becomes an object of the preposition *by* or is absent from the sentence entirely, as in the third example below.

> Passive voice: Children <u>are supported</u> by good parents.
> The cat <u>was crushed</u> by a car.
> A movie <u>will be shown</u> in class.

Notice that active and passive verbs can be in any tense. Present, past, and future tense verbs are used in both sets of examples above. Can you tell which is which?

Passive voice verbs are formed by using a form of *be* + the past participle form of the verb. This is another situation where you need to know the past participle form of irregular verbs; for instance, in the third example above, the correct passive construction is *will be shown*, not *will be showed*. In the examples below, note the different tenses and pay special attention to the passive voice verb forms.

	Active	**Passive**
present	The boss signs the cheque.	The cheque is signed by the boss.
past	The boss signed the cheque.	The cheque was signed by the boss.
future	The boss will sign the cheque.	The cheque will be signed by the boss.
present progressive	The boss is signing the cheque.	The cheque is being signed by the boss.
past progressive	The boss was signing the cheque.	The cheque was being signed by the boss.

Exercise 12.5

Underline the verbs in the sentences with two lines. Then identify them as either active (A) or passive (P). The first one is done for you. The answers to the exercises in this part of the chapter begin on page 445.

1. __A__ The professor <u>checks</u> our homework every day.

2. _____ The report is being prepared by the marketing department.

3. _____ The car was being driven by a chauffeur.

4. _____ Clyneria will invite Kiefer to the party.

5. _____ The CN Tower is visited by hundreds of people every day.

6. _____ My best friend designed this bracelet.

7. _____ *The English Patient* was written by Canadian author Michael Ondaatje.

8. _____ Hollywood made the book into a successful movie.

9. _____ The song was performed by Eminem.

10. _____ A hurricane is destroying your village!

Exercise 12.6

Now rewrite the sentences in Exercise 12.5, changing active voice verbs to passive and passive voice verbs to active. We've done the first sentence for you as an example.

1. Our homework is checked by the professor every day.
2.
3.
4.
5.
6.
7.
8.
9.
10.

Active voice verbs are more direct and emphatic than passive verbs. Good writers use the active voice unless there is a specific reason to use the passive. There are three situations in which the passive voice is preferable.

1. The person or agent that performed the action is not known.

The telephone <u>had been left</u> off the hook for two days.
Primate Road is the name that <u>has been given</u> to our street.
This work stations <u>is</u> not ergonomically <u>designed</u>.

2. You want to place the emphasis on the person, place, or object that was affected by an action rather than on the subject performing the action.

The computer lab <u>was broken</u> into by a group of angry students.

This sentence focusses the reader's attention on the computer lab rather than on the students. If we reconstruct the sentence in the active voice, we produce a quite different effect.

A group of angry students <u>broke</u> into the computer lab.

3. You are writing a technical report, a scientific report, or a legal document.

Passive verbs are the appropriate choice when the focus is on the facts, methods, or procedures involved in an experiment, situation, or event rather than on the person(s) who discovered or performed them. Passive verbs establish an impersonal tone that is appropriate to these kinds of writing. Contrast the emphasis and tone of these sentence pairs:

Passive: The heat <u>was increased</u> to 150°C and <u>was maintained</u> at that temperature.
Active: My lab partner and I <u>increased</u> the heat to 150°C and <u>maintained</u> it at that temperature.

Passive: Our annual report <u>was approved</u> by the board on February 15.
Active: The board <u>approved</u> our annual report on February 15.

In general, because active verbs are more concise and forceful than passive verbs, they add focus and strength to your writing. When you find a passive verb in your writing, think about *who* is doing *what* to *whom*. Ask yourself why the *who* is not the subject of your sentence. If there is a good reason, then use the passive voice. Otherwise, change the verb.

Exercise 12.7

Rewrite the sentences below, changing the verbs from passive to active voice. You may need to add a word or word group to identify the doer of the action expressed by the verb.

1. The puppy was named by Lisa.

2. A great sigh of relief was let out by me.

3. His business card was given to me by the sales representative.

4. An error in your bill was made by our computer.

5. The short route home was taken by my brother.

6. On our first anniversary, our portrait was taken by a professional photographer.

7. American election practices are not always understood by Canadians.

8. Very little about Canada is known by most Americans.

9. In today's class, their research papers will be worked on by all students.

10. All the information you need to become a competent writer is contained in this book.

Exercise 12.8

Rewrite the sentences below, changing the verbs from passive to active voice. Then compare your revision to the original and, with the three reasons for choosing the passive voice in mind (page 154 and 155), decide which sentence is more effective.

1. The professor was told by Bambi that she was finding the course too difficult.

2. This document was not typed by a member of our staff.

3. A group of pedestrians was almost run into by a Ford Explorer running a red light.

4. My ability to read was helped by my new bifocals.

5. The body had been dragged for almost 2 km before being hidden in the underbrush.

6. At 4:00 each afternoon, the linens are laid and the tables are set by the dining room servers.

7. In the parade around the stadium, the Olympic flag was carried by a biathlete.

8. The project was delayed because of poor communication between the members of the team.

9. His bookcase is used by my brother to hold his bowling trophies and empty fast food containers.

10. A state of emergency has been declared and a special fund to aid the victims of the flood has been set up by the provincial government.

GO TO WEB

EXERCISES 12.3, 12.4

Exercise 12.9

Rewrite the following paragraph, changing passive voice verbs to active where appropriate.

(1) After graduation, Sati was hired by a large publishing company to sell humanities textbooks to college professors. (2) Her first call was made at a university with a huge arts faculty. (3) Her company's books were being used by many of the professors, so Sati was not too worried about having to sell aggressively. (4) The popular history text on her list, however, had not been adopted by all faculty in the history department, so that is where her visit was begun. (5) A list of all the faculty members in the department was provided to Sati by the secretary. (6) Her book was not being used by professors Maheu, Jaffer, and Vacant, so the search for their offices was begun. (7) According to the schedule posted on his door, a class was being taught by Professor Maheu for the next two hours. (8) Professor Jaffer was found by Sati to be receptive and pleasant, but the text was not appropriate for the courses being taught by her. (9) Last, Sati went to find Professor Vacant, and his office was finally located by her. (10) She knocked on the door and was told to come in. (11) When Professor Vacant was asked for by Sati, the woman at one of the desks in the office looked blank. (12) She said there

was no person in the history department by that name. (13) The fact that Professor Vacant's name was on the list Sati had been given was politely pointed out by her. (14) The woman at the desk looked at the list and began to laugh. (15) Finally, the joke was understood by Sati. (16) There was no Professor Vacant; the history department had a vacant position.

13

Mastering Subject–Verb Agreement

Singular and Plural

One of the most common writing errors is lack of agreement between subject and verb. Both must be singular, or both must be plural. If one is singular and the other plural, you have an agreement problem. You have another kind of agreement problem if your subject and verb are not both in the same "person" (see Chapter 17).

Let's clarify some terms. First, it's important to distinguish between **singular** and **plural**.

- "Singular" means one person or thing.
- "Plural" means more than one person or thing.

Second, it's important to know what we mean when we refer to the concept of **person**:

- "First person" is the person(s) speaking or writing: *I, me; we, us*
- "Second person" is the person(s) being addressed: *you*
- "Third person" is the person(s) being spoken or written about: *he, she, it; they, them*

Here's an example of the singular and plural forms of a regular verb in the present tense.

	Singular	Plural
first person	I win	we win
second person	you win	you win
third person	she wins (*or* he, it, the horse wins)	they win (*or* the horses win)

The form most often causes trouble is the third person because the verb endings do not match the subject endings. Third-person singular present tense verbs end in -s, but their singular subjects do not. Third-person plural verbs never end in -s, while their subjects normally do. Look at these examples.

A <u>fire</u> <u>burns</u>.
The <u>car</u> <u>skids</u>.
The <u>woman</u> <u>cares</u> for the children.

The three singular verbs, all of which end in -s (*burns*, *skids*, *cares*), agree with their singular subjects (*fire*, *car*, *woman*), none of which ends in -s. When the subjects become plural, the verbs change form, too.

Four <u>fires</u> <u>burn</u>.
The <u>cars</u> <u>skid</u>.
The <u>women</u> <u>care</u> for the children.

Now all of the subjects end in -s, and none of the verbs does.
This is **subject–verb agreement**:

Subjects and verbs must either be both singular or both plural.

This rule causes difficulty only when the writer doesn't know which word in the sentence is the subject and so makes the verb agree with the wrong word. As long as you decode the sentence correctly (see Chapter 5), you'll have no problem making every subject agree with its verb. Here's an example of how errors occur.

Only one of the 2000 ticket buyers are going to win.

What is the subject of this sentence? It's not *buyers*, but *one*. The verb must agree with *one*, which is clearly singular. The verb *are* does not agree with *one*, so the sentence is incorrect. It should read

Only <u>one</u> ~~of the 2000 ticket buyers~~ <u>is</u> going to win.

If you are careful about identifying the subject of your sentence, even when it is separated from the verb by other words or phrases, you'll have no difficulty with subject–verb agreement. Before you try the exercise below, reinforce what you've learned by studying these examples.

Incorrect: One of my sisters speak five languages.

Correct: <u>One</u> ~~of my sisters~~ <u>speaks</u> five languages.

Incorrect: Xue, one of the few girls on the team, keep trying for a perfect score.

Correct: <u>Xue,</u> one ~~of the few girls on the team,~~ <u>keeps</u> trying for a perfect score.

Incorrect: One of the students continually write graffiti on the walls of the staff room.

Correct: <u>One</u> ~~of the students~~ continually <u>writes</u> graffiti ~~on the walls of the staff room.~~

Exercise 13.1

Underline the subject in each sentence. Answers for exercises in this chapter begin on page 446.

1. The key to power is knowledge.
2. Here are the invoices for this shipment of software.
3. In the future, instead of live animals, people may choose intelligent machines as pets.
4. At the front of the line stands Professor Temkin, waiting to see Santa.
5. Jupiter and Saturn, the solar system's largest planets, appear close together in the western sky.

Exercise 13.2

Change the subject and verb in each sentence from plural to singular. Underline the subject once and the verb twice. Then check your answers.

1. Girls just want to have fun.

2. Our dogs bark at strangers.

3. The technicians have gone to a conference in Vancouver.

4. Under our back porch live two huge raccoons.

5. Have the lucky winners collected the lottery money?

6. The articles in this journal give you the background information you

   need.

7. Hotels within walking distance of the arena are a necessity for our team.

8. Only recently have our track coaches become interested in chemistry.

9. So far, only two of your answers have been incorrect.

10. The pressures of school work and part-time work have caused many students to drop out.

GO TO WEB

EXERCISE 13.1

Exercise 13.3

Rewrite each sentence, switching the positions of the main elements and revising the verb accordingly. Then check your answers. For example:

Nachos <u>are</u> my favourite snack.
My favourite <u>snack</u> <u>is</u> nachos.

1. Hockey players are a good example.
2. A healthy type of oily fish is sardines.
3. Hand held computers are a necessity in my job.
4. What irritates us is noisy speedboats on our quiet lake.
5. Fresh fruits and vegetables are an important part of a balanced diet.

Exercise 13.4

This exercise will challenge your ability to use singular and plural subjects and verbs correctly. Rewrite the following paragraph, changing its nouns and verbs from plural to singular. Then check your answers. Your first sentence will be "A **dog seems** to understand the **mood** of **its owner**."

Dogs seem to understand the moods of their owners. They are tuned in

to any shifts in emotion or changes in health of the humans they live with.

Doctors will often suggest adding pets to households where there are people suffering from depression or emotional problems. Dogs are sympathetic companions. The moods of elderly people in retirement homes or even hospital wards can be brightened by visits from pet owners and their dogs. Dogs never tire of hearing about the "good old days," and they are uncritical and unselfish in giving affection. Doctors will often encourage epilepsy sufferers to adopt specially trained dogs. Such dogs are so attuned to the health of their owners that they can sense when seizures are about to occur long before the owners can. The dogs then warn the owners of the coming attack, so the owners are able to take safety precautions.

So far, so good. You can find the subject, even when it's hiding on the far side of the verb or separated from the verb by one or more prepositional phrases. You can match up singular subjects with singular verbs and plural subjects with plural verbs. Now let's take a look at a few of the complications that make subject–verb agreement such a disagreeable problem.

Four Special Cases

Some subjects are tricky. They look singular but are actually plural, or they look plural when they're really singular. There are four kinds of these slippery subjects, all of them common and all of them likely to trip up the unwary writer.

1. Multiple subjects joined by *or*; *either . . . or*; *neither . . . nor*; or *not . . . but*.

Most multiple subjects we've dealt with so far have been joined by *and* and have required plural verbs, so agreement hasn't been a problem. But watch out when the two or more elements of a compound subject are joined by *or*; *either . . . or*; *neither . . . nor*; or *not . . . but*. In these cases, the verb agrees in number with the nearest subject. That is, if the subject closest to the verb is singular, the verb will be singular; if the subject closest to the verb is plural, the verb must be plural too.

> Neither the <u>federal government</u> nor the <u>provinces</u> effectively <u>control</u> pollution.

> Neither the <u>provinces</u> nor the <u>federal government</u> effectively <u>controls</u> pollution.

Exercise 13.5

Circle the correct verb for each of the following sentences. Then check your answers.

1. Either Pierre or his sisters (live lives) at home, but not both.
2. Neither the photos nor the painting (reveal reveals) her true beauty.
3. Not one teacher but more than a dozen students (has have) come to help.
4. Fast cars, powerful boats, or any video about them (fascinate fascinates) five-year-old Josh.
5. Neither the landlord nor the tenants (know knows) who is responsible for the break-in.

GO TO WEB

EXERCISE 13.2

2. Subjects that look multiple but really aren't.

Don't be fooled by phrases beginning with words such as *with, like, as well as, together with, in addition to,* and *including.* These prepositional phrases are NOT part of the subject of the sentence. Since they do not affect the verb, you can mentally cross them out.

> My math professor, ~~as well as my counsellor~~, has advised me to change my major.

Two people were involved in the advising; nevertheless, the subject (math professor) is singular, so the verb must be singular (<u>has advised</u>).

All my courses, ~~including English~~, are easier this term.

If you mentally cross out the phrase "including English," you can easily see that the verb (<u>are</u>) must be plural to agree with the plural subject (<u>courses</u>).

Exercise 13.6

Circle the correct verb for each of the following sentences. Then check your answers.

1. Anar, like her sisters, (want wants) to be a nurse.
2. One hotdog with ketchup, mustard, and pickles (has have) more calories than you can imagine.
3. In addition to a tripod and three rolls of film, my camera (was were) stolen from my van.
4. Eddie, together with his band, (is are) featured tonight in the student pub.
5. "People" skills, such as a sense of humour, (doesn't don't) usually appear on a résumé although they are essential in the workplace.

GO TO WEB

EXERCISE 13.3

3.   Words ending in *-one*, *-thing*, or *-body*.

When used as subjects, the words below are always singular. They require singular verbs.

anyone	anything	anybody
everyone	everything	everybody
no one	nothing	nobody
someone	something	somebody

The last part of the pronoun subject is the tip-off here: every*one*, any*thing*, no*body*. If you focus on this last part, you'll remember to use a singular verb with these subjects. Usually, these words cause trouble only when modifiers crop up between them and their verbs. For example, you would never write "Everyone are here." The trouble starts when you insert a group of words in between the subject and the verb. You might, if you weren't careful, write this: "Everyone involved in implementing the company's new policies and procedures are here." The meaning is plural: several people are present. But the subject (*everyone*) is singular, so the verb must be *is*.

Exercise 13.7

Circle the correct verb for each of the following sentences. Then check your answers.

1. Everyone in my photos (has have) red eyes.
2. Nothing (succeed succeeds) like success.
3. Somebody in one of the other offices (wants want) to borrow our coffee maker.
4. Everything we do to try to help them (make makes) things worse.
5. No one carrying a pager or a cell phone (is are) permitted into the theatre.

GO TO WEB

EXERCISE 13.4

4. Units of money, time, mass, length, and distance.

These expressions require singular verbs.

Eight dollars is too much to pay for a hamburger.

Two hours seems like four in our sociology class.

Eighty kilograms is the mass of an average man.

Ten kilometres is too far to walk.

Exercise 13.8

Circle the correct verb for each of the following sentences. Then check your answers.

1. Do you think $30 (is are) too much to pay for a used set of Jim Carrey videos?
2. I think 12 kg (is are) going to be too much turkey for ten people.
3. If you have good equipment and move at a steady speed, the 19 km of the ski trail (go goes) by very quickly.
4. Five hundred grams of grapes (was were) more than I could eat.
5. Five centimetres of ice and slush (take takes) longer to clear than the same amount of snow.

GO TO WEB

EXERCISE 13.5

In the following exercises, correct the errors in subject–verb agreement. Check your answers to each exercise before going on. Answer for this section of the chapter begin on page 447.

Exercise 13.9

1. Not only cat hairs but also ragweed make me sneeze.

2. If either of the twins wear blue, the other is sure to wear green.

3. Neither high wind nor heavy rains was enough to stop our hike on the Coastal Trail.

4. Every one of the winners have accepted an invitation to the awards ceremony.

5. None of the winners want to have her picture taken for publicity.

6. The mother panda, together with her cubs, two handlers, a vet, and three tonnes of food, are being shipped on a chartered jet.

7. In every group project, there is one member of the team who always get stuck with most of the work.

8. According to a survey by my fitness club, either weight lifting or aerobic workouts was what most members wanted.

Exercise 13.10

There are ten errors in this exercise.

1. Each day that passes bring us closer to the end of term.

2. A Quetchua Indian living in the Andes Mountains have two or three more litres of blood than people living at lower elevations.

3. The sisters as well as their obnoxious brother plans to visit us, but each of them want a personal invitation first.

4. Neither your e-mail messages nor your telephone call were passed along to me because the office are short staffed this week.

5. The original model for the king in a standard deck of playing cards are thought to be King Charles I of England.

6. A large planet together with two small stars are visible on the eastern horizon.

7. Each of the three heavenly bodies appear to be a pale, silvery blue.

8. One faculty member in addition to a group of students have volunteered to help us clean out the lab.

GO TO WEB

EXERCISES 13.6, 13.7

Exercise 13.11

Find and correct the ten errors in the following paragraph.

The rewards of obtaining a good summer or part-time job goes well beyond the money you earn from your labour. Contacts that may be valuable in the future and experience in the working world is an important part of your employment. Even if the jobs you get while attending school has nothing to do with your future goal, they offer many benefits. For example, when considering job applicants, an employer always prefer someone who can be counted on to arrive at the work site on time, get along with fellow workers, and follow directions. Neither instinct nor instruction take the place of experience in teaching the basic facts of working life. These long-term considerations, in addition to the money that is the immediate reward, is what makes part-time work so valuable. Everyone who have worked part time while going to school are able to confirm these observations.

GO TO WEB

EXERCISE 13.8

Exercise 13.12

Complete the sentences in the exercises below using present-tense verbs. After you complete each set, check the answer section to see whether your verbs should be singular or plural.

1. Neither my boss nor the receptionist

2. Everybody with two or more pets

3. Not the lead singer but the musicians

4. A flock of birds

5. Every one of his employees

6. Ten dollars

7. The whole family, including two aunts and six cousins

8. The actors, as well as the director

9. Either a Big Mac or a Whopper

10. No one among the hundreds present

Exercise 13.13

Write your own sentences, choosing your subjects as indicated and using present-tense verbs.

1. Use a unit of time as your subject (e.g., your age).

2. Use a multiple subject.

3. Use *no one* as your subject.

4. Use *everything* as your subject.

5. Use *neither . . . nor*.

6. Use *either . . . or*.

7. Use a singular subject + *together with*.

8. Use a plural subject + *in addition to*.

9. Use your own height as your subject.

10. Use a multiple subject joined by *or*.

The box below contains a summary of the rules governing subject–verb agreement. Review them carefully before you try the mastery test for this chapter.

Summary

1. Subjects and verbs must agree. Both must be singular, or both must be plural.
2. Subjects joined by *and* are always plural.
3. When subjects are joined by *or; either . . . or; neither . . . nor;* or *not . . . but,* the verb must agree with the subject that is closest to it.
4. The subject is never in a prepositional phrase. Ignore phrases beginning with *as well as, including, in addition to, like, together with,* etc., when deciding whether to use a singular or plural verb.
5. Pronouns ending in *-one, -thing,* or *-body* are singular and require singular verbs.
6. Units of money, time, mass, length, and distance are always singular.

Exercise 13.14

As a final check of your mastery of subject–verb agreement, correct the 15 errors in the following exercise.

Travel Advisory

Anyone travelling abroad are advised to remember that other countries are not like home. Caution with respect to food, language, and customs are advisable. The French, for example, consumes vast quantities of butter and garlic with their beloved *escargots*; however, no amount of butter and garlic piled on snails disguise the fact that they are slugs in a shell. And although delectable croissants is available everywhere in France, no foreigner attempting to pronounce the word *croissant* are likely to be understood. Many other nations besides France offers local foods that the cautious traveller will want to avoid. Pizza Hut, McDonald's, and Holiday Inn provides familiar food, and every wary traveller are advised to eat in these locations only. Another problem for the unadventurous is that foreigners insist on speaking languages with which no one (other than the natives) are familiar. Neither speaking loudly nor pronouncing slowly and carefully seem to have any effect on the natives' ability to understand English. As for foreign customs, every country in the world have traditions that those of us who have led sheltered lives find bizarre or dangerous. Even a few days in foreign lands are enough to spell disaster. Spanish bulls, Italian drivers, German beer drinkers, Japanese subways, Brazilian beaches: each of them are to be avoided by the prudent traveller who want to return safe and sound to loved ones at home. In fact, those who are likely to be made uncomfortable by anything unfamiliar, exotic, or even new, should either stay at home or vacation in the West Edmonton Mall.

14

Keeping Your
Tenses Consistent

Verbs are time markers. Changes in tense express changes in time: past, present, or future.

I (was) hired yesterday; I (hope) this job (will last) longer than my last one.

    past   *present*   *future*

Sometimes, as in the sentence above, it is necessary to use several different tenses in a single sentence to get the meaning across. But most of the time, whether you're writing a sentence or a paragraph, you use one tense throughout. Normally, you choose either the past or the present tense, depending on the nature of your topic. (Few paragraphs are written completely in the future tense.) Here is the rule to follow.

> Don't change tense unless meaning requires it.

Readers like and expect consistency. If you begin a sentence with "I argued, protested, and even appealed to his masculine pride," the reader will tune in to the past tense verbs and expect any other verbs in the sentence to be in the past tense too. So, if you finish the sentence with ". . . but he looks at me with those big brown eyes and gets me to pay for dinner," your readers will be jolted abruptly out of one time frame into another. This sort of jolting is uncomfortable, and readers don't like it.

Shifting tenses is like shifting gears: it should be done smoothly and when necessary—never abruptly, out of carelessness, or on a whim. Avoid causing verbal whiplash; keep your tenses consistent.

Consider these two examples, both of which mix tenses inappropriately.

Problem: I'm standing right behind Sula when she suddenly screamed.
Solution 1: I was standing right behind Sula when she suddenly screamed.
Solution 2: I'm standing right behind Sula when she suddenly screams.

Problem: Tony delayed until the last possible minute and then begins to write his paper. When he gets halfway through, he decided to change his topic.
Solution 1: Tony delayed until the last possible minute and then began to write his paper. When he got halfway through, he decided to change his topic.
Solution 2: Tony delays until the last possible minute and then begins to write his paper. When he gets halfway through, he decides to change his topic.

Now look at this example, which expresses a more complex idea.

Problem: I handed my paper in just before the deadline. The next day, however, when I see the professor, she says that it was late, so I will lose marks.

This sentence is a hopeless muddle. It begins with the past tense, shifts to the present for no reason, and ends with the future.

Solution: I handed my paper in just before the deadline. The next day, however, when I saw the professor, she said that it was late, so I will lose marks.

Here the past tense is used consistently until the last clause, where the shift to future tense is appropriate to the meaning.

In the following exercises, most—but not all—of the sentences contain unnecessary tense shifts. Use the first verb in each sentence as your time marker and change the tense(s) of the other verb(s) to agree with it. Answers for exercises in this chapter begin on page 448.

Exercise 14.1

1. When the Leafs scored a goal, the crowd applauds politely.

2. Alain went home and tells Gulçan what happened.

3. Gil tried to laugh, but he is too upset even to speak.

4. After his fiancée broke up with him, she refuses to return his ring.

5. Some people believe that, in the future, people will live for 200 years.

6. The rebellion failed because the people do not support it.

7. I enjoy my work, but I was not going to let it take over my life.

8. Prejudice is learned and will be hard to outgrow.

9. A Canadian is someone who thinks that an income tax refund was a gift from the government.

10. Janelle goes to the gym every day, where she will work out and have a sauna.

GO TO WEB

EXERCISE 14.1

Exercise 14.2

1. We need proof that the picture was genuine.

2. When Madonna came on stage, the crowd goes crazy.

3. The couple living in the next apartment had a boa constrictor that keeps getting loose.

4. The property next door has been sold; soon a house will be built on it.

5. It was getting dark, but Stanley is not afraid.

6. I had about 30 computer games on my hard drive until my brother accidentally erases them.

7. My deadline is Friday, and I had to submit an outline and a rough draft by then.

8. A person who lacks a sense of humour may not appreciate the numerous jokes in this book.

9. I drank a half litre of milk, then I eat two protein- and veggie-stuffed wraps, and I am ready for anything.

10. It was great music for dancing, and it's being played by a super band.

GO TO WEB

EXERCISE 14.2

Exercise 14.3

Correct the 15 faulty time shifts in the following paragraph. Use the italicized verb as your time marker. Then check your answers.

My most embarrassing moment *occurred* just last month when I meet an old friend whom I have not seen in years. We greet each other and begin to chat, and I tell her that I have been reading her daughter's columns in the newspaper. I congratulate her on her daughter's talent. I tell her that she must be very proud to see her offspring's name in print. My friend looks puzzled for a minute, then she laughs and tells me that the writer I am praising so highly isn't her daughter. My friend had divorced long ago; her former husband remarries, and the columnist is her ex-husband's new wife.

GO TO WEB

EXERCISE 14.3

Exercise 14.4

Using the italicized verb as your time marker, correct the 15 faulty tense shifts in the following paragraph.

As a young boy, Erik *had* a remarkable knack for making accurate predictions about the future. When he is seven, he tells everyone that he would be a millionaire by the time he is old enough to vote. At eleven, he predicts that he would star in a major motion picture before he reaches legal driving age. At fourteen, he prophesies that he will be elected to political office before his twenty-fourth birthday. Amazingly, all his predictions will come to pass, one after the other. At sixteen, Erik becomes the youngest person ever to star in a James Bond movie. Good financial advice and careful investing will make him a multimillionaire in two years. With all that money behind him, there will be no stopping Erik's political career. He becomes, at twenty-three, the youngest mayor in Nanaimo's history. None of his early successes, however, prepare Erik for political life in British Columbia. At the age of twenty-five, having lost his office, his fortune, his friends, his family, and even his chauffeur-driven limousine, Erik, like so many ex-politicians before him, at last finds his true calling: he becomes a talk-show host.

15

Choosing the Correct Pronoun Form

"Pronoun? That's just a noun used by a professional!" When a character in a television sitcom spoke this line, the audience cracked up. His TV wife corrected him, pointing out that a pronoun is a word that stands in for a noun, replacing it in a sentence so the noun doesn't have to be repeated. His response: "Both answers are acceptable."

Of course, he's wrong, and his wife is right. The audience seemed to know this (or maybe they just knew that in sitcoms, the wife is always right). Generally, pronouns are not well understood. In this chapter and the two following, we will look at the three aspects of pronoun usage that can trip you up if you're not careful: pronoun **form**, **agreement**, and **consistency**. We will also consider the special problem of using pronouns in a way that produces sexist language.

There are three kinds of pronouns that are likely to cause difficulty for writers:

personal pronouns	I, we, she, they, etc.
relative pronouns	who, which, that, etc.
indefinite pronouns	any, somebody, none, each, etc.

(You will find a complete list of these pronouns on page 419.)

The first thing you need to do is be sure you are using correct pronoun forms. Look at these examples of incorrect pronoun usage:

Her and me offered to pick up a video.
Between you and I, I think Paul's mother does his homework.

How do you know which form of a pronoun to use? The answer depends on the pronoun's place and function in your sentence.

There are two forms of personal pronouns. One is used for subjects, and one is used for objects. Pronoun errors occur when you confuse the two. In Chapter 5, you learned to identify the subject of a sentence. Keep that information in mind as you learn the following basic rule.

When the subject of a sentence is (or is referred to by) a pronoun, that pronoun must be in **subject form**; otherwise, use the **object form**.

Subject Pronouns

Singular	Plural
I	we
you	you
he, she, it, one	they

She and *I* <u>decided</u> to rent a video.
(The pronouns are the subject of the sentence.)

The lucky <u>winners</u> of the free tickets to the World Wrestling Championships <u>are</u> *they*.
(The pronoun refers to the subject of the sentence, "winners.")

The only <u>person</u> who got an A in the course <u>was</u> *she*.
(The pronoun refers to the subject of the sentence, "person.")

We serious <u>bikers</u> <u>prefer</u> Harleys to Hondas.
(The pronoun refers to the subject of the sentence, "bikers.")

Object Pronouns

Singular	Plural
me	us
you	you
him, her, it, one	them

Between you and *me*, I <u>think</u> Paul's mother is doing his homework.
("Me" is not the subject of the sentence; it is one of the objects of the preposition "between.")

<u>Sasha</u> <u>saw</u> *him* and *me* copying from each other.
("Him" and "me" are not the subject of the verb "saw"; Sasha is, so the pronouns must be in the object form.)

The <u>police</u> <u>are</u> always suspicious of *us* bikers.
("Us" does not refer to the subject of the sentence, "police"; it refers to "bikers," the object of the preposition "of.")

Be especially careful with pronouns that occur in multiple subjects or following prepositions. If you remember the following two rules, you'll be able to eliminate most potential errors in pronoun form.

1. Any pronoun that is part of a multiple subject is *always* in subject form.
2. Any pronoun that comes after a preposition is *always* in object form.

<u>*She*</u> and <u>*I*</u> <u>have</u> season's tickets.
(The pronouns are used as a multiple subject.)

We are very happy for *you* and *her*.
(The pronouns follow the preposition "for.")

I can't believe Chandra would break up with me after me and her got matching tattoos and navel rings.

Here's a practically foolproof way for native English speakers to tell which pronoun form is needed. (ESL speakers, unfortunately, must rely on memorizing the rules.) When the sentence contains a pair of pronouns, mentally cross one out and check the sentence with one pronoun at a time. Applying this technique to the first example above, you get "*She* has tickets" and "*I* have tickets," both of which sound right and are correct. In the second sentence, if you try the pronouns separately, you get "We are happy for *you*" and "We are happy for *her*." Again, you know by the sound that these are the correct forms. You would never say "*Her* had tickets," or "*Me* had tickets," or "We are happy for *she*." If you deal with paired pronouns one at a time, you are unlikely to choose the wrong form.

Exercise 15.1

Choose the correct pronouns from the words given in parentheses. Answers for exercises in this chapter begin on page 449.

1. The photographer and (I me) agree that you look better out of focus.
2. Mohamed wants to go to the concert with Annie and (I me).
3. (Her She) and I disagree on the kind of music to play in the car.
4. Except for Pauli and (her she), there's no one else who knows the system.
5. (They Them) and our professor made up the schedule.
6. The work will go much faster if Roland and (he him) do it by themselves.
7. Sami and (he him) shot and edited the whole film.
8. According to (them they) and their supporters, we are responsible for missing the deadline.
9. Neither (they them) nor (us we) deserve to be treated like this.
10. I can't believe Chandra would break up with me after (her she) and (I me) got matching tattoos and navel rings.

Exercise 15.2

Correct the ten errors in pronoun form in the following sentences.

1. Have you and her ever tried sky diving?

2. My boyfriend and me have completely different tastes in music.

3. It is not up to you or I to discipline your sister's children.

4. She and Xan took the videos back before Tami or me had seen them.

5. The rest is up to he and his team, because us volunteers have done enough.

6. Do you insist on seeing they, or could us possibly help you?

7. Him and Marie finished on time; except for they and their staff, no one else met the deadline.

GO TO WEB

EXERCISES 15.1, 15.2

Choosing the correct pronoun form is more than just a matter of not wanting to appear ignorant or careless. Sometimes the form you use determines the meaning of your sentence. Consider these two sentences:

Giesele treats her dog better than *I*.
Giesele treats her dog better than *me*.

There's a world of difference between the meaning of the subject form—"Giesele treats her dog better than *I* [do]"—and the object form—"Giesele treats her dog better than [she treats] *me*."

When using a pronoun after *than*, *as well as*, or *as*, decide whether you mean to contrast the pronoun with the subject of the sentence. If you do, use the subject form of the pronoun. If not, use the object form.

Meiling would rather listen to Ricky Martin than I.
(*I* is contrasted with *Meiling*.)

Meiling would rather listen to Ricky Martin than me.
(*Me* is contrasted with *Ricky Martin*.)

Here's a quick way to check that you've used the correct pronoun form. If you've used a subject form, insert a verb after it. If you've used an object form, insert a preposition before it. If your sentences make sense, you have chosen correctly. For example,

Meiling would rather listen to Ricky Martin than I [would].
Meiling would rather listen to Ricky Martin than [to] me.

Some writers prefer to leave the additional verb or preposition in place.

Exercise 15.3

Correct the errors in the following sentences.

1. The prize is sure to go to Omar and she.

2. No one likes our cooking class more than me.

3. In fact, nobody in the class eats as much as me.

4. It's not surprising that I am much bigger than them.

5. My mother would rather cook for my brother than I because he never complains when dinner is burned or raw.

6. At last I have met someone who loves barbecued eel as much as me!

7. More than me, Yuxiang uses the computer to draft and revise his papers.

8. He doesn't write as well as me, but he docs write faster.

9. Only a few Mexican food fanatics can eat as many jalapeño peppers as him.

10. I think you have as much trouble with English as me.

GO TO WEB

EXERCISE 15.3

Exercise 15.4

Revise the following paragraphs below to correct the ten errors in pronoun form.

Most of we humans, it seems, feel nostalgic about "the golden days" of our youth. But the experiences of earlier generations often sound more grim than golden to we who've heard their stories. My grandparents used to tell my sister and I about the "good old days" when them and their friends walked to school through giant snow drifts. Some of their friends were very poor, and them had nothing to wear in winter but shoes with holes. My sister and me didn't think this sounded like much fun.

Our parents claim that the "good old days" were when us children were babies, and there were no computers or CDs or cell phones. These sound like bad old days to my sister and I, who can't imagine life without computers, CDs, and cell phones.

For those of we in our twenties, now is probably our "good old days." Perhaps in ten years we'll be reminiscing about the early 2000s, while our sons and daughters wonder what on Earth we're talking about. As we grow older, I hope my friends and me will remember both the good and the bad about the days of our youth.

16

Mastering Pronoun-Antecedent Agreement

"I am writing in response to your ad for a waiter and bartender, male or female. Being both, I am applying for the position."

Pronoun confusion can take several forms, and some of the resulting sentences can be unintentionally hilarious. In this chapter, we'll look at how to use pronouns consistently throughout a sentence or paragraph to avoid confusing and embarrassing mistakes.

Pronoun-Antecedent Agreement

The name of this pronoun problem may sound difficult, but the idea is simple. Pronouns are words that substitute for or refer to the name of a person, place, or thing mentioned elsewhere in your sentence or your paragraph. The word(s) that a pronoun substitutes for or refers to is called the **antecedent**.

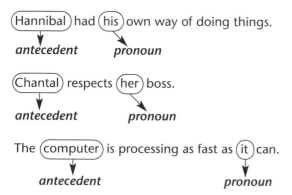

Usually, as in these three examples, the antecedent comes before the pronoun that refers to it. Here is the rule to remember.

A pronoun must agree with its antecedent in
- number (singular or plural)
- person (first, second, or third)
- gender (masculine, feminine, or neuter)

Most of the time, you follow this rule without even realizing that you know it. For example, you would never write

Hannibal had *your* own way of doing things.

Chantal respects *its* boss.

The computer is processing as fast as *she* can.

You know these sentences are incorrect even if you may not know precisely why they are wrong.

There are three kinds of pronoun–antecedent agreement that you do need to learn about. They lead to errors that, unlike the examples above, are not obvious, and you need to know them so you can watch out for them. The rules you need to learn involve **relative pronouns; indefinite pronouns ending in *-one*, *-body*, or *-thing*; and vague references**.

Relative Pronouns

The first potential difficulty with pronoun–antecedent agreement is how to use relative pronouns—*who/whom*, *which*, and *that*—correctly. Relative pronouns must refer to someone or something already mentioned in the sentence. Here is the guideline to follow.

Use *who* and *whom* to refer to people.
Use *that* and *which* to refer to everything else.

The chef *who* prepared this meal deserves a medal.

The servers *who* presented it deserve to be fired.

The appetizer *that* I ordered was covered with limp cilantro.

My mother's soup, *which* was cold, arrived at the same time as her main course.

My father's meal, *which* was delicious, demonstrated the talent *that* the chef is famous for.

Whether you need *who* or *whom* depends on the pronoun's place and function in your sentence. Apply the basic pronoun rule.

If the pronoun is, or refers to, the subject of the sentence, use *who*. Otherwise, use *whom*. Or you can revise the sentence to eliminate the pronoun.

Who decided we had to take English? (The pronoun *who* is the subject of the sentence.)

It was Sheila *who* filled out the form that won us the trip to Moose Factory. (The pronoun refers to the subject of the sentence, *Sheila*.)

The trip's promoters were willing to settle for *whom* they could get. (The pronoun does not refer to the subject, *promoters*; it is the object of the preposition *for*.)

A better solution is to solve the problem by rewriting the sentence so you don't need either *who* or *whom*.

Sheila filled out the form that won us the trip to Moose Factory.

The trip's promoters were willing to settle for anyone they could get.

That is required more often than *which*. You should use *which* only in a clause that is separated from the rest of the sentence by commas.

The moose *that* I met looked hostile.

The moose, *which* was standing right in front of my car, looked hostile.

Exercise 16.1

Correct the errors in the following sentences. Answers for exercises in this chapter begin on page 449.

1. Chi Keung is the technician that can fix the problem.

2. Halema plays the violin just like the musician that taught her to play.

3. A grouch is a person which knows himself and isn't happy about it.

4. The student that was asked to read claimed to have laryngitis.

5. I wish I could find someone in the class which could help me with my homework.

6. My quilt was bought by a woman that was looking for a gift for her grandchild.

7. The faculty which were present rejected the union steward's proposal.

8. Anyone that says he can see right through women is missing a lot.

   (Groucho Marx)

9. Is this the dog who bit the mail carrier that carries a squirt gun?

10. Anar has just started on the term paper, that was assigned a month ago, for her political science course.

Pronouns Ending in *-one*, *-body*, *-thing*

The second tricky aspect of pronoun–antecedent agreement involves these **indefinite pronouns**:

anyone	anybody	anything
everyone	everybody	everything
no one	nobody	nothing
someone	somebody	something
each (one)		

In Chapter 13, you learned that, when these words are used as subjects, they are singular and require singular verbs. So it makes sense that the pronouns that stand for or refer to them must also be singular.

Antecedents ending in *-one*, *-body*, and *-thing* are singular.
They must be referred to by singular pronouns: *he, she, it; his, her, its.*

Everyone deserves a break from *her* children now and then.

Everything has *its* place and should be in it.

Everyone got your message in *his* electronic mailbox.

No one has the courage to open *his* mouth and complain.

But take another look at the last two sentences. Until about 30 years ago, the pronouns *he, him,* and *his* were used with singular antecedents and referred to both men and women. Most modern readers are sensitive to sex bias in writing and think that it is not appropriate to use the masculine pronoun when referring to both sexes. As a writer, you should be aware of this sensitivity. If you want to appeal to the broadest possible audience, you should avoid what some readers may consider to be sexist language.

In informal usage, it has become acceptable to use plural pronouns with *-one*, *-body*, and *-thing* antecedents. Although they are grammatically singular, they are often plural in meaning, and in conversation we tend to say

Everyone got your message in *their* electronic mailbox.

No one has the courage to open *their* mouth and complain.

This usage is acceptable in speech, but it is not acceptable in standard written English. Writers sometimes make errors in pronoun–antecedent agreement because they are trying to write without indicating whether the person referred to is male or female. "Everyone got your message in *their* electronic mailbox" is incorrect, as we have seen; however, it does avoid making "everybody" male. The writer could replace the plural *their* with the singular and non-sexist *his or her*—"Everyone got your message in *his or her* electronic mailbox"—but *his or her* sounds clumsy if it is used frequently.

There are two better ways to solve the problem.

1. Revise the sentence to leave the pronoun out.

Everyone got your message via electronic mail.

No one has the courage to complain.

Such creative avoidance of sex-specific language or incorrect constructions can be an interesting intellectual challenge. The results sometimes sound a little artificial, however. The second solution is easier to accomplish.

2. Revise the sentence to make both the antecedent and the pronoun plural.

We all got your message in *our* electronic mailboxes.

The *staff* haven't the courage to open *their* mouths and complain.

Here are a couple of examples for you to study:

Problem: Everybody has been given his assignment.
Revision 1:   Everybody has been given an assignment.
Revision 2:   All of the students have been given their assignments.

Problem: Not one of the writers wants his copy edited.
Revision 1:   Not one of the writers wants copy editing.
Revision 2:   All of the writers object to having their copy edited.

 If you are writing on a word processor, you can use the search function to ensure agreement between pronouns and their antecedents. Search your paper for every occurrence of *their* and *they*, and check each one to be sure its antecedent is not a pronoun ending in *-one*, *-body*, or *-thing*.

Exercise 16.2

Identify the most appropriate word(s) from the choices given in parentheses. Check your answers carefully before continuing.

1. Each of the apartments we looked at was appealing in (its their) own way.
2. Would someone kindly lend (his, her, their, a) copy of the text to Mei Yee?
3. Everyone is expected to pay (his or her, their, a) portion of the expenses.
4. No one who cares about (her their) children will smoke in the house, or let (her their) husband or friends smoke, either.
5. No one on the wrestling team has been able to get (his their) parents to donate (his or her, their) house for the party.
6. None of our best jokes was enough by (themselves itself) to get us hired by Tom Green.
7. Anyone who wants a high mark for (his, their, this) essay should see me after class and write out (his, their, a) cheque.

GO TO WEB

EXERCISE 16.1

Correct the errors in the following sentences, being careful to avoid awkward repetition and sexist language. Because there is more than one way to correct these errors, your answers may differ from our suggestions.

1. Anyone that invests all their disposable income hopes to retire rich.

2. Every investor must find a level of risk they are comfortable with.

3. For someone who can tolerate high risk, the return on their money can be huge; however, it is also possible that they can lose everything they've invested.

4. Every investment counsellor in this firm uses a Ouija board to make their stock predictions.

5. For each person that invests their money in the stock market, there is someone that would rather keep their money in a savings account.

Vague Reference

Avoiding the third potential difficulty with pronoun–antecedent agreement requires common sense and an ability to put yourself in your reader's place. If you look at your writing from your reader's point of view, it is unlikely that you will break the following rule.

A pronoun must refer clearly to the correct antecedent.

The mistake that occurs when you fail to follow this rule is called **vague reference**.

Luc pointed to his brother and said that he had saved his life.

Who saved whom? Here's another:

Danielle wrote a song about her sister when she was five years old.

Is the song about a five-year-old sister, or was Danielle a musically talented child?

In sentences like these, you can only guess the meaning because you don't know who is being referred to by the pronouns. The antecedents are not clear. You can make such sentences less confusing either by using proper names (Luc, Danielle) more frequently or by changing the sentences around. These solutions aren't difficult; they just take a little time and some imagination. Try them on our examples.

Another type of vague reference occurs when there is no antecedent in the sentence for the pronoun to refer to.

Zoe loves watching dog shows and is going to enter hers when it's old enough. (Enter what?)

Snowboarding is Anna's favourite sport, and she's hoping to get one for her birthday. (One what?)

How would you revise these sentences?

Make sure that every pronoun has a clear antecedent and that every pronoun agrees with its antecedent. Both must be singular, or both must be plural. Once you have mastered this principle, you'll have no trouble with pronoun–antecedent agreement.

Exercise 16.4

Correct the following sentences where necessary. There are several ways to fix these sentences. In some cases, the antecedent is missing, and you need to supply one. In other cases, the antecedent is so vague that the meaning of the sentence can be interpreted in more than one way; you need to rewrite these sentences to make the meaning clear.

1. The frustrated programmer whacked the computer with his hand, breaking it.

2. Every time David looked at the dog, he barked.

3. When I realized that smoking was the cause of my asthma, I gave them up for good.

4. Jack seems to have lost his scoring touch; he hasn't got one in six games.

5. Yasmin told her sister that their teacher liked her essay.

6. Telling time seems to be a challenge for my girlfriend, so I'm getting her one for her birthday.

7. At our college, they strictly enforce the "no smoking" policy.

8. Ali sat down next to Muhsin and began to eat his lunch.

9. During the all-candidates debate, Stockwell told Preston that he was not the man he used to be.

10. He didn't see that she had fallen overboard, which was because he was concentrating on landing his fish.

Every time David looked at the dog, he barked.

GO TO WEB

EXERCISE 16.2

Exercise 16.5

Revise the following paragraph, which contains ten errors representing the three different kinds of pronoun–antecedent agreement error. If you change a subject from singular to plural, don't forget to change the verb to agree. Some of your answers may differ from our suggestions and still be correct.

It seems that everyone in North America is keen on playing games involving useless bits of information called trivia. The trivia player is expected to have at their fingertips the names of obscure musical groups, statistics for unimportant sports events, details of world geography, and total knowledge of the film industry. Team trivia contests have become important fund raisers for charitable organizations, with each member of the team expected to answer questions in their own area of expertise while as many as 300 rivals in the room cheer or jeer their answers. Television offers a variety of programs in which the contestant must demonstrate their knowledge of useless information. In some games, the host gives the contestant a selection of answers; he may also give him clues or aids to answering the question if he wants. In other games, the contestant has competitors whom they must challenge in order to take home the prize. Whether a person plays alone, with a group at home, in a team at a fund raiser, or on television, they shouldn't take a trivia game too seriously. After all, it's the only game in which the winner must admit that they have a more trivial mind than the loser.

Before you try the final exercise for this chapter, it may be helpful for you to review the rules for pronoun–antecedent agreement.

Summary

- Every pronoun must agree with its antecedent (a word or word group that appears earlier in the sentence or paragraph); both must be singular, or both must be plural.
- Use *who/whom* to refer to people; use *that* and *which* to refer to animals, objects, and ideas.
- Antecedents ending in *-one*, *-body*, and *-thing* are singular and must be referred to by singular pronouns: *he, she, it; his, her, its.*
- A pronoun must clearly refer to a specific antecedent.

Exercise 16.6

Correct the 15 errors in the following paragraph. Part of the challenge in this exercise is to make the paragraph not only grammatically correct but also free of sexist language.

A triathlon is a race consisting of three parts who are called "legs": swimming, cycling, and running. Anyone that has competed in one knows that intensive training is an absolute necessity, not only for their success, but also for their survival. Swimming is one of the toughest contests because it demands cardiovascular fitness as well as strength. While each of the three parts has their own challenges, the cycling leg is the event that separates serious athletes from weekend fitness buffs. An amateur will find they can't summon enough energy after the swim to stay close to his opponent if he has trained harder than he has. The serious athlete will begin to assert their dominance now, and by the end of the bike ride, anyone that has achieved a high level of physical efficiency through their training will have a chance of a high placing. For competitors in a triathlon, survival is often the primary goal. The body's reserves are called on, and only highly dedicated, well trained athletes will be able to do it. For most athletes, reaching the finish line is a personal test: each athlete competes against their own previous finish times. Anyone that still has winning in mind after the swim, the cycle race, and the run has physical and mental reserves beyond the ordinary.

17

Maintaining Person Agreement

So far, we have focussed on using pronouns correctly and clearly within a sentence. Now let's turn to the problem of **person agreement**, which means using pronouns consistently throughout a sentence or a paragraph. There are three categories of person that we use when we write or speak:

	Singular	**Plural**
first person	I; me	we; us
second person	you	you
third person	she, he, it, one; her, him and all pronouns ending in -one, -body, -thing	they; them

Here is the rule for person agreement.

Do not mix "persons" unless meaning requires it.

In other words, be consistent. If you begin a sentence using a second-person pronoun, you must use second person all the way through. Look at this sentence:

If *you* wish to succeed, *one* must work hard.

This is the most common error—mixing second-person *you* with third-person *one*.

Here's another example:

One can live happily in Vancouver if *you* have a sturdy umbrella.

We can correct this error by using the second person throughout:

(1) *You* can live happily in Vancouver if *you* have a sturdy umbrella.

We can also correct it by using the third person throughout:

(2) *One* can live happily in Vancouver if *one* has a sturdy umbrella.

or

(3) *One* can live happily in Vancouver if *he or she* has a sturdy umbrella.

These last three sentences raise two points of style that you should consider.

1. Don't overuse *one*.

All three revised sentences are grammatically correct, but they make different impressions on the reader, and impressions are an important part of communication.

- The first sentence, in the second person, sounds the most informal—like something you would say. It's a bit casual for general writing purposes.
- The second sentence, which uses *one* twice, sounds the most formal—even a little pretentious.
- The third sentence falls between the other two in formality. It is the one you'd be most likely to use in writing for school or business.

Although it is grammatically correct and non-sexist, this third sentence raises another problem. Frequent use of *he or she* in a continuous prose passage, whether that passage is as short as a paragraph or as long as a paper, is guaranteed to irritate your reader.

2. Don't overuse *he or she*.

He or she is inclusive, but it is a wordy construction. If used too frequently, the reader cannot help shifting focus from what you're saying to how you're saying it. The best writing is transparent—that is, it doesn't call attention to itself. If your reader becomes distracted by your style, your meaning gets lost. Consider this sentence:

A student can easily pass this course if he or she applies himself or herself to his or her studies.

Imagine being the unfortunate reader who has to struggle through a paper—or even a single paragraph—filled with this clumsy construction. Readers deserve more consideration than this awkward solution to the problem of sexist language allows them.

There are two better solutions to this problem, and they are already familiar to you because they are the same as those for making pronouns ending in *-one*, *body*, or *thing* agree with their antecedents.

• You can change the whole sentence to the plural.

Students can easily pass this course if they apply themselves to their studies.

• You can rewrite the sentence without using pronouns.

A student can easily pass this course by applying good study habits.

Exercise 17.1

Choose the correct word(s) from the choices given in parentheses. Answers for exercises in this chapter begin on page 450.

1. You shouldn't annoy the instructor if (one wants, you want, he or she wants) to get an A.
2. A person can succeed at almost anything if (you have, they have, he or she has) enough talent and determination.
3. When we came up for air, (we, one, you) couldn't see the boat!
4. After you have assembled the unit, (one, you, we) should give it a coat of paint.
5. You can save a great deal of time if (one fills, you fill, we fill) out the forms before going to the passport office.
6. Have you decided on a topic for (one's, your) major project yet?
7. Our opinions will never be heard unless (one makes, we make, you make) a serious effort to reach the public.
8. I wish that (one, we) had a few more options to choose from.
9. Anyone with a telephone can get (his or her, one's, their, your) voice heard on the radio.
10. Call-in programs give everyone the opportunity to make sure the whole world knows (one's, our, your) ignorance of the issues.

GO TO WEB

EXERCISE 17.1

Exercise 17.2

Correct the errors in pronoun consistency in the following sentences.

1. One is never too old to learn, but you are never too young to know everything.

2. One always removes your shoes when entering a mosque.

3. When you wish upon a star, one's dreams come true.

4. One ought to remember to keep a tight reign on your temper.

5. No one can blame you for trying to do your best, even if one does not always succeed.

6. Experience is that marvellous thing that enables us to recognize a mistake when you make it the second time. (F.P. Jones)

7. If you can't cope with the pressure, one must be expected to be replaced by someone who can.

8. We all need some unconditional love when you're having a bad day.

9. I find that unconditional love is most reliably offered by one's dog.

10. One's colleagues and superiors can make us feel stupid and insignificant, but my dog's whole world revolves around me.

GO TO WEB

EXERCISE 17.2

Exercise 17.3

Correct the five consistency errors in the following paragraph. Look for errors in number agreement (singular vs. plural) as well as person agreement. Try to avoid sexist language and wordy constructions in your revision.

Those of us who enjoy baseball find it difficult to explain one's enthusiasm to non-fans. We baseball enthusiasts can watch a game of three hours or more as one follows each play with rapt attention. We true fans get excited by a no-hitter—a game in which, by definition, nothing happens. They claim that the game offers more pleasures than mere action, but non-fans must be forgiven if you don't get the point. To them, watching a baseball game is about as exciting as watching paint dry.

Exercise 17.4

Rewrite the following paragraph in the first person plural, using *we*, *our*, and *us* as your base pronouns. As you revise, correct the 12 errors in agreement of person and number. Be sure to change verbs, where necessary, to agree with their revised subjects. (The quotation from Robert Frost has been altered to suit the purpose of this exercise.)

When one is at the beginning of our careers, it seems impossible that you may one day wish to work less. The drive to get ahead leads many of us to sacrifice one's leisure, one's community responsibilities, even one's family life for the sake of your career. Normally, as you age, one's priorities begin to change, and career success becomes less important than quality of life. Not everyone, however, experiences this shift in your priorities. Indeed, some people work themselves to death, while others are so committed to their work throughout their lives that they die within months of your retirement—presumably from stress caused by lack of work. The poet Robert Frost once observed, "By working faithfully eight hours a day, one may eventually get to be a boss. Then you can work twelve hours a day." Those of you who are living and working in the early years of the 21st century would be wise to take Frost's words to heart.

Exercise 17.5

Find and correct the 15 pronoun agreement errors—in both person and number—in the following paragraph.

Canadians who complain about winter might just as well complain about your height or hair colour. The experience of winter is part of being Canadian. In November, we take out of storage your heavy wool socks, your scarves and mitts and toques. You clean your down-filled coats, fill the windshield washer reservoir in your cars, and put on your snow tires. All this preparation is as much a part of being Canadian as strapping on one's skis, cheering for one's hockey team, or complaining about your government. While most of the world is paralyzed by a few centimetres of snow that brings traffic to a halt and closes schools and businesses, we Canadians just get up a few minutes earlier to shovel out one's driveways, scrape the snow off the car, and chip the ice from the windshield with that specially designed scraper that they always carry in our cars between

October and April. As comedian Rick Mercer once observed, very little

unites Canadians, but they all know how to pull up your heavy wool socks

and pump your brakes.

_____**Exercise 17.6**

Think of a significant experience you've had since coming to college. (If you don't like "significant," try embarrassing, enlightening, frightening, or surprising.) Write an account of this experience, telling your story in the third person. That is, instead of using _I_, use _he_ or _she_. When you have finished your paper, reread it carefully. Check the sentence structure. Check your spelling. Check the agreement of your subjects and verbs and of your pronouns and antecedents. Finally, check to be sure your verb tenses and pronouns are consistent throughout the paper.

UNIT 4

Punctuation

Punctuation

The following quick quiz will let you see at a glance which chapters of Unit 4 you need to focus on. The paragraphs below contain 20 errors: commas, semi-colons, colons, quotation marks, punctuation of titles, and end punctuation. When you've made your corrections, turn to page 451 and compare your version with ours. For each error you miss, the answer key directs you to the chapter you need to work on.

1   When we go to a movie most of us like to sit back, munch away on a bucket of popcorn, and get lost in a good story filled with great-looking people. We forget that a film is a complex technical construct put together by huge teams of professionals who are responsible for its look sound and overall effect. Occasionally a "blooper"—a clumsy technical error—will remind us just what a complicated artifact a movie really is.

2   One kind of blooper is the anachronism something in the movie that is inconsistent with the time period in which the movie is set. For example, in *Gladiator*, set 2,000 years ago in Roman times tractor tracks are visible in the field that the hero Maximus walks by on his way home. You'll also see saddles with stirrups, an invention that didn't occur until nearly 800 years

later. If you look carefully at the cigarettes that characters in *Titanic* are smoking, you'll see filter-tipped models that weren't invented until the 1940s. The ship sank in 1912. In Francis Coppola's classic film, "The Godfather," two characters walk past a Volkswagen Beetle in 1945. The Beetle didn't come to the United States until well into the 1950s.

3   Then there is the "continuity" goof. Individual shots and scenes in a movie are filmed one at a time and often out of sequence, therefore it is important to make sure that if for instance a character takes a drink from a glass in one shot, the glass has to be less full rather than more full in the next shot. Characters' hair, beards, and even fingernails have to be consistent over entire sequences. So do props. For example when Sonny Corleone is blown away in *The Godfather,* the windshield of his car is shattered by a blast of machine, gun fire. Seconds later in the next scene, his bodyguards arrive. They are too late to save Sonny but somehow the windshield is miraculously intact; a classic continuity blooper.

4   Close viewers are also alert to geography errors. In the 1980 comedy "Caddyshack," a character says he lives in Nebraska (a prairie state) as he rides by a palm tree in the opening credits. When the doomed ship first appears in *Titanic*, New York's Statue of Liberty is in the background, the geographical problem is that the ship left Southampton, England, and was bound for New York when the iceberg intervened.

5   Another blooper is visible film equipment or crew but you have to be alert to catch these lapses. If you look closely at *The Matrix* you'll see a few inches of wire on either side of Neo's hands when he backflips off the train tracks onto the platform. You can also spot a crew member in "blue jeans" sauntering around the background in a scene of *Gladiator.*

6   There are also factual errors. In *Charlie's Angels*; for example, the door of a commercial airline at cruising speed is opened up. Such a thing could not really occur because of the higher air pressure in the cabin. Even if it could happen, everything inside the cabin—people, and objects—would be sucked outside the aircraft, ruining all the fun.

7   Perhaps ruining the fun is what's happening here. When we encounter a work of art, we want to achieve what the poet Coleridge called the willing suspension of disbelief. We need to believe because getting lost in the story is the essence of a great movie. Bloopers can interfere with this belief, but so can looking too hard for mistakes!!!

18

The Comma

Many writers-in-training tend to sprinkle punctuation like pepper over their pages. Do not use punctuation either to spice up or to decorate your writing. Punctuation marks are functional: they indicate to the reader how the various parts of a sentence relate to one another. By changing the punctuation, you can change the meaning of a sentence. Here are two examples to prove the point.

1. An instructor wrote the following sentence on the board and asked the class to punctuate it appropriately: "woman without her man is nothing."

   The men wrote, "Woman, without her man, is nothing."
   The women wrote, "Woman! Without her, man is nothing."

2. Now it's your turn. Punctuate this sentence: "I think there is only one person to blame myself."
   If you wrote, "I think there is only one person to blame, myself." the reader will understand that you believe only one person—who may or may not be known to you—is to blame.
   If you wrote, "I think there is only one person to blame: myself." the reader will understand that you are personally accepting responsibility for the blame.

The comma is the most frequently used—and misused—punctuation mark in English. Perhaps nothing is so sure a sign of a competent writer as the correct use of commas, so it is very important that you master them. This chapter presents five comma rules that cover most instances in which you need to use commas. If you apply these five rules faithfully, your reader will never be confused by missing or misplaced commas in your writing.

And if, as occasionally happens, the sentence you are writing is not covered by one of our five rules, remember the first commandment of comma usage: when in doubt, leave it out.

Five Comma Rules

> 1. Use commas to separate items in a series of three or more.

The required subjects in this program are math, physics, and English.

Drive two blocks north of Main, turn left, go past two traffic signals, and turn right.

Wing-Kee went to the movies, Jan and Yasmin went to play pool, and I went to bed.

The comma before the *and* at the end of the list is optional, but we advise you to use it. Occasionally, misunderstandings can occur if it is left out.

Exercise 18.1

Insert commas where necessary in the following sentences. Answers for exercises in this chapter begin on page 453.

1. Hirako held two aces a King a Queen and a Jack in her hand.
2. This food is spicy colourful nourishing and delicious.
3. In Canada, the seasons are spring summer fall winter winter and winter.
4. Just let me have a bath and a haircut before you judge my appearance.
5. Cell phones hand-held computers and DVD players are three popular new technologies.
6. You need woolen underwear showshoes Arctic boots but very little money to go winter camping.
7. Sleeping through my alarm dozing during sociology napping in the library after lunch and snoozing in front of the TV all are symptoms of my overactive nightlife.
8. Once you have finished your homework taken out the garbage and done the dishes, you can feed the cat clean your room and do your laundry.

9. Don't forget to bring the photo album videotape and souvenirs of your trip to Australia.
10. Both my doctor and my nutritionist agree that I should eat better exercise more and give up smoking.

---

2. Use commas to set off any word or phrase that is not ESSENTIAL to the main idea of the sentence.

To find out whether a word, phrase, or clause is essential, try crossing it out. If the main idea remains unchanged and the sentence still makes sense, the crossed-out expression is *non-essential* and should be set off by commas. Study the following four examples.

Writing a good letter of application isn't difficult, ~~if you're careful~~.

The phrase "if you're careful" is not essential to the main idea of the sentence, so it's separated from the rest of the sentence by a comma.

Writing a letter of application ~~that is clear and concise~~ is a challenge.

If you take out "that is clear and concise," you change the meaning of the sentence. Not all letters of application are a challenge to write: only clear and concise ones. Writing vague and wordy letters is easy; anyone can do it. The words "that is clear and concise" are therefore essential to the meaning of the sentence, so they are not set off by commas.

~~One of Canada's best-known novelists,~~ Alice Munro spends the summer in Clinton and the winter in Comox.

The phrase "one of Canada's best-known novelists" is not essential to the main idea; it just gives us additional information about Alice Munro. Leaving it out does not change the meaning, so it is set off by a comma.
    When non-essential or supplementary information occurs in the middle of the sentence, rather than at the beginning or the end, be sure to put commas both before and after it.

In *Selling Illusions*, ~~published in 1994~~, Neil Bissoondath explains why he thinks Canada's multiculturalism policy has done more harm than good.

The phrase "published in 1994" is a supplementary detail. It is not essential to the meaning of the sentence, so it is set off by commas.

Exercise 18.2

Insert commas where necessary in the following sentences. Check your answers before going on.

1. Our family doctor like our family dog never comes when we call.
2. This photograph taken when I was only four embarrasses me whenever my parents show it.
3. Mira's boyfriend who looks like an ape is living proof that love is blind.
4. Isn't it strange that the poor who are often bitterly critical of the rich buy lottery tickets?
5. Several premiers and a former political advisor a man now well into his eighties accompanied the prime minister on his trade mission to China.
6. My car made it all the way to Saskatoon without anything falling off or breaking down a piece of good luck that surprised us all.
7. A popular mathematics instructor Professor Lam won the distinguished teaching award again this year.
8. We're going to the shopping mall a weekly ritual we all enjoy.
9. No one who has seen Patrick Roy play can doubt that he is a superstar.
10. Classical music which I call Prozac for the ears can be very soothing in times of stress.

---

3. Put a comma between independent clauses when they are joined by these transitional words:

for	but	so
and	or	
nor	yet	

(You can remember these words easily if you notice that their first letters spell "fanboys.")

I hope I do well in the interview, for I really want this job.

I like José Carreras, but I prefer Placido Domingo.

We shape our tools, and our tools shape us. (Marshall McLuhan)

I knew I was going to be late, so I went back to sleep.

Be sure that the sentence you are punctuating contains two independent clauses rather than one clause with a single subject and a multiple verb.

<u>We</u> <u>loved</u> the book but <u>hated</u> the movie.
(<u>*We*</u> is the subject, and there are two verbs, <u>*loved*</u> and <u>*hated*</u>. Do not put a comma between two or more verbs that share a single subject.)

<u>We</u> both <u>loved</u> the book, but <u>Kim</u> <u>hated</u> the movie.
(This sentence contains two independent clauses—<u>*We*</u> <u>*loved*</u> and <u>*Kim*</u> <u>*hated*</u>—joined by *but*. The comma is required here.)

Exercise 18.3

Insert commas where they are needed in the following sentences and check your answers.

1. This has been a perfect day and you have been a perfect host.
2. We have a plan and a budget yet we still don't have the staff we need.
3. Talk shows ran out of things to say years ago but they haven't stopped talking yet.
4. We discovered that we both had an interest in art so we made a date to go to an exhibition at the gallery next Friday.
5. Canadians are proud of their country but don't approve of too much flag waving.
6. Take good notes for there will be an exam on Tuesday.
7. You won't get any sympathy from us nor will we help you explain to your parents.
8. The car swerved wildly and just missed the crossing guard.
9. I have travelled all over the world yet my luggage has visited many more places than I have.
10. Jet lag makes me look haggard and sick but at least I resemble my passport picture.

4. Put a comma after a word or group of words that comes before an independent clause.

Lucas, you aren't paying attention.

No matter how hard I try, I will never forget you.

Exhausted and cranky from staying up all night, I staggered into class.

If that's their idea of a large pizza, we'd better order two.

Until she got her promotion, she was quite friendly.

Exercise 18.4

Insert commas where they are needed in the following sentences and check your answers.

1. Unfortunately, we'll have to begin all over again.
2. Mr. Dillinger, the bank wants to speak with you.
3. In the end, the quality of your performance counts more than the effort you put into it.
4. Treading water, we waited for the boat to return and rescue us.
5. Even though this photograph is out of focus, it does show that Remi did take part in the Polar Bear swim.
6. Finally understanding what she was trying to say, I apologized for being so slow.
7. After an evening of watching television, I have accomplished as much as if I had been unconscious.
8. Since my doctor recommended that I get more exercise and eat less, I have been walking around the block during my lunch break.
9. Having munched our way through a large bag of peanuts while watching the game, we weren't interested in food by supper time.
10. Whenever a police officer pulls over an optimist, the optimist thinks it's to ask for directions.

> 5. Use commas between coordinate adjectives but not between cumulative adjectives.

Coordinate adjectives are those whose order can be changed, and the word *and* can be inserted between them without changing the meaning of the sentence.

Our company is looking for energetic, courteous salespeople.

The adjectives *energetic* and *courteous* could appear in reverse order, and you could put *and* between them: "Our company is looking for courteous and energetic salespeople."

In a series of **cumulative adjectives**, however, each adjective modifies the word that follows it. You cannot change their order, nor can you insert *and* between them.

The bride wore a pale pink silk dress, and the groom wore a navy wool suit.

You cannot say "The bride wore a silk pink pale dress" or "The groom wore a navy and wool suit," so no commas are used with these adjectives.

Exercise 18.5

Insert commas where they are needed in the following sentences. Check your answers before continuing.

1. The desk was made of dark brown carved oak.
2. Do you want your portrait in a glossy finish or a matte finish?
3. Bright yellow fabric that repels stains is ideal for rain gear.
4. Toronto in the summer is hot smoggy and humid.
5. Today's paper has an article about a new car made of lightweight durable aluminum.
6. Using the new improved model should increase your productivity.
7. This ergonomic efficient full-function keyboard comes in a variety of pastel shades.
8. We ordered a large nutritious salad for lunch, then indulged ourselves with a whipped cream topped dessert.
9. Danni bought a cute cuddly pure-bred puppy.
10. Ten months later that cute puppy turned into a vicious man-eating monster.

The rest of the exercises in this chapter require you to apply all five comma rules. Before you start, write out the five rules and keep them in front of you as you work through the exercises. Refer to the rules frequently as you punctuate the sentences. After you've finished each exercise, check your answers and make sure you understand any mistakes you've made.

Exercise 18.6

1. I call my salary "take home pay" for home is the only place I can afford to go on what I make.

2. Madalena won my heart by laughing at my jokes admiring my car and tolerating my obsession with sports.
3. Though I try to remember my password I seem to forget it at least once a month.
4. Leo went to the bank to withdraw enough money to pay for his tuition books and the student activity fee.
5. At her wedding reception Luisa had an argument with her new mother-in-law about the guest seating.
6. The happiest years of my life in my opinion were the years I spent in college.
7. Sabina spends all day sleeping in bed so she can spend all night dancing in the clubs.
8. Doing punctuation exercises is not very exciting but it's cleaner than tuning your car.
9. This year instead of the traditional gold watch we will be giving retiring employees a framed photograph of our company's president.
10. Called Frobisher Bay until 1987 Iqaluit is a major centre on Baffin Island in Canada's eastern Arctic.

GO TO WEB

EXERCISES 18.1, 18.2

Exercise 18.7

Insert the 15 commas that are missing in this paragraph.

To his surprise a newly married man noticed that his wife always cut off both ends of a roast before she cooked it. When he asked her why she did this she told him that her mother had always cut off both ends of the roast so trimming the roast must be the proper technique for cooking it. In time the young man got to know his in-laws well enough that he felt he could ask his mother-in-law why she cut the ends off the roast before putting it in the oven. In answer to his question the mother-in-law replied that she did it because her own mother had always done it and her mother was a wonderful cook. The young man made a special trip to Calgary the city where his wife's grandmother lived followed the directions to her house and knocked on the door. He introduced himself and the plump grey-haired old woman invited him to join her for tea. After a pleasant conversation over tea with homemade scones and jam he felt comfortable enough to ask his grandmother-in-law why she cut off the ends of a roast before cooking it. The old lady replied that when she was a young mother she had only one cooking pot and it was too small to hold a roast large enough for the family. So she trimmed the roast to fit the pot. And thus a family tradition was born.

GO TO WEB

EXERCISES 18.3, 18.4

Exercise 18.8

Insert the 15 commas that are missing from this paragraph.

Not long ago in a remote part of the Yukon three men became lost in the woods. After floundering around in a panic for two days they came upon a trapper's cabin. Luckily the door was unlocked so they entered to take shelter. To their surprise the large cast iron stove that heated the cabin was suspended from the ceiling by heavy wire. When they had warmed up and had had something to eat from the supplies in the cabin the three men began to speculate on why the stove was hanging from the ceiling. One was sure the reason was to provide more floor space in the small cabin while another thought it might be so that the trapper wouldn't have to bend over to add wood to his fire. The third after long and serious thought suggested that the elevated stove was a more efficient way to distribute the heat in the cabin. Just before midnight the trapper arrived welcomed the lost men to his home and promised to help them find their way. Before they all went to sleep for the night one of the men finally asked the trapper why he had suspended his stove from the ceiling. His answer was simple: "I had lots of wire but I didn't have much stove pipe."

19

The Semicolon

The semicolon and the colon are often confused and used as if they were interchangeable. They serve very different functions, however, and their correct use can dramatically improve a reader's understanding of your writing. Here is one function of the semicolon.

A semicolon can replace a period; in other words, it can appear between two independent clauses.

You should use a semicolon when the two clauses (sentences) you are joining are closely connected in meaning, or when there is a cause-and-effect relationship between them.

I'm too tired; I can't stay awake any longer.

Montreal is not the city's original name; it was once called Ville Marie.

A period could have been used instead of a semicolon in either of these sentences, but the close connection between the clauses makes a semicolon more effective in communicating the writer's meaning.

Some connecting or transitional words are sometimes put between independent clauses to show a cause-and-effect relationship or the continuation of an idea. Words or phrases used in this way are usually preceded by a semicolon and followed by a comma.

; also,	; furthermore,	; nevertheless,
; as a result,	; however,	; on the other hand,
; besides,	; in addition,	; otherwise,
; consequently,	; in fact,	; then,
; finally,	; instead,	; therefore,
; for example,	; moreover,	; thus,

The forecast called for sun; instead, we got snow.

My monitor went blank; however, I continued to type my essay.

I'm not offended by dumb blonde jokes because I know I'm not dumb; besides, I also know I'm not blonde. (Dolly Parton)

In other words, *a semicolon + a transitional word/phrase + a comma* = a link strong enough to come between two related independent clauses.

Note, however, that, when the shaded words and phrases are used as non-essential expressions rather than as connecting words, they are separated from the rest of the sentence by commas (Chapter 18, Rule 2, page 211).

However hard I try, I just can't seem to master particle physics.

The emissions test, moreover, will ensure that your car is running well.

To make a COMPLEX LIST easier to read and understand, put semicolons between the items instead of commas.

A complex list is one in which at least one component part already contains commas. Here's an example:

In the near future, devices such as phones, faxes, and even computers will be part of our clothing; surgical implants will enable us to communicate instantly with each other and with computers; and machines such as cars and household appliances will become programmable and multifunctional.

Exercise 19.1

Put a check mark (✓) before the sentences that are correctly punctuated. Answers for exercises in this chapter begin on page 455.

1. _____ We'll have to go soon; for it's getting late.

2. _____ Truth is often stranger than fiction; my experience this morning proves it.

3. _____ I don't remember if my childhood was happy or not; I was only a kid at the time.

4. _____ Here's a book you should read; it's about improving your manners.

5. _____ Make good notes on this topic; for it could be on the exam.

6. _____ If a tree falls in the woods where no one can hear it; does it make a noise?

7. _____ Cooking tasty food is easy; anything with enough garlic in it will be delicious.

8. _____ Invented by a Canadian in the late 19th century; basketball is one of the world's most popular sports.

9. _____ My neighbour works for a high-tech company; but he can't program his own VCR.

10. _____ I think; therefore, I'm single. (Liz Winstead)

Exercise 19.2

Correct the faulty punctuation in Exercise 19.1.

Exercise 19.3

Insert commas and semicolons where necessary in these sentences, then check your answers.

1. We're late again, this is the third time this week.

2. I'm reading a book on levitation, I can't put it down.

3. The sun is shining, and the temperature has risen ten degrees; we can finally go to the beach.

4. Catalina enjoys listening to music; but her tastes are much different from mine.

5. If you ever need a loan or a helping hand; just call Michel.

6. Travelling in Italy broadens the mind, eating Italian food broadens the behind.

7. North America's oldest continuously run horse race; the Queen's Plate, pre-dates the Kentucky Derby by 15 years.

8. We can't afford dinner at an expensive restaurant, instead we'll eat some of my famous pork and beans at home.

9. She spends her days playing solitaire on the computer watching daytime television whenever there's something interesting on drinking coffee which she makes so strong you could float a loonie on it and talking on the phone to her other stay-at-home friends.

10. I am a marvellous housekeeper, every time I leave a man I keep his house. (Zsa Zsa Gabor)

GO TO WEB

EXERCISE 19.1

Exercise 19.4

Correct the punctuation in these sentences by deleting or inserting commas and semicolons where necessary. Check your answers carefully before continuing.

1. An apple a day keeps the doctor away; however, an onion a day keeps everyone away.

2. Cash your pay cheque right away; this company might be out of business by morning.

3. The telephone has been ringing all day; but there's no one home to take the call.

4. This note says that we are supposed to be at the interview by 9:00 a.m.; consequently, we'll have to leave home by 7:30.

5. Some people are skilled in many fields; Kumari, for example, is both a good plumber and a great cook.

6. The proposal, which was unanimously accepted at the last meeting of our committee, is now sitting on someone's desk.

7. The school counsellors maintain that to succeed at this level, you need excellent note-taking skills, organized study habits, and, most of all, superior time-management strategies.

8. Canada's history is not a very violent one; however, we've had several rebellions of note.

Some people are skilled in many fields; Kumari, for example, is both a good plumber and a great cook.

9. In 1813, Laura Secord trekked 25 km to warn the British and the Canadians of an American attack, her information resulted in victory at the Battle of Beaverdams.

10. Many years later, her name became famous; and a chocolate company was named after her.

GO TO WEB

EXERCISE 19.2

Exercise 19.5

Have you mastered the semicolon? Try this exercise and find out. Insert semicolons and change commas to semicolons and semicolons to commas where necessary in the following sentences.

1. Concluding that we weren't really welcome; we left and went to Tim Hortons for coffee.

2. Horton was a native of Cochrane, Ontario, there's a very popular Tim Hortons shop in his hometown.

3. He played hockey for the Toronto Maple Leafs at a time when they were league champions, he was a key player on their defensive line.

4. Sadly, Horton was killed in a car accident in St. Catharines, Ontario, while commuting from Toronto to Buffalo.

5. Horton ended his career playing for the Buffalo Sabres, nevertheless it is as a member of the Toronto Maple Leafs that he is best remembered.

6. The donut chain that he started has made his name a household word in Canada and even in parts of the United States.

7. The word "donut" is an abbreviated form of the original "dough nought;" meaning a zero made from dough.

8. Deep fried in fat and made from starch and sugar, donuts cannot be considered health food, as a result, some Tim Hortons outlets have installed reinforced seating for their patrons.

9. No one thought the idea of a smoke-free Tim Hortons would work, since coffee and cigarettes seem as natural a pairing as Beavis and Butthead, instead the concept has increased the popularity of the restaurant.

10. I enjoy going to Tim Hortons just to watch the smokers encased behind glass in their little cage, it's more fun than going to the zoo.

20

The Colon

The **colon** functions as an introducer. When a statement is followed by a list, one or more examples, or a quotation, the colon between the statement and what follows alerts the reader to what is coming.

> When I travel, I am never without three things: sturdy shoes, a money belt, and my journal.

> There is only one enemy we cannot defeat: time.

> We have two choices: to study or to fail.

> Early in his career, Robert Fulford did not think very highly of intellectual life in Canada: "My generation of Canadians grew up believing that, if we were very good or very smart, or both, we would someday *graduate* from Canada."

The statement that precedes the colon must be a complete sentence (independent clause). Therefore, a colon can never come immediately after *is* or *are*. Here's an example of what *not* to write.

> The only things I am violently allergic to are: cats, ragweed, and country music.

This is incorrect because the statement before the colon is not a complete sentence.

The colon, then, follows a complete statement and introduces a list or example(s) that defines or amplifies something in the statement. The information after the colon often answers the question "what?" or "who?"

I am violently allergic to three things: (what?) cats, ragweed, and country music.

Business and industry face a new challenge: (what?) e-commerce.

The owner has found the ideal candidate for the position: (who?) his brother.

And finally, the colon is used after a complete sentence introducing a quotation.

Lucille Ball observed that there were three secrets to staying young: "Live honestly, eat slowly, and lie about your age."

The uses of the colon can be summed up as follows.

The colon follows an independent clause and introduces one of three things: an example, a list, or a quotation.

Exercise 20.1

Put a check mark (✓) next to those sentences that are correctly punctuated. Answers for questions in this chapter begin on page 456.

1. _____ The best way to concentrate on what you are reading is to turn off the TV.

2. _____ I stay fit by: cycling and swimming.

3. _____ I read only one kind of book: technical manuals.

4. _____ We agree on the most important things in life: food and music.

5. _____ My car is so badly built that, instead of a warranty, it came with: an apology.

6. _____ There are many species of fish in this lake, including: pike, bass, and walleye.

7. _____ In the words of H.L. Mencken: "Some people don't recognize opportunity when it knocks because it comes in the form of hard work."

8. _____ Although the results are not yet conclusive, the experiment proved one thing: we're on the right track.

9. _____ This apartment would be perfect if it had more storage: there aren't enough closets, bookshelves, or even drawers.

10. _____ After a day at school, I look forward to: a cool drink, a tasty snack, and an afternoon nap.

Exercise 20.2

Correct the faulty punctuation in Exercise 20.1.

GO TO WEB

EXERCISE 20.1

Exercise 20.3

Correct the following sentences as necessary.

1. If at first you don't succeed: become a consultant and teach someone else how to do it.

2. The trees in this park are all native BC species, Douglas fir, arbutus, and dogwood.

3. Our dog knows only one trick, pretending to be deaf.

4. There is a reason I have always felt my little brother was a mean, spiteful child, he always hit me back.

5. She spends too much time: shopping at the malls, talking on the phone, and watching TV.

6. Milton Berle might have been talking about our city's team when he said: "Our team lives hockey; it dreams hockey; it eats hockey. Now, if only it could play hockey."

7. This essay lacks three important features, a title page, a Works Cited page, and some content in between.

8. The shortstop on our baseball team caught only one thing all season, mononucleosis.

9. My mother always wanted a successful son, so I did my part, I urged her to have more children.

10. When someone starts to reminisce about how wonderful everything used to be and how terrible everything is now, just quote the words of Robert Benchley: "Nothing is more responsible for the good old days than a bad memory."

GO TO WEB

EXERCISE 20.2

Exercise 20.4

As a test of your ability to use colons correctly, correct these sentences where necessary.

1. Here's a tip, never go to a job interview on a skateboard.

2. Luis wooed Carmela with three never-fail tactics daily phone calls, weekly flowers, and constant flattery.

3. I have two friends who never let me down no matter how poorly the rest of the world treats me, my dog and my hamster.

4. One of Canada's most famous war heroes was born in the little Ontario town of Owen Sound and became the greatest fighter pilot on the Imperial side in WWI, Billy Bishop.

5. Credited with 72 victories in air battles, he was awarded Britain's highest military honour: the Victoria Cross.

6. Bishop won the Victoria Cross for a single-handed raid on a German air-field in: June of 1917.

7. His last victory came a year later when, in a single day, he accomplished an amazing feat, he shot down five enemy aircraft.

8. A fellow pilot once described him as: "a fantastic shot, but a terrible pilot."

9. A 1982 National Film Board film challenged many of Bishop's claims and even suggested he didn't make the raid that won him the Victoria Cross, the attack on the German airfield.

10. During World War II, Bishop was an honorary air marshal in the organization he was partly responsible for creating, the Royal Canadian Air Force.

Exercise 20.5

The following paragraph will test all you have learned in the last three chapters. Insert commas, semicolons, and colons where appropriate in this passage. There are 15 errors.

Imagine if you can Mario's surprise on being told that he had won a big prize in the lottery, one million dollars. At first he didn't believe it it was simply too good to be true. Once the reality had sunk in however he began to make plans for his fortune. As he thought about how to spend the money he kept one goal in mind "I want to help others as well as myself." He talked to the counsellors at the college who advised him that setting up a scholarship would be a good use of his funds. Every year five thousand dollars would go to three students who were doing well in school but who couldn't afford to continue with their education without assistance. It was a perfect way for Mario to share his good fortune with others. Of course he also bought himself the car of his dreams a sleek silver Porsche.

21

Quotation Marks

Quotation marks (" ") are used to set off short passages of quoted material and some titles. They are a signal to the reader that the words in quotation marks are not yours but someone else's. Quotation marks come in pairs; there must be a set to show where the quotation or title begins and a set to show where it ends. You must be certain that whatever appears in quotation marks is stated *exactly* as it is in the source you are using.[1] The only other thing you need to know about quotation marks is the punctuation needed to introduce and conclude them.

Quoted Material

When you quote a **short passage** (three lines of print or less), you can work it into your own sentence using appropriate punctuation.

1. Normally, you use a comma to introduce a quotation of one or more sentences and include normal sentence punctuation within the quotation marks.

> According to Margaret Atwood, "If you like men, you can like Americans. Cautiously. Selectively. Beginning with the feet. One at a time."

---

[1] If you wish to omit a word or words and can do so without changing the meaning of the original, use ellipses (three spaced dots: . . .) to indicate the omission. If you need to add or change a word (e.g., to maintain tense consistency), put square brackets [ ] around the change. See the documented essay by Nell Waldman on page 410 for examples.

"As you grow old," wrote Richard Needham, "you lose your interest in sex, your friends drift away, your children ignore you. There are other advantages, of course, but these would seem to me the outstanding ones."

"My idea of long-range planning is lunch," confesses Frank Ogden, Canada's foremost futurist.

2. If your own introductory words form a complete sentence, use a colon to introduce the quotation.

Frank Ogden, Canada's foremost futurist, confesses that he has little respect for traditional business-planning cycles: "My idea of long-range planning is lunch."

3. If the passage you are quoting is a couple of words, a phrase, or anything less than a complete sentence, do not use any punctuation to introduce it.

Woody Allen's one regret in life is that he is "not someone else."

Neil Bissoondath argues that racism is based on "willful ignorance and an acceptance of—and comfort with—stereotype."

4. A quotation *within* a quotation is punctuated by single quotation marks.

According to John Robert Colombo, "the most widely quoted Canadian aphorism of all time is Marshall McLuhan's 'The medium is the message.' "

This year's winner of the Wacky Warning Label Contest is, "Never iron clothes while they are being worn."

All the lines of a **long quotation** (more than three lines of print) should be indented ten spaces from the left margin. (Long quotations are NOT enclosed in quotation marks.)

The block indentation indicates to the reader that the words set off in this way are not yours but some other writer's. (Turn to page 413 for an example of how to treat a long quotation.)

College writing normally requires that you indicate the source of any material you quote. The easiest way to do this is to give the author's surname (if it's not already included in your sentence), and the page reference in parentheses at the end of the quotation.

For example:

An American humorist once noted, "I never let schooling interfere with my education" (Twain 97).

American humorist Mark Twain once observed, "I never let schooling interfere with my education" (97).

These source identifications are called parenthetical citations.

Some instructors prefer footnotes or endnotes to parenthetical citations. Find out what format your instructor requires and follow it. In any library or bookstore, you will find a variety of style guides and handbooks that explain different styles of documentation. Some instructors are very particular about format, so you would be wise to ask your instructor which format he or she wants you to use.

As a general rule, if you are writing a paper for a humanities course, we suggest you consult Joseph Gibaldi, *MLA Handbook for Writers of Research Papers*, 5th ed. (New York: MLA, 1999). A useful Web site for advice on MLA format is http://webster.commnet.edu/mla.htm, which includes a link to an online book that provides guidance on how to cite electronic sources.

For papers in the social sciences, the standard source is the *Publication Manual of the American Psychological Association*, 5th ed. (Washington, DC: APA, 2001). Check http://webster.commnet.edu/apa.htm for advice on using APA style, including instruction on citing electronic and online information.

The information and exercises that follow are based on MLA format.

Exercise 21.1

In the following sentences, place quotation marks where they are needed and insert any necessary punctuation before and after each quotation. Answers for this chapter begin on page 457.

1. The most famous quotation in the history of Canadian sports is Foster Hewitt's He shoots! He scores!

2. The beaver, which is Canada's national animal, was once described by Michael Kesterton as a distant relative of the sewer rat.

3. In the opinion of writer Barry Callaghan We Canadians have raised being boring to an art form.

4. All we want, jokes Yvon Deschamps, is an independent Quebec within a strong and united Canada.

5. Pierre Berton sums up the difference between Canadians and Americans as follows You ask an American how he's feeling, and he cries Great! You ask a Canadian, and he answers Not bad, or Pas mal.

Titles

Titles of books or other entire works should be *italicized* or <u>underlined</u>.

Titles of parts of books or other works should be put in quotation marks.

The title of anything that is published or produced as a separate entity (e.g., books, magazines, newspapers, pamphlets, plays, films, TV shows, albums) should be italicized or underlined. The title of anything that has been published or produced as part of a separate entity (e.g., articles, essays, stories, poems, a single episode of a TV series, songs) should be placed in quotation marks.

Why the difference? The way you punctuate a title tells your reader what sort of document you are quoting from or referring to: it may be a complete work that the reader can find listed by title, author, or subject in a library, or it may be an excerpt that the reader can find only by looking up the name of the work in which it was published.

Below is an example of a bibliography—a list of works consulted or cited (referred to) in a research paper—showing how titles of different kinds of publications are punctuated.

Works Cited

WWW Home page

Beaudreau, Sylvie. "Sylvie's Canadian Comedy Page." 12 Mar. 2001 <http: faculty.plattsburgh. edu/sylvie.beaudreau/sylvies_canadian_ comedy.html>.

Newswire story from an online database

"Bravo U.S. Buys 'Made in Canada,' the Satirical Series about the TV Industry." *Canadian Press* 27 Feb. 2001. Online: Ebsco. Canadian MAS FullTEXT Elite. 6 Mar. 2001.

Article in an electronic magazine

"GG Fatbusting at the Y." *Frank: Canada's Definitive Satirical Magazine* 12 Mar. 2001. 13 Mar. 2001. <http://www.frankmag.net/>.

Personal e-mail

Jones, George. "Check this Web site for a Laugh." E-mail to Mary Smith. 14 July 2000.

Essay or article in an anthology or collection

Leacock, Stephen. "Small Town: Mariposa, Ont." *The Oxford Anthology of Canadian Literature.* Ed. Robert Weaver and William Toye. Toronto: Oxford University Press, 1973. 274-278.

Article in a newspaper from an online database

Mackowycz, Bob. "Canuck in King George's Court." *The Toronto Star* 18 Feb. 2001. Online: Electric Library Canada. 8 Mar. 2001.

Poem in an anthology

Ondaatje, Michael. "The Strange Case." *The Maple Laugh Forever: An Anthology of Canadian Comic Poetry.* Ed. Douglas Barbour and Stephen Scobie. Edmonton: Hurtig, 1981. 107.

Article in an encyclopedia on CD-ROM

Rosen, David. "Comedy." *The 1998 Canadian & World Encyclopedia* CD-ROM. Toronto: McClelland and Stewart, 1998.

Article in a print encyclopedia

Scobie, Stephen. "Humorous Writing in English." *The Canadian Encyclopedia: 2nd ed.* Toronto: McClelland & Stewart, 1999.

Television program

"The Sharpest Tongue in the East: Rick Mercer Profile." *The Fifth Estate.* CBC. 10 Jan. 2001.

Article in a magazine

Walker, Ruth. "Why Canucks Provide the Yuks." *Christian Science Monitor* 15 July 1999: 1.

Exercise 21.2

Insert the necessary punctuation (quotation marks, italics, or underlining) in the following sentences. Check your answers before continuing.

1. For me, the most helpful chapter of The Bare Essentials Plus is Cracking the Sentence Code.

2. Canada's national anthem is derived from a French song, Chant national, which was first performed in Quebec City in 1880.

3. O Canada, the English version of Chant national, was written by R. Stanley Weir, a Montreal judge and poet, and was first performed in 1908.

4. In Shakespeare's play The Winter's Tale, there is a peculiar stage direction that has baffled scholars for 400 years: Exit, pursued by a bear.

5. Crouching Toad, Hidden Lizard, a humorous documentary made by our college's television students, was shown on the CBC program Short Shots.

6. The video documentary A War of Their Own is the story of the Canadian troops in World War II who fought in the long, bloody Italian campaign.

7. The CD Sparkjiver features some great blues songs, such as Harlem Nocturne and Try a Little Tenderness, performed by an unusual trio of electric organ, sax, and drums.

8. Go to The Globe and Mail's Web page if you want to follow the links to Steve Galea's article Thunder in the Snow, which describes the appeal and the dangers of snowmobiling.

9. The Diana Krall album When I Look in Your Eyes has three of my favourite jazz vocals: Devil May Care, I Can't Give You Anything But Love, and Do It Again.

10. The Outdoors Channel is playing reruns of old Survivor episodes to show viewers, as TV Guide puts it, how to live off the land while surrounded by cameras, microphones, TV technicians, and an obnoxious host.

GO TO WEB

EXERCISES 21.1, 21.2

EXERCISES 21.1, 21.2

Exercise 21.3

This exercise is designed to test your understanding of how to punctuate short quotations and titles in your writing. When and where do you use quotation marks? Italics (or underlining)? Which punctuation marks precede and follow a quotation?

1. Nothing escaped the humorous attention of Mark Twain, not even vegetables The cauliflower is nothing but cabbage with a college education.

2. I've been on a constant diet for the last two decades complains Erma Bombeck. I've lost a total of 789 pounds. By all accounts, I should be hanging from a charm bracelet.

3. I lost 10 kg by following Richard Watson's advice in his book The Philosopher's Diet: How to Lose Weight and Change the World. The first chapter, entitled Fat, begins Fat. I presume you want to get rid of it. Then quit eating so much (3).

4. The other chapters in the book are Food, Roughage, Running, Sex, How to Live, and How to Die.

5. On her Home page, which she calls My Life and Welcome to It, Gina provides links to all her favourite Web sites.

6. The headline in the Halifax Chronicle Herald reads Legend of Bluenose Strong After 80 Years.

7. The main source for my essay on maple syrup was Leo Werner's article entitled Maple Sugar Industry from the Canadian Encyclopedia CD-ROM.

8. The CBC radio program Choral Concert played a magnificent version of Verdi's Requiem in honour of the 100th anniversary of the composer's death.

9. An article on potential overcrowding at Canada's colleges and universities, called The University Crunch can be found on the Maclean's magazine Web site, www.Macleans.ca.

10. In the film Casablanca, Humphrey Bogart never actually says Play it again, Sam, even though that has become one of the most famous lines associated with the film.

22

Question Marks, Exclamation Marks, and Punctuation Review

The Question Mark

Everyone knows that a **question mark** follows an interrogative, or asking, sentence, but we all sometimes forget to include it. Let this chapter serve as a reminder not to forget!

Put a question mark at the end of every interrogative sentence.

The question mark gives your readers an important clue to the meaning of your sentence. "There's more?" (interrogative) means something quite different from "There's more!"(exclamatory), and both are different from "There's more."(declarative). When you speak, your tone of voice conveys the meaning you intend; when you write, your punctuation tells your reader what you mean.

The only time you don't end a question with a question mark is when the question is part of a statement.

Question	Statement
Are you going?	I asked whether you were going.
Do you know them?	I wonder if you know them.
Is there enough evidence to convict him?	The jury deliberated whether there was enough evidence to convict him.

Exercise 22.1

Put a check mark (✓) before each sentence that is correctly punctuated. Answers for exercises in this chapter begin on page 458.

1. _____ Who's on first?

2. _____ I want to know what's going on?

3. _____ Why do they bother to report power outages on TV.

4. _____ Were you aware that half of the population is below average?

5. _____ If corn oil comes from corn, I wonder where baby oil comes from?

6. _____ We question your conclusions.

7. _____ I'm curious about where you are going for your vacation?

8. _____ Theo wanted to know if Maria was going to the concert?

9. _____ Do you know another word for *thesaurus*.

10. _____ As a Canadian, I often wonder if God ever considered having snow fall up?

GO TO WEB

EXERCISE 22.1

Exercise 22.2

Revise the sentences in Exercise 22.1 that were incorrect.

The Exclamation Mark

Consider the difference in tone between these two sentences:

There's a man behind you.
There's a man behind you!

In the first sentence, information is being supplied, perhaps about the line of people waiting their turn at a grocery store checkout counter. The second sentence might be a shouted warning about a mugger.

Use an **exclamation mark** as end punctuation only in sentences requiring extreme emphasis or dramatic effect.

Note that the exclamation mark will have "punch" (dramatic effect) only if you use it sparingly. If you use an exclamation mark after every other sentence, how will your readers know when you really mean to indicate excitement? Overuse of exclamation marks is a technique used by comic book writers to try to heighten the impact of their characters' words. Ironically, the effect is to neutralize the impact. You will seldom find exclamation marks in academic or business writing.

Practically any sentence could have an exclamation mark after it, but remember that the punctuation changes the meaning of the sentence. Read the following sentences with and without an exclamation mark, and picture the situation that would call for each reading.

They've moved   Don't touch that button
The file was empty   Listen to that noise

Exercise 22.3

Supply the necessary punctuation in the following sentences. Then compare your answers with our suggestions. (Answers will vary, depending on the tone and impact the writer wants to convey.)

1. I quit
2. Stop thief
3. Don't you dare
4. He's on the stairway right behind you
5. We won I can't believe it
6. Brandishing her new credit card, Tessa marched through the mall shouting, "Charge it "
7. Take the money and run
8. I can't believe it's over

Exercise 22.4

Using a variety of punctuation marks (periods, question marks, and exclamation marks) supply appropriate end punctuation in the following sentences. Then compare your answers with our suggestions.

1. The question was whether it would be better to stay in bed or to go to the clinic
2. Gregory asked Nell if she'd ever been to Nanaimo
3. Hurry, or we'll be late
4. Did you ever notice that the early bird gets the worm, but the second mouse gets the cheese
5. Just imagine   In only three hours they are going to draw my ticket number in the lottery
6. Is it true that those who live by the sword get shot by those who don't
7. Don't stop   Do you want the bus behind us to run into our rear end
8. Shoot the puck   Why won't he shoot the puck

Exercise 22.5

Supply appropriate punctuation for the 15 sentences in the following paragraph.

(1) I wonder why it is that I cannot dance (2) My girlfriend would go out dancing every night of the week if she didn't have morning classes (3) And can she ever dance (4) When she is really into the music, I've seen her

receive applause from an entire club as she leaves the dance floor (5) They applaud me, too, but it's because they're glad to see me sit down (6) Why is it that every part of my body moves to a different rhythm (7) When my hips find the beat, my feet are half a beat behind, and my shoulders move around on their own as if I had some horrible nervous disorder (8) Is it because I'm tall, and nerve impulses have to travel a long way to get from one part of my frame to another (9) I've been told that, when dancing, I look like a stork with an uncontrollable itch in a vital part of its anatomy (10) Talk about embarrassing (11) "What can I do " I ask myself (12) Should I subject myself to weeks of torture and take dancing lessons when I suspect they wouldn't help in the least (13) Is there no medical cure for my condition (14) I must have been born without a rhythm gene (15) I wonder if it's too late to get a transplant

Punctuation Review

The exercises that follow are designed to test your knowledge of the punctuation marks you have studied in Unit 4. All of the sentences below contain errors: punctuation is either missing or misused. Work through the exercises slowly and carefully. Check your answers to each set before continuing. If you make a mistake, go back to the chapter that deals with the punctuation mark you missed, and review the explanation and examples. If you're still confused, log on to the Web site for *Bare Essentials Plus* and ask the authors to help you solve your problem.

Exercise 22.6

1. Good health, according to my doctor, should be defined as: the slowest possible rate at which one can die.

2. The fast pace of life does not concern me at all, it's the sudden stop at the end that has me worried.

3. My friend Gordon doesn't think much of a healthy lifestyle; he often says Eat well exercise regularly and die anyway.

4. Did you know that the word "karate" in English means empty hands.

5. The prescription for a healthy life is well known eat a balanced diet, get regular exercise, even if it's just a five minute walk each day, get regular checkups, and avoid stress.

6. I wonder how many people know that the first episode of the television series Star Trek, broadcast in September, 1966, was called The Man Trap?

7. If you want to make your living as a comedian you must: remember the punch line and deliver it with perfect timing.

8. My computer is so old that I can't use it to play any games developed since 1985, I can't use it to access the Internet, it has a two-colour monitor, and believe it or not it uses 5-1/4-inch floppy disks.

9. When he saw Charlie Chaplin imitating Hitler in the movie The Great Dictator Douglas Fairbanks said This is one of the most fortuitous tricks in the history of civilization, that the greatest living villain in the world and the greatest comedian should look alike.

10. One of my favourite Canadian quotations comes from Charlotte Whitton, the first woman mayor of Ottawa, who said To succeed, a woman must be twice as good as a man. Fortunately that isn't difficult.

GO TO WEB

EXERCISE 22.2

Exercise 22.7

Insert the 20 punctuation marks that are missing from the following paragraphs.

A well-known Canadian politician a prominent member of the federal cabinet was asked to make a major speech to an audience of business people Since he enjoyed the services of several assistants one of whom was a professional speech writer he called the writer and outlined for her who the audience for his speech would be what government policies and programs he would like to speak about and what sort of tone and approach he wanted to take with this important audience The speech writer asked only one question she wanted to know how long the speech would be The politician checked his notes and told her that it should be exactly 20 minutes long.

On the day after the big speech had been given the speech writer was at her desk early she was curious to learn how her boss had performed. When he called she could tell from the tone of his voice that he was not pleased in fact he was very angry. He told her that the speech had been a disaster, and it was her fault. He bellowed I asked for a 20 minute speech but you gave me a 60 minute speech. Before I was finished more than half the audience had left the hall! The speech writer replied that she had given him exactly what he asked for notes for a 20 minute speech and two copies.

Exercise 22.8

Write a paper of approximately two pages explaining how to do or make something or how to get somewhere. When you've finished, review your paper carefully, checking spelling, sentence structure, and grammar. Pay particular attention to punctuation. Be sure you have put a question mark at the end of every interrogative sentence and used exclamation marks only when necessary, for emphasis. Check your placement of commas, semicolons, and colons. If you quote, either in dialogue or from a source, check the position of your quotation marks and the punctuation that introduces and concludes each quotation. Here are some topics you might explore.

1. How to choose a good school (hair stylist, professor, spiritual adviser, etc.)
2. How to dance (play golf, tend bar, babysit a spoiled child, etc.)
3. How to survive winter (unemployment, a family reunion, etc.)
4. How to win (or lose) an argument
5. How to prepare for a job interview (a parental interrogation, an interview with the dean, etc.)
6. How to cure a cold (the blues, insomnia, an addiction, etc.)
7. How to raise a family while going to school

UNIT 5

Writing a
College Paper

23

Finding Something to Write About

Every writer knows that content is important. Not so many seem to know that form is just as important. In fact, you can't really separate the two: *what you say is how you say it.* Writing a paper (or an essay, or a report, or a letter, or anything else) is like doing a chemistry experiment: you need the right amount of the right ingredients put together in the right proportions and in the right order. There are five steps to follow.

1. Choose a satisfactory subject
2. Select the main points of your subject
3. Write a thesis statement
   and/or
   Write an outline
4. Write the paragraphs
5. Revise the paper

If you follow these steps faithfully, in order, we guarantee that you will write clear, organized papers.

Note that, when you get to step 3, you have a choice. You can choose to organize your paper by means of a thesis statement or by means of an outline. The thesis statement approach works well for short papers—those no longer than about 500 words. An outline is necessary for longer papers and is often useful for organizing shorter papers. Ideally, you should learn to use both methods of organizing your writing; in fact, your teacher may require that you do so.

Steps 1, 2, and 3 make up the planning stage of the writing process. Be warned: done properly, these three steps will take you at least as long as steps 4 and 5, which involve the actual writing. The longer you spend on planning, the less time you'll spend on drafting and revising, and the better your paper will be.

Step 1
Choose a Satisfactory Subject

Unless you are assigned a specific subject by a teacher or supervisor, choosing your subject can be the most difficult part of writing a paper. Apply the following guidelines carefully, because no amount of instruction can help you to write a good paper on something you don't know anything about or on something that is inappropriate for your audience or purpose. Your subject should satisfy the **4-S test**.

A satisfactory subject is SIGNIFICANT, SINGLE, SPECIFIC, and SUPPORTABLE.

1. Your subject should be **significant**. Write about something that your reader needs to know or might want to know. Consider your audience and choose a subject that they will find significant. This doesn't mean that you can't ever be humorous, but, unless you're another Stephen Leacock, an essay on "How I Deposit Money in My Bank" will probably be of little significance to your readers. The subject you choose must be worthy of the time and attention you expect your readers to give to your paper.

2. Your subject should be **single**. Don't try to cover too much in your paper. A thorough discussion of one topic is more satisfying to a reader than a skimpy, superficial treatment of several topics. A subject such as "The challenge of government funding cutbacks to colleges and universities" includes too much to deal with in one paper. Limit yourself to a single topic, such as "How private sector donations are helping our college meet the challenge of funding cutbacks."

3. Your subject should be **specific**. This requirement is closely tied to the "single" requirement. Given a choice between a general topic and a specific one, you should choose the latter. In a short paper, you can't hope to say anything new or significant about a large topic: "Employment opportunities in Canada," for example. But you could write an interesting, detailed discussion on a more specific topic, such as "Employment opportunities in Nova Scotia's hospitality industry."

You can narrow a broad subject by applying one or more **limiting factors** to it. Try thinking of your subject in terms of a specific *kind*, or *time*, or *place*, or *number*, or *person* associated with it. To come up with the hospitality topic, for example, we limited the subject of employment opportunities in Canada in terms of both place and kind.

4. Your subject must be **supportable**. You must know something about the subject (preferably, more than your reader does), or you must be able to find out about it. Your discussion of your subject will be clear and convincing only if you can include examples, facts, quotations, descriptions, anecdotes, and other details. Supporting evidence can be taken from your own experience or from the experience of other people. In other words, your topic may require you to do some research.

Exercise 23.1

Imagine that you have been asked to write a 500-word paper and given this list of subjects to choose from. Test each subject against the guidelines we've given and identify what's wrong with it. Answers for exercises in this chapter begin on page 459.

1. The theory of evolution
2. The five senses
3. Caring for your cuticles
4. The positive and negative effects of TV on children under 12
5. My best friend: my dog
6. Career opportunities in banking and financial advising
7. Democracy is good
8. Problems our children will face as parents
9. How to parachute or bungee-jump safely
10. On-the-job training

Exercise 23.2

Apply the 4-S guidelines to the following subjects. Some are possibilities for short papers (300 to 500 words) but fail to satisfy one or more of the guidelines. Others are hopeless. Revise the "possible" subjects to make them significant, single, specific, and supportable.

1. Water is necessary to life
2. Some people are very attractive
3. The proper way to stack the dishwasher
4. The Russian economy
5. Canadian women worth knowing

6. How to mix paint
7. Predicting the future
8. The challenges facing Canada's immigrants

Exercise 23.3

List five subjects that you might choose to write about. Be sure each subject is *significant*, *single*, *specific*, and *supportable*.

Step 2
Select the Main Points of Your Subject

Now that you have an appropriate subject for your paper, give some thought to the approach you're going to take to develop it. There are many possible ways of thinking and writing about a subject. In a short paper, you can deal effectively with only a few aspects of your topic. How do you decide which aspects of your subject to discuss, which **main points** to make and explain? One way is to make a list of everything you can think of that you might want to say about the subject. Some preliminary research may help too. You may discover some points about the subject that you hadn't thought of.

Another way—especially useful if you find you're stuck for ideas—is to ask yourself questions about your subject. Run your subject through this list of questions and see which one "fits" it best. (The symbol S stands for your subject.)

1. How do you make or do S? (What are the main steps to follow in accomplishing S?)
2. How does S work?
3. What are the main parts or components of S?
4. What are the main functions of S?
5. What are the important features or characteristics of S?
6. What are the main kinds or types of S?
7. What are some significant examples of S?
8. What are the causes of S?
9. What are the effects or consequences of S?
10. What are the main similarities and/or differences between S and _____ ?
11. What are the main advantages (or disadvantages) of S?
12. What are the reasons for (or against) S?

These questions suggest some common ways of looking at or thinking about a subject. Most subjects will yield answers to more than one of these questions. You should focus on the question that produces the answers that are closest to what you want to say about your subject. These answers will become the main points that you will discuss in your paper.

Here's how the procedure works. Assume you've been assigned a 300–500 word essay on the topic "Dressing for success." If you can't think of an approach that you like, run down the list of questions until you find the one you can answer best. The process might go something like this:

1. How do you dress for success?
   Here's a good start. There's much to say about how to select a look that is likely to improve your chances of getting a job or a promotion.

2. How does dressing for success work?
   Answering this question will require research into the ways that appearance can contribute to success. Why does one's appearance matter so much? The subject is certainly significant, but it may require more time and effort than you have to spend.

3. What are the main parts or components of dressing for success?
   This question doesn't get us anywhere. Let's move on.

4. What are the main functions of dressing for success?
   Another question that doesn't apply.

5. What are the important features or characteristics of dressing for success?
   This question is a good possibility for a short paper. Focussing on two or three different jobs as examples, you could detail what kind of clothing contributes to a positive image and describe how to create a look that will enhance one's chances for career success.

6. What are the main kinds or types of dressing for success?
   This question makes no sense in terms of this subject. Let's move on.

7. What are some significant examples of dressing for success?
   This question has possibilities but will probably require research. You would need to find examples of two or three people who gained positions and/or promotions after dramatically changing their physical appearance. (Preston Manning comes to mind.)

8. What are the causes of dressing for success?
   The answer is obvious: you want to get ahead. Don't waste time explaining the obvious.

9. What are the effects/consequences of dressing for success?
   Another good possibility. Once you have achieved a successful "look," what reaction might you expect from customers or clients, co-workers, and managers? What benefits might result from your new image?

10. What are the main similarities/differences between dressing for success and _____ ?
    This question makes no sense. Let's skip it.

11. What are the main advantages of dressing for success?
    This question can be answered, but the answers are, for the most part, obvious. A less obvious question would be a better choice.

12. What are the reasons for/against dressing for success?
    Again, the answers are obvious—and overlap with those generated by question 8.

Applying this list of questions to your potential subject is often a time-consuming process because it requires you to explore your subject from all angles. Nevertheless, the task is well worth your time and effort. Having gone through the list, it is unlikely that you will miss any aspect of your subject worth writing about. This is important because the more you have to say about your subject and the more comfortable you are with the approach you take, the more likely it is that you will produce a good paper. Take the time to go through all the questions thoughtfully. As we've said before, the more time you spend on planning your paper, the less time you'll need to draft and revise it.

Below you will find seven sample subjects, together with some of the main points that were discovered by applying the list of questions on page 252. Study this chart until you are sure you understand how to find useful main points for any subject.

Subject	Selected Question	Main Points
The ideal job	5. What are the important characteristics of the ideal job?	• satisfying work • good location • compatible co-workers • good pay and benefits
Refugees in Canada	8. What are the main causes of refugees coming to Canada?	• persecution in homeland • war in homeland • poverty in homeland

Subject	Selected Question	Main Points
Cell phones	11. What are the main disadvantages of using cell phones?	• prevent escape from work • create disturbance in theatres, restaurants, etc. • put drivers at risk • possible medical hazard
Cell phones	11. What are the advantages of using cell phones?	• to contact help in an emergency • to keep in touch with family • to conduct business away from the office
Nursing as a career	11. What are the main advantages of a career in nursing?	• opportunity to help people • opportunity for travel • career security
Mental retardation	8. What are the causes of mental retardation?	• genetic defects • brain damage • early environmental deprivation
A successful party	1. How do you give a successful party?	• invite the right mix of people • plan the entertainment • prepare the food in advance • provide a relaxed, friendly atmosphere
Quitting smoking	6. What are some ways to quit?	• cold turkey • taper off gradually • chemical support (pills, gum, patch)
A good teacher	5. What are the characteristics of a good teacher?	• knowledge of subject • ability to communicate • respect for students

As a general rule, you should try to identify between *two* (the absolute minimum) and *five* main ideas to support your subject. If you have only one main idea, your subject is suitable for one paragraph. If you have discovered more than five main ideas that require discussion, you have too much material for a short paper. Either select the most important aspects of the subject, or take another look at it to see how you can focus it more specifically.

Exercise 23.4

In this exercise, select a question from the highlighted list on page 252 and generate good main points for each subject.

Subject	Selected Question	Main Points
1. My future career	•	• • •
2. My first romantic break-up	•	• • •
3. My family's (or my ancestor's) immigration to Canada	•	• • •
4. Leaving home	•	• • •
5. Internet search engines	•	• • •

Subject	Selected Question	Main Points
6. Globalization	•	•
		•
		•
7. Computer games	•	•
		•
		•
8. Hip-hop (or another kind of) music	•	•
		•
		•

Exercise 23.5

For each of the five subjects you chose in Exercise 23.3, list two to five main points. To discover suitable main points, apply to your subject the 12 questions highlighted on page 252, one at a time, until you find the question that fits best. The answers to that question are your main points.

TESTING YOUR MAIN POINTS

Now take a close look at the main points you've chosen for each subject in Exercise 23.5. It may be necessary to revise some of them before going any further. Are some points too trivial to bother with? Do any of the points overlap in meaning? Are there any points that are not directly related to the subject?

Main points must be SIGNIFICANT, DISTINCT, and RELEVANT.

To be satisfactory, the main points you have chosen to write about must all be **significant**: worth writing a paragraph or more on. You shouldn't have any trivial ideas mixed in with the important ones.

Each of the main points you've chosen must also be **distinct**. That is, each must be different from all the others. There must be no overlap in meaning. Check to be sure you haven't given two different labels to what is really one aspect of the subject.

Finally, each main point must be **relevant**; it must be clearly **related** to the subject. It must be an aspect of the subject you are writing about, not some other subject. For example, if you're writing about the advantages of a subject, cross out any disadvantages that may have appeared on your list.

Exercise 23.6

Each of the following subjects is followed by some possible main points. Circle the unsatisfactory point(s) in each group.

1. Popular Canadian sports teams
   - Toronto Blue Jays
   - Winnipeg Blue Bombers
   - Montreal Canadiens
   - Seattle Mariners
   - Hamilton Tiger Cats

2. The advantages of being physically fit
   - improved muscle tone
   - improved looks
   - improved stamina
   - improved appearance
   - improved social life

3. Problems faced by new immigrants in Canada
   - travelling
   - finding suitable work
   - shovelling snow
   - learning a new language
   - finding a suitable place to live
   - adjusting to the climate

4. Reasons for drug abuse among adolescents
   - peer pressure
   - school pressure
   - alcohol
   - boredom

5. The functions of a travel counsellor
   - plan the client's itinerary
   - book the required arrangements
   - make travel plans
   - get a passport
   - ensure client is satisfied

6. The main kinds of daytime
   television

   • talk shows
   • quiz shows
   • soap operas
   • Oprah
   • game shows

7. Types of dangerous weather systems

   • hurricanes
   • blizzards
   • tornadoes
   • earthquakes
   • typhoons

8. Characteristics of sharks

   • tiny brains
   • white shark
   • skeletal system is cartilage
   • several sets of needle-sharp
     teeth
   • hammerhead shark
   • not all are dangerous to
     humans

GO TO WEB

EXERCISE 23.1

Exercise 23.7

Study the main points you chose in Exercise 23.5 on page 257. Cross out any that are not *significant*, *distinct*, or *relevant* to the subject. If necessary, add new main points so that you end up with at least three main points for each subject.

ORGANIZING YOUR MAIN POINTS

Now that you've decided on three or four main points to discuss, you need to decide in what order you wish to present them in your paper. Choose the order that is most appropriate for your particular subject.

There are four basic ways to arrange main points in an essay: CHRONOLOGICAL, CLIMACTIC, LOGICALLY LINKED, and RANDOM order.

1. **Chronological order** means in order of time sequence, from first to last. Here's an example:

Subject	Main Points
The development of a relationship	• attraction • meeting • discovery • intimacy • disillusionment

2. **Climactic order** means presenting your strongest or most important point last. Generally, you would discuss your second-strongest point first and the others in between, like this:

Subject	Main Points
Disadvantages of cigarette smoking	• danger to those around you • disapproval of others • expense • danger to yourself

3. **Logically linked order** means that the main points are connected in such a way that one point must be explained before the next can be understood. Consider this example:

Subject	Main Points
Main causes of gang involvement	• lack of opportunity for work • lack of recreational facilities • boredom • need for an accepting peer group

The logical link here is this: because of unemployment, recreational facilities are needed, and because of both unemployment and inadequate recreational facilities, boredom becomes a problem. Bored by having nothing to do and nowhere to go, young people need an accepting peer group to bolster their self-esteem. The first three points must be explained before the reader can fully understand the fourth.

4. **Random order** means the points can be satisfactorily explained in any order. A random arrangement of points is possible only if the main points are *equally significant* and *not chronologically or causally linked*, as in this example:

Subject	Main Points
Reasons for the garbage disposal crisis	• disposal sites are hard to find • costs are high • new technologies are not yet fully developed

Exercise 23.8

Below we have identified eight subjects, together with several main points that could be used to develop them. For each subject, number the points so that they are arranged in the order suggested.

Subject	Order		Main Points
1. How to start a gas lawn mower	chronological	_____	make sure there is enough gas in tank
		_____	turn switch to start
		_____	put lawn mower on flat ground
		_____	when running, adjust to proper speed
		_____	pull cord
		_____	mow!
2. Differences between spoken and written language	climactic	_____	speech is transitory; writing is permanent
		_____	speech is direct and personal; writing isn't
		_____	speech can't be revised; writing can
3. How to write a research paper	chronological	_____	read and take notes on selected research sources
		_____	draft the paper
		_____	compile a working bibliography of research sources
		_____	define the subject
		_____	type and proofread paper
		_____	prepare footnotes, if needed, and reference list
		_____	revise the paper

Subject	Order	Main Points
4. How colleges benefit society	logical	_____ they provide the individual with a higher level of general education
		_____ society benefits from increased productivity and commitment of an educated populace
		_____ they provide the individual with job skills
5. Effects of malnutrition	logical	_____ malnutrition affects the productivity and prosperity of nations as a whole
		_____ malnutrition impedes the mental and physical development of children
		_____ undernourished children become sickly adults unable to participate fully in their society
6. Why pornography should be banned	chronological	_____ it degrades the people involved in making it
		_____ it brutalizes society as a whole
		_____ it desensitizes the people who view it
7. Why pornography should not be banned	climactic	_____ organized crime benefits from illegal distribution
		_____ censorship violates individual civil rights
		_____ banning pornography would lead to censorship of legitimate art and literature

8. Reasons for student   climactic   _____   lack of parental
   poverty   assistance
                                            _____   lack of government
                                                    loan assistance
                                            _____   inability to manage
                                                    money effectively
                                            _____   inability to find
                                                    part-time work

---

Exercise 23.9

Using your list of subjects and main points from Exercise 23.7, arrange the main points for each subject in the most appropriate order. (*Note:* Keep your answer sheet. You will need it in some of the exercises that follow.)

In this chapter, you've learned how to choose a satisfactory subject and how to select and arrange the main points of that subject—the first two steps in the five-step process we outlined at the beginning of the chapter. Now it's time to decide whether you'll develop your paper by the thesis statement method or by the outline method. We think the former generally works best for short papers and the latter for long papers, but this distinction isn't hard and fast. Your wisest choice is to learn both ways to structure a paper. You will often get the best results if you use them together.

24

Writing the Thesis Statement

In Chapter 23, you chose a topic and selected some aspects of it to discuss. Now you're ready for the third step in developing a paper. If you're writing a short paper, we recommend that you use the method presented in this chapter. If you're writing a longer paper, or if your teacher prefers the outline method, you may prefer to turn now to Chapter 25, "Writing the Outline."

Step 3
Write a Thesis Statement

The key to a clearly organized paper is a **thesis statement**—a statement near the beginning of your paper that announces its subject and scope. The thesis statement helps both you and your readers because it plans your paper for you, and it tells your readers exactly what they are going to read about. In fiction, telling readers in advance what they are going to find would never do. But for practical, everyday kinds of writing, advance notice works well. Term papers, technical reports, research papers, office memoranda, and business letters are no place for suspense or surprises. In these kinds of writing, you're more likely to get and keep your readers' attention if you indicate the subject and scope of your paper at the outset. The thesis statement acts like a table of contents, giving a clear indication of what follows. It's a kind of map of the territory covered in your paper: it keeps your reader (and you) on the right track.

A thesis statement is a sentence that clearly and concisely indicates the SUBJECT of your paper, the MAIN POINTS you will discuss, and the ORDER in which you will discuss them.

To write a thesis statement, you join your **subject** to your **main points,** which you have arranged in order. To join the two parts of a thesis statement, you use a **link**. Your link can be a word or a phrase such as *are, include, consist of, because,* or *since,* or it can be a colon.[1] Here is a simple formula for constructing a thesis statement.

$$S \text{ consists of } 1, 2, 3 \dots n.$$

subject   *link*   *main points*

Here's an example:

Three characteristics of a good business letter (are) conciseness, clarity, and courtesy.

      subject   *link*   *main points*

Exercise 24.1

In each of the following thesis statements, underline the subject with a wavy line, circle the link, and underline the main points with a straight line. Answers for this chapter begin on page 461.

1. The essential features of a good novel are interesting characters, a stimulating plot, and exceptional writing.

2. My boss enjoys two hobbies: improving his golf game and tormenting his employees.

3. Well-known stars, stunning technical effects, and a hugely expensive advertising campaign are the requirements for a blockbuster movie.

4. A typical computer system consists of a CPU, monitor, printer, scanner, and interface devices.

5. If I were you, I would avoid eating in the cafeteria because the food is expensive, tasteless, and unhealthy.

6. The original Volkswagen Beetle, the Citröen CV, and the Morris Minor are three cars that will be remembered for their endearing oddness.

---

[1] Remember that a colon can be used only after an independent clause. See Chapter 20 if you need a review.

7. *The Simpsons* amuses and provokes viewers with its depiction of a smart-aleck, under-achieving son; a talented, high-achieving daughter; and a hopeless, blundering father.

8. Because they lack basic skills, study skills, or motivation, some students run the risk of failure in college.

9. Fad diets are not the quick and easy fixes to weight problems that they may seem to be; in fact, they are often costly, ineffective, and even dangerous.

10. The Canadian political culture differs from American political culture in terms of attitudes to universal health care, gun control, and capital punishment.

When you combine your subject with your main points to form a thesis statement, there is an important rule to remember.

The main points should be **grammatically parallel**.

This rule means that, if main point 1 is a word, then main points 2 and 3 and so on must be words too. If main point 1 is a phrase, then the rest must be phrases. If your first main point is a dependent clause, then the rest must be dependent clauses. Study the model thesis statements you analyzed in Exercise 24.1. In every example, the main points are in grammatically parallel form. For each of those thesis statements, decide whether words, phrases, or dependent clauses were used. If you think your understanding of parallelism is a bit wobbly, review Chapter 9 and do the following Web exercise before continuing.

GO TO WEB

EXERCISE 24.1

Exercise 24.2

Put a check mark (✓) before the sentences that are grammatically parallel. When you have completed the exercise, check your answers on page 461.

1. _____ A good counsellor must have knowledge, insight, patience, and compassion.

2. _____ Good writing involves applying the principles of organization, sentence structure, spelling, and you have to punctuate correctly.

3. _____ Our company requires employees to be knowledgeable, totally honest, disciplined, and we have to be able to rely on them.

4. _____ Hobbies are important because they provide us with recreational activities, stimulation, and they are relaxing.

5. _____ Some of the negative effects of caffeine are nervousness, you have difficulty sleeping, and heart palpitations.

Exercise 24.3

Now revise the incorrect sentences in Exercise 24.2.

GO TO WEB

EXERCISE 24.2

Exercise 24.4

Revise the following draft thesis statements. Be sure that the main points of each statement are significant, distinct, relevant, and grammatically parallel. Some sentences contain more than one kind of error. Make corrections as needed; then compare your revisions with our suggested answers.

1. The four kinds of prose writing are description, narrative, exposition, and argumentation.

2. Intramural sports offer students a way to get involved in their school, an opportunity to meet new friends, uniforms, and they can stay fit.

3. Increasingly, scientists are finding links between the weather and diseases such as colds, cancer, arthritic ailments, and aging.

4. The most prolific producers of pretentious language are politicians, teachers and administrators, those who write advertising copy, educators, and sports writers.

5. There are three categories of students with whom teachers find it difficult to cope: those who skip class, sleeping in class, and those who disrupt class.

Exercise 24.5

For each of the following subjects, assess the main points we've provided to see if they are suitable for inclusion in a short essay. Then, using the points that pass the test, write a grammatically parallel thesis statement. Underline the subject with a wavy line, circle the link, and underline the main points with straight lines. We've done part of the first question for you as an example.

1. Subject: Watching television is a valuable way to spend time

Choose main points that support the subject

- learn things? Yes, you can learn many things watching TV

- relax and laugh? Yes, TV provides good entertainment

- wastes time? No, TV may do that, but this point doesn't support the thesis

- provides topics for discussion? Yes, talking about shows we've watched brings us together with friends and family

- violent video games? No (why?) _____

A. Thesis Statement: Watching television is a valuable way to spend time because it teaches us many things, it provides laughter and relaxation, and it supplies us with topics to discuss with others.

Now re-write the thesis statement using a colon as a link.

B. There are three reasons _____

2. Vancouver is a wonderful place to live

- moderate climate

- traffic

- Museum of Anthropology

- scenery that is beautiful

- rain

- cultural attractions

A. Three reasons why Vancouver is a wonderful place to live _____

_____

_____

_____

Re-write the thesis statement using *because* as a link.

B. _____   _____

_____

_____

_____

3. Immigration is a good policy for Canada

- immigrants offer new skills

- immigrants may find it difficult to adjust to life in Canada

- immigrants may bring investment dollars

- immigrants must often learn a new language

- immigrants enrich Canadian culture

A. Immigration is a good policy for Canada because _____

_____

_____

_____

Re-write the thesis statement using a colon as the link.

B. _____

_____

_____

_____

4. People love to take vacations, but the kind of vacation depends on the kind of person.

- beach resorts
- Las Vegas
- gambling trips
- Cancun, Mexico
- Buckingham Palace
- adventure vacations
- too much sun
- mountain climbing
- lose money
- touring cultural attraction vacations
- can be dangerous

A. Different people like different kinds of vacation; for example, <u>some people like to relax at a beach resort</u>, _____

_____

_____

Re-write the thesis statement using *are* as a link.

B. _____

_____

_____

_____

5. The following question comes from the illustration on pages 253 and 254 that explained how to use questions to generate main points for an essay. The topic is "Dressing for success." First, decide which points are usable, then write two different versions of a thesis statement for the subject.

- career in sales or public relations
- installing computer networks
- career in high-level corporate environment
- career in technical field
- CEO
- software sales representative

A. Thesis statement: _____

_____

_____

_____

B. Thesis statement: _____

_____

_____

_____

_____

Exercise 24.6

For each of the topics below, provide main points and write a thesis statement.

1. Learning a new language

-
-
-

Thesis statement: _____

_____

_____

_____

2. What I've learned from my family since I became an adult

-
-
-

Thesis statement: _____

_____

_____

_____

3. Using the Internet

-
-
-

Thesis statement: _____

_____

_____

_____

4. What makes us laugh

-
-
-

Thesis statement: _____

_____

_____

_____

5. What a college education means to me

-
-
-

Thesis statement: _____

_____

_____

_____

_____

Exercise 24.7

Find the subjects and main points you produced for Exercise 23.9 in Chapter 23. Combine each subject with its main points to make a thesis statement. Be sure the main points are expressed in parallel form.

We said at the beginning of this chapter that a thesis statement outlines your paper for you. Before we turn to the actual writing of the paper, you should have a general idea of what the finished product will look like.

In a short paper, each main point can be explained in a single paragraph. The main points of your subject become the **topics** of the paragraphs, as shown below in the model format for a paper with three main points.

Title

paragraph 1: contains your introduction and thesis statement

S consists of 1, 2, and 3.

paragraph 2: explains your first main point

Topic sentence introducing main point 1. ____

paragraph 3: explains your second main point

Topic sentence introducing main point 2. ____

paragraph 4: explains your third main point

Topic sentence introducing main point 3. ____

paragraph 5: states your conclusion

Notice the proportions of the paragraphs in the model format. This format is for a paper whose main points are approximately equal in significance, so the body paragraphs are approximately equal in length. (In a paper in which your last main point is more important than the other points, however, the paragraph that explains it will probably be longer than the other paragraphs.)

Notice, too, that the introductory and concluding paragraphs are much shorter than the ones that explain the main points. Your introduction should not ramble on, and your conclusion should not trail off. Get to your main points as quickly as you can, and end with a bang, not a whimper.

Exercise 24.8

An example of a paper that follows the model format exactly is Nell Waldman's "Bumblers, Martinets, and Pros," which appears in Appendix A. Read it through; then go back and underline the thesis statement and the topic sentences.

25

Writing the Outline

For longer compositions—business and technical reports, research papers, and the like—an outline is often necessary. A good outline maps out your paper from beginning to end. It shows you before you begin to write what you have to say about each of your main points. Outlining spares you the agony of discovering too late that you have too much information about one point and little or nothing to say about another.

Step 3
Write an Outline

Once you've chosen a satisfactory subject and main points to discuss, the next step is to expand what you have into an organized plan for your finished paper. To do this, you may need to do some more thinking or reading to gather additional information and supporting details. (For ideas about what kinds of information you might use, see "Developing Your Paragraphs" in Chapter 26.) After you've assembled all the information you think you'll need, prepare the outline.

First, write down your main points in the order you've decided is best for your presentation. Leave at least a half-page between points. Using Roman numerals (I, II, III, and so on), number your main points. Now, under each main point, indent and list the examples, facts, quotations, or other supporting information you're going to use to explain it. Again, leave lots of space. Check to be sure these items are arranged in an order that will be clear to your reader.[1] Label your supporting points *A, B, C,* and so on.

---

[1] The four kinds of order explained in Chapter 23 apply to the arrangement of ideas within a paragraph as well as to the arrangement of main points in a paper.

If some of these supporting points need to be explained or developed, indent again and list the second level of supporting points, numbering them *1, 2, 3,* and so on. Third-level supporting details, if there are any, should be indented under the points to which they relate and labelled *a, b, c,* and so on. Add the introduction and the conclusion, and you're done. Your outline might look something like this.

Introduction
    Attention-getter
    Thesis statement/statement of subject

I. First main point
    A. Item that develops first main point
    B. Item that develops first main point
        1. Supporting material that develops item B
        2. Supporting material that develops item B

II. Second main point
    A. Item that develops second main point
    B. Item that develops second main point
    C. Item that develops second main point

III. Third main point
    A. Item that develops third main point
        1. Supporting material that develops item A
          a. Detail
          b. Detail
        2. Supporting material that develops item A
    B. Item that develops third main point

Conclusion
    Summary
    Memorable statement

Questions about how to arrange your information under each main point and how much time to spend on a particular point should be cleared up at the outline stage. If, for example, you find you have six subheadings under main point I and only one under main point II, you need to do some rethinking to balance your paper. Main points should be supported by approximately equal amounts of information.

Preparing a satisfactory outline takes time. Be prepared to spend time adding, deleting, and rearranging your ideas and supporting details until you're completely satisfied with the arrangement and proportions of your outline.

If you have access to a word-processing program with an outline feature, be sure to try it out! These programs can be very helpful to an inexperienced writer faced with a writing assignment and little knowledge of how to organize it.

After you have written and revised your outline, you are ready to draft your paper. Make the main points into paragraph divisions, explain the supporting points in sentences, and add an introduction and a conclusion. Chapter 26 explains how.

To show you the relationship between an outline and the final product, we've re-created the outline that was used to write "Bumblers, Martinets, and Pros," which you will find in Appendix A.

Introduction

Attention-getter: Quotes from George Bernard Shaw ("Those who can, do. Those who can't, teach") and Woody Allen ("Those who can't teach, teach gym). We've all had teachers who fit these definitions, and we've also had some who do their jobs cheerfully and well.

Thesis statement: Most teachers fit into one of three categories: Bumblers, Martinets, and Pros.

I. The Bumbler

   A. Definition: A teacher who is so uncoordinated she trips over the doorjamb while entering the classroom

   B. Characteristics
      1. Clumsy
      2. Flustered
      3. Disorganized
      4. Unable to cope with technology
      5. Unable to concentrate on the lesson or the class
      6. Forgets to collect assignments or give assigned tests

   C. Effectiveness: Students can only learn from this teacher if they take the initiative

II. The Martinet

   A. Definition: A strict disciplinarian

   B. Characteristics
      1. Authoritarian
      2. Never smiles
      3. Harsh voice
      4. Humiliates students
      5. Classes follow unvarying routine

      6. Intolerant of questions or digressions
      7. Assignments are long and tedious
      8. Tests are unreasonably difficult
  C. Effectiveness
      1. Only by memorizing can students pass tests
      2. Students lose patience and suffer loss of self-esteem

III. The Professional
  A. Definition: A teacher who genuinely likes and respects students as well as his or her subject
  B. Characteristics
      1. Well-organized but flexible
      2. Encourages questions
      3. Class atmosphere is relaxed, friendly
      4. Atmosphere stimulates students to focus on learning
      5. Assignments are designed to reinforce and enhance learning
      6. Tests are rigorous but fair
  C. Effectiveness: Students are eager and able to learn

Conclusion
  Summary: The Bumbler, Martinet, and Pro represent the best and worst qualities of individual teachers as well as the extremes of different types of teachers.
  Memorable Statement: In an ideal world, students would be able to choose their teachers. Who would opt for a Bumbler or a Martinet, given the chance to sign up for a Pro?

Once you've mapped out your plan in an outline, the task of writing the essay is much easier. You can see where you're going and how to get there. Remember, the more time you spend on planning, the less time you will spend on writing and the better your paper will be.

Exercise 25.1

Read "Bumblers, Martinets, and Pros" in Appendix A. Find the paragraphs that correspond to the various headings and subheadings in the outline on pages 277–278. Label the paragraphs and sentences to show where they fit into the outline: I, A, B, 1, 2, and so on.

Exercise 25.2

Read D'Arcy McHayle's "The Canadian Climate" in Appendix A and write an outline for it. Then turn to pages 463–464 to compare your outline with ours.

Exercise 25.3

Turn to the subjects and main points you developed for Exercise 23.9 in Chapter 23 and create an outline for a paper on one of those subjects.

26

Writing the Paragraphs

You are now at step 4 in the writing process. With either your thesis statement or your outline before you, you are ready to turn your main points into paragraphs. Does that sound like a magician's trick? It isn't. The only skills involved are knowing what a paragraph looks like and how to put one together.

A paragraph looks like this:

Three or more sentences that specifically support or explain the topic go in here.

{

A sentence that introduces the **topic** (or main idea) of the paragraph goes here.

_____

_____

_____

_____

_____

_____

A sentence that concludes your explanation of the topic goes here.

Sometimes a main point can be explained satisfactorily in a single paragraph. If the main point is complicated and requires lots of support, several paragraphs are needed. Nevertheless, whether it is explaining a main point of a paper or an item supporting a main point, every paragraph contains two things: a **topic sentence** (usually the first sentence in the paragraph) and several sentences that develop the topic.

A sentence that clearly states your main idea is a good way to start a paragraph. The sentences that follow should support or expand on the topic. The key to making the paragraph *unified* (an important quality of English paragraphs) is to make sure that each of your supporting sentences relates directly to the main idea introduced in the topic sentence.

Turn to Appendix A and read Brian Green's "The Case Against Quickspeak." Study the fourth, fifth, and sixth paragraphs and find in each the three basic components of a paragraph: the topic sentence, the supporting sentences, and the conclusion. Compare your answer with ours. Answers for exercises in this chapter begin on page 464.

Developing Your Paragraphs

How do you put a paragraph together? First, write your topic sentence, telling your reader what topic (main point or idea) you're going to discuss in the paragraph. Next, develop your topic. An adequately developed paragraph gives enough supporting information to make the topic completely clear to the reader. An average paragraph runs between 75 and 200 words (except for introductions and conclusions, which are shorter), so you will need lots of supporting information for each point.

Unless you are writing from a detailed outline and have all the supporting material you need listed in front of you, you need to do some more thinking at this point. Put yourself in your reader's place. What does your reader need to know in order to understand your point clearly? If you ask yourself the six questions listed below, you'll be able to decide what **kinds of development** to use to support a particular topic sentence. The kinds of development you use is up to you. Decide on the basis of your topic and what the reader needs to know about it.

1.   Is a **definition** necessary?

If you're using a term that may be unfamiliar to your reader, you should define it. Use your own words in the definition. Your reader needs to know what *you* mean by the term—and, besides, quoting from the dictionary is a boring way to develop a paragraph. In the following paragraph, Brian Green defines what fly fishing means to him. (Other fly fishers would not necessarily agree with him.) Included in the overall definition of fly fishing are two subordinate definitions. Can you find them?

> Fly fishing is the art and science of using expensive technical equipment
> to capture an animal with the intelligence of a hubcap. The challenge in
> fly fishing is to launch a lure—an artificial fly made of feathers and fur so

light it will float—out to where the fish are lurking, presumably waiting to eat it. Try throwing a cotton ball across the room, and you'll understand the challenge. The fishing line used in fly fishing is the secret weapon that enables the fisher to accomplish this seemingly impossible task. It is a thick, fairly heavy line made of vinyl coated Dacron. Using a light, highly flexible graphite or fibreglass fishing rod, the caster launches the line (with fly attached) backward in an arc, then whips it forward across the water, all the while letting the line's weight and momentum pull more line from the reel. Once enough line is in the air, the fisher stops the motion, the line drops to the water, and the fly lands (if the fisher is sufficiently skilful) on the water in front of the quarry. If the fish thinks the bits of fur and feather thus presented to it resemble a bug that has conveniently landed on the water right before his nose, he will attempt to eat it and be caught. Compared to dropping a hook decorated with a worm in the water and waiting for a strike, fly fishing is maddeningly complicated. Perhaps that's its attraction. (5–6)

You should include a definition, too, if you're using a familiar term in a specific or unusual way. In the following paragraph, Andrew Nikiforuk defines how he interprets the familiar phrase "back to the basics":

Let me reiterate what "back to the basics" means. It means teaching subjects that matter—such as English, math, history, geography, and science—because they contain the codes for power in a technological society as well as the only tools for criticizing and analyzing it. It means giving teachers more control over how their classrooms are organized and taught as well as making them more accountable for the results. It means skills in the context of disciplines (that's critical thinking) with the honest realization that not all students will become critical thinkers. It means fair tests and even standardized tests, because product matters in this culture. And finally, it means using the varied cultural backgrounds of students to explore common ground and Canadian realities. (106)

Source: Nikiforuk, Andrew. *School's Out: The Catastrophe in Public Education and What We Can Do about It*. Toronto: MacFarland, 1993.

Exercise 26.2

Write a paragraph in which you define one of the following terms:

a good (or bad) parent	a good (or bad) friend	success
community	creativity	boredom
racism	a good (or bad) job	a good (or bad) marriage

2. Would **examples** help to clarify the point?

Listing a number of examples is probably the most common method of developing a topic. Readers become confused, even suspicious, when they read unsupported generalizations or statements of opinion. One of the most effective ways of communicating your idea is by providing clear, relevant examples. In the following paragraph, excerpted from a reading in Appendix A, Sun-Kyung Yi uses examples to explain why her job with a Korean company proved to be a "painful and frustrating experience."

> When the president of the company boasted that he "operated a little Korea," he meant it literally. A Canadianized Korean was not tolerated. I looked like a Korean; therefore, I had to talk, act, and think like one, too. Being accepted meant a total surrender to ancient codes of behaviour rooted in Confucian thought, while leaving the "Canadian" part of me out in the parking lot with my '86 Buick. In the first few days at work, I was bombarded with inquiries about my marital status. When I told them I was single, they spent the following days trying to match me up with available bachelors in the company and the community. I was expected to accept my inferior position as a woman and had to behave accordingly. It was not a place to practice my feminist views, or be an individual without being condemned. Little Korea is a place for men (who filled all the senior positions) and women don't dare to speak up or disagree with their male counterparts. The president (all employees bow to him and call him Mr. President) asked me to act more like a lady and smile. I was openly scorned by a senior employee because I spoke more fluent English than Korean. The cook in the kitchen shook her head in disbelief upon discovering that my cooking skills were limited to boiling a package of instant noodles. "You want a good husband, learn to cook," she advised me. (405–406)

Source: Yi, Sun-Kyung. "An Immigrant's Split Personality." *The Globe and Mail* 12 Apr. 1992. Reprinted by permission of Sun-Kyung Yi.

Sometimes one example developed in detail is enough to allow the reader to understand what you mean. In the following paragraph, Nell Waldman describes one familiar kind of teacher.

> Every student gets a Bumbler at least once. She's the teacher who trips over the doorjamb as she makes her first entrance. She looks permanently flustered, can't find her lesson plan, and dithers as she scrambles through her mess of books and papers. The Bumbler can't handle the simplest educational technologies: chalk self-destructs in her fingers, overhead

projectors blow up at her touch, and VCRs jam if she so much as looks in their direction. Organization isn't Ms. Bumbler's strong point either. She drifts off in mid-sentence, eyes focussed dreamily out the window. Students can easily derail her with off-topic questions. She'll forget to collect assignments or to give the test that everyone has studied for. The Bumbler is an amiable sort, but her mind is on a perpetual slow boat to nowhere. Students can learn in her class, but only if they are willing to take a great deal of initiative. (400)

Source: Waldman, Nell. "Bumblers, Martinets, and Pros." *Canadian Content*. Ed. Sarah Norton and Nell Waldman. Toronto: Harcourt, 1988. 108–110.

Exercise 26.3

Write a six- to ten-sentence paragraph based on one of the topic sentences below, using examples to develop it.

Most Americans do not understand why their country is so unpopular abroad.
Life in the big city is not for me.
Living away from home is hard to adjust to.
The terrorists acts of September 11, 2001, have changed forever the world we live in.

3. Is a **series of steps** or **stages** involved?

Sometimes the most effective way to develop the main idea of your paragraph is by explaining how to do it—that is, by relating the process or series of steps involved. Make sure you break the process down into its component parts and explain the steps logically and precisely. Below, Brian Green explains the process of writing a good e-mail message. As you read through this paragraph, number the steps the author identifies as the parts of the process. Has he left anything out?

E-mail is no different from any other business correspondence: it must be clear and concise. Achieving clarity and conciseness is not difficult, but it does require planning. Begin with an introduction that briefly explains the purpose of your message. Next, outline how you are going to develop that message. Use numbered or bulleted points to guide the reader from your position statement through your reasoning to your conclusion. Reinforce your message with a conclusion that states any follow-up actions you require and that confirms the time, place, and responsibilities of those who are contributing to the project. Next, re-read your message as if you were seeing it for the first time. Revise to be sure that you have included all the necessary details: dates, reference numbers, times and places of meetings, and whatever other information is needed to get the right people together in the right places, on the right days, at the right times, with the right information in their briefcases. Use a spell-checker, but don't count on it to catch all your errors and typos. Remember: A clear message, clearly delivered, is the essence of effective communication. (402)

Exercise 26.4

Write a paragraph developed as a series of steps telling your reader how to make or do something you are good at. (Choose a significant topic, not a trivial one.)

4. Would **specific details** be useful?

Providing your reader with concrete, specific, descriptive details can be an effective way of developing your main point. In the following paragraph, underline the specific details that help to make effective the author's explanation of a wine taster's vocabulary:

> Wine tasters have developed a vocabulary that often seems eccentric, exaggerated, or even pretentious to the uninitiated. However, a little experience and some education in wine tasting can demonstrate the appropriateness of some of the descriptors used by wine enthusiasts. Interestingly, there are no smells or tastes that are unique to wine, so the descriptions used are all comparative, as in "it tastes <u>like</u>. . . ." The "nose" of a wine is its smell in the glass, so a white wine—a Sauvignon Blanc, for example—may have a "grassy" or "herbaceous" nose, or have suggestions of grapefruit, lychee, green apple, or lemon. A red wine such as a Pinot Noir may have all sorts of red berry flavours in the nose: red currant, raspberry, strawberry, or cassis. As they age, some red wines take on hints of leather, tar, licorice, or tobacco. Not everyone can detect such odours at first, but wine experts, with years of practice, can consistently catch these and many other unlikely smells in a glass of wine. (Green 2)

In some paragraphs, numerical facts or statistics can be used to support your point effectively. Ever since Benjamin Disraeli's immortal comment that the media print "lies, damned lies, and statistics," however, critical readers tend to be suspicious of statistics, so be very sure that your facts are correct and that your statistics are current.

> Canadians are great travellers. We not only travel around our own country, exploring every nook and cranny from Beaver Creek in the Yukon

Territory to Bay Bulls in Newfoundland, but we also can be found touring around every other country on Earth. Statistics Canada reports that we take about 150 million overnight trips a year within our own borders. Abroad, we favour our next door neighbour by a wide margin above other destinations, averaging around 15 million overnight trips a year to the United States. The United Kingdom is our second favourite destination, with over 800 thousand visits, followed by Mexico (over 600 thousand) and France (over 400 thousand). Of the Caribbean islands, Cuba is our favourite winter escape. Cuba ranks fifth overall, with 350 thousand annual visits by Canadians. Of the Asian nations, Hong Kong, in tenth place, tops the list with 115 thousand visits. Australia, in fourteenth place with about 90 thousand visits, ranks just ahead of Japan. Rounding Canada's population off to about 30 million, we can use these figures to deduce that, on average, a Canadian travels within Canada five times every year and takes a trip abroad twice in three years. (Green 3)

Exercise 26.5

Write an eight- to ten-sentence paragraph describing one of the following topics. Try to include details that involve several of the physical senses: sight, hearing, touch, smell, and taste. Be sure to begin with a clearly identifiable topic sentence.

A restaurant (store, workplace, school, etc.) you will never go back to
The place where you feel most at ease
An infant (your own, or a child you have cared for)
Something of personal value to you
A rave
An embarrassing incident
A locker room after a game
A classroom during an exam
A city (or town or village) under attack

5. Would a **comparison** or **contrast** help to clarify your point?

A **comparison** points out similarities between objects, people, or ideas; it shows how two different things are alike. A **contrast** points out dissimilarities between things; it shows how two objects, people, or ideas are different. A **comparison and contrast** identifies both similarities and differences. In the paragraph below, Sun-Kyung Yi contrasts the two sides of her "split personality."

When I was younger, toying with the idea of entertaining two separate identities was a real treat, like a secret game for which no one knew the rules but me. I was known as Angela to the outside world, and as Sun-Kyung at home. I ate bologna sandwiches in the school lunch room and rice and kimchee for dinner. I chatted about teen idols and giggled with my girlfriends during my classes, and ambitiously practiced piano and studied in the evenings, planning to become a doctor when I grew up. I waved hellos and goodbyes to my teachers, but bowed to my parents' friends visiting our home. I could also look straight in the eyes of my teachers and friends and talk frankly with them instead of staring at my feet with my mouth shut when Koreans talked to me. Going outside the home meant I was able to relax from the constraints of my cultural conditioning, until I walked back in the door and had to return to being an obedient and submissive daughter. (404–405)

Source: Yi, Sun-Kyung. "An Immigrant's Split Personality." *The Globe and Mail* 12 Apr. 1992. Reprinted by permission of Sun-Kyung Yi.

In the following paragraph, the writer develops his topic—how lack of planning can kill a city—by comparing the anatomy of a city to that of the human body.

A poorly planned city dies from the centre out. When an unplanned urban area is growing rapidly, businesses and residential developments spring up wherever it is advantageous for them to locate. In time, they become plaque deposits on the very arteries that they chose to build on, gradually narrowing and choking the city's passages. New routes cannot be constructed without major surgery, nor can the old ones be widened because of the poorly planned developments that line them. Without sufficient flow along its arteries, an organism begins to experience high pressure . . . whether from traffic or blood. As the pressure builds, those who live and work in the city core seek to relocate to more convenient, less stressful surroundings, and the centre begins to die. Keeping arteries open and healthy requires advance planning and constant vigilance. In the human organism, a healthy diet and physical exercise will keep the blood flowing; in the urban organism, mass transit and well-planned traffic corridors will do the trick. (Green 4)

Exercise 26.6

Write a paragraph comparing or contrasting two cities (or countries, co-workers, instructors, careers, or employers). Begin your paragraph with a clearly identifiable topic sentence.

6. Would a **quotation** or **paraphrase** be appropriate?

Occasionally, you will find that someone else—an expert in a particular field, a well-known author, or a respected public figure—has said what you want to say better or more convincingly than you could ever hope to say it. In these cases, quotations—as long as they are kept short and not used too frequently—are useful in developing your topic. In the following paragraph, Brian Green quotes Robert Benchley and a Portuguese proverb to sum up wittily and concisely what many of us have often thought but not been able to express so well.

> "Nothing is more responsible for the good old days than a bad memory." Robert Benchley got it right. Those who continually praise the past and decry the present are victims of selective memory. They are people who are dissatisfied with their present lives and want to believe that conditions in the past were better. To these pessimists, today's glass is half empty, while yesterday's was half full. Seldom does their preference for the way things were stand up under factual scrutiny. Even when one or two conditions from times past may be preferable to conditions in the present, innumerable other factors will have improved. The Portuguese have a proverb that captures the pessimists' selective nostalgia: "What was hard to bear is sweet to remember." (5)

A **paraphrase** is a summary in your own words of someone else's idea. Remember to indicate whose idea you are paraphrasing, the way the author of "The Myth of Canadian Diversity" (in Appendix A) does in the following paragraph.

> . . . [O]ur much-discussed ethnic differences are overstated. Although Canada is an immigrant nation and Canadians spring from a variety of backgrounds, a recent study from the C.D. Howe Institute says that the idea of a "Canadian mosaic"—as distinct from the American "melting pot"—is a fallacy. In *The Illusion of Difference*, University of Toronto sociologists Jeffrey Reitz and Raymond Breton show that immigrants to Canada assimilate as quickly into the mainstream society as immigrants to the United States do. In fact, Canadians are less likely than Americans to favour holding on to cultural differences based on ethnic background. If you don't believe Mr. Reitz and Mr. Breton, visit any big-city high school, where the speech and behaviour of immigrant students just a few years in Canada is indistinguishable from that of any fifth-generation classmate. (407)

Source: "The Myth of Canadian Diversity." *The Globe and Mail* 13 June 1994: A12. Reprinted by permission of *The Globe and Mail*.

College writing normally requires that you indicate the source of any material you quote. The easiest way to do this is to give the reference in parentheses at the end of your quotation. If the author's name is already mentioned in your introduction to the quotation, you need give only the page number(s) on which you found the quotation. If the author's name is not given in your introduction to the quotation, you need to include it along with the page number(s). Go back and see how we've cited the sources of all the quoted material in this chapter. When a paragraph has been excerpted from one of the essays in the Appendix, the page numbers given are those on which you will find the excerpt at the back of the book.

If your quotation is short and included in your sentence, you use the same citation format, but you insert the parenthetical reference—author (if not already mentioned) and page number—before the end punctuation. For example:

According to Brian Green, "Fly fishing is the art and science of using expensive technical equipment to capture an animal with the intelligence of a hubcap" (5).

One writer takes a fairly cynical view of the sport of fly fishing: "Fly fishing is the art and science of using expensive technical equipment to capture an animal with the intelligence of a hubcap" (Green 5).

At the end of your paper, include a Works Cited list, which is a list in alphabetical order by authors' surnames of all the books, articles, and other publications from which you have quoted in your paper. See page 235 for an example of the format to use. Follow the instructions given in whatever style guide your instructor recommends, or consult the authorities on MLA or APA style given in Chapter 21 (page 233).

When you plan the paragraphs of your essay, remember that you will often need to use more than one method of development to explain each point. The six methods outlined above can be used in any combination. Choose whichever kinds of development will be most helpful to your reader in understanding what you have to say.

Exercise 26.7

Identify the kinds of development used in the following paragraphs (more than one kind may be present in each). Then check your answers.

1. "The Case Against Quickspeak," paragraph 5
2. "Bumblers, Martinets, and Pros," paragraph 3
3. "Bumblers, Martinets, and Pros," paragraph 2

4. "The Canadian Climate," paragraph 1
5. "The Canadian Climate," paragraph 2
6. "The Case Against Quickspeak," paragraph 4
7. "The Myth of Canadian Diversity," paragraph 1
8. "The Myth of Canadian Diversity," paragraph 2
9. "An Immigrant's Split Personality," paragraph 4
10. "An Immigrant's Split Personality," paragraph 10

Exercise 26.8

Choose one of the following topic sentences (or make up one of your own) and write a paragraph of about 100 words using one of the methods of paragraph development we have discussed. Then write a second paragraph based on a different topic sentence and a different method of development.

1. _____ is an Internet site worth visiting.
2. Life is like a game of _____.
3. Cheating on college tests is simple and safe.
4. We are entertaining ourselves to death.
5. You are what you wear.
6. _____ is an enjoyable and potentially profitable hobby.
7. History (or any other subject) is (not) a useful subject for college.
8. There are many ways to learn a new language.
9. Canadians don't appreciate how lucky they are.
10. Few Canadians understand what it means to be a refugee.

Writing Introductions and Conclusions

Two paragraphs in your paper are not developed in the way we've just outlined: the introduction and the conclusion. All too often, these paragraphs are dull or clumsy and detract from a paper's effectiveness. But they needn't. Here's how to write good ones.

The introduction is worth special attention because that's where your reader either sits up and takes notice of your paper or sighs and pitches it into the wastebasket. Occasionally, for a short paper, you can begin simply with your thesis statement or statement of subject. More usually, though, an **attention-getter** comes before the thesis statement. An attention-getter is a sentence or two designed to get the reader interested in what you have to say.

There are several kinds of attention-getter to choose from.

1. A quotation or paraphrase (see "Bumblers, Martinets, and Pros")
2. A little-known or striking fact (see "An Immigrant's Split Personality")
3. A statement of opinion you intend to challenge (see "The Myth of Canadian Diversity")
4. An interesting incident or anecdote related to your subject (see "The Case Against Quickspeak")
5. A question (see "The Second-Language Struggle")

Add your thesis statement to the attention-getter and your introduction is complete.

The closing paragraph, too, usually has two parts: a **summary** of the main points of your paper (phrased differently, please—not a word-for-word repetition of your thesis statement or your topic sentences) and a **memorable statement**. Your memorable statement may take several forms.

1. Refer back to the content of your opening paragraph (see "Bumblers, Martinets, and Pros").
2. Include a relevant or thought-provoking quotation, statement, or question (see "The Myth of Canadian Diversity").
3. Emphasize the value or significance of your subject (see "The Case Against Quickspeak").
4. Make a suggestion for change (see "An Immigrant's Split Personality").
5. Offer a solution, make a prediction, or invite the reader to get involved (see "The Canadian Climate").

Exercise 26.9

Using as many of the different kinds as you can, write an attention-getter and a memorable statement for each of the following topics.

1. Movies today are better (worse) than ever before.
2. I love (hate) hockey (baseball, basketball, football, etc.).
3. Honesty is (not) always the best policy.
4. College professors should (not) be required to take courses in how to teach.
5. Travel is the best form of education.
6. College students should (not) be paid by the government to complete their programs of study.

7. The experience of war changes one in unexpected ways.
8. Canada's new immigration policy will (not) benefit the country over time.
9. The notion of employer-supported lifelong learning (i.e., continual retraining throughout my career) is (not) appealing to me.
10. Credit card catastrophe.

Keeping Your Reader with You

As you write your paragraphs, keep in mind that you want to make it as easy as possible for your reader to follow you through your paper. Clear **transitions** and an appropriate **tone** can make the difference between a paper that confuses or annoys readers and one that enlightens and pleases them.

TRANSITIONS

Transitions are those words or phrases that show the relationship between one point and the next, helping a paragraph or a paper to read smoothly. Like turn signals on a car, they tell the person following you where you're going. Here are some common transitions you can use to keep your reader on track.

1. *To show a time relation:* first, second, third, next, before, during, after, now, then, finally, last
2. *To add an idea or example:* in addition, also, another, furthermore, similarly, for example, for instance
3. *To show contrast:* although, but, however, instead, nevertheless, on the other hand, in contrast, on the contrary
4. *To show a cause—effect relation:* as a result, consequently, because, since, therefore, thus

Here is a paragraph that has adequate development but no transitions:

There are several good reasons why you should not smoke. Smoking is harmful to your lungs and heart. It is annoying and dangerous to those around you who do not smoke. Smoking is an unattractive and dirty habit. It is difficult to quit. Most worthwhile things in life are hard to achieve.

Not very easy to read, is it? Readers are jerked from point to point until, battered and bruised, they reach the end. This kind of writing is unfair to readers. It makes them do too much of the work. The ideas may all be there, but the readers have to figure out for themselves how they fit together. After a couple of paragraphs like this one, even a patient reader can become annoyed.

Now read the same paragraph with the transitions added:

> There are several good reasons why you should not smoke. *Among them, three stand out as the most persuasive. First,* smoking is harmful to your lungs and heart. *Second,* it is *both* annoying and dangerous to those around you who do not smoke. *In addition to these compelling facts,* smoking is an unattractive and dirty habit. *Furthermore, once you begin,* it is difficult to quit; *but then,* most worthwhile things in life are hard to achieve.

In the revised paragraph, readers are gently guided from one point to the next. By the time they reach the conclusion, they know not only what ideas the writer had in mind but also how they fit together. Transitions make the reader's job easier and more rewarding.

TONE

One final point. As you write the paragraphs of your paper, be conscious of your **tone.** Tone is simply good manners on paper. The words you use, the examples, quotations, and other supporting materials you choose to help explain your main points—they all contribute to your tone.

When you are trying to explain something to someone, particularly if it's something you feel strongly about, you may be tempted to be highly emotional in your discussion. If you allow yourself to get emotional, chances are you won't be convincing. What will be communicated is the strength of your feelings, not the depth of your understanding or the validity of your opinion. To be clear and credible, you need to restrain your enthusiasm or anger and present your points in a calm, reasonable way.

Here are a few suggestions to help you find and maintain the right tone.

- Never insult your reader, even unintentionally. Avoid phrases such as "Any idiot can see," "No sane person could believe," and "It is obvious that. . . . " What is obvious to you isn't necessarily obvious to someone who has a limited understanding of your subject or who disagrees with your opinion.

- Don't talk down to your readers as though they were children or hopelessly ignorant. Don't use sarcasm, profanity, or slang.

- Don't apologize for your interpretation of your subject. Have confidence in yourself. You've thought long and hard about your subject, you've found good supporting material to help explain it, and you believe in its significance. Present your subject in a positive manner. If you hang back, using phrases such as "I may be wrong, but . . . " or "I tend to feel that . . . ", your reader won't be inclined to give your points the consideration they deserve. Keep your reader in mind as you write, and your writing will be both clear and convincing.

Exercise 26.10

Rewrite the following paragraph, adding transitions where we've indicated they are needed, and correcting the lapse in tone. Then compare your revision with ours.

My friends and family find it hard to believe. [transition] I've become a fan of classical music. Recently, I had a serious operation. [transition] I was forced to stay in bed for almost three weeks while I recovered. I quickly grew tired of the boring, repetitive programs on daytime television. [transition] I began listening to the radio. Soon I discovered CBC 2, which is, as any intelligent person ought to know, a network of stations across Canada that plays classical music by great composers of the past and the present. I don't yet know very much about the music I'm listening to. [transition] I am learning. [transition] I can now recognize many of the more popular works by composers such as Beethoven, Mozart, and Bach. Now that I have discovered this magnificent music, [transition], I don't enjoy pop songs as much as I used to. [transition] I am confident that I've gained much more than I've lost.

Exercise 26.11

Do either A or B.

A. Using one of the thesis statements you prepared in Chapter 24, Exercise 24.6, write a paper of approximately 400 words.

B. Using the outline you prepared in Chapter 25, Exercise 25.3, write a paper of approximately 500 words.

27

Revising Your Paper

No one can write in a single draft an essay that is perfectly organized and developed, let alone one that is free of errors in sentence structure, grammar, spelling, and punctuation. The purpose of the first draft is to get down on paper something you can work with until you're satisfied it will meet your reader's needs and expectations. Planning and drafting should take about half the time you devote to writing a paper. The rest should be devoted to revision.

Revision is the process of refining your writing until it says what you want it to say in a way that enables your readers to understand your message and to receive it favourably. These two goals, clear understanding and favourable reception, constitute good communication. You can accomplish these goals only if you keep your readers in mind as you revise. Because it reflects the contents of the writer's mind, a first draft often seems all right to the writer. But in order to transfer an idea as clearly as possible from the mind of the writer to the mind of the reader, revision is necessary. The idea needs to be honed and refined until it is as clear to your reader as it is to you. By revising from your reader's point of view, you can avoid misunderstandings before they happen.

What Is Revision?

Revision means "re-seeing." It does *not* mean recopying. The aim of revision is to improve your writing's organization, accuracy, and style. Revising is a three-stage process. Each step requires that you read through your entire essay, painful though this may be. The goal of your first reading is to ensure that your reader's information needs are met. In your second reading, you focus on structure. Your third reading concentrates on correctness. Here are the steps to follow in revising a paper.

1. Improve the whole paper by revising its content and organization.
2. Refine paragraph and sentence structure, and correct any errors in grammar.
3. Edit and proofread to catch errors in word choice, spelling, and punctuation.

Inexperienced writers often skip the first two stages and concentrate on the third, thinking they will save time. This is a mistake. In fact, they waste time—both theirs and their readers'—because the result is writing that doesn't communicate clearly and won't make a positive impression.

The best way to begin revising is to do nothing to the early version of your paper for several days. Let as much time as possible pass between completing your first draft and rereading it. Ten minutes, or even half a day, is not enough. The danger in rereading too soon is that you're likely to "read" what you *think* you've written—what exists only in your head, not on the paper. But if, like many writers, you haven't allowed enough time for this cooling-off period, don't despair. There are two other things you can do to help you get some distance from your draft. If your first draft is handwritten, type it out. Reading your essay in a different form helps you to "re-see" its content. Alternatively, read your paper aloud and try to hear it from the point of view of your reader. Listen to how your explanation unfolds, and mark every place you find something unclear, irrelevant, inadequately developed, or out of order.

Step 1
Revise Content and Organization

As you read your paper aloud, keep in mind the three possible kinds of changes you can make at this stage:

1. You can **rearrange** information. This is the kind of revision that is most often needed but least often done. Consider the order in which you've arranged your paragraphs. From your reader's point of view, is this the most effective order in which to present your ideas? If you are not already using a word-processing program, now is the time to begin. With a good word processor, moving blocks of text around is as easy as dealing a deck of cards.

2. You can **add** information. Adding new main ideas or more develop-ment is often necessary to make your message interesting and con-vincing as well as clear. It's a good idea to ask a friend to read your draft and identify what needs to be expanded or clarified. (Be sure to return the favour. You can learn a great deal by critiquing other people's writ-ing.)
3. You can **delete** information. Now is the time to cut out anything that is repetitious, insignificant, or irrelevant to your subject and reader.

Use the checklist that follows to guide you as you review your paper's form and content.

CONTENT AND ORGANIZATION CHECKLIST

ACCURACY
Is everything you have said accurate?
- Is your information consistent with your own experience and observa-tions or with what you have discovered through research?
- Are all your facts and evidence up-to-date?

COMPLETENESS
Have you included enough main ideas and development to explain your subject and convince your reader? Remember that "enough" means from the reader's point of view, not the writer's.

SUBJECT
Is your subject
- significant? Does it avoid the trivial or the obvious?
- single? Does it avoid double or combined subjects?
- specific? Is it focussed and precise?
- supportable? Have you provided enough evidence to make your mean-ing clear?

MAIN POINTS
Are your main points
- significant? Have you deleted any unimportant ones?
- distinct? Are they all different from one another, or is there an overlap in content?
- relevant? Do all points relate directly to your subject?
- arranged in the most appropriate order? Again, "appropriate" means from the reader's perspective. Choose chronological, climactic, logical, or random order, depending on which is most likely to help the reader make sense of your information.

INTRODUCTION
Does your introduction
- catch the reader's attention and make him or her want to read on?
- contain a clearly identifiable thesis statement?
- identify the main points that your paper will explain?

CONCLUSION
Does your conclusion
- contain a summary or reinforcement of your main points, rephrased to avoid word-for-word repetition?
- contain a statement that effectively clinches your argument and leaves the reader with something to think about?

TONE
Is your tone consistent, reasonable, courteous, and confident throughout your essay?

When you have carefully considered these questions, it's time to move on to the second stage of the revision process.

Exercise 27.1

Here is a draft outline for a short essay on how to write effective e-mail in a business environment. Rearrange the main points in chronological order, write an appropriate thesis statement, and delete any unnecessary supporting points to produce a good working outline for the essay. Then compare your answer with our suggestion. Answers for exercises in this chapter begin on page 465.

E-Mail Excellence

Attention-getter: As the recipient of approximately 1,000 business-related e-mail messages every month, I am something of an expert on what is effective and what is not in e-mail correspondence.

Thesis statement: _____

_____

_____

_____

Main points:

I. Subject line

    A. always include one

    B. make sure it states clearly what the message is about

    C. never use vague subject lines such as "hello," or "message," or "are you there?"

    D. never leave the subject line blank

II. Attachments

    A. use sparingly

    B. may carry viruses

    C. take time to transfer and to open

    D. attach text-only files, unless a graphic is absolutely necessary

    E. use only if necessary

III. Message

    A. Content

        1. be concise and to the point

        2. tell the reader what action is needed, by whom, and when

        3. don't be a novelist or a "Chatty Cathy"

        4. use plain English, not "cyberspeak"

        5. use an appropriate level of language in your message as well as in your salutation and signature

    B. Appearance

        1. use bullets to identify points you want to emphasize

        2. leave white space between points

        3. avoid sending your message in upper case letters (shouting)

        4. avoid smilies and other "cute" computer shorthand symbols

Summary: If you follow my recommendations on these three points whenever you write an e-mail, you will make the recipient of your
message very happy.

Memorable statement: Especially if you're writing to me.

Step 2
Revise Paragraphs and Sentences

Here, too, you should allow time—at least a couple of days—between your
first revision and your second. Enough time must elapse to allow you to
approach your paper as if you were seeing it for the first time. Once again,
read your draft aloud, and use this list of questions to help you improve it.

PARAGRAPH AND SENTENCE CHECKLIST
PARAGRAPHS
Does each paragraph
- begin with a clear, identifiable topic sentence?
- develop one—and only one—main idea?
- present one or more kinds of development appropriate to the main idea?
- contain clear and effective transitions to signal the relationship between
  sentences? Between paragraphs?

SENTENCES

Sentence Structure
1. Is each sentence clear and complete?
   - Are there any fragments or run-ons?
   - Are there any misplaced or dangling modifiers?
   - Are all lists (whether words, phrases, or clauses) expressed in parallel
     form?
2. Are your sentences varied in length? Could some be combined to
   improve the clarity and impact of your message?

Grammar
1. Have you used verbs correctly?
   - Are all verbs in the correct form?
   - Do all verbs agree with their subjects?

- Are all verbs in the correct tense?
- Are there any confusing shifts in verb tense within a paragraph?
2. Have you used pronouns correctly?
- Are all pronouns in the correct form?
- Do all pronouns agree with their antecedents?
- Have any vague pronoun references been eliminated?

When you're sure you've answered these questions satisfactorily, go to the third and last stage of the revision process.

Exercise 27.2

Here is the first draft of the essay on e-mail. Revise it to correct errors in paragraph structure, sentence structure, and grammar. Then compare your answer with our suggestion on page 466.

1   As the recipient of approximately 1,000 business-related e-mail messages every month, I am something of an expert on what is effective and what is not in e-mail correspondence. The three areas that need attention in most e-mail messages are the subject line, the content, and appearance of the message and the use of attachments.

2   Some people leave the subject line blank, this is a mistake. I want to know what the message is about before I open it so I can decide if it needs my immediate attention. Or can wait until later. A message with no subject line or with a line that didn't tell me nothing about the content of the e-mail get sent to the bottom of my "to-do" list. There are lots of readers like me busy people who receive tons of e-mail, much of it unsolicited advertising that clutter up their in-boxes. For this reason the subject line should always clearly state the subject of the message and should never be vague or cute like "hello" or "message" or "are you there?"

3   As for the message itself, it's function should be to tell the reader what action one wants, you need to be clear about this and be as brief as possible. What is it that you want the recipient to do. Who else needs to be involved. By when does the action need to take place. Communicate your message in plain English, not in "cyberspeak" Not everyone knows Net lingo, and even some who are famliar with it find it irritating not charming. Use an appropriate level of language (general level Standard English will always be appropriate) to convey you're message. Use the same level of language in you're salutation and closing or "signature." One should definitely not sign off a message to you're client or you're boss with "love and kisses." Format you're message so that the recipient will be able to read it quickly and understanding it easily. Use bullets to identify points you want to emphasize, separate the bullets with white space so they can be read at a glance and reviewed individually if necessary. There are some important points of e-mail etiquette that you should observe. Don't type you're message in upper case letters, that's considered "shouting." Do avoid "smilies" and other "cute" computer shorthand symbols. Some of you're readers won't understand them others will have seen them so often they will be turned off.

4   Attachments should be included only if they are really necessary, for one thing, they may carry virruses and some people won't open them.

Another disadvantage is that they take time to send download and open. Unless I am sure that an attachment is both urgent and vitally important—the agenda of tomorrow's meeting, for example—I don't bother to open it, for all I know, it might contain not only a virus but also footage of the sender's toddler doing her latest photogenic trick. As a general rule attach only what you must and attach text-only files. Try to include everything you need to say in the message itself and use attachments only as a last resort. Think of them as equivalent to footnotes supplementary to the message not an essential part of it.

5   If you follow my recommendations on these three points whenever you write an e-mail, you will make the recipient of your message very happy, especially if you're writing to me.

Step 3
Edit and Proofread

By now you're probably so tired of refining your paper that you may be tempted to skip **editing**—correcting errors in word choice, spelling, and punctuation—and **proofreading**—correcting errors in typing or writing that appear in the final draft. But these final tasks are essential if you want your paper to make a positive impression.

Misspellings, faulty punctuation, and messiness don't always create misunderstandings, but they do cause the reader to form a lower opinion of you and your work. Careful editing and proofreading are necessary if you want your writing to be favourably received.

Most word-processing programs include a grammar checker and a spellchecker. It is worthwhile running your writing through these programs at

the editing stage. The newer programs have some useful features. For example, they will question (but not correct) your use of apostrophes; they will sometimes catch errors in subject–verb agreement; and they will catch obvious misspellings and typos.

But don't make the mistake of assuming these programs will do all your editing for you. Many errors slip past a computer's database, no matter how comprehensive the salesperson told you it is. Only you or a knowledgeable and patient friend can find and correct all errors.

If spelling is a particular problem for you, you should first run your paper through a spell-checker. After that, you're on your own. Read your paper backward word by word, from the end to the beginning. Reading backward forces you to look at each word by itself and helps you to spot those that look suspicious. Whenever you're in doubt about the spelling of a word, look it up! If you find this task too tedious to bear, ask a good speller to read through your paper for you and identify any errors. (Then take this person out for dinner. If you get an A, add a show.)

Here are the questions to ask yourself when you are editing.

EDITING CHECKLIST

WORDS

Usage

Have you used words to "mean" rather than to "impress"?

- Have you eliminated any clichés, slang, and pretentious language?
- Have you cut out any unnecessary words?
- Have you corrected any "abusages"?

Spelling

Are all words spelled correctly?

- Have you double-checked any sound-alikes or look-alikes?
- Have you used capital letters where they are needed?
- Have you used apostrophes correctly for possessives and omitted them from plurals?

PUNCTUATION

Within Sentences

- Have you eliminated any unnecessary commas and included commas where needed? (Refer to the five comma rules as you consider this question.)
- Have you used colons and semicolons where appropriate?
- Are all quotations appropriately marked?

Beginnings and Endings

- Does each sentence begin with a capital letter?
- Do all questions—and only questions—end with a question mark?
- Are all quotation marks correctly placed?

Exercise 27.3

Now go through the revised first draft of the e-mail essay that you produced in Exercise 27.2. This is your last chance to make this essay error-free. Use the Editing Checklist above and the Tips for Effective Proofreading below to guide you as you make your final pass through this document. Then compare your answer with our suggestion on page 466.

TIPS FOR EFFECTIVE PROOFREADING

By the time you have finished editing, you will have gone over your paper so many times you may have practically memorized it. When you are very familiar with a piece of writing, it's hard to spot the small mistakes that may have crept in as you produced your final copy. Here are some tips to help you find those tiny, elusive errors.

1. Read through your essay line by line, using a ruler to guide you.
2. If you've been keeping a list of your most frequent errors in this course, scan your essay for the mistakes you are most likely to make.
3. Use the "Quick Revision Guide" on the inside front cover of this book to make a final check of all aspects of your paper.

Your "last" draft may need further revision after your proofreading review. If so, take the time to re-write the paper so that the version you hand in is clean and easy to read. If a word processor is available to you, use it. Computers make editing and proofreading almost painless, since errors are so easy to correct.

At long last, you're ready to submit your paper. If you've followed the three steps to revision conscientiously, you can hand it in with confidence that it says what you want it to say, both about your subject and about you. One last word of advice.

DON'T FORGET TO KEEP A COPY FOR YOUR FILES!

GO TO WEB

EXERCISE 27.1

Exercise 27.4

Turn to the draft paper you wrote for Exercise 26.11 in Chapter 26. Revise the paper by applying to it the three steps of the revision process.

For ESL Learners: A Review of the Basics

Introduction

As a college student, you are preparing for a meaningful and rewarding career. If you are preparing for this career in a language that is not native to you, English, we acknowledge your accomplishment. Your hard work and your ability to use two (or more) languages suggest that you are able to achieve a high level of success.

However, you may feel that your communication skills in English are holding you back. Even if your command of spoken English is good, you may lack fluency with standard written English (SWE), and poor writing skills can hinder your opportunities for academic and career success.

The ability to use SWE well helps you in three ways. First, it gives you the power to express your ideas clearly. Second, it helps you win the respect of your readers. And third, it increases the number of people with whom you can communicate. That's why employers look for people who can use SWE effectively.

Unit 6 of *The Bare Essentials Plus* is designed specifically to help the second-language writer master the conventions of SWE. It focusses on the most common problems that ESL students experience when they write English. These include verb tense and formation, plural forms/quantity expressions, articles, and prepositions. Even highly sophisticated ESL writers occasionally make mistakes in these constructions and identify their second-language background to native speakers. Working on these problem areas will develop and improve your ability to write in English.

These chapters provide concise explanation, likely less explanation than you have come to expect in advanced grammar texts. But there are many exercises and much opportunity for you to practise specific writing skills. Grammatical explanation can certainly help you to understand what constitutes correct English, but ultimately you must gain confidence in your ability to write correctly without constant reference to grammar rules. This confidence is what will make you a fluent writer of English.

A Review of the Basics

The following quick quiz will let you see at a glance which chapters of Unit 6 you need to focus on. The paragraphs below contain 25 errors: verb tense, negative verb formation, participial adjectives, modal auxiliaries, singular and plural forms, articles, and prepositions. When you've made your corrections, turn to page 467 and compare your version with ours. For each error you miss, the answer key directs you to the chapter you need to work on.

1   Humans learn very early how to use their first language. Most of us understand spoken words and respond to them since the time we are two or three years old. It takes another few years for us to learn how to read and write, but we acquire our first language fairly easily. By most of us, however, learning a second language is slow and exasperating process. Most people who study the English as a second language are especially frustrating by three of its peculiarities: its unsystematic pronunciation, its inconsistent spelling, and its enormous vocabulary.

2   English is having sounds that are difficult for speakers of other languages. The *th* sound is one of them. Why is it pronounced differently in words such as *this* and *think*? The consonant sounds *l*, *r*, and *w* also present problems. Many new English speakers don't hear the differences between *light*, *right*, and *white*, and so they not pronounce them. There are also more vowel sound in English than in most other language. The *a* sound in the words *bat* and *mat* is peculiar to English, so second-language learners often

pronounce *bet, bat,* and *but* identically. To native speakers of English, these words are having quite distinct sounds that many second-language learners do not hear and so cannot pronounce. Many ESL speaker find it difficult to pronounce the unusual vowel sounds that occur to the words *bird, word,* and *nurse.* The fact that the same sound occurs in words with three different vowels—*i, o,* and *u*—is example of second major difficulty with English: its inconsistent spelling system.

3 Most native speakers would be agreeing that English spelling is challenging. Why do *tough* and *stuff* rhyme when their spelling is so different? Shouldn't *tough* rhyme with *cough*? But *cough* rhymes with *off.* Why does *clamour* rhyme with *hammer* while *worm* and *storm*—which should rhyme— don't? There isn't no single answer, but part of the reason is that English is language that has absorbed many words and sounds from other languages, along with their spellings. Almost 75 % of English words are having regular spellings, but, unfortunately, the most frequently used words in English are the irregular one. All of us, second-language learners and native speakers alike, simply have to learn to cope.

4 English also has a huge vocabulary, in part because it borrows freely for other languages. The roots of English are Germanic, but the Celts, Romans, French, and many other have contributed heavily to the language. The gigantic *Oxford English Dictionary* lists about 500,000 words and does not include about another half million technical and scientific word.

5 English is difficult language for all of these reason, but it's a rich and satisfied one that is well worth the effort to learn.

28

Choosing the Correct Verb Tense

In English, the tense of a verb signals the time of an action: present, past, or future.

> I *work* hard every day.
> I *worked* at the library yesterday.
> I *will work* at the library next summer.

Of course, as you know, there is more to the English tense system than this simple example suggests. English verbs change in complicated and subtle ways to describe complex time relations.

> I *am working* at the library now, but I *have worked* at a number of different jobs in the past. I *will be working* for most of my life, so it *is* important that I *develop* more skills than I *have done* so far.

Trying to sort out the tenses of the verbs in these sentences is a real headache for second-language learners. Another headache is the fact that some verb tenses have the same meaning, or close to the same meaning. Most native speakers will not hear a difference in meaning between *I am working at the library now* and *I work at the library now*. However, native speakers will certainly pick up the mistake if you say or write *I am been working at the library now* or *I will work at a number of different jobs in the past*. To write clearly, you require a thorough understanding of—and lots of practice with—the English verb tense system. This chapter will provide you with both.

To see at a glance how the English tense system expresses past, present, and future time, study the Time Line on the inside of the back cover of this book. The symbol key below explains how to interpret the Time Line and also the graphic illustrations of tenses covered in this chapter.

- ▲ indicates *now,* the present moment.
- ● represents *a completed action or state of being.*
- ○ indicates *an event that occurred or will occur sometime after the action represented by the black dot took place.*
- 〜〜 represents *a continuing action or condition,* both of which are expressed by the progressive forms of a verb.
- ------- indicates that *the action or condition may continue* into the future.

Now that you have an overview of the six basic tenses and the "times" they represent, let's look at how the various tenses are formed. Then we will focus on how to use each one.

Verb Tense Formation

The chart below shows how the different tenses are formed. It provides two examples, *work* (a regular verb) and *grow* (an irregular verb), to illustrate the changes. The principal parts of the verbs (see pages 143 to 148) are presented first because all tenses are formed from them.

Principal parts:

Base/Infinitive	Present Participle	Past	Past Participle
(to) work	*working*	*worked*	*(has) worked*
(to) grow	*growing*	*grew*	*(has) grown*

Tense	Example *(work)*	Example *(grow)*
Simple present (*base; base + s* for third-person singular)	work/works	grow/grows
Present progressive (*am/is/are + present participle*)	am/is/are working	am/is/are growing
Present perfect (*has/have + past participle*)	has/have worked	has/have grown
Present perfect progressive (*has/have + been + present participle*)	has/have been working	has/have been growing

Tense	Example *(work)*	Example *(grow)*
Simple past (*past form*)	worked	grew
Past progressive (*was/were + present participle*)	was/were working	was/were growing
Past perfect (*had + past participle*)	had worked	had grown
Past perfect progressive (*had + been + present participle*)	had been working	had been growing
Simple future (*will + base*) OR (*am/is/are going to + base*)	will work am/is/are going to work	will grow am/is/are going to grow
Future progressive (*will be + present participle*)	will be working	will be growing
Future perfect (*will + have + past participle*)	will have worked	will have grown
Future perfect progressive (*will + have been + present participle*)	will have been working	will have been growing

The chart above shows how to form all the English tenses. Some tenses, however, such as the future perfect progressive, are rarely used because the same meaning can usually be expressed in a less complicated manner. So while this chapter will provide an overview of all tenses, we will concentrate on the most commonly used ones in order to make sure that you understand how to form them correctly and use them appropriately.

Exercise 28.1

Practice by filling in the "missing pieces" (either a principal part or an auxiliary) to form the required verb tense. Use the verb *go* and then use the verb *see*. The first one is done for you. Answers to exercises for this chapter begin on page 469.

	GO	SEE
1. present perfect:	He <u>has</u> been <u>going</u>.	He <u>has</u> been <u>seeing</u>.
2. past progressive:	I was _____.	I was _____.
3. simple present:	He _____. They _____.	He _____. They _____.
4. present progressive:	You _____ _____.	You _____ _____.
5. simple past:	We _____.	We _____.
6. future progressive:	She _____ be _____.	She _____ be _____.
7. present perfect progressive:	He _____ been _____ .	He _____ been _____.
8. past perfect:	We had _____.	We had _____.
9. simple future:	You _____ _____.	You _____ _____.
10. past perfect progressive:	Someone had ____ ____.	Someone had ____ ____.

Exercise 28.2

This exercise requires you to practise with the "pieces" (auxiliaries and principal parts) that are used to form various verb tenses. Use only one word for each blank. Identify the verb tense you used after you have filled in each blank.

1. He will _____ going with us. (Tense: _____)

2. The new year _____ on January 1. (Tense: _____)

3. Jerome _____ always _____ attractive to women. (Tense:

   _____)

4. Linda and Joy _____ leaving for China a week from now. (Tense:

   _____)

5. Wolf _____ played in the band for six years, but he quit a year

   ago. (Tense: _____)

6. You _____ _____ working very hard, so why not take a break?

   (Tense: _____)

7. The movie _____ _____ playing for 30 minutes by the time we

   got there. (Tense: _____)

8. I _____ with my manager yesterday. (Tense: _____)

9. I _____ taking off my running shoes right now because they

_____ killing my feet. (Tense: _____)

10. He _____ watching TV when I _____ him last night. (Tense:

_____ ; _____)

The Present Tenses

A. THE SIMPLE PRESENT TENSE

The simple present is used to express present time (especially with non-action linking verbs), general truths, and regular or habitual activity.

> Gianni *is* a handsome man.
> I *hope* that you *are* happy now.
> People *need* food and water to survive.
> Sarah *swims* every day.

B. THE PRESENT PROGRESSIVE TENSE

The present progressive is used to express an activity that is *in progress now* or one that is ongoing. Sometimes the activity is in progress over a period of time such as *this week*, *month*, or even *year*.

> I *am talking* on my cell phone.
> They *are driving* home right now.
> Lorne *is taking* golf lessons this year.

It is important to know that some English verbs are not used in any of the progressive tenses. "Nonprogressive" verbs describe conditions or states of being, not actions in progress. Often, nonprogressive verbs express mental (cognitive) or emotional states, possession, or sense perception. Study the following list. (We will come back to the asterisked words later.)

States of being: appear*, be*, cost, exist, look, seem, weigh*

Mental (cognitive) or emotional states: appreciate, believe, care, dislike, doubt, envy, fear, feel, forget, hate, imagine, know, like, love, mean, mind, need, prefer, realize, recognize, remember, suppose, think*, understand, want

Possession: belong, have*, own, possess

Sense perception: appear*, be, feel*, hear, see*, smell*, taste*

To repeat, these "states of being" verbs are not used in the progressive tenses. You wouldn't say "I am liking her very much." You would use the simple present: "I like her very much." Revise the following sentences by replacing the incorrect verbs with correct ones.

I *am hearing* that you *are owning* a laptop computer. I *am needing* to bor-

row one for today's class. I *am knowing* that you *are hating* to lend your

things, but I *am promising* to return it this evening.

Note that ten of the verbs on the list—the ones marked with an asterisk (*)—can be used to describe actions as well as states of being or conditions.

State of being	**Action**
Solaya *weighs* 65 kg.	Solaya *is weighing* herself to see how much she has gained.
Tom *appears* old and tired.	Tom *is appearing* in a Broadway play.
The curry *tastes* delicious.	The chef *tastes* the curry while it is cooking.

Often, you have to decide whether the verb is expressing a state of being or an action before you can decide whether or not to use a progressive tense.

Incorrect: He *is having* a car.
            She *is smelling* of cigarette smoke.
            I *am knowing* you for a long time.

Correct: He *has a* car.
            She *smells* of cigarette smoke.
            I *have known* you for a long time.

Exercise 28.3

Fill in each blank with the appropriate tense—simple present or present progressive—of the verb given in parentheses. Then check your answers.

1. It (snow) _____ again today. In my country, it often (rain)

   _____ , but it never (snow) _____ .

2. Marc usually (work) _____ as a lifeguard, but this summer he

   (work) _____ in his family's restaurant.

3. Ellistine (want) _____ to fix her car, but she (need)

   _____ someone to help her.

4. A ticket home (cost) _____ so much that I (doubt)

   _____ that I can afford the trip.

5. We still (believe) _____ we have a good team, and now we

   (try) _____ to develop a winning strategy.

6. My mother usually (phone) _____ me every day at 6:00, but it

   is now 6:30 and I am (wait, still) _____ for her call. I wonder

   what she (do) _____ .

7. The baby (cry) _____ again. He always (cry) _____

   when his mother (leave) _____ .

8. What (do, you) _____ right now? I (learn) _____

   English verb tenses.

9. The little girl (look) _____ tired, but right now she (look)

   _____ at her favourite storybook.

10. Jamala (study) _____ in the library almost every evening.

    Tonight she (has) _____ difficulty concentrating because the

    student who (sit) _____ at the next table (talk) _____

    on his cell phone.

GO TO WEB

EXERCISES 28.1, 28.2

C. THE PRESENT PERFECT TENSE

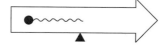

The present perfect tense is used to express three different meanings.

1. Events that occurred (or didn't occur) at some unspecified time in the past, the consequences of which persist in the present.

> The rain *has stopped.*
> I *have*n't *voted* yet.

2. Events that were repeated several or many unspecified times in the past and are likely to occur again in the present and future.

> It *has rained* practically every day this month.
> I *have* always *voted* for the Green Party.

3. Events that began at some unspecified time in the past and continue into the present.

> Yu *has lived* in Canada for a long time.
> Alessandro *has been* a good boy.

Sentences requiring the present perfect tense frequently contain words or phrases that suggest action beginning in the past and persisting into the present; e.g., *for, since, for a long time, already, so far, always, often, during, recently, this year.*

Note that *for* is used with a period of time and *since* is used with a specific time.

> I have lived in Canada *for* a long time.
> I have lived in Canada *since* 1979.

Exercise 28.4

Answer the questions using the present perfect tense and completing the time phrases correctly.

1. Do you like to travel?

   Yes, I do. I (go) _____ to many different places during my life. I

   (visit) _____ both Central America and South America (since/for)

   1999.

2. Are you taking an ESL course this semester?

No, I (take, already) _____ it. I (study) _____ English

(since/for) 11 years.

3. Do you love me?

Yes, I (love, always) _____ you. I (know) _____ you

(since/for) I was a little girl, and I (love, never) _____ anyone

but you.

4. Do you get much e-mail?

Yes, my old computer crashed, and I (buy, recently) _____ a

new computer with a high speed connection. Lots of people write to

me. For example, I (get, already) _____ 47 e-mail messages

(until/so far) this morning.

5. When did you move here?

I moved here in _____ . I (be) _____ here (since/for)

_____ years.

D. THE PRESENT PERFECT PROGRESSIVE TENSE

The present perfect progressive tense puts more emphasis on the duration of an action than the present perfect tense does, but other than that subtle difference, the two tenses are practically equivalent in meaning. The present perfect progressive is used to express actions that began at some unspecified time in the past and continue in the present moment or to emphasize the duration of a single past-to-present action. Time phrases such as *for, since, all afternoon, all day, all year* are often used with the present perfect progressive tense to emphasize the period of time over which the action has been taking place.

The class *has been working* on verb tenses. (And they are still working on them.)

I *have been sitting* here all day. (And I am still sitting here.)

Your husband *has been waiting* for you for over an hour. (And he is still waiting.)

The present perfect progressive and present perfect tenses often express the same meaning, especially when the sentence contains *since* or *for*.

Hans *has been living* here since 1997.   Hans *has lived* here since 1997.

I *have been working* here for 20 years.   I *have worked* here for 20 years.

Exercise 28.5

Fill in the blanks with the correct form of the present perfect progressive.

1. (snow) It _____ all day.

2. (study) They _____ physics for three days straight.

3. (think) Desi _____ about taking a trip to Belize.

4. (talk) I _____ to my professors about dropping a course.

5. (ring) The phone _____ all morning.

Exercise 28.6

Fill in the blanks in the sentences below with either the present perfect or the present perfect progressive form of the verb provided. In some sentences, either tense may be used. Compare your answers with ours on page 470.

1. It (rain) _____ all night, and the basement is flooded.

2. There (be) _____ four big rainstorms already this week.

3. I (sent) _____ several e-mails but got no reply. I (phone/also) _____ them every day.

4. The children (be) _____ to the beach. They are covered with sand because they (build) _____ sandcastles.

5. How long (you/live) _____ in Canada?

GO TO WEB

EXERCISES 28.3, 28.4

The Past Tenses

A. THE SIMPLE PAST TENSE

The simple past tense indicates an action or a state that began and ended in the past. It can be used to refer to one event completed in the past or to repeated events completed in the past.

I *ate* too much last night.
The weather *was* horrible last winter.
Binh *lived* in Hong Kong before he *moved* to Montreal.

B. THE PAST PROGRESSIVE TENSE

The past progressive tense is used to express an action or condition that began and ended sometime in the past. It emphasizes the duration—or ongoing quality—of an event that is now completed.

The boys *were watching* television all morning.
I *was flying* home from Halifax.
What *were* you *doing* in Halifax?

The past progressive is also used to indicate an action that was taking place when another occurred. It is often used with time words such as *for* or *since*, or with a clause that uses *when* or *while* to denote simultaneous occurrences.

Julieta *was driving* to school when the accident happened.
While I *was cooking* dinner, the power went off.

Sometimes there is little difference in meaning between the past and the past progressive: "It snowed last night" and "It was snowing last night" mean the same thing, and both are correct.

Exercise 28.7

Fill in each blank with the appropriate tense—simple past or past progressive—of the verb given in parentheses. Then check your answers on page 470.

1. Three of us (smoke) _____ in the upstairs washroom when the

boss (walk) _____ in.

2. The cat (hide) _____ behind the fish tank when I (see) _____ his tail twitch and (catch) _____ him.

3. While their sister (prepare) _____ their lunch, the children (run) _____ into the house and (turn) _____ on the television.

4. When the movie *Crouching Tiger, Hidden Dragon* (play) _____ in the theatre, I (see) _____ it four times. Later I (buy) _____ the DVD.

5. Marco (try) _____ to park his new SUV in the narrow driveway when he (hit) _____ the neighbour's hedge. The branches (make) _____ deep scratches in the paint.

6. As Julio (tell) _____ his friends about his new job, one of them (ask) _____ how he (find) _____ the position.

7. Wai-Lan (walk) _____ home when the rain (begin) _____ . To stay dry, she (wait) _____ under a tree until a taxi (drive) _____ by and rescued her.

8. I (hear, not) _____ you arrive last night because I (sleep) _____ .

9. Miranda (dislike) _____ the play because she (think) _____ it (be) _____ long and boring.

10. I (study) _____ in the college library when I (become) _____ ferociously hungry and (know) _____ that I (have) _____ to eat.

C. THE PAST PERFECT TENSE

Sometimes two different actions or conditions that occurred in the past are included in the same sentence. The past perfect tense is used to depict an action that was completed before another event (or time) in the past. It is the "further-back-in-the-past" tense. In other words, the action that happened first chronologically is expressed by the past perfect; the action that occurred after it is expressed in the simple past.

I *had left* the building before the bomb *exploded*.

Obviously the "leaving" happened first (and is in the past perfect tense)—before the explosion (in the simple past tense)—or I wouldn't be around to tell the story.

The past perfect tense is frequently used with time expressions such as *after*, *before*, and *when*.

Kareem realized his mistake after he *had spoken*.
The class *had left* before the instructor found the room.

To be fair, however, we should acknowledge that if the time sequence is clear from other elements in the sentence, the past perfect is often not necessary. Most native speakers would not hear an error in the following sentences:

I *left* the building before the bomb *exploded*.
The class *left* before the instructor *found* the room.
Kareem *realized* his mistake after he *spoke*.

However, in sentences with *just, already, scarcely, hardly,* and *no sooner than,* the past perfect is required.

My boyfriend *had already gone* home when I *arrived*.
We *had hardly unpacked* our suitcases when the fun *began*.

In these sentences, using the simple past (*already went* and *hardly unpacked*) would be incorrect.

Exercise 28.8

Fill in the blanks with the appropriate tense—simple past or past perfect—of the verbs in parentheses.

1. Sven was late for class. The professor (give, just) _____ a quiz

   when he (get) _____ there.

2. Yesterday my friend Ronit (see) _____ an old friend whom she

   (see, not) _____ in years.

3. I almost missed my flight. Everyone (board, already) _____ the

   plane by the time I (rush) _____ in.

4. After our guests (leave) _____ , we (clean) _____ up the kitchen.

5. Devondra (swim, hardly) _____ a single lap of the pool when the rain (start) _____ .

D. THE PAST PERFECT PROGRESSIVE TENSE

The past perfect progressive tense emphasizes the duration of a past event that took place before another event. Often it is used to refer to a past event that was in progress before being interrupted by another event.

He *had been waiting* in the doctor's office for an hour before she arrived.
They *had been talking* about Carol when she walked in.

The exercise below will help you with the time sequencing of English verbs by reminding you of the difference between the present perfect progressive (*has/have + been + present participle*) and the past perfect progressive (*had + been + present participle*).

Exercise 28.9

Fill in the blanks in the sentences below with the present perfect progressive tense or the past perfect progressive tense as appropriate.

1. It is 6:00 p.m. I (work) _____ for ten hours straight, so it is time to go home.

2. It was 6:00 p.m. I (work) _____ for ten hours straight, so it was time to go home.

3. I woke up feeling strange this morning because I (dream) _____ about dinosaurs all night.

4. The child is sad. She (cry) _____ all morning.

5. Barbara (sell) _____ real estate for 25 years when she realized that she wanted a new career.

Exercise 28.10

Fill in each blank with the most appropriate tense—simple past, past perfect, or past perfect progressive—of the verb in parentheses. In some sentences, more than one answer is possible. Compare your answers with ours on page 471.

1. By the time I (realize) _____ that I needed an elective to graduate, I (drop, already) _____ my history course.

2. Aunt Mina (promise) _____ to leave her fortune to Jacob, but unfortunately she (die) _____ before making a will.

3. Karin's sister (arrive) _____ about ten minutes after Karin (leave) _____ .

4. Felipe (plan) _____ a formal dinner party for his father's fiftieth birthday until his mother (suggest) _____ a backyard barbecue instead.

5. By the time Kim (work) _____ the night shift for three months, she (think) _____ that she would never have a social life again.

6. We (look) _____ forward to our vacation for months when my wife (get) _____ a promotion, and we (have) _____ to cancel our plans.

7. If I (know) _____ how difficult this course (be) _____, I would have signed up for something easier.

8. When he (retire) _____, Professor Green (teach) _____ creative writing for 30 years.

9. We (decide) _____ to sell our condominium, but we (change) _____ our minds when the real estate agent (tell) _____ us the low price we would get.

10. I (realize, never) _____ how difficult it would be to work for Ms. Wright. She (be) _____ a very demanding boss.

GO TO WEB

EXERCISES 28.5, 28.6

Exercise 28.11

Review the present and past tenses by filling in the blanks using any of the tenses we have studied so far.

1. Ky and Shona (meet) _____ last September and (go) _____

   out together ever since.

2. I (see, never) _____ any of Monet's paintings until I (go)

   _____ to the Museum of Modern Art in New York last year.

3. We (plan) _____ to renovate our house for a long time, but we

   (decide) _____ on a contractor only last week.

4. Hockey (be, always) _____ Canadians' favourite sport; we (play)

   _____ the game for more than 150 years.

5. Although Ali (live) _____ in Toronto since he was ten, he (visit,

   never) _____ the CN Tower.

6. Maria (hope) _____ to go to Newfoundland for a long time. Her

   sister (live) _____ there for a year, and she (convince) _____

   Maria that "the Rock" (be) _____ a place she must visit.

7. For six weeks, I (wait) _____ for my transcript to come in the mail.

   I wonder if the Registrar's Office (go) _____ on strike.

8. (you, know) _____ who (eat) _____ all the pizza last night?

9. Yesterday my father (make) _____ me go to the barber who (cut)

   _____ his hair for the past 20 years.

10. While I (wait) _____ for my turn, I (notice) _____ that I (be)

    _____ the only person in the shop under 50.

The Future Tenses

A. THE SIMPLE FUTURE TENSE

There are two ways to express the simple future tense:

1. *will + base form*:   I *will go* home. They *will see* you tomorrow.

2. *(be) + going to + base form*: I *am going to go* home. They *are going to see* you tomorrow.

Both constructions have the same meaning. In informal English, especially speech, *will* is usually contracted to *'ll* in the future tense:

I *'ll go* home. They *'ll see* you tomorrow.
You *'ll go* home. We *'ll see* them tomorrow.

Won't is the contraction for *will not*: You *won't see* me tomorrow.

The *(be) + going to + base form* is usually used when the sentence expresses a prior plan or decision. The *will + base form* is more likely to be used to express willingness or ability. The following examples illustrate the difference.

Prior plan: *(be) + going to + base*

Why did you buy these flippers?
I *am going to learn* how to snorkel. (Not "I *will learn* how to snorkel.")

Willingness: *will + base*

Help me! I'm broke, and my rent is due today.
Ask Roderigo. Maybe he *'ll lend* you some money. (Not "Ask Roderigo. Maybe he *is going to lend* you some money.")

Traditional grammar texts often describe different (and very subtle) changes in meanings expressed by the future tense—e.g., promise, prediction, permission, volition, supposition, concession—and prescribe using a specific form with each purpose. However, these meanings are often difficult to separate from futurity, and native speakers rarely hear lapses in these distinctions as grammar errors. Traditional grammar texts also teach that *shall* is used for first-person subjects (*I shall go home*) and *will* is used with second- and third-person subjects (*You/They will go home*). In North American English, this distinction is obsolete. In short, don't spend a lot of time worrying about the difference between *will/is going to* or *shall/will*.

Exercise 28.12

Fill in the blanks with the appropriate form of the future: *will + base form* or *(be) + going to + base form* of the verbs in parentheses. Check your answers on page 472.

1. Elie (work) _____ on his car tomorrow, but I (help, not)

    _____ him.

2. Until Yasmin's grades improve, her parents (let, not) _____ her get

    a part-time job. But as soon as she can, Yasmin (look) _____ for

    work in the fashion industry.

3. Since you (take) _____ an elective course next semester, I suggest

    you sign up for sociology. You (enjoy) _____ Professor Singh's

    sense of humour.

4. Our neighbours (build) _____ an addition onto their home next

    summer. I hope we (be) _____ on vacation when the construction

    begins.

5. I (buy) _____ a daytimer schedule because my counsellor says that

    it (help) _____ me put some order in my life.

B. THE FUTURE PROGRESSIVE TENSE

The future progressive tense expresses an action that will be in progress at a time in the future. There is often little difference in meaning between the future progressive and the simple future.

I *will be seeing* him later tonight.   I *will see* him later tonight.
Tomorrow you *will be dining* with us.   Tomorrow *you will dine* with us.

Exercise 28.13

Use the appropriate verb form—future or future progressive—to fill in the blanks in these sentences.

1. I have no idea where I (work) _____ next week, but I (let) _____ you know as soon as I found out.

2. My fiancée insists that I buy her a diamond ring before she (marry) _____ me, so I (buy) _____ a lot of lottery tickets.

3. I (have, not) _____ time to talk on the phone this afternoon because I (cook) _____ a traditional dinner for 14 people.

4. Ranjan is going to Bombay, where she (stay) _____ with her family for two months. They (be) _____ surprised to find how much she has changed in the last year.

5. If Ivo passes this year, he (go) _____ to school in Vancouver for his final year. He (live) _____ with his girlfriend.

C. THE FUTURE PERFECT TENSE

The future perfect expresses an action that will be completed before another time or action in the future.

By next June, we *will have graduated* from college.
Before the end of the semester, we *will have covered* a lot of grammar.
Before we *leave* Quebec City, we *will have seen* all of the tourist attractions.
(Note that the verb in the time clause is in the simple present tense.)

Often, use of the future perfect tense is not absolutely necessary. For instance, the simple future could be used in these sentences:

By next June, we *will graduate* from college.
Before the end of the semester, we *will cover* a lot of grammar.
Before we leave Quebec City, we *will see* all of the tourist attractions.

However, if *already* is used in the sentence, the future perfect is required as it is in this example:

Correct: I *will already have gone* to bed before you arrive.
Incorrect: I *will already go* to bed before you arrive.

D. THE FUTURE PERFECT PROGRESSIVE TENSE

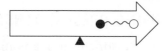

This tense is seldom used. It stresses the duration of an action in the future that takes place before another action in the future. Often, the future perfect progressive and the future perfect tenses have the same meaning, as in the examples below:

Our cousins *will have been studying* English for three months before they arrive in Canada.

Our cousins *will have studied* English for three months before they arrive in Canada.

Exercise 28.14

Fill in the blanks with a future tense of the verb in parentheses. More than one correct answer is possible in some of these sentences.

1. I (go) _____ to Florida with Josef next spring because by then he

   (earn) _____ enough money to pay for his share of the trip.

2. We are going to be late because of the terrible traffic. By the time we

   (reach) _____ the airport, Miryam's plane (arrive, already)

   _____. She (worry) _____ that something has happened to

   us.

3. My cat (have) _____ another litter. If she continues to produces

   litters at her present pace, she (give) _____ birth to 68 kittens by

   the time she is ten years old.

4. You were born in _____. By the year 2050, you (live) _____

   for _____ years. You (see) _____ many changes!

5. By the time Michelle (be) _____ ready to leave the party, William

   (drink) _____ beer all evening, so she plans to drive home.

USING PRESENT TENSES TO INDICATE FUTURE TIME

As if distinguishing among all these tenses were not complicated enough, there is another convention you need to know about. In English, the simple present and present progressive tenses are also used to express future time in several circumstances.

1. A few simple present tense verbs—*arrive, begin, close, come, end, finish, leave, open, return, start*—are used with scheduled events to express future time. Usually the sentences contain future time words or phrases; these are underlined in the three examples below.

   Sunil's flight *arrives* <u>at midnight</u>.
   School *begins* <u>on September 8 next year</u>.
   The stores at the mall *close* <u>at 6:00 p.m. today</u>.

2. When the sentence contains a time or condition clause, the simple present tense is required in that clause even though the verb refers to future or conditional time. Consider these examples carefully; the underlined clauses express time or condition and the verbs must be in the simple present.

   Incorrect: I *will take* a vacation <u>after I *will quit* my job</u>.
   <u>If the snow *will continue*</u>, the president *will close* the college.

   Correct: I *will take* a vacation <u>after I *quit* my job</u>.
   <u>If the snow *continues*</u>, the president *will close* the college.

3. The present progressive is often used when a time word or phrase in the sentence indicates the future.

   I *am touring* Tuscany <u>next fall</u>.
   Jess *is meeting* Deb and Tamara in New York <u>on the weekend</u>.

Exercise 28.15

Fill in the blanks with the correct form of the verb in parentheses.

1. As soon as Val (graduate) _____ , he (leave) _____ for Africa.

2. If Ms. Drecho (have) _____ twins, she (name) _____ them Fay and May or Bob and Rob.

3. Sophie (answer) _____ the phones while Ravi (be) _____ on

vacation next week.

4. If it (rain) _____ on the weekend, we (cancel) _____ our

plans for a beach party.

5. Pierre (be) _____ here in Canada for at least another year before

he (return) _____ home to Haiti and (get) _____ a job.

GO TO WEB

EXERCISES 28.7, 28.8

Exercise 28.16

Complete the following paragraphs using only the progressive forms of the present, past, and future tenses. The first verb has been converted for you.

Many of us (study) *are studying* computers as part of our college pro-

grams. In fact, computer skills have become essential for success in almost

all of the jobs we (do) _____ in the next decade. Most Canadians take

the presence of a computer in the home, at work, and at school for granted.

It is astonishing, therefore, to reflect that not that many years ago, many

people (treat) _____ computers as a mere fad. During the 1940s, for

example, engineers (predict) _____ that computers in the future

would weigh over a tonne. In the same decade, the chairman of IBM told

his company, "We (lose, not) _____ sleep over these machines." He

thought there would be a world market for "maybe five computers." A

decade later, book publishers (assure) _____ their employees that data processing was a fad that wouldn't last a year. In 1977, the president of

Digital Equipment Corporation (tell) _____ the company's share-

holders that there was no reason for anyone to want a computer in the

home.

Today, all of us who (use) _____ computers know about Bill Gates,

the president of Microsoft. In the years to come, his company (produce)

_____ many of the programs and applications that will become the

standard of the future. These programs will use gigabytes of memory. It is

hard to believe that in 1981 Bill Gates (tell) _____ anyone who would

listen, "640K ought to be enough for anybody."

Exercise 28.17

Go through Exercise 28.16 again. This time, assume the writer wishes to emphasize the events themselves, not the time over which they took place. Fill in the
blanks with the appropriate simple tenses (past, present, and future). Avoid
using any progressives. When you have finished, compare your two sets of paragraphs. Which version do you prefer? Why?

Exercise 28.18

In the following paragraphs, fill in the blanks with the most appropriate verb
tenses, choosing from the twelve tenses you have reviewed.

Just when I had begun to think about having children, my sister

(arrive) _____ from the west coast with her two young boys. I

(look) _____ forward to spending a quiet couple of weeks with my

sister and my nephews, getting to know them again after a long time

apart.

Within minutes of their arrival, the younger boy, Davy, (knock) _____ over the coffee table because the older one, Max, (encourage) _____ him to grab the plates of sandwiches and cookies that (lie) _____ on the table. By the time we (clean) _____ up that mess, Max (manage) _____ to pour honey all over the cat while Davy (burn) _____ my husband's treasured collection of baseball cards, using our best brandy as a fire starter. It was as if they had stored up their energy for months in order to run wild in our house.

Today is the third day of their visit, and for the past two nights my husband (sleep) _____ at his office. I suspect he (prepare) _____ divorce papers. I (see, not) _____ him since he (leave) _____. I (call) _____ him tomorrow because by then I (evict) _____ my sister and her two little monsters. The goldfish are dead, the cat (be) _____ in hiding, our lovely home (look) _____ like a disaster area, and the police (come) _____ twice.

My sister (be) _____ a saint—or maybe she's a fool. She (want) _____ a family for many years before Max was born. Now that she (have) _____ the two boys, she (seem) _____ willing to put up with anything they do. I (know, not) _____ how she stands it. With luck, by the time they come for their next visit, my husband _____ (return), the cat's hair (grow) _____ back, and we (continue) _____ to be child-free.

29

More about Verbs

In addition to verb formation and tense, there are three verbal constructions that present problems for second-language writers: negatives, participial adjectives, and modal auxiliaries.

Forming Negatives

Not expresses a negative idea. In a negative sentence, the word *not* comes immediately after the *to be* verb or an auxiliary verb. Auxiliary verbs are forms of *to be*, *to have*, *shall*, *will*, or a modal auxiliary. (Reminder: the forms of *to be* are *am/is/are/was/were/will be*. The forms of *to have* are *have/has/had*.)

Yes, the sun *is* out.	No, the sun *is not* out.
I *have learned* my lesson.	I *have not learned* my lesson.
They *will eat* a whole pizza.	They *will not eat* a whole pizza.
She *might visit* her family.	She *might not visit* her family.

If the main verb in the sentence does not have an auxiliary, the *to do* verb is added before the *not*; the main verb follows.

I *love* him.	I *do not love* him.
He *loves* me.	He *does not love* me.
I *loved* him.	I *did not love* him.

Not can be contracted to *n't*. *Isn't*, *aren't*, *wasn't*, *weren't*, *won't*, *doesn't*, *don't*, *didn't*, *hasn't*, *haven't*, *hadn't*, *can't*, *couldn't*, and *wouldn't* are examples of contracted negative verbs. What are the full forms of these contractions? (Note that *ain't* is not included in the list. Using *ain't* is a grammatical error.)

Grammatically, the word *not* is a negative adverb; it isn't actually part of the verb itself. Other negative adverbs that are used to express negative meanings are *never, rarely, seldom, scarcely (ever), hardly (ever),* and *barely (ever).* Here are some examples:

My wife and I *rarely* go out.
I *never* understand what my boyfriend really wants.
The train is *hardly ever* late.
My son *seldom* goes to school.

The word *no* can be used as an adjective in front of a noun to provide the same meaning as *not.* Just make sure that you do not use two negatives. If you do, you create a grammatical error known as a "double negative."

Correct: Ali *doesn't have* problems speaking English.
             Ali *has no* problems speaking English.

Incorrect: Ali *doesn't have no* problems speaking English. (Double negative)

Exercise 29.1

Rewrite the following sentences to make them negative. Include both the full form and the contracted form of the verbs. We've completed the first question for you as an example. Answers for exercises in this chapter begin on page 473.

1. The student needs help from the teacher.

   The student *does not* (or *doesn't*) *need* help from the teacher.

   ALSO CORRECT: The student *needs no* help from the teacher.

2. I trust the bank.

3. Barbara wants to visit Las Vegas.

4. The passengers have their passports in order.

5. You should have given the students a quiz on negatives.

6. Jabez likes to shop for clothes.

7. Ling forgot to pick us up yesterday.

8. We always stop for gas at the Big Apple.

9. José and Marta wanted to eat before the movie.

10. The class needs more exercises on verb forms.

Exercise 29.2

Change the following affirmative sentences to negative ones; make any negative clauses affirmative. Pay close attention to verb tense as you make these changes.

1. Mohammed and Hassan have enjoyed the winters in Canada.
2. I certainly want to see you.
3. I certainly wanted to see you.
4. We managed to find our way to the lost-and-found department.
5. Most of the class attended the reception for international students.
6. The Montreal Canadiens succeeded in winning many new fans last season.
7. Solaya always wants to come to the movies with us, even when we don't want her to join us.
8. Ivana is planning a party for her husband's birthday.
9. Ivana was planning a party for her husband's birthday.
10. She came to the meeting alone.

GO TO WEB

EXERCISES 29.1, 29.2

Participial Adjectives

Allan and Zeta went out on a date. It didn't go well. The two sentences that follow describe why the evening was not a success, but their meanings are different.

Version 1: Allan was a *boring* date.
Version 2: Allan was a *bored* date.

Boring and *bored* are adjectives that are formed from the participle forms of the verb *to bore*. *Boring* is the present participle; *bored* is the past participle. Choosing the correct participial adjective is often a problem for second-language writers. Let's go back to the story.

In version 1, Allan is a dull fellow. He is shy and has nothing to talk about. He bored Zeta. She found him *boring*. In version 2, Zeta is the dull person with nothing to talk about. Zeta bored Allan, so he was a *bored* date.

Are you *confused*? Is the choice *confusing*? Yes. First, we'll sort it out for you, and then we'll provide some practice with participial adjectives.

The present participle, the *-ing* form, conveys an active meaning. The noun it describes *is* or *does something*. Allan bores Zeta in version 1, so he is *boring*. Participial adjectives often confuse ESL writers, so these words are *confusing*.

The past participle conveys a passive meaning. The noun it describes *has something done to it*. Zeta bores Allan in version 2, so he is *bored*. Participial adjectives confuse ESL writers, so these writers are *confused*. Note that the past participle of irregular verbs may not end in *-ed*. (See Chapter 12, then check your dictionary for the past participle form of any irregular verb not covered in Chapter 12.)

Exercise 29.3

Complete each of the following sentences by filling in the blank with the correct participle of the italicized verb. Then check your answers on page 474.

1. Ivan *loves* Zeta. He is a _____ man.

2. Allan *loves* Clara. She is a _____ woman.

3. The movie *interests* the children. They are _____ children. They are watching an _____ movie.

4. The news *surprised* my brother. He is a _____ person. The news was quite _____.

5. The gorilla *frightened* the lady. The gorilla is a _____ animal. She is a _____ lady.

6. The teacher *irritates* the class. The class is _____. The teacher is _____.

7. The task *exhausted* me. I was _____ by this _____ task.

8. The cold, dreary weather *depresses* Sara. Sara is _____. The weather is _____.

9. The child's tantrum *embarrassed* his father. The father was _____. The child's tantrum was _____.

10. The test results *shocked* the whole town. The _____ people could hardly believe the _____ test results.

Exercise 29.4

In each of the following sentences, supply the correct present or past participle. The first one has been done for you as an example.

1. If a new friend *fascinates* you, how would you describe the person? *fascinating*

   How would you describe yourself? *fascinated*

2. If your neighbour *annoys* you, how would you describe the neighbour?

   _____

   How would you describe yourself? _____

3. If an accident *horrifies* you, how would you describe the accident?

   _____

   How would you describe yourself? _____

4. If the garbage *disgusts* you, how would you describe yourself?_____
   How would you describe the garbage? _____

5. If a meal *satisfies* you, how would you describe the meal? _____
   How would you describe yourself? _____

6. If a problem *worries* your friend, how would you describe your friend?

   _____

   How would you describe the problem? _____

7. If the work *tires* your mother, how would you describe the work?

   _____

   How would you describe your mother? _____

8. If the music *pleases* you, how would you describe yourself? _____

   How would you describe the music?_____

9. If the answer *amazes* you, how would you describe the answer? _____

   How would you describe yourself? _____

10. If a story *astonishes* a child, how would you describe the child? _____

    How would you describe the story? _____

GO TO WEB

EXERCISES 29.3, 29.4

Modal Auxiliaries

As we have seen, the verbs *am, is, are, was, were; do, does, did; has, have, and had* can stand alone as the only verb in a sentence. They can also work in an auxiliary capacity; that is, they can combine with the main verb in a sentence to change time zones or to form a negative construction.

There is another kind of auxiliary verb called a "modal" auxiliary. These words provide different shades of meaning to the main verb. The modal auxiliaries are listed below:

can	might	should
could	must	will
may	shall	would

Some common verb phrases also function as modals:

be able to	have to	supposed to
be going to	ought to	used to

We will discuss these and other modal phrases in detail below.

The examples that follow will show you how modals change the meaning of the main verb.

Modal	Interpretation
I *can* work.	I am able to do the job.
I *could* work.	If someone would offer me a job.
I *may* work.	But, then again, maybe I won't.
I *must* work.	My family needs the money.
I *should* work.	My mother is nagging me to get a job.
I *would* work.	If you paid me enough.
I *used to* work.	But I don't anymore.

The good news about modals is that they are always followed by the base form of the verb (e.g., *work*) with no *-s* added to the third-person singular or *-ed* added to the past tense. Unlike *do* and *has*, the modal auxiliaries don't change number and, except for *can/could* and *will/would*, they don't change time.

The bad news about modals is that they often suggest subtle changes in meaning that confuse second-language writers. Traditional grammar texts use a great deal of ink attempting to distinguish "obligation" versus "advisability" and "polite" versus "impolite" requests. The following chart will help you sort out the meanings of modals. But while you're struggling to learn the differences among various modals, keep in mind that native speakers almost never hear a difference between your telling them that you *may work tomorrow* and you *might work tomorrow*.

Single-Word Modal Auxiliaries

Auxiliary	Meaning	Example (Present/Future)	Example (Past)
can	1. ability	I *can swim* well.	I *could swim* when I was two.
	2. informal request	*Can* I *call* you tonight?	
could	1. past tense of *can*		I *could swim* when I was two.
	2. polite request	*Could* I please *speak* to your wife?	
	3. low level of certainty	It *could rain* tonight, or it *could be* clear.	
may	1. polite request	*May* I please *speak* to your wife?	
	2. low level of certainty	It *may rain* tonight, but it *may* not [*rain*].	
	3. possibility	Harvey says he *may go* with us.	

Auxiliary	Meaning	Example (Present/Future)	Example (Past)
might	1. low level of certainty	It *might rain* tonight, but it *might* not [*rain*].	
	2. possibility	I *might visit* Paris this summer.	
	3. past tense of *may*		Harvey said he *might go* with us.
must	1. strong necessity	You *must drink* water.	
	2. high level of certainty	The teacher isn't here, so she *must be* ill.	
shall	1. polite question	*Shall* I *help* you across the street?	
	2. future (with *I/we*)	I *shall see* you tomorrow. (or *will see* . . .)	
should	1. advisable	You *should lose* a few pounds.	
	2. high level of certainty	You study hard, so you *should do* well in the course.	
	3. obligation	He *should support* his children.	
will	1. complete certainty	They *will eat* dinner with us tonight.	
	2. willingness	I*'ll cook* a beautiful meal for them.	
	3. polite request	*Will* you please *tell* me what you think?	
would	1. preference (with *rather*)	I *would rather eat* at a restaurant.	
	2. polite request	*Would* you please *tell* me what you think?	
	3. repeated action in past		We *would* always *phone* home on weekends when we lived abroad.
	4. conditional with *if* clause	I *would go* outside if it stopped raining.	

Exercise 29.5

Complete the sentences in the following exercise by using one modal auxiliary together with one main verb from the choices we have provided. Use each modal and main verb only once. Be careful: two of the sentences require negations. When you have completed this exercise, check your answers on page 474.

Modal Auxiliaries		Main Verbs	
can	shall	tell	say
could	should	answer	talk
may	will	~~fall~~	prepare
~~might~~	would	go	take
must		hand	

Example: 1. If you lean out of the window, you <u>might</u> <u>fall</u>.

2. _____ you please _____ me the phone?

3. You _____ _____ Rani about the party because we want it to

   be a surprise for her.

4. The baby is just learning to talk but he _____ _____ five or

   six words. A few weeks ago he _____ _____ at all.

5. _____ I _____ your arm as we cross the street?

6. _____ I _____ a room for the guests?

7. I didn't get much sleep last night, so I _____ _____ to bed

   early tonight.

8. He makes me angry because he _____ _____ his cell phone

   even in a movie theatre.

The chart on page 347 summarizes modal and other auxiliaries that are made up of more than a single word. *Ought to* and *used to* do not require any change in the verb form. Like the single-word modals, they simply precede the base form of the main verb. For example, "She used to (*modal*) love (*base form of verb*) me." *Be able to, be going to, be supposed to*, and *has/have to* present an extra challenge. Because they include the verb *to be*, they require a change in the auxiliary itself to mark tense and number. Study the examples below.

We *were able to* finish the assignment.
You *are going to* have trouble with that car.
I *am supposed to* teach a class at noon today.
She and I *were supposed to* teach a class yesterday.
He *has to* change his clothes.
They *had to* change their clothes.

When you are using past participles such as *supposed to* and *used to*, don't forget to include the *-d* at the end of the word. Omitting the *-d* is one of the most common errors made by student writers.

Incorrect: The show was suppose to begin an hour ago.
  I use to have more money.

Correct: The show was suppose*d* to begin an hour ago.
  I use*d* to have more money.

Phrasal Modal Auxiliaries

Auxiliary	Meaning	Example (Present/Future)	Example (Past)
be able to	ability (can)	He *is able to handle* the truck	He *was able to handle* the truck.
be going to	plan (for the future)	I *am going to help* you.	I *was going to help* you, but I changed my mind.
be supposed to	expectation	We *are supposed to meet* them.	We *were supposed to meet* them, but we forgot.
have/has/had to	necessity (must)	He *has to go* to the bank today.	He *had to go* to the bank on Tuesday.
ought to	1. advisability (should)	We *ought to bring* our raincoats and an umbrella.	
	2. high level of certainty	She studies hard and *ought to do* well in school.	
used to	repeated action		She *used to work* hard in school. He *used to weigh* 100 kg.

Exercise 29.6

Fill in each blank with one of the phrasal modal auxiliaries. More than one modal may be possible, but use each only once. Compare your answers with our suggestions on page 475.

1. It _____ rain later, so you _____ take your umbrella.

2. Sergei _____ be lazy about his schoolwork, so now he _____ work very hard to catch up.

3. We _____ go to the beach yesterday, but it was too cold. We hope that we _____ go tomorrow.

Exercise 29.7

Use one of the auxiliaries with each verb in parentheses. More than one auxiliary may be possible.

1. (see) The doctor _____ you later this afternoon.

2. (finish) If he works very hard, Paulo _____ the project before the deadline.

3. (complete) He _____ it on time if he wants to get paid.

4. (visit) You _____ your grandmother because she misses you.

5. (run) When Oswaldo was younger, he _____ very fast.

6. (love) Felix bought his girlfriend a beautiful engagement ring; he _____ her very much.

7. (drink) Her parents _____ heavily, but they have stopped entirely since joining Alcoholics Anonymous.

8. (collect) You _____ the children at daycare; how could you have forgotten them?

9. (help) It _____ you remember to pick them up if you tie this string around your finger.

10. (come, not) Wally is in the shower, so he _____ to the phone.

Exercise 29.8

Use a modal auxiliary (one word or a phase) in each of the blanks.

1. I wonder when the boat will arrive. It _____ be here an hour ago.

2. When we were in high school, my friends and I _____ do anything that sounded like fun.

3. If you have a food processor, you _____ prepare this salad in a few minutes.

4. What did you say? _____ you please repeat it?

5. We _____ fill up the gas tank or we _____ run out of fuel.

6. The mayor is not in her office; she _____ be at a meeting.

7. Their whole house is decorated in red; they _____ really love the colour!

8. After you thaw the chicken, you _____ cook it right away.

9. Our instructor _____ give us quizzes every day, but now he gives only three a semester.

10. _____ you _____ come to our party?

Exercise 29.9

Fill in each blank with an appropriate modal auxiliary.

I happened to meet my friend Selva yesterday, and we decided that we _____ get together soon. We _____ see each other every day at school, but we haven't _____ visit as often since we graduated and started to work. "I _____ call you tonight," Selva said as she hurried on her way.

Selva called as she had said she _____ . We planned to go to a show the following evening. We both decided we _____ see the new Keanu Reeves film.

Were we ever disappointed! The show was so boring that I _____ hardly keep my eyes open. "Keanu _____ be cute," I said, "but no one _____ accuse him of being a good actor." Selva and I left halfway through the film, and we went to a restaurant where we _____ catch up on each other's news.

GO TO WEB

EXERCISES 29.5, 29.6

Exercise 29.10

Edit these sentences to correct the errors in negative constructions, participial adjectives, and modal auxiliaries.

1. Claude doesn't very interesting in the movie; he found it bored.
2. All the plants in the office are dying. They may be getting enough sunlight.
3. I'm sorry, but I can go swimming today because of my earache. It causes an annoyed pain in my head.
4. It is amazed that you have hardly never had an earache.
5. Cao was disappointing because he was suppose to get a good grade on the test and he failed.
6. When our boss gone to Hawaii for a conference, she did'nt leaves us with any work to do.
7. Neither Amit nor Helene is going to work on the weekend, but they don't have no money to go to the clubs with us.
8. The whole beach was deserting. We couldn't see nothing but sand.
9. Don't a person has to be rich to lead an excited life?
10. Who is knocking on the door? It can be Victoria because she is out of town, so it shall be Marcella or it used to be Brian. Why you don't open the door and found out?

30

Solving Plural Problems

Singular vs. Plural Nouns

Nouns in English are words that name people, places, things, or ideas. For example, *Julia Roberts*, *Manitoba*, *hedgehog*, and *honesty* are all examples of nouns. The first three examples are **concrete** nouns; in other words, they refer to physical objects that we can see or touch. The fourth example, *honesty*, is an **abstract** noun that refers to a concept that exists in our minds; it cannot be seen or touched.

Singular nouns refer to one person, place, thing, or idea: *mother*, *bedroom*, *book*, *justice*. Plural nouns refer to more than one person, place, or thing: *mothers*, *bedrooms*, *books*. Abstract nouns are not usually found in the plural form.

To form the plural of most nouns, you add *-s* to the singular form.

Singular	Plural	Singular	Plural
classroom	classrooms	idea	ideas
cousin	cousins	truck	trucks
friend	friends	umbrella	umbrellas

Exercise 30.1

Rewrite the following sentences in the plural. Make sure that your verbs and pronouns agree with the plural nouns; you may also have to delete an article (*a* or *an*). The first question is done for you. Answers for exercises in this chapter begin on page 476.

1. The book is on her table.

   The books are on their tables.

2. Your little girl loves her new toy.

3. A student learns to take a test.

4. A good doctor listens to her patient.

5. The taxi crashed into the house.

6. The boy visits his girlfriend every night.

7. This room is very large.

8. An angry dog is a dangerous animal.

9. Would he like a new car?

10. My store has the item you need.

Unfortunately, there are many exceptions to the "add -*s* for plural" rule. The most common exceptions are listed below.

1. Irregular plural forms

Most of these are very common words, but they are based on an older form of English. You need to memorize them and get used to their irregular nature.

Singular	Plural	Singular	Plural
child	children	mouse	mice
foot	feet	ox	oxen
goose	geese	tooth	teeth
man	men	woman	women

2. Nouns ending in "soft" sounds of *-s, -x, -z, -ch, -sh*: add *-es*

Singular	Plural
box	boxes
buzz	buzzes
church	churches
class	classes
dish	dishes
kiss	kisses

If the *-ch* is a "hard" sound—as in *stomach*—add *-s* only: *stomachs*.

3. Nouns ending in *-y* preceded by a consonant: change the *-y* to *-i* and add *-es*

Singular	Plural
country	countries
lady	ladies
penny	pennies
reply	replies

Nouns ending in *-y* preceded by a vowel are regular. Add *-s* to pluralize them.

boys	keys
delays	valleys

4. Nouns ending in *-f* or *-fe*: add *-ves* if the plural is pronounced with a *-v* sound

Note that the word *self* is in this category. This rule has important consequences for the "self" words.

calves	himself → themselves
knives	yourself → yourselves
thieves	herself → themselves
wives	myself → ourselves

5. If the plural noun keeps its *-f* sound, add only *-s.*

beliefs	chiefs
chefs	proofs

6. Some nouns ending in *-o* pluralize by adding *-es*; other nouns ending in *-o* add only *-s.* Check your dictionary if you're not sure.

echoes	BUT	pianos
heroes		sopranos
potatoes		studios
tomatoes		zoos

7. Some nouns are used in the singular form only, for both singular and plural.

caribou	elk	salmon
carp	moose	sheep
deer	pickerel	trout

8. Some nouns are used in the plural form only, even though they refer to a single unit.

glasses	pyjamas
jeans	scissors
pants	shorts

9. Some foreign language nouns retain their original plural form.

Singular	Plural	Singular	Plural
analysis	analyses	larva	larvae
criterion	criteria	phenomenon	phenomena
fungus	fungi	stimulus	stimuli
hypothesis	hypotheses	thesis	theses

Exercise 30.2

Fill in the blank with the missing form (singular or plural) of the noun or pronoun given in each item below. The first one is done for you.

Singular	**Plural**
1. one movie	two <u>movies</u>
2. look at yourself (one person)	look at _____ (two people)
3. the category	three different _____
4. a _____	the women
5. one sheep	many _____
6. my foot	their _____
7. an _____	thick eyelashes
8. one phenomenon	many _____
9. the man himself	the men _____
10. a photo	several _____
11. the piano	two _____
12. a _____	many tomatoes
13. one _____	four criteria
14. the monarch	two _____
15. one thesis	several _____
16. a thief	a pack of _____
17. my husband	my friends' _____
18. his only _____	all your teeth
19. the hero	these _____
20. one valley	two _____

Exercise 30.3

Insert the correct plural forms of the nouns provided before each sentence.

cigarette, match   1. Since I quit smoking, I never carry either

_____ or _____.

mushroom, berry

2. Some wild _____ and _____ might be poisonous, so be careful about eating them.

tree, leaf

3. It is difficult to identify _____ by their bark, but it's easy if you have some _____ from the tree.

course, quiz

4. We are lucky to have only three _____ this semester because each of them has weekly _____.

library, wolf

5. Tomas has been to four _____ in search of information about _____.

city, community

6. Most Canadian _____ are home to many different ethnic _____.

inquiry, reply

7. Ming mailed out a dozen _____ about jobs, but she received only six _____.

knife, fork

8. Are there enough _____ and _____ for everyone on the table?

ninety, attorney

9. When my grandmother was in her _____, she hired several _____ to manage her business.

activity, study

10. Marcel has so many after-school _____ that he has no time left for his _____.

GO TO WEB

EXERCISES 30.1, 30.2

Count vs. Noncount Nouns

Count nouns are words for separate persons, places, or things that can be counted: *one apple, two apples, three apples*. Count nouns can be made plural in one of the ways explained above. Count nouns name individual, distinct items: e.g., *college, job, meal, student, toy*. Note that the *-s* ending makes each of these count nouns plural: *colleges, jobs, meals, students, toys*.

Noncount nouns are words that identify things that cannot be counted. Many noncount nouns refer to a "whole" that is made up of different parts. For instance, a room may contain two sofas, three tables, four chairs, and a television. All of these items can be counted—and the words can be made plural. However, all of these items can be considered as a "whole" and described as *furniture*, which is a noncount noun that cannot be pluralized.

Incorrect: two chair, furnitures
Correct: two chairs, furniture

There are several categories of noncount nouns.

- Abstract nouns (words for concepts that exist as ideas in our minds): e.g., *courage, fun, hatred, health, information*. You acquire data in bits and pieces, but you acquire *information* as a whole. You wouldn't say that you have gathered *informations* as you acquire more data.
- Words that identify a quantity or mass: e.g., *air, coffee, food, rice, salt, sugar, water*. These words identify substances that are made up of particles too numerous to count. You can count *bottles of water* or *bowls of rice*, but you cannot count *water* or *rice*.
- The names of many sports: e.g., *golf, hockey, tennis*
- The names of some illnesses: e.g., *diabetes, flu, osteoporosis*
- Subjects of study, whether their form is singular (*astronomy, biology, chemistry*) or plural (*economics, mathematics, physics*)
- Weather and other natural phenomena: e.g., *electricity, fire, lightning, sunshine*

The important thing to remember about noncount nouns is that they have only one form, not different forms for singular and plural. The count or noncount quality of a noun also determines the articles and modifiers that are used before the noun. (We will review articles and modifiers in Chapter 31.) For now, keep in mind that you do not add plural inflections to noncount nouns, although some of them, such as the academic disciplines listed above, have an *-s* ending.

Incorrect: I should do my homeworks.
Correct: I should do my homework.

Incorrect: We always have funs on our vacations.
Correct: We always have fun on our vacations.

Incorrect: My friends and I are concerned about our healths.
Correct: My friends and I are concerned about our health.

Incorrect: The airline lost our luggages.
Correct: The airline lost our luggage.

Exercise 30.4

Choose the correct word from the list below for the blank in each sentence. Write a C above the word in the sentence if it is a count noun; write NC above the word in the sentence it if it is a noncount noun. Make the word plural if necessary. Use each word only once. Check your answers on page 476.

advice	vegetable	coffee
health	sugar	dinner
soil	problem	equipment
milk	knowledge	vitamin
math	beef	computer

1. Put some _____ and _____ in my _____, please.

2. I need your _____ to solve two _____ .

3. Your _____ of _____ is better than mine.

4. I love to eat _____ for _____ .

5. The old _____ in the library are examples of the outdated

_____ that the college needs to replace.

6. The _____ in our area of the city is too polluted with chemicals

to allow people to grow _____ .

7. You have to take your _____ if you want to regain your

_____ .

So far so good, but there is one complication that makes the count/non-count issue very tricky. Some nouns can be both count and noncount, depending on how they are used. If the noun has a general, as-a-whole kind of meaning, it is noncount and is not pluralized; e.g., "We often have chicken for dinner." If the noun has a specific, count-them-up kind of meaning, it is a count noun and can be pluralized; e.g., "Four chickens were running around in the yard." Therefore, some noncount nouns may be used in a countable sense and have a plural form. Study the four examples given below.

Exercise
Noncount (in a general sense): *Exercise* is good for you.
Count (a specific movement or example): Carmen does *exercises* every morning.

Food
Noncount (in a general sense): *Food* is an important part of every culture.
Count (specific cuisines): There were *foods* from all over the world at the party.

Experience
Noncount (in a general sense): You need *experience* for this job.
Count (specific happenings): I had some interesting *experiences* in class this semester.

Fire
Noncount (in a general sense): When did humans learn to use the power of *fire*?
Count (specific blazes): We could see several different *fires* on the beach.

Check an advanced learner's dictionary if you are unsure whether a noun is count or noncount. Sometimes noncount nouns are identified as "uncountable" (a *U* in your dictionary). "Noncount" and "Uncountable" mean the same thing.

Exercise 30.5

Write the correct form of the word—either singular or plural—in the blanks below.

money, luck   1. They often win _____ in the lottery, so
         I guess you could say they have good

         _____ .

luggage, suitcase

2. After the _____ arrived at the hotel, we found that two _____ were missing.

effort, work

3. It takes _____ to study all of the _____ of Shakespeare.

advice, homework

4. Our teacher gave us good _____ about doing all the _____ he assigns.

change, penny

5. I have a great deal of _____ in my pocket, but it is all _____.

light

6. As the sun set and the _____ faded, we turned on all the _____ in the cottage.

time

7. How many _____ do I have to tell you that _____ is important?

garbage, work

8. Taking out the _____ every week is not much _____.

history, music

9. Carmine studied the _____ of _____ while he was at university.

lightning, golf

10. The _____ storm prevented us from playing _____.

Exercise 30.6

Correct the errors in the following sentences, then check your answers on page 477.

1. Robert is going bald and wants to know where he can get informations on hairs replacement.

2. I found a couple of hairs in my soup.

3. You can have funs in sports, but the enjoyments disappear if you play too much hockeys or footballs.

4. The children brought several footballs and their hockey sticks to the field.

5. The riches get richer, and the poors get poorer.

6. Benicio lives on a beautiful ranch with a large herd of cattles.

7. All of my relatives had advices for me when I came to Canada.

8. We continue to work in sunshines and in darkness; in fact, neither rain nor snow nor sleet nor lightning nor wind can interfere with our determination to get the works done.

9. We didn't hear much laughters coming from the back of the van as we drove through the rush-hour traffics.

10. Why don't you change your dirty clothings?

Robert wants information about hairs replacement.

Exercise 30.7

Rewrite the following paragraph, changing the appropriate nouns from singular to plural. Don't forget to make your verbs and pronouns agree with your plural nouns, and prepare to omit some articles (*a, an*)—the subject of Chapter 31. Your paragraph will begin "Canadians who enjoy winter are strange people. With their noses red and their fingers frozen, they actually take . . . ." Check your answers before continuing.

A Canadian who enjoys winter is a strange person. With his nose red and his fingers frozen, he actually takes pleasure in shovelling the huge mound of snow in his driveway. He doesn't mind when his water pipe freezes or his car doesn't start. With a smile on his face, he bundles up in thermal underwear, flannel shirt, sweater, down jacket, scarf, boots, and woolen toque. Then this peculiar creature goes out into the bitter cold and howling wind to engage in an activity that leaves a normal person completely baffled. He looks for a rink, or a trail, or a hill on which to skate or ski. While a sensible person stays indoors, huddles close to the stove, and warms himself with a hot drink, the winter-loving Canadian is outside behaving like a child with a new toy. Should he be admired or pitied?

GO TO WEB

EXERCISES 30.3, 30.4, 30.5

Quantity Expressions

The English language contains many words and phrases that tell us the quantity or amount of something. For instance, *one prize, three prizes,* and *fifty prizes* state the exact number of prizes; *many prizes, several prizes,* and *a few prizes* tell us that there is more than one prize, but not exactly how many there are. Whether a noun is count or noncount determines the appropriate expression of quantity that is used with the noun. But before we study the chart that summarizes the correct quantity expressions, there is an important rule to remember.

When a quantity expression contains the word *of,* any count noun that follows it must be plural.

Incorrect: We ate a couple of pizza.
Correct: We ate a couple of pizzas.

Incorrect: She grew a lot of vegetable in the garden.
Correct: She grew a lot of vegetables in the garden.

Incorrect: Several of the teacher were very kind.
Correct: Several of the teachers were very kind.

Note that it is also correct to omit the *of* in this last sentence, but the noun *teachers* remains plural: *Several teachers were very kind.*

The chart below uses a count noun (*dollars*) and a noncount noun (*money*) to illustrate how quantity expressions are used with count and noncount nouns.

Quantity Expression	Count Noun	Noncount Noun
SINGULAR	DOLLAR(S)	MONEY
one	one dollar	——
each	each dollar	——
every	every dollar	——
PLURAL		
a couple of	a couple of dollars	——
a few	a few dollars	——
a number of	a number of dollars	——
both	both dollars	——
few	few dollars	——

Quantity Expression	Count Noun	Noncount Noun
PLURAL	DOLLAR(S)	MONEY
many	many dollars	——
several	several dollars	——
two, three, etc.	two dollars	——
a great deal of	——	a great deal of money
a little	——	a little money
much	——	much money
all	all dollars	all money
a lot of	a lot of dollars	a lot of money
hardly any	hardly any dollars	hardly any money
lots of	lots of dollars	lots of money
not any/no	not any/no dollars	not any/no money
most	most dollars	most money
plenty of	plenty of dollars	plenty of money
some	some dollars	some money

Exercise 30.8

Each of the following sentences has a blank indicating where a quantity expression is required. Several choices of quantity expression are given in parentheses following each sentence. Using the information in the chart above, cross out the quantity expressions that *cannot* be appropriately used in the blank. Then check your answers.

1. I will read _____ reports. (*four, several, much, a great deal of, some, few, a lot of, too many, every, most, a little*)

2. I will study _____ information. (*three, each, much, a lot of, several, a great deal of, plenty of, a few, a little, hardly any*)

3. Shakira owns _____ beautiful dresses. (*too much, hardly any, eleven, a few, a great deal of, no, plenty of, some, every*)

4. Shakira owns _____ beautiful clothing. (*a few, three, one, some, several, a number of, much, a lot of, lots of, a couple of*)

Note that *a few* and *few* have different meanings, as do *a little* and *little*. A *few* and *a little* have a positive meaning: for example, "I have a few friends" and "I have a little money" suggest that I have at least some friends and some funds. I'm not completely alone, nor am I completely broke. On the other hand, *few* and *little* have negative connotations. "I have few friends" and "I have little money" suggest that I am a lonely person who has almost no money to spend.

Exercise 30.9

The following sentences require that you fill in each blank either with an appropriate expression of quantity (choose from the list on pages 363–364) or with an appropriate noun. When you've completed this exercise, compare your answers with our suggestions.

1. _____ extra money is good to have.

2. Several of the _____ are hiring waiters.

3. Roberto has _____ friends here in Canada, so he feels very homesick.

4. _____ of the _____ found the course very boring. Only two or three people found it interesting.

5. After Tom Hanks' plane crashed in the movie *Cast Away*, he had _____ chance of being rescued.

6. My best friend has _____ good-looking brothers, so I like to spend as _____ time at her house as I can.

7. _____ one of her _____ is tall, dark, handsome, and smart.

8. I like my coffee sweet, so I put _____ of _____ in it; sometimes I also put _____ cream in it.

9. It takes _____ practice to learn how to ice skate.

10. _____ of us got home from the game quickly because there was _____ traffic.

GO TO WEB

EXERCISES 30.6, 30.7

Exercise 30.10

Correct the 25 errors in plural form in this paragraph. Be sure to revise verbs and pronouns to agree with any nouns you change from singular to plural.

Many people think that moonlights influence the lifes of human, animal, and even plant. Police surveyes show that more criminal activitys occur when the moon is full. People who like to fish are convinced that the fishes bite better during the full moon. Some newspaper publish datas on the phases of the moon, showing the best times to catch various species of fish. I know I always catch more salmons and trouts when the moon is full. Many gardener will not plant anything during a full moon, believing that crops such as tomatos and corns will not grow properly if they do. We know that mushroom and other funguses grow faster when the moon is new. Finally, in many societys we find legend of werewolfs: man and woman who turn into wolfs when the moon is full. Are these storys true? Probably not. But only we ourselfs know what influence the moon has on us as individuals.

31

Using Articles
Accurately

People who learn English as their first language rarely have problems with these three little words: *a*, *an*, and *the*. But if you learned English as a second language, articles are a potential minefield of trouble for you. One reason is that the use or non-use of articles often depends on meaning that is implied rather than stated. Look at these sentences, for example:

A woman is waiting in your office.
The woman is waiting in your office.

Both sentences are correct, but the meanings they convey are quite different. Whether you choose *a* or *the* is determined by what you know about the woman, not by the grammar of the sentence. If she is an unknown, *indefinite* woman, you use the **indefinite article**, *a*. But if she is a known, *definite* person whom you recognize, you use the **definite article**, *the*. Both articles *can* be used; which one you *should* use depends on what you mean to say. There are few hard-and-fast rules that govern the use of these troublesome little words. You need to take time and practise until you become familiar with them. There are, however, some general guidelines that will help you use articles correctly. In this chapter, we explain the guidelines and give you practice in applying them.

The Indefinite Article: *A/An*

The indefinite article marks a non-specific noun. In other words, *a/an* is used to refer to a common noun in a general, un-particularized way. Here are some examples:

A woman is waiting in your office. (could be any woman)
I ate *an* apple. (any apple, not a specific piece of fruit)
A shark is a dangerous creature. (the whole species of shark, not a specific fish)

One rule that always applies (no exceptions) tells you whether to use *a* or *an*.

> Use *a* if the word that follows it begins with a consonant or the sound of a consonant.
>
> Use *an* if the word that follows it begins with the vowel or the sound of a vowel.

Consonant or Consonant Sound	Vowel or Vowel Sound
a party	an event
a sunset	an umbrella
a great evening	an awful trip
a tiny elf	an oak tree
a university (*university* begins with a vowel, but it sounds like the consonant -*y*)	an honour (*honour* begins with a consonant, but it sounds like the vowel -*o*)

Exercise 31.1

Complete this exercise with the correct indefinite article, *a* or *an*. Don't use *the*. Answers for exercises in this chapter begin on page 478.

It was _____ dark day when I walked into _____ old dilapidated house. There I met _____ peculiar old man. He was wearing _____ yellow shirt and _____ frayed pair of overalls. He was holding _____ sword, and _____ evil-looking pistol was stuffed into his pocket. "You look like _____ brave young fellow," he said. "Would you like to see _____ impressive collection of stuffed animals upstairs?" My heart was pounding as I politely declined his offer and made

_____ hasty retreat.

Now let's look at how to use indefinite articles accurately. Study the five guidelines and examples that follow.

> 1. Use the indefinite article with singular count nouns. (See Chapter 30 for an explanation of count and noncount nouns.)

- *A/an* is never used with plural nouns.
  Incorrect: A women are waiting in your office.
  Correct: Women are waiting in your office.

- *A/an* is never used with noncount nouns.
  Incorrect: We moved a new furniture into the office.
  Correct: We moved new furniture into the office.
  Also correct: We moved a new desk into the office. (count noun)

> 2. Many nouns have a count meaning as well as a noncount meaning. The indefinite article *a/an* is required if the noun is being used as a singular count noun.

For example, the noun *life* is usually thought to be noncount and is not pluralized; e.g., "Life is good." The noun *life*, though, also has a count sense and can be pluralized; e.g., "Six lives were lost in the earthquake" or "The hurricane did not take a single life." To take another example, consider the difference between these two sentences:

Incorrect: Life of poverty is very difficult.
Correct: A life of poverty is very difficult. (*life* is being used as a singular count noun)

Again, the meaning—as well as the grammar of your sentence—determines whether or not you need the article.

There are other nouns usually considered to be noncount that are also used as count nouns. For example, liquids thought of as contained items (such as *coffee* in a cup) are count nouns and can be used with *a*. These nouns can also be pluralized.

Coffee is grown in South America. (*Coffee* is used as a noncount noun.)

Please bring me *a* coffee. (*Coffee* is used as a singular count noun.)

Please bring us two coffees. (*Coffee* is used as a plural count noun.)

3. The indefinite article is used with certain quantity expressions such as *a few, a little, a couple of* (see pages 363 and 364).

I'll speak to him if I have *a little* time left after class.

We have *a couple of* questions for you.

4. The indefinite article is used in certain time expressions, such as *half an hour* and *a half hour*. The phrases *once an hour, twice a day, three times a week, several times a month* and similar expressions use *a/an* to express frequency.

Can you meet me in *half an hour*?

We usually get together at least *twice a year*.

5. Many idioms require the indefinite article.

You should be familiar with the common idioms listed below.

as a rule	lend a hand
do a favour	make a living, make a point of, make a
for a long time	difference, make a fool of
give me a break (informal)	once in a while
have a headache	stand a chance
in a hurry	take a trip, take a break, take a look at
keep an eye on	tell a lie

Exercise 31.2

In the following sentences, fill in the blanks with the correct indefinite article (*a/an*), if it is required. Do not write in the blanks where *a/an* is not required. Do not use the definite article (*the*) in this exercise.

1. The Russian government came to depend on _____ regular transfer of _____ information from _____ secret agent in the Canadian government.

2. _____ child learns affection through the love of _____ parents.

3. Reggie asked for _____ last drink before the bar closed even though he had already drunk _____ half bottle of whiskey.

4. _____ cummerbund is _____ article of clothing that you wear with _____ tuxedo.

5. As _____ rule, _____ rich person should be prepared to help others who are less fortunate.

6. I waited for _____ hour and _____ half to see _____ counsellor.

7. Twice _____ year, I take _____ adventure trip with _____ friend or two.

8. _____ baby needs to drink _____ milk.

9. We left _____ few items in the car, so please do me _____ favour and get them.

10. Sorry, dear, I have _____ headache.

GO TO WEB

EXERCISES 31.1, 31.2

The Definite Article: *The*

The is a word that makes a noun specific or definite. It distinguishes the known from the unknown. In the sentence "The woman is waiting in your office," we know something about the woman. She isn't a stranger off the street. She is a definite person. Nouns can be particularized—made definite or specific—in several ways. The following guidelines and examples show how nouns are particularized and will help you figure out how to use the definite article.

> 1. Use the definite article with familiar objects, places, and people in the external environment.

For instance, we speak about *the* Earth, *the* sun, *the* apartment we live in, *the* school we attend, *the* doctor we consult, and *the* TV shows we watch. All of these things are particularized (made definite) because we are familiar with them. We know who or what we have in mind when we use the word, and the reader or listener is going to be thinking about the same thing.

The Earth rotates around *the* sun.

I drove to *the* college and parked *the* car in *the* faculty lot.

> 2. Nouns can be made definite from the context of the sentence. (This principle is called the anaphoric—or second mention—use of *the*.)

Once you refer to an unknown person, place, or thing using the indefinite article, that person, place, or thing becomes a known—or definite—entity the next time you refer to him, her, or it. Consider this example:

A strange woman is waiting in your office. *The* woman is wearing *an* interesting suit. *The* suit is made of blue silk and is held together with giant safety pins.

The first time we mention the woman, she is unknown and referred to as "*a* woman." This first mention makes her definite, so we refer to her as "*the* woman" in the second sentence. Can you explain the shift in the articles that modify the suit she is wearing?

Exercise 31.3

Complete the exercise below using *a/an* or *the* correctly in the blanks.

When you move to ___a___ new city, you have to think about your

housing needs. If you are going to be there for only ___a___ short time,

you can rent ___a___ furnished apartment. ___The___ apartment

should be in ___a___ convenient location. Perhaps you should locate

yourself in ___the___ downtown area near public transportation.

___The___ furnished apartment you rent needs to have ___a___ decent kitchen. ___The___ kitchen should have ___a___ working stove and refrigerator. ___The___ place where you live is ___an___ important factor in your adjustment to your new city.

---

3. The definite article can be used with singular and plural nouns and with count and noncount nouns.

The woman is waiting in your office. (singular noun)

The women are waiting in your office. (plural noun)

We moved *the* new desk into your office. (count noun)

We moved *the* new furniture into your office. (noncount noun)

4. The definite article can also be used with a singular generic noun; that is, it can be used when you are making a generalization about a class of things.

Usually, the indefinite article can also be used in a such a sentence. Both of the sentences below have the same meaning, and both are correct.

The shark is dangerous. (the whole species of fish)

A shark is dangerous. (the whole species of fish)

Do not use *the* with a plural count noun in the generic sense. Instead, use the plural form with no article: "Sharks are dangerous." If you are referring to specific animals, though, you can use *the* with the plural count noun: "The sharks off the east coast of Australia are dangerous." Here is another example to illustrate the correct use of articles with generic and specific plural count nouns.

Problem: The teenagers are often moody and irritable with their parents.

This use of *the* is incorrect if you are referring to teenagers as a class of people; it is correct if it refers to a specific group of teenagers.

Correct: Teenagers are often moody and irritable with their parents.

Also correct: The teenagers in that family are often moody and irritable with their parents.

Exercise 31.4

Fill in each blank with *the* or leave it blank if *the* is not required. Do not use *a/an* in this exercise.

1. _____ elderly deserve _____ support of society.

2. _____ lightning can be very dangerous, so people should take cover when _____ electrical storms occur.

3. Do we know who invented _____ wheel?

4. _____ Internet will play an increasingly large role in our lives.

5. _____ elephant and _____ whale are both huge animals that give birth to _____ live babies; in other words, they are _____ mammals.

6. I like to play games on _____ computers.

7. _____ life is very interesting, and _____ life of Thomson Highway has been especially interesting.

8. _____ college students need to spend _____ time studying if they want to be successful.

9. My computer crashed and that is _____ reason I didn't finish _____ assignment.

10. Thank you for _____ bananas; I love to eat _____ fruit.

GO TO WEB

EXERCISES 31.3, 31.4

5. The definite article is used in many quantity expressions that contain *of*; for example, *some of the coffee, most of the children, each one of the judges, all of the exams, both of the rings.*

In many of these phrases it is also correct to omit the "of the" part of the phrase.

Many of the models in fashion shows are very young.

Many models in fashion shows are very young.

Both sentences are correct and mean the same thing.

Note that you cannot omit the definite article from a quantity expression without omitting "of" as well.

Incorrect: Some of people in this building are very wealthy.

Correct: Some of the people in this building are very wealthy.

Also correct: Some people in this building are very wealthy.

6. Many idioms use the definite article.

Some common examples are

all the time	play the fool
clear the table	tell the truth
make the beds	wash the dishes

7. Other uses of the definite article are listed below.

- With superlative adjectives: He is *the* ugliest man I know.

- With number words (ordinals): *the* third child, *the* tenth chapter

- In phrases that specify time or space sequence: *the* next day, *the* end, *the* last desk in *the* row

- In phrases that rank things: *the* main reason, *the* only person

- With official titles: *the* prime minister, *the* president (When the person's name is attached, however, the definite article is omitted: Prime Minister Chrétien, President Fox.)

- With names of governmental and military bodies, both with common nouns (*the* parliament, *the* police, *the* army) and with proper nouns (*the* Liberal Party, *the* United Nations, *the* Pentagon)

- With historical periods or events: *the* Renaissance, *the* Ming Dynasty, *the* 1960s, *the* Quebec Referendum

- With legislative bills and acts: *the* Canadian Charter of Rights and Freedoms, *the* Meech Lake Accord

Exercise 31.5

Fill in the blanks in the sentences below with *a*, *an*, or *the*. Do not leave the blank empty.

1. I want to find _____ interesting book to read on _____ next flight, but _____ book that Harvey gave me looks quite dull.

2. _____ phase of _____ moon is one of _____ causes of ocean tides.

3. I bought _____ new CD online yesterday, and _____ CD should be here by tomorrow.

4. What is _____ name of _____ student you were talking to this morning? He is _____ first person I talked to in class, and I would like to know his name.

5. Though I had never seen her before, I spoke to _____ beautiful young woman in _____ supermarket this morning; she is one of _____ loveliest human beings I have ever seen.

6. _____ kind of vacation I enjoy most is _____ long train ride.

7. I don't need _____ special destination when I board _____ train; for me _____ most important thing is _____ journey.

8. Today it is not difficult for _____ woman to succeed as _____ lawyer; 50 years ago, however, _____ woman who entered law school faced many obstacles.

9. Thinking it would give him an image as _____ super salesperson, Tony longed for _____ big, fancy car. To tell _____ truth,

_____ small, plain car his company provided was _____ big disappointment to him.

10. In many parts of Canada, _____ college student who begins school in _____ last part of August finishes _____ school year in April.

GO TO WEB

EXERCISES 31.5, 31.6

No Article (Zero Article)

No article is used in general statements with noncount and plural nouns unless the noun is particularized or made specific in some way. Study the following guidelines and examples.

> 1. Do not use an article with noncount nouns: Water is necessary for life. Rice is China's staple food. Gold is valuable.

No article is required with *water*, *life*, *rice*, *food*, and *gold* in these sentences.

> 2. In general statements, no article is required with plural nouns: We like bananas. Sharks are dangerous creatures. People need friends.

To decide whether or not you need an article with a plural noun, you must determine whether the word is being used in a general or a specific sense. The following exercise will give you practice in making the correct decision.

Exercise 31.6

Use either *the* or no article in the blanks below. Do not use *a/an*.

1. I like to study _____ history; I have learned that _____ history of Bosnia is tragic.

2. Writer Tom Wolfe always wears _____ spats; _____ spats he wears are white leather coverings for his shoes.

3. Everyone has _____ problems in _____ life. _____ problems may be big or small, but everyone must cope with them.

4. _____ venison is _____ meat that comes from _____ deer. _____ venison we ate last night was delicious.

5. Some of _____ most important products that Canada buys from India are _____ tea, _____ cotton, and _____ rice.

6. _____ milk is my baby's favourite drink, but she often spills _____ milk that I put in her cup.

7. _____ kindness is an attractive quality in people, and _____ kindness of that woman is known to all of us.

8. _____ jewellery is a popular gift; my boyfriend loved _____ jewellery that I gave him.

9. Paula is studying _____ architecture in university, and she is going to Los Angeles to look at _____ architecture of Frank Gehry.

10. _____ boots are a necessary item of winter clothing in Canada, but _____ boots I bought last year were not very warm.

Using *The* or No Article in Geographical Names

Place names in English are inconsistent in their requirement for the definite article or no article. For example, you use *the* with oceans (*the Pacific Ocean, the Indian Ocean*) but not with lakes (*Lake Ontario, Shuswap Lake*). Why? Is there a guiding principal here? Unfortunately, no. You must learn the conventions that govern the use of articles in geographical and other place names.

No Article	**Examples**
Continents	Asia, Australia, Europe, South America
Countries	Canada, China, Italy, Laos, Mexico
Cities	London, Paris, Penticton, Rio de Janeiro
Lakes, bays, falls	Lake Simcoe, Hudson Bay, Niagara Falls
Streets and parks	Princess Street, Portage Avenue, High Park
Colleges or universities (with *College* or *University* after name)	Humber College, Red Deer College, Oxford University, Trent University
Halls	Carnegie Hall, Convocation Hall

Definite Article (The)	**Examples**
Plural place names	the Americas, the Balkans, the Maritimes
Countries (or other bodies) that refer to a political union or association	the United Kingdom, the United States
Mountain ranges	the Himalayas, the Rocky Mountains
Groups of islands, *but* not individual islands	the Philippine Islands, the Thousand Islands, the West Indies, *but* Long Island, Manitoulin Island, Vancouver Island
Oceans	the Arctic Ocean, the Atlantic Ocean, the Indian Ocean
Groups of lakes	the Finger Lakes, the Great Lakes
Rivers, seas, straits	the St. Lawrence River, the Caribbean, the Straits of Magellan
Colleges and universities that have *of* in the name	the College of the Americas, the University of New Brunswick, the University of Saskatchewan
Buildings, towers, bridges, hotels, libraries, museums	the Empire State Building, the CN Tower, the Granville Street Bridge, the Banff Springs Hotel, the Library of Parliament, the Bata Shoe Museum
Deserts, forests, peninsulas	the Sahara Desert, the Black Forest, the Gaspé Peninsula
Points of the globe or compass	the Equator, the Tropic of Capricorn, the Middle East, the North Pole, the Southern Hemisphere

Exercise 31.7

Use either *the* or no article in the blanks below.

1. _____ earthquakes sometimes happen in _____ British Columbia, but they almost never occur in _____ prairie provinces, _____ central Canada, _____ Quebec, or _____ Maritimes.

2. Many of _____ geographical names in Canada are derived from _____ languages of Aboriginal peoples who lived here for thousands of _____ years before _____ first European settlers arrived.

3. For example, _____ Manitoulin Island, in _____ Lake Huron, got its name from the Algonkian word *Manitou*, which means "spirit."

4. _____ Queen Charlotte Islands (also known as Haida Gwaii) off _____ British Columbia coast consist of about 150 islands, the largest of which are _____ Graham Island and _____ Moresby Island.

5. _____ Saskatchewan, _____ province of Ontario, _____ Magnetawan River, _____ Lake Okanagan, and even _____ name "Canada" itself are all examples of _____ influence of native people's languages on Canada's place names.

6. I enjoyed _____ speech by Ms. Gonzalez last night. She spoke

about _____ life in _____ Peru.

7. _____ Mojave Desert is in _____ state of California, not too

far from _____ Sierra Nevada Mountains.

8. We had a wonderful holiday in _____ Dominican Republic on our

way back from _____ South America.

9. _____ St. Lawrence River forms _____ boundary between

_____ Ontario in _____ Canada and _____ New York

in _____ United States.

10. _____ Bering Strait is between _____ state of Alaska and

_____ former U.S.S.R, now known as _____ Russia.

GO TO WEB

EXERCISES 31.7, 31.8

Exercise 31.8

Fill in each space with the correct article or leave it blank if no article is required.

You can tell all you need to know about _____ person from

_____ shoes he or she wears. Our economics teacher, for example,

wears _____ worn-out, old brown leather loafers. These shoes tell us

that he doesn't care about _____ appearances, that he likes to save

_____ money, and that he enjoys _____ comfort more than

_____ style. On the other hand, our computer teacher is _____

fashionably dressed woman who wears _____ different pair of shoes

almost every day. My favourites are her black patent leather pumps with

gold buckles on _____ toes. Such _____ stylish selection of

_____ shoes tells me that she is _____ fashion-conscious person

who cares what _____ people think of her appearance. She appreci-

ates quality and is willing to spend money to buy it. If my theory about

_____ relationship between _____ character and footwear is

valid, I would be interested in _____ analysis of my English professor,

who wears _____ black army boots for two days, _____ white

running shoes _____ next day, then _____ pair of cowboy boots,

and ends the week with _____ pair of platform disco shoes.

Exercise 31.9

Correct any misused or missing articles in the paragraph below.

Ramon was searching a supermarket shelves for box of detergent when

he noticed sugar spilling from broken bag in his shopping cart. He put bro-

ken bag of sugar back on shelf and put new bag in cart. Then, as he went

up and down the aisles of supermarket, he added coffee, orange juice, the

jar of jam, and a fruit to his cart. After selecting bunch of grapes and bas-

ket of peaches, Ramon went to vegetable counter where he picked up broc-

coli, beans, carrots, and kilogram of tomatoes. Finally, he added package of cookies and made his way to a cash register. Only after he had paid for his purchases and left store did he realize that he had forgotten a detergent.

Exercise 31.10

Correct any misused or missing articles in the paragraph below.

The goldfish make the terrific pets. I bought three goldfish at local pet store for five dollars, a price that wouldn't even buy collar for dog. Goldfish are also easy to care for. I change water in their bowl once the week, throw the pinch of food in bowl twice the day, and they seem happy and healthy. Furthermore, goldfish are very interesting to watch. I can spend an hours watching them cruise around their little world, occasionally nuzzling or fighting each other. The goldfish may not bark at intruders or rub against my leg when I come home, but for me they are as close to the perfect as pets can get.

Exercise 31.11

Edit these paragraphs for errors in the use of articles. There are 25 errors.

I love the travelling and have been to many interesting places around world. My favourite places are the China and the Morocco because they are very different from Canada in culture, language, architecture, and cuisine. When I go to United States or the Great Britain or Australia, I find an experiences much like those here in Canada. In China and Morocco, I am always conscious that I am far away from a home.

In Morocco, I sampled couscous, which is very popular dish in the North Africa. In the markets, people dress in long, flowing robes and a tasseled red hats called fez. The buildings are all made of the clay, and many of cities are surrounded by large walls.

The China, too, is fascinating to me as the Canadian because it is so different. The Beijing is the very interesting city to visit, and I also enjoyed a trip to a Great Wall. In a countryside, an oxen are used to plow fields, and bicycles are more common than automobiles. The food is very spicy in some areas of country, and visitors will be surprised by variety of foods in different regions.

Morocco and China are not the countries like Canada where food, dress, and architecture are same wherever you go. Travel is wonderful way to learn about the world.

32

Practising with Prepositions

Prepositions are small words that often cause big problems for second-language learners. People who speak English as a first language are never confused by the distinction between *in* and *on* or *from* and *for*. But these little words often puzzle and frustrate second-language learners.

Prepositions have no special endings or inflections that make them easy to identify. (For instance, *-ous* endings usually indicate adjectives; e.g., *prosperous*; and *-ity* endings suggest nouns; e.g., *prosperity*.) The only characteristic that prepositions have in common is that most of them are short words.

Sometimes two short prepositions are joined to make a one-word compound (e.g., *into, without, upon*). People who learn English as a second language must memorize these words and their sometimes multiple meanings. There is no other way to learn how to use prepositions correctly.

A preposition is a word that begins a group of words known as a **prepositional phrase** (preposition + object).

after lunch   *to* school

during the week   *under* the car

in the closet   *with* my brother

In each of these phrases, the first word is a **preposition**. You can see from these examples that prepositions often clarify such relationships as time, place, or direction. Every prepositional phrase requires an **object** (a noun or pronoun); *lunch, week, closet, school, car, brother* are the objects in the prepositional phrases above.

Below is a list of common prepositions used in English.

above	beneath	into	throughout
about	beside	like	till
across	between	near	to
after	beyond	of	toward
against	by	off	under
along	despite	on	underneath
among	down	out	until
around	during	outside	up
at	for	over	upon
before	from	past	with
behind	in	since	within
below	inside	through	without

We'll break up this long list into four categories to make it easier for you to learn the various uses of prepositions. Each of the four charts below is organized according to the relationship that the preposition points to. The charts also provide brief definitions and examples of prepositions used correctly.

One of the reasons that prepositions are confusing is that the same word can be used with more than one meaning; hence, some occur in more than one chart. See *at*, *by*, and *from*, for example. Please note that the following charts include only the most common prepositions and their meanings. Your dictionary provides more extensive definitions and examples.

Check your understanding of prepositions by doing the exercises that follow each chart. Occasionally, there is more than one preposition that could be used correctly in a blank. Answers for exercises in this chapter begin on page 480. If you make any mistakes, study the chart again, and do the Web exercises that we have provided.

PREPOSITIONS THAT INDICATE TIME RELATIONSHIPS

Preposition	Uses/Meaning	Examples
after	one event follows another event	We will have dinner *after* the concert.
at	used with a specific time of the day	The bell rang *at* midnight. He has dinner *at* 7:00.
before	one event comes before (precedes) another	Mail your tax return *before* April 30.
by	no later than	Finish your assignment *by* Friday.
during	indicates a period of time, usually undivided	I usually sleep *during* a long flight.
for	indicates a quantity of time	The photographer needs you *for* an hour.
from	indicates the time in the future when something starts	The concert is three days *from* now.
in	used with a part of the day/month/year/season	I'll see you *in* the morning. My birthday is *in* March. Jessamyn was born *in* 1976. Birds fly south *in* the fall.

Preposition	Uses/Meaning	Examples
in	identifies a period of time by which something will happen; also means *during*	I'll see you *in* an hour. Traffic congestion has gotten much worse *in* recent years.
of	used with a date and month	People light fireworks on the first *of* July.
on	used with a day of the week or a specific date	I work *on* Saturday. Passover begins *on* April 7 this year.
since	from one time until now	I have not eaten *since* breakfast.
until, till	as far as the time when another event will occur	I won't have anything to eat *until* dinner.
within	not more than the specified period of time	Call me if you don't receive a cheque *within* a week.

Exercise 32.1

1. If you don't pay your credit card bill _____ the due date, the company will add interest charges to next month's bill.

2. The blood tests are supposed to be taken _____ the morning on an empty stomach, so don't eat anything _____ your arrival at the lab.

3. _____ Adil lost interest in his classes, it has been difficult for him to stay awake _____ lectures.

4. You will finish your degree a year _____ now, and I would like to have a party for you when you graduate _____ June.

5. Francisco arrived _____ the summer; he was born _____ noon _____ July 11, 1962.

GO TO WEB

EXERCISE 32.1

PREPOSITIONS THAT INDICATE PLACE OR POSITION

Preposition	Uses/Meaning	Examples
above	directly higher	His apartment is *above* ours.
across	on the other side	She lives *across* the street.
among	included in a group (more than two)	She sat *among* her 12 grandchildren.
at	indicating a specific location; also with specific addresses	Xhonghong is *at* school. We live *at* 1507 Marine Drive.
behind	in back of	The grizzly bear is *behind* you!
below	directly lower	Her apartment is *below* ours.
beneath	under	Your coat is *beneath* mine in the pile.
beside	next to	Please sit *beside* me.
between	in the middle of two	She sat *between* her two grandchildren.
by	very near to, beside	He has a house *by* the river.
in	within an area or space	St. John's is *in* Newfoundland.
near	close to; within a short distance	I live *near* the subway.
on	covering or forming part of a surface	Please write *on* the blackboard.

Preposition	Uses/Meaning	Examples
over	higher than something else	The helicopter flew *over* the highway.
under	lower than something else	The subway runs *under* this theatre.
underneath	beneath, close under	Her purse was *underneath* the bed.
within	not farther than the distance from	The school is *within* a kilometre of her apartment.

Exercise 32.2

1. Either put the dishes _____ the table or put them away _____ the cupboard.

2. What time does my plane land _____ Vancouver, and who will take me to my hotel, which is _____ Main and Hastings?

3. _____ a wrestling match, there are ropes _____ the wrestlers and the audience.

4. The young man sat down right _____ the teacher who was sitting _____ 15 of his other students.

5. Skunks live _____ holes called burrows, and that awful smell suggests you have a skunk burrow _____ a few metres of your back door.

GO TO WEB

EXERCISE 32.2

PREPOSITIONS THAT INDICATE DIRECTION OR MOVEMENT

Preposition	Uses/Meaning	Examples
across	from one side to the other	She walked *across* the room.
around	indicating movement within a larger area; moving past something in a circle	The sprinters ran *around* the track. Assad sailed *around* the world.
by	moving past someone or something	Michel walked *by* his ex-wife without speaking. The car drove *by* the restaurant.
down	from a higher to a lower level	I walked quickly *down* the stairs to the basement.
from	indicating place where movement away began	Our flight to Vancouver left *from* Hong Kong.
into	moving to a point inside	Nguyen dove *into* the cold water.
out of	moving away from	She jumped *out of* bed happily.
past	moving by someone or something	Michel walked *past* his ex-wife without speaking. The car drove *past* the restaurant.
through	passing from one side to another	The Assiniboine River flows *through* Winnipeg.
to	movement in the direction of a specific place	She walks *to* school every day.
toward	in the general direction of something	Walk *toward* the ocean and enjoy the beautiful sunset.
up	from a lower to a higher point	I walked quickly *up* the stairs to the attic.

Exercise 32.3

1. We drove _____ your house last night, but we didn't stop because no one seemed to be home.

2. After Javier reached the top of the hill, he walked back _____ the slope heading _____ the cabin.

3. The 401 highway goes directly _____ the city of Toronto, but the newer 407 highway goes _____ the outskirts of the city.

4. In order to get _____ Florida at the end of their holiday, they had to take a flight _____ Miami back home to Halifax.

5. The thief climbed _____ the ladder and crawled _____ the house _____ an open upstairs window.

GO TO WEB

EXERCISE 32.3

OTHER PREPOSITIONAL RELATIONSHIPS: RELATION, SOURCE, MANNER, POSSESSION, QUANTITY

Preposition	Uses/Meaning	Examples
about	on the subject of someone or something	This book is *about* love. We know *about* your family.
about	concerning something	We can do something *about* the problem.
for	indicating the person receiving something	The message is *for* you. What can I do *for* you?
for	with regard to purpose or function	Tharshini received roses *for* her birthday. He works *for* a car dealership.

Preposition	Uses/Meaning	Examples
from	indicating the source of someone or something; indicating the product or material from which something is made	Réné comes *from* the Gaspé. Wine is made *from* grapes. Penicillin is an antibiotic that was originally made *from* mould.
from	indicating the reason for something	The baby cried *from* hunger.
from	used to make a distinction between two things	English is very different *from* French.
of	belonging to somebody or something	He is a friend *of* mine. Please close the lid *of* the box.
of	concerning, relating to, or showing something	This is a photograph *of* my boyfriend. Do you have a map *of* Mexico?
of	indicating what is measured, counted, or contained	We drank a litre *of* wine.
of	used with *some, many, a few*, etc.	Some *of* the students failed the exam. A few *of* the CDs were stolen.
with	in the company of someone or something	I took a vacation *with* my husband. Please leave the keys *with* the parking attendant.
with	having or carrying something	The child *with* the red hair is her son. Take the coffee *with* you.
with	indicating the manner or condition	She did her homework *with* care. He was trembling *with* rage.
with	indicating the tool or instrument used	You can see the stars *with* a telescope.

Preposition	Uses/Meaning	Examples
without	not having, not using	No one can live *without* water. Can you see *without* your glasses?

Exercise 32.4

1. Farida took only one picture _____ me together _____ you.

2. After spending a day _____ the twins, we recognized that they are very different _____ one another.

3. Some _____ us were surprised to learn that Scotch whiskey is made _____ barley.

4. I know very little _____ the man except that he treats his children _____ real tenderness.

5. Immigrants _____ South America often find that working in Canada is difficult _____ a good knowledge of English or French.

GO TO WEB

EXERCISE 32.4

The exercises that follow will give you practice in using prepositions correctly. Fill in the blanks with appropriate prepositions chosen from those listed on page 386. When you have completed the exercise, compare your answers with our suggestions on page 481.

Exercise 32.5

1. We wake up _____ 7:00 and finish our breakfast sometime _____ 7:30.

2. _____ the argument, the two men would not speak _____ each other.

3. No one is permitted to leave _____ the conclusion _____ the performance.

4. I'll meet you _____ front of the restaurant that is located _____ the corner _____ Princess and Division Streets _____ Kingston.

Exercise 32.6

1. Did you get any of the work done _____ class time or will you have to finish the assignment _____ class?

2. There was a pool _____ oil _____ the car, so we knew that we would have to take it _____ a mechanic _____ repairs.

3. He came _____ the house quickly, jumped _____ his car, and sped _____ the street right _____ a police car.

Exercise 32.7

1. I saw him _____ the first time _____ midnight _____ a club _____ downtown Montreal _____ Saturday, October 31.

2. If you look _____ the painting _____ the wall, you will find a safe _____ a lot _____ money _____ it.

3. This is a secret _____ you and me: the police came _____ the house _____ midnight because the children had been left alone _____ their parents.

4. I work _____ 8:00 _____ the morning _____ 8:00 _____ night, and I am usually exhausted _____ the end _____ that time.

Exercise 32.8

My friend Jamil goes _____ school _____ the King Edward campus _____ Vancouver Community College. _____ the same time, he works full-time _____ his family's grocery business. The store is _____ the street _____ the college, so Jamil doesn't have to travel very far _____ school and work. He has to leave school _____ 4:00 p.m. every day so that he can work _____ the counter of the store selling goods _____ customers. _____ September, Jamil has been studying computer and business courses at the college, and he puts a lot _____ effort _____ his school work. Because he works every night _____ midnight, he sometimes does his homework _____ quiet moments _____ the store. _____ his hard work, Jamil's family couldn't keep the store going. Jamil is working _____ two important goals: he is determined to succeed _____ his studies, and he is equally determined to help his family prosper.

GO TO WEB

EXERCISE 32.5

Exercise 32.9

Fill in the blanks with appropriate prepositions chosen from the list on page 386.

1. We fixed the hole _____ the ceiling _____ duct tape.

2. Wally, why don't you go _____ the house and fix dinner _____ us?

3. The money will be split _____ the four people who bought the winning lottery ticket _____ January 25.

4. We don't live very far _____ the airport, so I'll be glad to get you there _____ your flight.

5. Michelle has a very large nose _____ a pair of small, close-set eyes. She wears a lot _____ heavy make-up _____ her face.

6. They told us all _____ their trip _____ Australia _____ their return _____ Canada.

7. _____ the opposition _____ the neighbours, they are going to go ahead and build a fence _____ the two properties.

8. Even if you have been speaking English _____ a long time, it is easy to make occasional mistakes _____ prepositions.

Appendixes

Readings

BUMBLERS, MARTINETS, AND PROS
Nell Waldman

1   The playwright George Bernard Shaw provided us with the memorable definition, "Those who can, do. Those who can't, teach." The film director Woody
Allen took the definition one step further: "Those who can't teach, teach gym."
At one time or another, most of us have suffered these truisms. We've all
encountered teachers who fit Shaw's definition, as well as some who manage
to do their jobs successfully, even cheerfully. Overall, most teachers fit into one
of three categories: Bumblers, Martinets, and Pros.

2   Every student gets a Bumbler at least once. She's the teacher who trips over
the doorjamb as she makes her first entrance. She looks permanently flustered,
can't find her lesson plan, and dithers as she scrambles through her mess of
books and papers. The Bumbler can't handle the simplest educational technologies: chalk self-destructs in her fingers, overhead projectors blow up at her
touch, and VCRs jam if she so much as looks in their direction. Organization isn't
Ms. Bumbler's strong point either. She drifts off in midsentence, eyes focussed
dreamily out the window. Students can easily derail her with off-topic questions.
She'll forget to collect assignments or to give the test that everyone has studied for. The Bumbler is an amiable sort, but her mind is on a perpetual slow boat
to nowhere. Students can learn in her class, but only if they are willing to take
a great deal of initiative.

3   Martinet was the name of a seventeenth-century French general who
invented a particularly nasty system of military drill. Thus, the word itself has
come to mean a strict disciplinarian, a stickler for the rules, a tough "drill ser-
geant." As a teacher, the Martinet is an uptight, rigid authoritarian who sends
shivers down students' spines. He rarely smiles, certainly not during the first

month. His voice is harsh, biting, and he specializes in the barbed response and the humiliating putdown. His classes unfold in a precise and boring manner. Each minute is accounted for, as he scouts the room for any disruptive or slumbering captives to be brought to heel. He tolerates no searching questions or interesting digressions. His assignments are lengthy and tedious; his tests are notoriously fearsome. Instead of the critical inquiry into ideas, rote learning takes place in the Martinet's classroom. And it takes place at the expense of the patience and self-esteem of his students.

4   Every once in a while, a student is blessed with a teacher who can be described as a Professional. The Pro is characterized by a genuine liking and respect for students and is motivated by enthusiasm for the subject matter. This teacher is organized enough to present lessons clearly, but not so hidebound as to cut off questions or the occasional excursion along an interesting sideroad of learning. The Pro's classroom is relaxed, friendly, yet stimulating enough to keep students concentrating on the task at hand. Assignments are designed to enhance learning; tests are rigorous but fair. Landing in the Pro's class is a stroke of luck. Such a teacher is a gift, for the Pro imparts the desire and ability to learn to the students he or she encounters.

5   These characterizations of the Bumbler, the Martinet, and the Pro are, of course, extreme portraits of some of the worst and best qualities a teacher can possess. Indeed, some teachers, in Jekyll-and-Hyde fashion, display characteristics of two or more types, sometimes in a single class period! In an ideal world and a perfect course, the student would be given a choice of instructors. Who would opt for a Bumbler or a Martinet given the chance to sign up for a Pro?

Source: Waldman, Nell. "Bumblers, Martinets, and Pros." *Canadian Content*. Ed. Sarah Norton and Nell Waldman. Toronto: Harcourt, 1988. 108–110.

THE CASE AGAINST QUICKSPEAK

Brian Green

"Thx fr yr rply. no prob. ill call mtg fr tues @ 9 ok? :-)"

1   If you aren't familiar with e-mail jargon, this message may look like something in military code or from outer space. Those who use e-mail regularly, however, will recognize it as an example of a new form of communication that I call "quickspeak." Many people these days are in such a hurry that they can't take time to spell, punctuate, or write complete sentences in their electronic correspondence. Of course, these folks wouldn't dream of writing messages like this on paper, but there's something about e-mail that makes them think it's acceptable, even fashionable, to ignore everything they ever knew about writing, in

order to "save time." Call me a dinosaur, an antique from the days of the inkwell and quill pen, but I will not succumb to quickspeak. I will continue to ensure that my e-mail is as structured and correct as any other mail I send. Why? Because I want my message to be clearly understood, I want to send messages that are thoughtful and complete, and I want to present a positive image to my readers.

2   "But you know what I mean!" protests an e-mail correspondent (written as "bt u no wht i meen :-]".) And it's true that, with some effort, I can make out what I think she means, but I'd also understand if she said, "Duh . . . , we gonna eat soon?" while scratching her stomach. Any written message, whether stored in print or electrons, communicates more than the bare meaning of its words. It tells the reader something about the importance of the message, the ability and intelligence of the writer, and the writer's consideration for the reader.

3   Quickspeak tells the reader that the writer doesn't care much about the message or the reader. It also implies that the writer may not be capable of writing correctly. At the very least, quickspeak betrays a writer as sloppy and disorganized. My father used to describe this approach to communication as "slapdash," and that's as good a term as any. A slap-dash writer is unlikely to make it into the executive suite.

4   Although I am usually able to decipher the gist of quickspeak, I'm seldom sure that I have translated the message accurately. In many cases, this failure stems from the fact that the writer didn't provide complete or accurate information. Take the example that introduces this essay. I know there will be a meeting (about what?) on Tuesday (which week?) at 9:00 (a.m. or p.m.?). Where is this meeting? Who will be present? What documents am I expected to bring? Without the answers to these questions, how can I prepare? Far from saving time, quickspeak actually wastes it. Now I have to respond to the e-mail sender to find out the answers to these questions. At least three messages will be needed where one would have done. If only the writer had recognized this basic rule of writing: to be brief takes time!

5   E-mail is no different from any other business correspondence: it must be clear and concise. Achieving clarity and conciseness is not difficult, but it does require planning. Begin with an introduction that briefly explains the purpose of your message. Next, outline how you are going to develop that message. Use numbered or bulleted points to guide the reader from your position statement through your reasoning to your conclusion. Reinforce your message with a conclusion that states any follow-up actions you require and that confirms the time, place, and responsibilities of those who are contributing to the project. Next, reread your message as if you were reading it for the first time. Revise to be sure that you have included all the necessary details: dates, reference numbers, times and places of meetings, and whatever other information is needed to get the right people together in the right places, on the right days, at the right times, with the right information in their briefcases. Use a spell-checker, but don't rely on it to catch all your errors and typos. Remember: A clear message, clearly delivered, is the essence of effective communication.

6   People who write in quickspeak ignore the reason that rules for correct writing evolved in the first place. Writing that communicates accurately depends upon precise thinking. A message with a statement of purpose, logically arranged points, and a confirming summary is the work of a writer whose message has been thought through and can be trusted. In contrast, quickspeak, which can be bashed out in no time, reflects no planning, little coherent thought, and no sense of order or priority. The message, the reader, and, ultimately, the writer all suffer as a result.

7   My co-worker who wrote the e-mail message that introduces this argument is "slap-dash" and may be semi-literate. That, at least, is the impression she gives. She has wasted not only my time but also her own. And, by using quickspeak, she hasn't taken advantage of the power of precise, structured language to produce clear, complete messages. Her trendy message communicates more about her than it does about the subject of her e-mail, and what it says is far from flattering.

THE CANADIAN CLIMATE
D'Arcy McHayle

1   The student who comes to Canada from a tropical country is usually prepared for cold Canadian winters, a sharp contrast to our hot northern summers. What the student may not be prepared for is the fact that Canadian personalities reflect the country's temperature range but are less extreme. Canadian personalities fall into two categories: warm and cool. The two groups share the Canadian traits of restraint and willingness to compromise, but they are dissimilar in their attitudes both to their own country and to the newcomer's country of origin.

2   Warm Canadians are, first of all, warm about Canada and will, at the first sound of a foreign accent, describe with rapture the magnificence of the country from the Maritimes to the West Coast, praising the beauty of the Prairies, the Rockies, and even the "unique climate of the Far North." Canadian leisure activities are enthusiastically described, with a special place reserved for hockey. "So you've never skated? You'll learn. Come with us; you'll have a great time." The Warm Canadian wants the newcomer to share in the pleasures of life in Canada. When she turns her attention to the foreign student's homeland, she seeks enlightenment, asking questions about its geography, social and economic conditions, and other concerns not usually addressed in travel and tourism brochures. The Warm Canadian understands that the residents of tropical countries are not exotic flower children who sing and dance with natural rhythm but are individuals who, like Canadians, face the problems of earning a living and raising a family.

3   Compared to the Warm Canadian, who exudes a springlike optimism, the Cool Canadian is like November. Conditions may not be unbearable for the moment, but they are bound to get much colder before there is any sign of a thaw. The Cool Canadian's first words on hearing that the foreign student is from a warm country are, "How could you leave such a lovely climate to come to a place like this?" Not from him will one hear of Banff, or Niagara Falls, or anything except how cold and dark and dreary it gets in the winter. It sometimes seems that the Cool Canadian's description of his own country is designed to encourage newcomers to pack their bags and return home at once. As for the foreign student's country of origin, the Cool Canadian is not really interested, although he may declare, "I hear it's beautiful. I'd love to go there." Beyond that, however, he has no interest in information that may shake the foundations of his collection of myths, half-truths, and geographic inaccuracies. This type of Canadian, if he does travel to a tropical country, will ensure that he remains at all times within the safe confines of his hotel and that he returns to Canada with all his preconceived ideas intact.

4   Foreign students should not be upset by the Cool Canadian; they should ignore his chilliness. Besides, like a heat wave in March, an unexpected thaw can occur and create extraordinary warmth. Likewise, a Warm Canadian may become a little frosty sometimes, but, like a cold spell in June, this condition won't last. And when the weather changes, foreign students will find an opportunity to display their own qualities of understanding, tolerance, and acceptance of others as they are.

Source: McHayle, D'Arcy. "The Canadian Climate." *Essay Essentials with Readings.* 2nd ed. Ed. Sarah Norton and Brian Green. Toronto: Harcourt, 1999. 170–171. Reprinted by permission of Harcourt Canada.

AN IMMIGRANT'S SPLIT PERSONALITY
Sun-Kyung Yi

1   I am Korean-Canadian. But the hyphen often snaps in two, obliging me to choose to act as either a Korean or a Canadian, depending on where I am and who I'm with.

2   When I was younger, toying with the idea of entertaining two separate identities was a real treat, like a secret game for which no one knew the rules but me. I was known as Angela to the outside world, and as Sun-Kyung at home. I ate bologna sandwiches in the school lunch room and rice and kimchee for dinner. I chatted about teen idols and giggled with my girlfriends during my classes, and ambitiously practised piano and studied in the evenings, planning to become a doctor when I grew up. I waved hellos and goodbyes to my teach-

ers, but bowed to my parents' friends visiting our home. I could also look straight in the eyes of my teachers and friends and talk frankly with them instead of staring at my feet with my mouth shut when Koreans talked to me. Going outside the home meant I was able to relax from the constraints of my cultural conditioning, until I walked back in the door and had to return to being an obedient and submissive daughter.

3   The game soon ended when I realized that it had become a way of life, that I couldn't change the rules without disappointing my parents and questioning all the cultural implications and consequences that came with being a hyphenated Canadian.

4   Many have tried to convince me that I am a Canadian, like all other immigrants in the country, but those same people also ask me which country I came from with great curiosity, following with questions about the type of food I ate and the language I spoke. It's difficult to feel a sense of belonging and acceptance when you are regarded as "one of them." "Those Koreans, they work hard. . . . You must be fantastic at math and science." (No.) "Do your parents own a corner store?" (No.)

5   Koreans and Canadians just can't seem to merge into "us" and "we."

6   Some people advised me that I should just take the best of both worlds and disregard the rest. That's ideal, but unrealistic when my old culture demands a complete conformity with very little room to manoeuvre for new and different ideas.

7   After a lifetime of practice, I thought I could change faces and become Korean on demand with grace and perfection. But working with a small Korean company in Toronto proved me wrong. I quickly became estranged from my own people. My parents were ecstatic at the thought of their daughter finally finding her roots and having a working opportunity to speak my native tongue and absorb the culture. For me, it was the most painful and frustrating two and one-half months of my life.

8   When the president of the company boasted that he "operated a little Korea," he meant it literally. A Canadianized Korean was not tolerated. I looked like a Korean; therefore, I had to talk, act, and think like one, too. Being accepted meant a total surrender to ancient codes of behaviour rooted in Confucian thought, while leaving the "Canadian" part of me out in the parking lot with my '86 Buick. In the first few days at work, I was bombarded with inquiries about my marital status. When I told them I was single, they spent the following days trying to match me up with available bachelors in the company and the community. I was expected to accept my inferior position as a woman and to behave accordingly. It was not a place to practise my feminist views, or be an individual without being condemned. Little Korea is a place for men (who filled all the senior positions) and women don't dare speak up or disagree with their male counterparts. The president (all employees bow to him and call him Mr. President) asked me to act more like a lady and smile. I was openly scorned

by a senior employee because I spoke more fluent English than Korean. The cook in the kitchen shook her head in disbelief upon discovering that my cooking skills were limited to boiling a package of instant noodles. "You want a good husband, learn to cook," she advised me.

9   In less than a week I became an outsider because I refused to conform and blindly nod my head in agreement to what my elders (which happened to be everybody else in the company) said. A month later, I was demoted because "members of the workplace and the Korean community" had complained that I just wasn't "Korean enough," and I had "too much power for a single woman." My father suggested that "when in Rome do as the Romans." But that's exactly what I was doing. I am in Canada so I was freely acting like a Canadian, and it cost me my job.

10   My father also said, "It doesn't matter how Canadian you think you are, just look in the mirror and it'll tell you who you *really* are." But what he didn't realize is that an immigrant has to embrace the new culture to enjoy and benefit from what it has to offer. Of course, I will always be Korean by virtue of my appearance and early conditioning, but I am also happily Canadian and want to take full advantage of all that such citizenship confers. But for now I remain slightly distant from both cultures, accepted fully by neither. The hyphenated Canadian personifies the ideal of multiculturalism, but unless the host culture and the immigrant cultures can find ways to merge their distinct identities, sharing the best of both, this cultural schizophrenia will continue.

Source: Yi, Sun-Kyung. "An Immigrant's Split Personality." *The Globe and Mail*, 12 Apr. 1992. Reprinted by permission of Sun-Kyung Yi.

THE MYTH OF CANADIAN DIVERSITY

1   Canadians cling to three myths about their country. The first is that it is young. In fact, Canada is well advanced into middle age. At 127, it has existed as a unified state for longer than either Italy (unified in 1870) or Germany (1871). Less than a third of the 180-odd nations now belonging to the United Nations existed in 1945, when Canada was already a mature 78. We were 51 when Iraq and Austria—two countries many think of as old—came into being.

2   The second myth is that, in everything but geography, Canada is a small country—small in population, small in economic heft. In fact, our population of 27 million is a fair size by international standards, bigger than that of Austria, Hungary, Sweden, Norway, Finland, Romania, Greece, Algeria, Peru and Venezuela, to name only a few. Our economy, by traditional measures, is the seventh-largest in the world.

3   But the most important myth about Canada—the one that distorts our self-image, warps our politics and may one day tear us apart—is the myth of

Canadian diversity. Almost any Canadian will tell you that his Canada is a remarkably varied place. "Canada, with its regional, linguistic and cultural diversity, has never been easy to govern," wrote *The Globe and Mail* when Jean Chrétien became Prime Minister. . . . Provincial politicians routinely parrot this myth to push for greater regional powers; federal politicians repeat it to let people know what a hard job they have.

4   In fact, Canada is one of the most homogeneous countries in the world. A foreign visitor can travel from Vancouver in the West to Kingston in the centre without finding any significant difference in accent, in dress, in cuisine or even, in a broad sense, in values. A highschool student in Winnipeg talks, looks and acts much like his counterpart in Prince George. Where they do exist, our regional differences are no match for those of most other countries.

5   Canada may have a few regional accents in its English-speaking parts—the salty dialect of Newfoundland, the rural tones of the Ottawa Valley—but these are nothing compared with the dozens in the United States or Britain. It may have two official languages, but that is unlikely to impress India, which has 14.

6   To be certain, we have our French–English divide, two "nations" living under one roof. That hardly makes us unique either. Spain has the Catalans and the Basques. Russia has the Tatars, Ukrainians, Belarussians, Chechens, Moldavians, Udmurts, Kazakhs, Avars and Armenians. And, although few would dispute that francophone Quebec is indeed a distinct society, the differences between Quebec and the rest of Canada are diminishing over time. As Lucien Bouchard himself has noted, we share a host of common attitudes—an attachment to the Canadian social system, tolerance of minorities, a respect for government and law.

7   Even our much-discussed ethnic differences are overstated. Although Canada is an immigrant nation and Canadians spring from a variety of backgrounds, a recent study from the C.D. Howe Institute says that the idea of a "Canadian mosaic"—as distinct from the American "melting pot"—is a fallacy. In *The Illusion of Difference*, University of Toronto sociologists Jeffrey Reitz and Raymond Breton show that immigrants to Canada assimilate as quickly into the mainstream society as immigrants to the United States do. In fact, Canadians are less likely than Americans to favour holding on to cultural differences based on ethnic background. If you don't believe Mr. Reitz and Mr. Breton, visit any big-city highschool, where the speech and behaviour of immigrant students just a few years in Canada is indistinguishable from that of any fifth-generation classmate.

8   This is not to say that Canada is a nation of cookie-cutter people. The differences among our regions, and between our two main language groups, are real. But in recent years we have elevated those differences into a cult. For all our disputes about language and ethnicity and regional rifts, our differences shrink beside our similarities, and the things that unite us dwarf those that divide us.

Source: "The Myth of Canadian Diversity." *The Globe and Mail* 13 June 1994: A12. Reprinted by permission of *The Globe and Mail*.

METAMORPHOSIS
Sarah Norton

1   Meet newborn Jeanie. Weak and helpless as a caterpillar, Jeanie's only defence against hunger and pain is the one sound she can make at will: crying. Eighteen months later, Jeanie will be a busy toddler who asks questions, expresses opinions, and even makes jokes. From helplessness to assertiveness: how does this wondrous transformation take place? To discover how we learn to speak, let's follow Jeanie as she develops from infant to toddler, from caterpillar to butterfly.

2   Infancy, the first stage of language development, literally means "unable to speak." For the first six months of her life, Jeanie isn't able to talk, but she can respond to speech. Shortly after birth, she'll turn her head toward the sound of a voice. By two weeks of age, she will prefer the sound of a human voice to non-human sounds. Between two and four months, she will learn to distinguish the voices of her caregivers from those of strangers, and she knows whether those voices are speaking soothingly or angrily. By the time she is two months old, Jeanie will have learned to coo as well as cry, and she coos happily when people smile and talk to her. Now she can express contentment as well as discomfort. At around four months of age, Jeanie's happy sounds become more varied and sophisticated: she registers delight on a scale ranging from throaty chuckles to belly laughs. All this vocal activity is actually a rehearsal for speech. As Jeanie cries and coos and laughs, her vocal cords, tongue, lips, and brain are developing the co-ordination required for her to speak her first words.

3   At six or seven months of age, Jeanie is no longer an infant; she's moved on to the baby stage of language development. Like a pupa in its cocoon, Jeanie is undergoing a dramatic but (to all but her closest observers) invisible change. She looks at her mother when someone says "Mama." She responds to simple directions: she'll clap her hands or wave "bye-bye" on request. By the time she is a year old, Jeanie will recognize at least twenty words. The sounds Jeanie produces at this stage are called babbling, a word that technically describes a series of reduplicated single consonant and vowel sounds and probably derives its name from a common example: "ba-ba-ba-ba." About halfway through this stage of her development, Jeanie progresses to variegated babbling, in which sounds change between syllables. "Da-dee, da-dee, da-dee," she burbles, to the delight of her father (who doesn't know that Jeanie cannot yet connect the sounds she makes to the meaning they represent to others). But by the time Jeanie celebrates her first birthday, the variety, rhythm, and tone of her babbling have become more varied, and her family begins to sense consistent meaning in the sounds she makes. "Go bye-bye!" is as clearly meant as it is spoken—Jeanie wants to get going!

4   Jeanie's recognition of the link between sounds and meanings signals her entry into the toddler stage—twelve to eighteen months. At eighteen months, Jeanie will understand approximately 250 words—more than ten times the number she understood at twelve months. Most of what she says are single-word utterances: "kitty" for a cat in her picture book, "nana" for the bananas she loves to squish and eat. But even single words now function as complex communications depending on the intonation Jeanie gives them. "Kitty?" she inquires, looking at a picture of a tiger. She demands a "nana!" for lunch. About halfway through the toddler stage, Jeanie begins to link words together to make sentences. "Mama gone," she cries when her mother leaves for work. "Me no go bed," she tells her father. Though it marks the beginning of trouble for her parents, this development marks a triumph for Jeanie. She has broken out of the cocoon of passive comprehension into the world of active participation.

5   In less than two years, Jeanie has metamorphosed from wailing newborn to babbling baby to talking toddler. Through language, she is becoming her own woman in the world. Now she can fly.

Source: Norton, Sarah. "Metamorphosis." *Canadian Content*. 4th ed. Ed. Sarah Norton and Nell Waldman. Toronto: Harcourt, 2000. 120–122. Reprinted by permission of Harcourt Canada.

THE SECOND-LANGUAGE STRUGGLE
Nell Waldman

The essay below is an example of a short research paper written in the MLA style. The annotations point out some features of MLA format and documentation. If your instructor requires a separate title page, ask for guidelines.

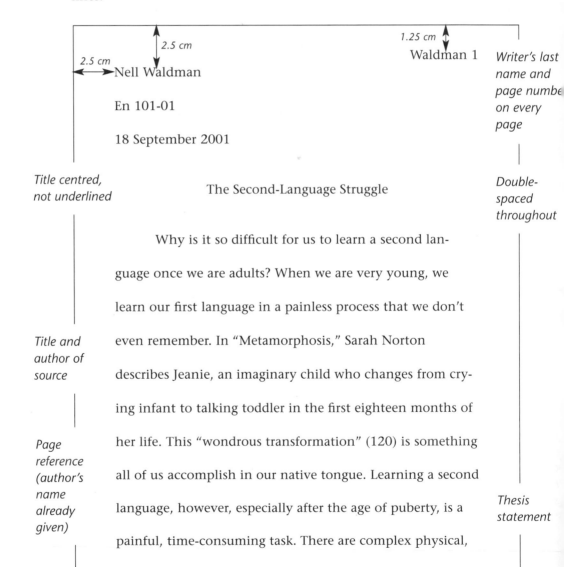

2.5 cm

2.5 cm

1.25 cm

Waldman 1

Nell Waldman

En 101-01

18 September 2001

The Second-Language Struggle

Why is it so difficult for us to learn a second language once we are adults? When we are very young, we learn our first language in a painless process that we don't even remember. In "Metamorphosis," Sarah Norton describes Jeanie, an imaginary child who changes from crying infant to talking toddler in the first eighteen months of her life. This "wondrous transformation" (120) is something all of us accomplish in our native tongue. Learning a second language, however, especially after the age of puberty, is a painful, time-consuming task. There are complex physical,

Writer's last name and page number on every page

Title centred, not underlined

Double-spaced throughout

Title and author of source

Page reference (author's name already given)

Thesis statement

Waldman 2

intellectual, and emotional factors that make acquiring a

second language difficult.

Paragraphs
indented
five spaces

     An important part of acquiring a language is learning

to speak, which is a physical skill. As any athlete will tell

you, it is an advantage to start learning a physical skill at a

young age. There are hundreds of muscles used in human

speech: mouth, lips, tongue, larynx, vocal cords, and throat.

A young child who babbles her way to articulate speech is

practising the physical skills of her native language. In addi-

tion, young children have a vast capacity for sound produc-

tion that is lost as they mature. Hence, even adults who

become fluent in a second language are likely to retain an

accent that is a vestige of their first language.

     An adult has intellectual and cognitive skills that a

child lacks. An adult can think abstractly and is able to

Paraphrase
+ author
and page
reference of
source

memorize and use dictionaries (Crystal 373). These skills

might seem to make it easier to learn a new language.

However, an adult already has a firmly established first lan-

guage in his intellectual repertoire, and the native language

Waldman 3

actually interferes with mastering the second language.

H. Douglas Brown describes the process whereby remnants

Quotation introduced by complete sentence + colon

of the native language collide with the new language: "The

relatively permanent incorporation of incorrect linguistic

forms into a person's second language competence . . . [is]

Ellipses indicate word(s) omitted; square brackets ind. cate word(s) changed or added

referred to as *fossilization*" (217). The fossils of our native

language tend to keep turning up as errors in the new

language we are struggling to learn.

Emotional factors also complicate the process of

learning a second language. Young children are naturally

open and lack the self-consciousness that leads to inhibi-

tion. Adults, on the other hand, have a highly developed

language ego; their control of language is bound up with

Quotation introduced by phrase + comma

self-esteem. As Brown points out, "you must be willing

literally to make a fool of yourself in the trial-and-error

struggle of speaking and understanding a foreign lan-

guage" (62). Making mistakes, as any language learner

Page reference (author's name alread mentioned)

must do, makes an adult anxious, shy, and reluctant to

communicate in the new language. These emotions

Waldman 4

make the process of mastering it even more difficult.

Many linguists argue that humans are born with an innate capacity for learning language, that we have what is known as a "language acquisition device" (LAD) hard-wired into our genetic make-up (Crystal 234). This LAD is what makes it possible for us to learn our native language with such ease. Knowing more than one language is, of course, an extremely valuable ability. Yet acquiring that second language is a complex and demanding process for most people, especially if they undertake it as adults. Eva Hoffman writes movingly about language and identity and the troubling feelings that accompanied her struggle to master English and transfer her identity, so to speak, from her native Polish language:

> What has happened to me in this new world? I don't know. I don't see what I've seen, don't comprehend what's in front of me. I'm not filled with language anymore, and I have only a memory of fullness to anguish me with the knowledge that, in this dark and empty state, I don't really exist. (110)

Quotation integrated into writer's sentence, no punctuation required

Author and page reference of source

Long quotation set off 10 spaces (1.25 cm) from left margin

Waldman 5

*Entries are
alphabetized*

Works Cited

*Heading is
centred, not
underlined*

Brown, H. Douglas. *Principles of Language Learning and*

*Indent
5 spaces
or 2.5 cm*

←→*Teaching*. 3rd ed. Englewood Cliffs, NJ: Prentice Hall,

←→1994.

*Double-
spaced
throughout*

Crystal, David. *The Cambridge Encyclopedia of Language*.

Cambridge: Cambridge UP, 1992.

Hoffman, Eva. "Lost in Translation." *Canadian Content*. 4th

ed. Ed. Sarah Norton and Nell Waldman. Toronto:

Harcourt, 2000. 108–112.

Norton, Sarah. "Metamorphosis." *Canadian Content*. 4th ed.

Ed. Sarah Norton and Nell Waldman. Toronto:

Harcourt, 2000. 120–122.

APPENDIX B

List of Grammatical Terms

adjective   A word that modifies (describes, restricts, relates to, makes more precise) a noun or pronoun. Adjectives answer the questions **What kind? How many? Which?**—e.g., the *competent* student; *five* home runs; my *last* class.

When two or more adjectives modify a noun, they may require punctuation marks. See Chapter 18 for the difference between **coordinate** and **cumulative** adjectives.

adverb   A word that modifies a verb, adjective, or other adverb. Adverbs answer the questions **When? How? Where? Why? How much?**—e.g., Nino talks *fast* (*fast* modifies the verb *talks*); he is a *very* fast talker (*very* modifies the adjective *fast*); he talks *really* fast (*really* modifies the adverb *fast*). Adverbs often   but not always—end in *-ly*.

antecedent   The word that a pronoun refers to or stands for. Literally, it means "coming before, preceding." The antecedent usually comes before the pronoun that refers to it—e.g., *Karen* believes *she* is possessed. (*Karen* is the antecedent to which the pronoun *she* refers.)

article   A determiner that precedes a noun. A/an is the **indefinite article** that signals an unspecified one of others—e.g., *a* stockbroker, *an* accountant, *a* village, *an* animal, *an* opportunity. Use a/an with a singular count noun when making a generalization: *A* stockbroker's job is stressful.

The is the **definite article** that signals a particular person, place, or thing, that has been singled out from others—e.g., *the* stockbroker who lives next door; *the* accountant who audits our books; *the* village where I was born. The is used when the speaker or writer and the audience are thinking about the same specific person(s) or thing(s). The is also used when an unspecified noun is mentioned a second time: I bought a box of chocolates, and my roommate ate half *the* box.

	No article (zero article) is used in general statements with noncount and plural nouns unless the noun is particularized or made specific in some way—e.g., *Tea* contains less caffeine than *coffee. Diamonds* are a girl's best friend. See Chapter 31.
clause	A group of words that contains a subject and a verb. If the group of words can stand by itself and makes complete sense, it is called an **independent clause** (or **principal clause** or **main clause**). If the group of words does not make complete sense on its own but is linked to another clause (depends on the other clause for its meaning), it is called a **dependent** or **subordinate clause**. Here's an example: The porch collapsed. This group of words can stand by itself, so it is called an independent clause. Now consider this clause: When Kalim removed the railing with his tractor. This group of words has a subject, *Kalim,* and a verb, *removed,* but it does not make complete sense on its own. It depends for its meaning on *the porch collapsed*; therefore, it is a dependent clause.
colloquialism	A word or phrase that we use in casual conversation or in informal writing.
	Steve *flunked* his accounting exam. *Did* you *get* what the teacher said about job placement? I can't believe that *guy* is serious about learning.
comma splice	The error that results when the writer joins two independent clauses with a comma—e.g., The comma splice is an error, it is a kind of run-on sentence. See Chapter 7.
count noun	A common noun that has a plural form and can be preceded by an indefinite article *(a/an)* or a quantity expression such as *one, many, several, a few of, hundreds of.* Examples: car, letter, dollar. See Chapter 30.
dependent clause cue	A word or phrase that introduces a dependent clause—e.g., when, because, in order that, as soon as. See page 78.
modifier	A word or group of words that adds information about another word (or phrase or clause) in a sentence. See **adjective, adverb, dependent clause**, and Chapter 8.
noncount noun	A common noun that cannot be preceded by an indefinite article *(a/an)* or by a quantity expression (e.g., *one, several, many, a couple of)* and that has no plural form. Examples: traffic, mail, money. See Chapter 30.
noun	A word that names a person, place, thing, or concept and that has the grammatical capability of being possessive. Nouns are most often used as subjects and objects. There are two classes of nouns: concrete and abstract.

Concrete nouns name things we perceive through our senses; we can see, hear, touch, taste, or smell what they stand for. Some concrete nouns are **proper**: they name people, places, or things and are capitalized—e.g., Paul Martin, Beijing, Canada's Wonderland. Other concrete nouns are **common** (woman, city, car, coffee); still others are **collective** (group, audience, swarm, committee).

Abstract nouns name concepts, ideas, characteristics—things we know or experience through our intellect rather than through our senses—e.g., truth, pride, feminism, self-esteem.

See also **count noun** and **noncount noun**.

object
The "receiving" part of a sentence. The **direct object** is a noun or noun substitute (pronoun, phrase, or clause) that is the target or receiver of the action expressed by the verb. It answers the question **what?** or **whom?**—e.g., John threw the *ball*. (John threw *what?*)

> He wondered where the money went. (He wondered *what?*)
> Munira loves Abdul. (Munira loves *whom?*)

The **indirect object** is a noun or pronoun that is the indirect target or receiver of the action expressed by the verb in a sentence. It is *always* placed in front of the direct object. It answers the question **to whom?** or **to what?**

> Doug threw *me* the ball. (Doug threw *to whom?*)
> Lisa forgot to give her *essay* a title. (Give *to what?*)

The **object of a preposition** is a noun or noun substitute (pronoun, phrase, or clause) that follows a preposition—e.g., after the *storm* (*storm* is a noun, object of the preposition *after*); before *signing the lease* (*signing the lease* is a phrase, object of the preposition *before*); he thought about *what he wanted to do* (*what he wanted to do* is a clause, object of the preposition *about*). Notice that what follows a preposition is always its object; that is why the subject of a sentence or clause can never be found in a prepositional phrase.

participle
The form of a verb that can be used as an adjective (the *completed* work, the *weeping* willows) or as part of a verb phrase (am *succeeding,* have *rented*).

> The **present participle** of a verb ends in *-ing*.
> The **past participle** of a **regular verb** ends in *-d* or in *-ed*.
> For a list of **irregular verbs**, see pages 146–148.

person
A category of pronouns and verbs. **First person** refers to the person who is speaking (I, we). **Second person** refers to the

person being spoken to (you). **Third person** is the person or thing being spoken about (he, she, it, they). Verb forms remain constant except in the present tense third-person singular, which ends in *-s*.

phrase   A group of meaning-related words that acts as a noun, a verb, an adjective, or an adverb within a sentence. Phrases do not make complete sense on their own because they do not contain both a subject and a verb.

> Please order *legal-size manila file folders.* (phrase acting as noun)
> I *must have been sleeping* when you called. (verb phrase)
> *Sightseeing in Ottawa,* we photographed the monuments *on Parliament Hill.* (phrases acting as adjectives)
> Portaging a canoe *in this weather* is no fun. (phrase acting as adverb)

prefix   A meaningful letter or group of letters added to the beginning of a word either (1) to change its meaning or (2) to change its word class.

> 1. *a* + moral = amoral
>   *bi* + sexual = bisexual
>   *contra* + diction = contradiction
>   *dys* + functional = dysfunctional
> 2. *a* + board (noun) = aboard (adverb, preposition)
>   *con* + temporary (adjective) = contemporary (noun, adjective)
>   *de* + nude = denude (verb)
>   *in* + put (verb) = input (noun)

Some prefixes require a hyphen, as here:
all-Canadian
de-emphasize
mid-morning

preposition   A word that connects a noun, pronoun, or phrase to some other word(s) in a sentence. The noun, pronoun, or phrase is the **object** of the preposition.

> I prepared the minutes *of the union meeting.* (*of* relates *meeting* to *minutes*)
> One *of the parents* checks the children every half hour. (*of* relates *parents* to *One*)

prepositional phrase   A group of grammatically related words beginning with a preposition and having the function of a noun, adjective, or adverb. See the list on pages 65 and 66.

pronoun   A word that functions like a noun in a sentence (e.g., as a subject, or as an object of a verb or a preposition). Pronouns usually substitute for nouns, but sometimes they substitute for other pronouns.

> *He* will promote *anything that* brings in money.
> *Everyone* must earn *her* badges.

There are several kinds of pronouns:

> **personal:** *I, we; you; he, she, it, they; me, us; him, her, them*
> **possessive:** *my, our; your; his, her, its, their*
> **demonstrative:** *this, these; that, those*
> **relative:** *who, whom, whose; which, that*
> **interrogative:** *who? whose? whom? which? what?*
> **indefinite:** all *-one, -thing, -body* pronouns, such as *every-one, -something,* and *anybody; each; neither; either; few; none; several*

subject   In a sentence, the person, thing, or concept that the sentence is about (see Chapter 5). In an essay, the person, thing, or concept that the paper is about (see Chapter 23).

suffix   A letter or group of letters that is added to the end of a word (1) to change its meaning, (2) to change its grammatical function, or (3) to change its word class.

> 1. king + *dom* = kingdom
>   few + *er* = fewer
>   tooth + *less* = toothless
> 2. buy (base form) + *s* = buys (third-person singular, present tense)
>   eat (base form) + *en* = eaten (past participle)
>   instructor + *s* = instructors (plural)
>   instructor + *'s* = instructor's (possessive singular)
> 3. your (adjective) + *s* = yours (pronoun)
>   act (verb) + *ive* = active (adjective)
>   active (adjective) + *ly* = actively (adverb)
>   ventilate (verb) + *tion* = ventilation (noun)

Some words add two or more prefixes and/or suffixes to the base form. Look at antidisestablishmentarianism, for example. How many prefixes and suffixes can you identify?

tense   The different forms of the verb used to indicate past, present, or future time are called **tenses**. The verb ending (e.g., play*s*, play*ed*) and any helping verbs associated with the main verb (*is* playing, *will* play, *has* played, *had* played, *will have* played) indicate the tense of the verb.

There are simple tenses: **present:** ask, asks
                                            past: *asked*
                                            future: *will ask*

and perfect tenses: **present:** *has (have) asked*
                                            past: *had asked*
                                            future: *will (shall) have asked*

The simple and perfect tenses can also be **progressive:** am asking, have been asking, etc.

transition   A word or phrase that helps readers to follow the writer's thinking from one sentence to the next or from one paragraph to another. See Chapter 26.

verb   A word or phrase that says something about a person, place, or thing and whose form may be changed to indicate tense. Verbs may make a statement, ask a question, or give commands. They may express action (physical or mental), occurrence, or condition (state of being). See Chapter 5.

> Wesley *hit* an inside curve for a home run. (physical action)
> Laurence *believed* the Blue Jays would win. (mental action)
> Father's Day *falls* on the third Sunday of June. (occurrence)
> Reva eventually *became* interested in English. (condition)

Some verbs are called **linking verbs:** they help to make a statement by linking the subject to a word or phrase that describes it.

> William Hubbard *was* Toronto's first black mayor. (*was* links *William Hubbard* to *mayor*)
> Mohammed *looks* tired. (*looks* links *Mohammed* and *tired*)

In addition to am, is, are, was, were, and been, some common linking verbs are appear, become, feel, grow, look, taste, remain, seem, smell, sound.

Another class of verbs is called **auxiliary** or **helping verbs.** They show the time of a verb as future or past (*will* go, *has* gone) or as a continuing action (*is* reading). They also show the passive voice (*is* completed, *have been* submitted).

voice   Verbs may be **active** or **passive**, depending on whether the subject of the verb is *acting* (active voice) or *being acted upon* (passive voice).

> In 2000, the government *introduced* another set of tax reforms. (active)

> Another set of tax reforms *was introduced* in 2000. (passive)

Answers to Exercises

Answers for Unit 1 Quick Quiz: Spelling (pages 2 and 3)

The Atacama Desert in the **northern** part of Chile (which is in **South** America) is the driest place on Earth. It gets about one centimetre of rain each year. Amazingly, parts of the Atacama **receive** no recorded rainfall at all—ever. Yet the **desert**, in spite of **its** dryness, is **truly** beautiful. The **Atacama's** landscape looks **a lot** like the landscape of the moon, with craters, **loose** rocks, strange rock formations, and no vegetation. In fact, one of the uses of the Atacama is as a testing ground for the robot vehicles that explore the moon or Mars. If moon **rovers** in the remote Atacama can be **controlled** from Houston or Cape Canaveral, chances are good that they can be **equipped** to maneuver on the moon. Most of the Atacama is uninhabited, but **there** are a few **villages** scattered here and there. The area has become a popular tourist destination because of its dramatic desert landscape that includes volcanoes; thermal geysers at a **height** of 4500 metres in the Andes Mountains; and unusual forms of wildlife such as pink flamingoes, vicunas, and llamas. The Atacama Desert is a **lonely** place that most of us **hear** about only in **geography** class. Travellers who venture as far as northern Chile, however, are **completely** captivated by the **desert's** unearthly beauty.

IF YOU MISSED . . .	SEE
northern or South	Chapter 3, Capital Letters (Rule 2)
receive	Chapter 1, Three Suggestions. . . (Rule 3)
desert	Chapter 2, Sound-Alikes, Look-Alikes, and Spoilers
it's	Chapter 4, The Apostrophe
	Chapter 2, Sound-Alikes, Look-Alikes, and Spoilers
truly	Chapter 1, Three Suggestions. . . (Rule 1)
Atacama's	Chapter 4, The Apostrophe
a lot	Chapter 2, Sound-Alikes, Look-Alikes, and Spoilers
loose	Chapter 2, Sound-Alikes, Look-Alikes, and Spoilers
rovers	Chapter 4, The Apostrophe
controlled	Chapter 1, Three Suggestions. . . (Rule 2)
equipped	Chapter 1, Three Suggestions. . . (Rule 2)
there	Chapter 2, Sound-Alikes, Look-Alikes, and Spoilers
villages	Chapter 4, The Apostrophe
height	Chapter 1, Three Suggestions. . . (Rule 3)
lonely	Chapter 1, Three Suggestions. . . (Rule 1)
hear	Chapter 2, Sound-Alikes, Look-Alikes, and Spoilers
geography	Chapter 3, Capital Letters (Rule 6)
completely	Chapter 1, Three Suggestions. . . (Rule 1)
desert's	Chapter 4, The Apostrophe

Answers for Chapter 1: Three Suggestions for Quick Improvement (pages 4 to 17)

Exercise 1.1
1. *humor.* You must use the root *humor* when adding an ending: e.g., *humorous.*
2. The word is spelled *harassment.*

3. The word is spelled *tattoo* and can be used both as a noun and as a verb.
4. People in Saskatchewan are more likely to experience a *tornado*; a *tsunami* is a gigantic sea wave and a *typhoon* is a tropical storm.
5. *program, center, skilful, traveler, judgment.* The preferred spellings are *program, centre, skilful, traveller,* and *judgment.*

Exercise 1.2

1. ratios	5. crises	9. appendixes
2. criteria	6. data (the singular is datum)	(*or* appendices)
3. analyses	7. mothers-in-law	10. formulas
4. personnel	8. nuclei (*or* nucleuses)	(*or* formulae)

Exercise 1.3

1. delayed	5. repayment	8. easier
2. journeys	6. loneliness	9. laziness
3. player	7. policies	10. necessarily
4. destroying		

The root words in 1 to 5 end in a **vowel** plus *y*; these words do not change spelling when you add an ending. The root words in 6 to 10 end in a **consonant** plus *y*; change *y* to *i* when you add an ending to such words.

Exercise 1.4

1. dis-cuss	5. through (Words	7. so-lu-tion
2. man-age-ment	of one syllable	8. al-go-rithm
3. ac-com-mo-date	cannot be divided.)	9. con-science
4. dis-trib-ute	6. cha-os	10. busi-ness

Exercise 1.6

1. safely	6. improvement	8. usable
2. arguing	7. reducing	9. immediately
3. lovable	5. extremely	10. requiring
4. accelerating		

Exercise 1.7

1. boring	5. careful	8. providing
2. movement	6. advertisement	9. sensible
3. scarcely	7. excusable	10. improvement
4. unusable		

Exercise 1.9

1. planning	5. stirred	8. writing
2. stopping	6. suffering	9. mapping
3. admitted	7. allotted	10. interrupted
4. nailing		

Exercise 1.10

1. preferring	5. controller	8. forgotten
2. omitted	6. occurred	9. replacing
3. acquitted	7. equipping	10. quizzed
4. developing		

Exercise 1.11

1. deferred	5. trimmed	8. dependence
2. rebellious	6. subsistence	9. recurrence
3. referring	7. difference	10. insistence
4. concurred		

Exercise 1.12

Although I am just a **beginner**, I am finding cooking to be a **compelling** new skill. For many years, I have **suffered** from eating frozen dinners that look delicious in the pictures on the packages, but look and taste disgusting when **transferred** from freezer to plate. Now I am **rebelling** against packaged slop, and making **truly** delicious meals from scratch. If you have a **preference** for nutritious, tasty, and attractive meals, I suggest you stop paying **outrageous** amounts for pre-packaged food, and start cooking.

Exercise 1.14

1. brief	5. relief	8. mischievous
2. cashier	6. retrieve	9. deceitful
3. receive	7. ceiling	10. hygiene
4. pierce		

Exercise 1.15

1. piece	5. caffeine, ceiling	8. diet, protein, relief
2. Neither, brief	6. weird, mischievous	9. deceiving, weight
3. leisure, foreign	7. Seize, believe	10. neighbour, steins
4. species, either		

Exercise 1.16

My **friend** Sunil and I decided to go south for the spring break. At the last minute, our roommate, **Weird** Wayne, decided to join us. We all **believed** that a week's vacation would do us far more good than staying at home and studying. Unfortunately, our holiday experience was not **quite** the **leisurely** getaway we had planned. Our first near disaster **occurred** at the airport, where the police threatened to **seize** Yvonne's luggage because her high-tech hair dryer looked on the x-ray machine like a bomb. In Florida we all got sick from eating tainted **wieners** at a hot dog stand, and we all got sunburned lying on the beach. **Neither** Sunil nor Wayne can **believe** me when I say I'm going again next year.

Answers for Chapter 2: Sound-Alikes, Look-Alikes, and Spoilers (pages 18 to 33)

Exercise 2.1

1. This is a **course** that I should be able to pass easily.
2. My sister is a **woman** who **hears** everything and remembers even more.
3. We need **peace** in order to concentrate.
4. Do you suppose **they're** still sick from eating **too** much?
5. It certainly is **quiet** once **your** roommates leave for school.
6. I'd like to **lose** four kilos by New Year's, but I can't resist **desserts**.

Exercise 2.2

1. **It's** the wrong **site** for a house, but it might work for a barn.
2. If you submit your assignment any **later**, the professor won't **accept** it.
3. Our **morale** is so low, we wouldn't recognize a **compliment** if someone gave us one.
4. It is in **their** best interest to recognize the **effects** of bad eating habits.
5. It was the **fourth** quarter of the game, and we **led** by 20 points.

Exercise 2.3

1. Is there anyone **whose advice** you would listen to?
2. **Your** confidence in your own superiority is an **illusion**.
3. Occasionally, my **conscience** bothers me when I send **personal** e-mails on the office computer.
4. **Much** of the time, we decide **who's** going first by flipping a coin.
5. Are the political party's **principles** more important **than** its desire to get elected?

Exercise 2.4
1. We **led** them to the **site** of the old mine.
2. She **cited** my essay when she spoke about the **effects** of poor grammar.
3. I will **accept** your **counsel** if you can provide me with proof of what you say.
4. Were you still **conscious** after falling off your **stationary** bicycle?
5. We were **led** into the **dining** room by the maitre d'.

Exercise 2.5
1. No **woman** is going to be impressed by your insincere **compliments**.
2. "Buy low, sell high" is one of my **principles**; **besides**, it makes money.
3. Are you **implying** that I should **choose** another career goal?
4. I would rather have my shirt collar too **loose than** too tight.
5. As a **minor** she isn't allowed to have icewine with her **dessert**.

Exercise 2.6
1. Most people's ability to learn is **affected** by **their personal** well-being.
2. I'd much rather write a 2,000 word essay **than** do an oral report in front of our class.
3. During my six month review, my supervisor **implied** that I would do better to **choose** another line of work.
4. **There** will be no **peace** in **our** office until **morale** improves.
5. The **principal** causes of the **morale** problem are **too** much overtime and too few "perks."
6. The **advice** given us by the personnel firm we hired was to appoint a **woman** whose only qualifications were a huge ego and shoes that **complemented** her every outfit.

Exercise 2.7
I had a hard time **choosing** between two colleges, both of which offered the **courses** I wanted. Both had good placement records, and I just couldn't make up my mind. I asked my friends for **advice**, but they were no help. Several were surprised that any college would even **accept** me. Their negative view of my academic ability did nothing to improve my **morale**; in fact, it **led** me to re-evaluate my selection of friends. My school **counsellor**, a **woman whose** opinion I respect, didn't think one college was better **than** the other, so she suggested that I choose the school that was located where I preferred to live. I followed her advice, and I haven't regretted it.

Exercise 2.8
Many people today are **choosing** a quieter way of life, hoping to live longer and more happily by following the "slower is better" **principle**. Some, on the **advice** of **their** doctors, have been forced to slow down. One heart surgeon, for example, directs his patients to drive only in the slow lane rather **than** use the passing lane. They may arrive a few minutes later, but their blood pressure will not be **affected**. Others don't need to be prompted by their doctors. They **accept** that living at a slower pace doesn't mean **losing** out in any way. In fact, the opposite is true: choosing a healthy lifestyle benefits everyone. The **effect** of increased **peace** and **quiet** in your **personal** life leads to increased productivity, higher **morale**, and greater job satisfaction. Sometimes the improvements are **minor**, but as anyone who has **consciously** tried to slow the pace of life can tell you, the slow lane is the fast lane to longevity.

Answers for Chapter 3: Capital Letters (pages 34 to 40)

Exercise 3.1
1. **T**ime is nature's way of keeping everything from happening at once.
2. Brad sang, "**T**here's a light in the Frankenstein house."
3. **M**y parents have a bumper sticker that reads, "**M**oney isn't everything, but it sure keeps the kids in touch."

4. Richard Harkness, writing in *The New York Times*, said "**A** committee is a group of the unwilling, picked from the unfit, to do the unnecessary."

5. **I**n conclusion, I want you to consider the words of Wendell Johnson: "*Always* and *never* are two words you should always remember never to use."

Exercise 3.2

1. After a brief stay in the **M**aritimes, **C**aptain **T**allman and his crew sailed west up the **S**t. **L**awrence.

2. The **B**roadcast **D**epartment of **N**iagara **C**ollege has ordered six **S**ony cameras for their studios in **W**elland, **O**ntario.

3. Do you find that **V**isa is more popular than American **E**xpress when you travel to far away places such as **M**exico, **F**rance, or **J**upiter?

4. Our stay at the **S**eaview **H**otel overlooking the **P**acific **O**cean certainly beat our last vacation at the **B**ates **M**otel, where we faced west, overlooking the city dump.

5. As a member of the **A**lumni **A**ssociation I am trying to raise funds from companies like **D**isney, **G**eneral **M**otors, **C**orel, and the **C**B**C**, where our graduates have positions.

Exercise 3.3

1. The **C**rusades, which were religious wars between **M**uslims and **C**hristians, raged through the **M**iddle **A**ges.

2. The **H**indu religion recognizes and honours many gods; **I**slam recognizes one god, **A**llah; **B**uddhism recognizes none.

3. The **K**oran, the **B**ible, and the **T**orah agree on many principles.

4. The **J**ewish festival of **H**anukkah often occurs near the same time that **C**hristians are celebrating **C**hristmas.

5. After **W**orld **W**ar I, many **J**ews began to emigrate to Palestine, where they and the **M**uslim population soon came into conflict.

Exercise 3.4

1. My favourite months are **J**anuary and **F**ebruary because I love all **w**inter sports.

2. This **M**onday is **V**alentine's **D**ay, when messages of love are exchanged.

3. In the summer, big meals seem too much trouble; however, after **T**hanksgiving, we need lots of food to survive the winter cold.

4. A **n**ational **h**oliday named **F**lag **D**ay was once proposed, but it was never officially approved.

5. By **T**hursday, I'll have finished my **S**t. **P**atrick's **D**ay costume.

Exercise 3.5

1. The review of my book, *The Life and Times of a Chocoholic*, published in *The Globe and Mail*, was not favourable.

2. Clint **E**astwood fans will be delighted that the two early movies that made him internationally famous, *A Fistful of Dollars* and *For a Few Dollars More*, are now available on DVD.

3. Joseph Conrad's short novel *Heart of Darkness* became the blockbuster movie *Apocalypse Now*.

4. Her poem, "**A** **B**right and **S**ilent **P**lace" was published in the **A**pril issue of *Landscapes* magazine.

5. Botticelli's famous painting, "**B**irth of **V**enus," inspired my poem "**W**oman on the **H**alf **S**hell."

Exercise 3.6

1. After studying geography for two years, I began taking courses in ancient **G**reek and modern history.

2. correct

3. By taking Professor Subden's non-credit course, **I**ntroduction to **W**ine, I qualified to register for **O**enology 120 the next semester.

4. While math is her strong subject, Laurie has trouble with accounting, **E**nglish, and conversational **F**rench.

5. The prerequisite for **T**heology 210 is **I**ntroduction to **W**orld **R**eligions, taught by Professor Singh.

Exercise 3.7

1. There will be a fundraising spaghetti dinner in the **A**nglican church on **B**irch **A**venue next **T**hursday evening.

2. You must take some **s**cience courses, or you'll never get into the program you want at **M**alaspina **C**ollege in the **f**all.

3. It should come as no surprise that Gore Vidal, author of *The Best Man*, once said, "**I**t is not enough to succeed; others must fail."

4. After the **g**ame, we went to the **B**urger **P**alace for a late snack and then went home to watch *This Hour Has 22 Minutes* on televison.

5. In our **E**nglish course at **C**aribou **C**ollege, we studied *The Englishman's Boy,* a novel about life among the settlers of the **A**merican and **C**anadian west.

Exercise 3.8

1. Marg Delahunty's campaign to be elected mayor of our fair city ran into trouble on **F**riday when she was quoted as saying, "**O**ur political system is nothing but mob rule with taxes."

2. I wonder how our **c**ollege gets away with requiring students to take **E**nglish and **m**athematics courses in addition to our **m**ajor subjects.

3. Leonard Cohen first became famous as a novelist when he published *The Favourite Game* and *Beautiful Losers*.

4. Years later, **C**ohen's career was spectacularly revived with the release of albums such as *I'm Your Man* in 1988 and *The Future* in 1992.

5. I was raised a **B**aptist, but since taking **P**rofessor Chan's course, **I**ntroduction to **W**orld **R**eligions, I've been interested in **H**induism and **B**uddhism.

6. I plan to travel to **A**sia next **s**ummer to learn more about these religions.

Answers for Chapter 4: The Apostrophe (pages 41 to 52)

Exercise 4.1

1. can't	5. let's	8. won't
2. she'd	6. hasn't	9. she'll
3. he'll	7. you're	10. we'll
4. we'd		

Exercise 4.2

1. they're	5. everyone's	8. you're
2. I'll	6. couldn't	9. we'd
3. it's	7. who's	10. won't
4. can't		

Exercise 4.3

1. **We'd** help if **they'd** ask us.
2. There **won't** be any problem if **you've** got an invitation.
3. **I'm** sure that contractions **shouldn't** be used in formal writing.
4. You **can't** leave until the **show's** over.
5. **Don't** worry about your heart; **it'll** last as long as you do.
6. Your **sister's** very nice, but I think your **brother's** a nutbar.

7. **It's** certain that **he'll** be late.
8. **It's** best to begin your paper well before the deadline unless **you're** confident about getting an extension.
9. **Wouldn't** it be wonderful if everyone **who's** celebrating a birthday today could get together for a party?
10. **I'd** support the idea only if the party **wasn't** held anywhere near my apartment.

Exercise 4.4

I am writing to apply for the position of Web Master for BrilloVision.com that **you have** advertised in the *Daily News*. **I have** got the talent and background **you are** looking for. Currently, I work as a Web designer for an online publication, Vexed.com, where **they are** very pleased with my work. If you click on their Web site, I think **you will** like what you see. **There is** little in the way of Web design and application that I **have not** been involved in during the past two years. But **it is** time for me to move on to a new challenge, and BrilloVision.com promises the kind of opportunity **I am** looking for. I guarantee you **will not** be disappointed if I join your team!

Exercise 4.5

1. woman's beauty
2. heaven's gate
3. families' budgets
4. crew's mutiny
5. armed forces' uniforms
6. everyone's choice
7. the Gulf Islands' weather
8. the Simpsons' daughters
9. the oldest child's responsibility
10. our country's flag

Exercise 4.6

1. **Stanley's** greatest fear is his **mother's** disapproval.
2. **Bikers'** equipment is on sale this week at Leather **Larry's** Boutique.
3. My parents would like to know **whose** yogurt was left in **their** fridge for three months.
4. After only a **month's** wear, my **son's** new jacket fell apart.
5. Unfortunately, the **book's** cover was much more interesting than **its** contents.
6. Our **team's** biggest win came at the same time as our rival **teams'** (or **team's**) most serious losses.
7. Virtue may be **its** own reward, but I won't refuse **your** offer of cash.
8. **Texas'** record of executing people is one of the **United States'** most notorious statistics.
9. This year, our **family's** Thanksgiving celebration will be a quiet one, as we think of other **families'** poverty.
10. This **week's** *Fashion* magazine devotes four pages to **men's** clothing and twelve pages to **women's**.

Exercise 4.7

1. **There's** a rumour that **you're** going to quit smoking.
2. **It's** true. My family **doctor's** concerns about my health finally convinced me to quit.
3. **Who's** perfect? I am, in my **mother's** opinion, at least.
4. **It's** a fact that most **mothers'** opinions about their children are unrealistically positive.
5. Most **fathers'** opinions are highly negative when they first meet their **daughters'** boyfriends.

Exercise 4.8

1. The **candidates'** debate was deadly boring until the fans started fighting in their seats.
2. **Today's** styles and **tomorrow's** trends will be featured in our display window.
3. **Hockey's** playoff schedule puts the **finals** into the middle of June.
4. My **in-laws'** home is about four **hours'** drive north of Red Lake.
5. **Today's** paper features a short article entitled "**It's** Clear the **Apostrophe's** Days Are Numbered."

Exercise 4.9

1. When you feel like a snack, you can choose between apples or **Timbits**.
2. **Anna's** career took off when she discovered **it's** easy to sell **children's** toys.
3. Golfing requires the use of different **clubs**: woods for long shots, irons for short ones.
4. Poker's an easy game to play if you are dealt **aces** more often than your **opponents** are.
5. **Nobody's** perfect, but must the prime minister of our country display so many more **faults** than **virtues**?

Exercise 4.10

1. **I've** posted a sign on my front lawn: "**Salespersons'** visits are always welcome. Dog **food's** expensive."
2. A dog always knows **its owner's** (or **owners'**) mealtimes.
3. Do you really think your **employees** will be disappointed when they hear that you've cancelled the **company's** annual picnic?
4. In Canada, when it's warm enough to expose **your** skin to the sun, the **insects'** feeding season is at **its** height.

Exercise 4.11

1. Candy is dandy, but **liquor's** quicker. (Ogden Nash)
2. The storm devastated the two small **towns** in **its** path.
3. Thank you for the **flowers** you sent us on the occasion of the **twins'** graduation.
4. **Somebody's** going to be very disappointed when the panel releases its decision.
5. Four **months'** work was wasted by a few **minutes'** carelessness.
6. We will need **everybody's** maximum effort if we're going to meet **tomorrow's** deadline.

Answers for Unit 2 Quick Quiz: Sentence Structure (pages 55 and 56)

(Note: a triple asterisk (***) indicates that unnecessary words have been deleted. Each triple asterisk counts as one error.)

You know that the heart pumps blood through our bodies, but did you also know that the word "heart" pumps through the English language in interesting ways? Let's look at some of the idioms using the word "heart." An idiom **is** a group of words whose meaning is difficult to figure out from the meaning of its individual words, such as "heart of gold" and "heart of stone." The word "heart" is found in many idioms. Some have positive connotations, **some have** negative connotations, and some are neutral. Some have to do with love and loss**;** others have nothing at all to do with romance.

To begin with, there are heart idioms that apply to romance. You "lose your heart" to someone **you desire**; in other words, you fall in love. As the relationship develops, you have many "heart to heart talks," **and** you love each other "from the bottom of your hearts." There are also **many** positive heart idioms that don't refer to love, such as "to have your heart in the right place," which means to be sincere and kind. To be "good hearted" means to be a good person; a "heart-warming" story causes you to feel *** warm and happy.

3   Once the love affair **is over**, heart idioms can also be called upon to describe the pain. For example, you "cry your heart out" about your lover's "change of heart**,**" your "heart sinks" whenever you hear his or her name**,** you are "heartbroken,**" and** you believe that your lover is a "heartless" rogue. Other idioms with a negative connotation include "to lose heart," which means to become discouraged, and "to be sick at heart," **which means to feel fear or grief.**

4   Then there are the **many** heart idioms that express a variety of meanings with neither positive nor negative connotations. For instance, to learn something "by heart" is to memorize it; to "have your heart set" on something is to want it badly. **If you are scared out of your wits**, the "heart-stopping" movie you are watching is tense and exciting. The "heartland" **is** the most important part of a country. If you ask someone to "have a heart," **y**ou're asking her

to be sympathetic. When you describe people as "young at heart," it's meant to be a compliment, **but** it still means they are old.

5   ***English idioms using the word "heart" have a bewildering number of meanings that we learn **only** through experience. Experience teaches us not to say that those spicy Buffalo wings gave us "heartache," or that an ex-lover **caused** our "heartburn." *****My** "heart goes out to" the many language learners who are confused by the difference.

IF YOU MISSED . . .	SEE
Paragraph 1:	
an idiom being . . .	Chapters 5 and 6
negative connotations cling to others	Chapter 9
. . . love and loss others . . .	Chapters 5 and 7
Paragraph 2:	
For starters,	Chapter 11 (Slang)
hot for	Chapter 11 (Slang)
"heart to heart talks," you . . .	Chapters 5 and 7
tons of	Chapter 11 (Slang)
feel real warm and happy	Chapter 11 (Abusages)
Paragraph 3:	
has been terminated	Chapter 11 (Pretentious Language)
For example, you . . . rogue.	Chapters 5 and 7
meaning feeling fear or grief	Chapter 9
Paragraph 4:	
the myriad, almost innumerable	Chapter 11 (Pretentious Language, Wordiness)
Scared out of your wits, the "heart-stopping" movie . . .	Chapter 8 (Dangling Modifiers)
The "heartland" being . . .	Chapters 5 and 6
to "have a heart." You're . . .	Chapters 5 and 6
it's meant to be a compliment it	Chapters 5 and 7
Paragraph 5:	
To conclude, I personally think that . . .	Chapter 11 (Wordiness)
meanings that only we learn	Chapter 8 (Misplaced Modifiers)
effectuated	Chapter 11 (Pretentious Language)
Anyways	Chapter 11 (Abusages, Wordiness)

Answers for Chapter 5: Cracking the Sentence Code (pages 57 to 72)

Exercise 5.1
1. Canadians love donuts.
2. They eat more donuts than any other nation.
3. Most malls contain a donut shop.
4. Donuts taste sweet.
5. Glazed donuts are my favourite.
6. Hot chocolate is good with donuts.
7. [You] Try a bran donut for breakfast.
8. It is good for your health.
9. Donut jokes are common on television.
10. Dentists like donuts too, but for different reasons.

Exercise 5.2

1. My <u>computer</u> <u>is</u> usually reliable.
2. Today, however, <u>it</u> <u>keeps</u> crashing.
3. [<u>You</u>] <u>Turn</u> it off.
4. Maybe the <u>processor</u> <u>is</u> tired.
5. Perhaps the <u>operator</u> <u>needs</u> a vacation.
6. <u>Computing</u> <u>is</u> a necessary part of my life.
7. My <u>work</u> <u>depends</u> on it.
8. Without a functioning computer, <u>I</u> <u>feel</u> frustrated and angry.
9. Eventually, <u>I</u> <u>decided</u> to hit it with a hammer.
10. The <u>computer</u> <u>booted</u> right up!

Exercise 5.3

1. <u>Is</u> <u>Tomas</u> still on the team?
2. [<u>You</u>] <u>Consider</u> it done.
3. Here <u>are</u> the <u>answers</u> to tomorrow's quiz.
4. <u>Is</u> <u>winter</u> warmer this year than last?
5. Into the pool <u>leaped</u> the terrified <u>cat</u>.
6. Where <u>are</u> the <u>children</u>?
7. There <u>are</u> two new <u>students</u> in class today.
8. Which <u>elective</u> <u>is</u> easier?
9. <u>Are</u> <u>you</u> happy with your choice?
10. <u>Who</u> <u>let</u> the dogs out?

Exercise 5.4

1. My brother Ted <u>is calling</u> from Mexico.
2. His wife <u>will arrive</u> on Tuesday.
3. <u>Have</u> you <u>arranged</u> for a party to celebrate the election results?
4. The president <u>could have fixed</u> the election.
5. The party in power <u>might have won</u> again.
6. Xue <u>should have completed</u> her diploma by now.
7. <u>Do</u> you <u>know</u> anything about Linux?
8. We <u>have played</u> in the rain before.
9. I <u>will be looking</u> for verbs in my sleep.
10. We <u>must have practised</u> enough by now.

Exercise 5.5

1. <u>I</u> <u>am making</u> a nutritious breakfast.
2. <u>It</u> <u>does</u> not <u>include</u> Coca Cola.
3. <u>You</u> <u>can add</u> fresh fruit to the cereal.
4. The <u>toast</u> <u>should be</u> almost ready now.
5. My <u>doctor</u> <u>has</u> often <u>recommended</u> yogurt for breakfast.
6. <u>I</u> <u>could</u> never <u>eat</u> yogurt without fruit.
7. With breakfast, <u>I</u> <u>will drink</u> at least two cups of coffee.
8. <u>I</u> <u>don't</u> <u>like</u> tea.
9. <u>I</u> simply <u>cannot</u> <u>begin</u> my day without coffee.
10. <u>I</u> <u>should</u> probably <u>switch</u> to decaf.

Exercise 5.6

1. <u>Winners</u> <u>are</u> always <u>watching</u> for opportunities.
2. <u>Losers</u> <u>are</u> usually <u>looking</u> for lucky breaks.
3. <u>I</u> <u>should be riding</u> my bicycle to work.
4. My <u>bike</u> <u>has been broken</u> for nearly two years.

5. I cannot <u>ride</u> a broken bike.
6. My broken <u>bike</u> <u>is</u> really just an excuse.
7. Given the opportunity, I <u>will</u> always <u>drive</u>.
8. Also, I <u>have been waiting</u> for the bicycle fairy to fix it.
9. <u>Wouldn't</u> <u>that</u> <u>be</u> a lucky break?
10. Maybe I <u>should</u> simply <u>start</u> working on it myself.

Exercise 5.7
1. Many <u>people</u> ~~in the crowd~~ <u>were</u> confused.
2. <u>Fifty</u> ~~of her friends~~ <u>gave</u> her a surprise party.
3. The official <u>opening</u> ~~of the new city hall~~ <u>will be held</u> tomorrow.
4. ~~In the movies~~, the <u>collision</u> ~~of two cars~~ always <u>results</u> ~~in a fire~~.
5. A <u>couple</u> ~~of burgers~~ <u>should be</u> enough ~~for each of us~~.
6. [You] Please <u>decide</u> ~~on dessert~~ ~~before dinnertime~~.
7. Only a <u>few</u> ~~of us~~ <u>have finished</u> our homework.
8. ~~After the rain~~, the <u>flowers</u> ~~in the garden~~ <u>began</u> to bloom.
9. There <u>is</u> a <u>show</u> ~~about laser surgery on television~~ tonight.
10. ~~In the land of the blind~~, the one-eyed <u>man</u> <u>is</u> king. (Erasmus)

Exercise 5.8
1. A <u>party</u> ~~in our neighbours' apartment~~ <u>kept</u> us awake until dawn.
2. The <u>meeting</u> ~~of all students in our class~~ <u>solved</u> nothing.
3. ~~In front of the mirror~~ <u>stood</u> the wicked <u>stepmother</u>.
4. ~~According to the news~~, the <u>temperature</u> ~~in Yellowknife~~ <u>fell</u> 20°C overnight.
5. My <u>invention</u> ~~of a phoneless cord~~ <u>was designed</u> ~~for untalkative people~~.
6. <u>Nothing</u> ~~in this world~~ <u>travels</u> faster than a bad cheque.
7. ~~For many students~~, <u>lack</u> ~~of money~~ <u>is</u> probably their most serious problem.
8. The <u>plural</u> ~~of "choose"~~ <u>should be</u> "cheese."
9. ~~Despite her doubts about my condition~~, the <u>nurse</u> ~~on duty~~ ~~at the hospital~~ <u>admitted</u> me.
10. My <u>guarantee</u> ~~of an A in this course~~ <u>is</u> valid only ~~under certain conditions~~.

Exercise 5.9
1. ~~In my opinion~~, the <u>fear</u> ~~of flying~~ <u>is</u> entirely justifiable.
2. ~~In our basement~~ <u>are</u> <u>stacks</u> ~~of magazines~~ dating ~~from the 1950s~~.
3. The <u>rats</u> ~~in our building~~ <u>have written</u> letters ~~of complaint to the Board of Health~~.
4. When <u>did</u> the <u>president</u> ~~of your company~~ <u>decide</u> ~~on this policy~~?
5. ~~For reasons of privacy~~, I <u>am listed</u> ~~in the telephone book~~ ~~under my dog's name~~.
6. ~~Into the classroom~~ and ~~up to the front~~ <u>marched</u> a tall <u>woman</u> ~~with a determined look in her eyes~~.
7. <u>Most</u> ~~of the students in the class~~ instantly <u>decided</u> not to argue ~~with her~~.
8. ~~In future~~, [you] <u>be</u> sure to read ~~through your notes before the exam~~.
9. ~~In your brochure~~, <u>you</u> <u>advertise</u> a "semi-annual after-Christmas sale" ~~of quality items~~.
10. ~~According to my dictionary~~, the <u>word</u> "semi-annual" <u>means</u> twice a year.

Exercise 5.10
1. My <u>mother</u> and <u>father</u> <u>support</u> me ~~in college~~.
2. I <u>can save</u> or [can] <u>spend</u> the money.
3. My <u>parents</u> and the <u>rest</u> ~~of my family~~ <u>are expecting</u> me to do well in school.
4. <u>Entertainment</u> and <u>clothing</u> <u>are</u> not <u>included</u> ~~in my budget~~.
5. <u>Tuition</u>, <u>books</u>, <u>lab fees</u>, and <u>rent</u> <u>take</u> all my money.
6. A student's <u>life</u> <u>can be</u> sad and lonely.

7. ~~In my letters home~~, I <u>whine</u> and <u>moan</u> ~~at every opportunity about my lack of money~~.
8. Unfortunately ~~for me~~, my <u>mother</u> and <u>father</u> <u>were</u> students too and <u>had</u> the same experience.
9. They <u>laugh</u> and <u>shake</u> their heads and <u>tell</u> me ~~about their college days~~.
10. ~~According to my parents~~, they <u>ate</u> only Kraft Dinner, <u>lived</u> ~~in a shack~~, <u>wore</u> hand-me-down clothes, and <u>walked</u> ten kilometres ~~to school~~.

Exercise 5.11
1. <u>Verbs</u> and <u>subjects</u> <u>are</u> sometimes hard to find.
2. <u>Farmers</u>, <u>loggers</u>, and <u>fishers</u> <u>need</u> and <u>deserve</u> the support ~~of consumers~~.
3. [You] <u>Open</u> the bottle, <u>pour</u> carefully, <u>taste</u>, and <u>enjoy</u>.
4. When <u>can</u> the salesperson and her <u>clients</u> <u>visit</u> your home?
5. <u>Werner</u>, <u>Italo</u>, and <u>Pierre</u> <u>discussed</u> and <u>debated</u> recipes all night.
6. ~~During the following week~~, each <u>one</u> <u>chose</u> and <u>prepared</u> a meal ~~for the other two~~.
7. Werner's <u>sauerbraten</u> and Black Forest <u>cake</u> <u>amazed</u> and <u>delighted</u> his friends.
8. <u>Italo</u> <u>chopped</u>, <u>sliced</u>, <u>simmered</u>, and <u>baked</u> a magnificent Italian meal.
9. <u>Pierre</u> and his <u>sister</u> <u>worked</u> ~~in the kitchen for two days~~ and <u>prepared</u> a delicious cassoulet.
10. ~~By the end of the week~~, <u>Pierre</u>, <u>Italo</u>, and <u>Werner</u> <u>were</u> ready ~~for a diet~~.

Exercise 5.12
1. A <u>fool</u> and his <u>money</u> <u>are</u> soon <u>parted</u>.
2. I <u>dream</u> ~~of success~~ and <u>worry</u> ~~about failure~~.
3. <u>Nur</u> and <u>Aman</u> <u>paddled</u> and <u>portaged</u> ~~for ten days~~.
4. ~~From under an oak leaf~~ <u>stepped</u> a tiny <u>elf</u> and his equally tiny <u>companion</u>.
5. ~~In the mist of early morning~~, a <u>Brontosaurus</u> and a <u>Tyrannosaurus Rex</u> <u>sniffed</u> the moist air and <u>hunted</u> ~~for food~~.
6. [You] <u>Study</u> my methods, <u>use</u> my research, but <u>do</u> not <u>copy</u> my work.
7. Why <u>are</u> <u>goalies</u> ~~in hockey~~ and <u>kickers</u> ~~in football~~ so superstitious?
8. ~~In my dreams~~, the <u>maid</u>, <u>butler</u>, <u>housekeeper</u>, and <u>chef</u> <u>wash</u> the dishes, <u>vacuum</u> the floors, <u>do</u> the laundry, and <u>make</u> the meals.
9. ~~According to the official course outline~~, <u>students</u> ~~in this English course~~ <u>must take</u> notes ~~during every class~~ and <u>submit</u> their notes ~~to their instructor for evaluation~~.
10. ~~In the opinion of many Canadians~~, the <u>word</u> *politician* <u>means</u> "idiot."

Answers for Chapter 6: Solving Sentence-Fragment Problems (pages 73 to 84)

Exercise 6.1
Many different sentences can be made out of the fragments in this exercise. Just be sure that each of your sentences has both a subject and a verb.
1. F   This <u>chapter</u> <u>is</u> about sentence fragments.
2. F   <u>We</u> <u>were</u> glad to be able to help you.
3. F   Your <u>mother</u> <u>is hoping</u> to hear from you soon.
4. F   The <u>class</u> <u>was saved</u> by the bell from doing yet another exercise.
5. F   To prevent a similar tragedy from happening again, a policy and procedures <u>manual will be developed.</u>
6. F   <u>It</u> <u>was</u> not a good idea to leave the cat in the same room with the canary.
7. F   <u>Watching</u> television <u>is</u> a cheap form of entertainment.
8. S
9. F   Our new <u>car</u> <u>came equipped</u> with a computer with true artificial intelligence and full control of the vehicle.
10. S

Exercise 6.2

1. F	5. F	8. S
2. F	6. S	9. F
3. F	7. F	10. F
4. F		

Exercise 6.3 (suggested answers)

1. This apartment suits me in every way, **e**xcept for the price. I can't afford it.
2. In track and field, this college is very well respected. Our team won the championship last year, **s**etting three new provincial records.
3. Whenever I go fishing, the fish aren't biting, but the mosquitoes are. Maybe I should give up fishing **a**nd start collecting insects as a hobby instead.
4. My son is a genius. On his last birthday, he was given a toy that was guaranteed unbreakable. **He** <u>used</u> it to break all his other toys.
5. We weren't lost, but we were certainly confused. I realized this when we passed City Hall **f**or the third time.
7. My husband and I often go to the hockey arena, **n**ot to watch sports, but to hear the concerts of our favourite local bands. These concerts give new meaning to the word "cool."
9. I enjoy reading travel books **a**bout far-away, exotic places that I have never visited and will probably never get to see. The fun is in the dreaming, not the doing.
10. To spend the days skiing and the nights dining and dancing **is** how I picture my retirement. Unfortunately, by then I'll be too old to do it.

Exercise 6.4

1. S	4. S	7. S
2. F	5. F	8. F
3. F	6. F	9. S

Exercise 6.5 (suggested answers)

   I decided to take swimming lessons for several reasons. First, <u>I</u> <u>know</u> that swimming is one of the best activities for physical fitness. Second, <u>I am concerned</u> about safety. You never know when the ability to swim might save your life **o**r the life of someone you're with. Third, <u>I</u> <u>want</u> to be able to enjoy water sports such as diving and snorkeling instead of being stuck on shore watching others have fun. By summer, I hope to be a confident swimmer, **a**ble to enjoy myself in and on the water. I can hardly wait!

Exercise 6.6

1. F (After) class is over.	5. F (Who) encouraged us to keep
2. F (When) you wish upon a star.	trying until we succeeded.
3. S	
4. F (As soon as) the fog lifts.	6. S
	7. F (Even if) there is an earthquake.

Exercise 6.7

1. After class is over, <u>I am meeting</u> Manuel for coffee.
2. When you wish upon a star, your <u>dreams</u> <u>will come</u> true.
4. As soon as the fog lifts, <u>we</u> <u>can take</u> the boat out.
5. <u>It</u> <u>was</u> our coach who encouraged us to keep trying until we succeeded.
7. Even if there is an earthquake, <u>we</u> <u>should be</u> safe in our mountain retreat.

Exercise 6.8

1. Walking is probably the best form of exercise there is. *Unless you're in the water.* Then swimming is preferable.

2. Rain doesn't bother me. I love staying inside with a good book. *When the weather is miserable.*
3. Try this curry. *After you've tasted it.* I am sure it will be your favourite.
4. The report identifies a serious problem that we need to consider. *Whenever our Web site is revised or updated.* It is vulnerable to hackers.
5. Sanir and Jade asked us what we thought about their recent engagement. *Since they want to go to Canada's Wonderland for their honeymoon.* We concluded they were probably too young to get married.

Exercise 6.9
1. You keep the temperature in your apartment very low. *In order to save money.* I have to wear a sweater every time I visit.
2. Your idea that we should ask for directions was a good one. *If we had relied on the hand-drawn map we were given.* We would still be lost right now.
3. Home decoration isn't all that difficult. *When you don't have enough money for furniture, carpets, or curtains.* You have no choice but to be creative.
4. I believe that honesty is the best policy. *If I found a million dollars in the street and discovered it belonged to a poor homeless person.* I'd give it right back.
5. The names of many Canadian landmarks have been changed over the years. The Oldman River, for example, which runs through Lethbridge, used to be called the Belly River. *Until local residents petitioned for a change to a more dignified name.*

Exercise 6.10
Corrections to the fragments in Exercise 6.8
1. Walking is probably the best form of exercise there is **u**nless you're in the water. Then swimming is preferable.
2. Rain doesn't bother me. I love staying inside with a good book **w**hen the weather is miserable.
3. Try this curry. After you've tasted it**,** I am sure it will be your favourite.
4. The report identifies a serious problem that we need to consider. Whenever our Web site is revised or updated**, it** is vulnerable to hackers.
5. Sanir and Jade asked us what we thought about their recent engagement. Since they want to go to Canada's Wonderland for their honeymoon**, w**e concluded they were probably too young to get married.

Corrections to the fragments in Exercise 6.9
1. You keep the temperature in your apartment very low **i**n order to save money. I have to wear a sweater every time I visit.
2. Your idea that we should ask for directions was a good one. If we had relied on the hand-drawn map we were given**, w**e would still be lost right now.
3. Home decoration isn't all that difficult. When you don't have enough money for furniture, carpets, or curtains**, y**ou have no choice but to be creative.
4. I believe that honesty is the best policy. If I found a million dollars in the street and discovered that it belonged to a poor homeless person**,** I'd give it right back.
5. The names of many Canadian landmarks have been changed over the years. The Oldman River, for example, which runs through Lethbridge, used to be called the Belly River **u**ntil local residents petitioned for a change to a more dignified name.

Exercise 6.11
Because the chances of winning are so small**, l**otteries have been called a tax on people with poor math skills. Buying a lottery ticket will gain you about as much as betting that the next U.S. president will come from Moose Jaw**, or** that the parrot in the pet store speaks Inuktitut. While winning a lottery is not impossible**, it** is so unlikely that you'd do better to use your

money to light a nice warm fire. Though the winners are highly publicized, **n**o one hears about the huge numbers of losers **w**hose money has gone to pay the winners. In order for the lottery corporation to make its enormous profits, **m**illions of dollars must be lost whenever a lucky winner is declared.

Answers for Chapter 7: Solving Run-On Sentence Problems (pages 85 to 95)

Exercise 7.1
1. She's late again; she's always at least 15 minutes late.
2. Our manager works hard, **and** she is efficient.
3. It's getting dark, **so** we'd better hurry.
4. I think I have some change. **I**t's in my pocket.
5. Here's my number; give me a call.
6. We're going to Kim's; it's not very far.
7. Leo needs your help; his homework is too hard for him.
8. Press on the wound. **T**hat will stop the bleeding.
9. I'm busy right now, **so** you'll have to wait.
10. correct

Exercise 7.2
1. I hate computers; they're always making mistakes.
2. I'm trying to stop playing computer games, **for** they take up too much of my time.
3. This pie is delicious. **I** must have the recipe.
4. I'm innocent. **T**his is a case of mistaken identity.
5. This desk is made of pine with maple veneer, **and** the other is solid oak.
6. I'm going to stay up all night tonight **because** I don't want to miss my 8:30 class.
7. It's too bad you don't like hockey because I have two tickets to tomorrow's game. **I**t'll be a good one.
8. You can't take your money with you, **but** it's not a good idea to give it away too soon.
9. correct
10. The good may sleep better at night, **but** the bad seem to enjoy their waking hours more.

Exercise 7.3
1. His favourite music is the Blues **because** it complements his personality and temperament.
2. This restaurant is terribly slow. **I**t will be supper time when we finally get our lunch.
3. I'm investing all my money in this week's lottery **because** the jackpot is over ten million dollars.
4. Computers make it easier to do many things, **but** most of the time these things don't need to be done.
5. correct
6. If I never again see a fast-food breakfast, it will be too soon. **T**he last one I ate nearly put me in the hospital.
7. The fine art of whacking an electronic device to get it to work again is called "percussive maintenance." **N**ine times out of ten, it works.
8. The English language makes no sense. **W**hy do people recite at a play and play at a recital?
9. I write in my journal every day. **W**hen I'm ninety, I want to read about all the important events in my life.
10. We have not inherited the Earth from our ancestors; we are borrowing it from our children.

Exercise 7.4
1. Many parents will agree **that** the first sign of adulthood is the discovery that volume can be turned down as well as up. **T**his realization does not happen overnight. **F**or some people, the process takes years.

2. There are two students in this class named Xan. **O**ne is from China; the other is from Russia. **T**he latter's name is a nickname, a short form of Alexandra.

3. I'm reading a collection of unintentionally funny newspaper headlines**, and** they are hilarious. **T**he book contains hundreds of examples of headlines that did not say what their writers intended. **M**y favourite is from the sports pages, **and** it reads, "Grandmother of Eight Makes Hole in One."

4. Some of my other favourites include examples of the spectacular talent of headline writers for stating the obvious, such as "Smokers are Productive, but Death Cuts Efficiency**.**" **A**nother is "Man is Fatally Slain." **I**s the reader really supposed to think these headlines are news?

5. If you have trouble getting your child's attention, all you have to do is sit down and get comfortable, pick up a book, turn on the TV, or just relax. **Y**our child will be all over you in no time. **T**his is why, when children are out of school for summer holidays, parents begin to understand why primary school teachers deserve twice the salary they currently earn.

Exercise 7.5

Once upon a time, three travellers came upon a raging river **that** prevented them from continuing their journey. **L**uckily, however, they got to the river just in time to rescue a magic elf from the rushing water. **S**he was so grateful to them for saving her life that she told them she would grant each of them one wish. **T**he first man wished for the strength to be able to cross the river**,** and instantly his arms and legs developed powerful muscles that enabled him to swim easily to the other side. **T**he second man wished for a boat that would carry him across. **H**is wish was granted in the form of a sturdy rowboat and strong oars, **which** allowed him to make his way safely to the other side. The third man, having observed the success of his two companions, wanted to show that he could outsmart them, **so** he asked for the intelligence that would enable him to cross the water with the least possible effort. **H**e was immediately transformed into a woman who realized there was a bridge a few metres downstream and walked across it to the other shore.

Exercise 7.6

1. That joke isn't the least bit funny. **I**t's sexist**,** and I'm surprised you told it.
2. The snow continues to fall; **it** hasn't let up for three days.
3. I've always driven a small car. I think the huge boats driven by many North Americans are ridiculous **t**hough I agree they are comfortable.
4. Mike has given up meat and become a vegetarian. **C**ounting today and the day he started his new diet, he hasn't had a hamburger in two days.
5. I need a cup of coffee; a caffeine lift in the middle of a difficult day helps keep me alert.
6. CRNC is the home of the million dollar guarantee. **Y**ou give us a million dollars, **and** we guarantee to play any song you want.
7. Tamara plays violin in a professional orchestra, **so** it's unlikely she'll be impressed by my skill on the one instrument I can play, **the** tambourine.
8. The cat is attacking the curtains again. **S**ince yesterday, when you put up the bird feeder outside the window, she's been climbing the curtains all day long **t**o get at the birds.
9. Television is a mass medium, **and** comedians since the 1950s have suggested that it's called a mass medium because things on it are rarely well done. **This** joke was funny once but now is old and tired.
10. It's far too hot. **N**o one feels like working**,** **n**ot even people who claim to like summer temperatures.

Answers for Chapter 8: Solving Modifier Problems (pages 96 to 106)

Exercise 8.1
1. The president fired only those who had failed to meet their sales quotas.
2. We were nearly run over by every car that passed.
3. The flag was raised just at sunrise.
4. She was exhausted after walking merely 300 metres.
5. After the fire, she took her clothes with the most smoke damage to the cleaners.
6. The French drink wine with almost every meal, including lunch.
7. The suspect gave the police scarcely any information.
8. He was underwater for nearly two minutes before surfacing.
9. We camped during August in a national park with lots of wild life.
10. A huge tree, even one more than 300 years old, can be cut by any idiot with a chainsaw.

Exercise 8.2
1. They closed just before five.
2. I have nearly been fired every week that I have worked here.
3. A computer that frequently crashes needs to be replaced.
4. Matti couldn't force the loudly braying donkey to take a single step.
5. We have computers with little memory and constant breakdowns for all office staff.
6. Canadians enjoy almost the highest standard of living in the world.
7. We bought gifts with batteries included for the children.
8. Kevin bought only three lottery tickets this week.
9. This is a book with real weight and depth for avid readers.
10. Trevor crouched with binoculars behind a tree and watched the rabbit.

Exercise 8.3
1. When running competitively, you must have a thorough warm-up.
2. As a college teacher, I find dangling modifiers annoying.
3. After revising her résumé, filling out the application, and going through the interview, she lost the position to someone else.
4. Getting to the meeting room 20 minutes late, we found everyone had left.
5. After cooking all day long, we thought the gourmet meal was worth the effort.
6. Having arrived so late, our guests were served a cold meal.
7. Driving recklessly, André was stopped at a road block by the police.
8. Dressed in a new miniskirt, she looked terrific to her boyfriend.
9. After waiting 20 minutes, we finally got the attention of the server.
10. Having been convicted of breaking and entering, Bambi was sentenced to two years in prison.

Exercise 8.4
1. Travelling in Quebec, you will find a knowledge of French is useful.
2. Her saddle firmly cinched, the mare was led out of the barn.
3. After playing for the crowd all night, the band welcomed the applause.
4. Being terribly shy, she was given a quiet birthday party by the family.
5. Badly banged up in the collision, the boat was brought slowly into dock.
6. Standing in the cold water for more than an hour, he was numbed to the bone by the cold.
7. Being very weak in math, I found the job was out of my reach.
8. Looking for a job, you'll find a good résumé is vital to success.
9. Living kilometres from anything, I find a car is a necessity.
10. Having had the same roommate for three years, I was urged by my parents to look for another.

Exercise 8.5
 1. When you are running competitively, a thorough warm-up is necessary.
 2. Since I am a college teacher, I find dangling modifiers annoying.
 3. After she had revised her résumé, filled out the application, and gone through the interview, the position was taken by someone else.
 4. When we got to the meeting room 20 minutes late, everyone had left.
 5. Although we had cooked all day long, the gourmet meal was worth the effort.
 6. Since our guests arrived so late, the meal was cold.
 7. Because André was driving recklessly, the police stopped him at a road block.
 8. When she was dressed in her new miniskirt, her boyfriend thought she looked terrific.
 9. After we had waited 20 minutes, the server finally came to our table.
 10. After she had been convicted of breaking and entering, the judge sentenced Bambi to two years in prison.

Exercise 8.6
 1. When you are travelling in Quebec, a knowledge of French is useful.
 2. As soon as the mare's saddle was firmly cinched, Marie led her out of the barn.
 3. After the band had played for the crowd all night, the applause was welcome.
 4. Because she was terribly shy, the family gave her a quiet birthday party.
 5. Because the boat had been badly banged up in the collision, Kathy brought it slowly into dock.
 6. When he had stood in the cold water for more than an hour, it numbed him to the bone.
 7. Since I am very weak in math, the job was out of my reach.
 8. When you are looking for a job, a good résumé is vital to success.
 9. Since I live kilometres away from anything, a car is a necessity.
 10. Because I've had the same roommate for three years, my parents suggested that I look for another.

Exercise 8.7
 1. The sign said that only students were admitted to the pub.
 2. While sleeping, I kicked the blankets off the bed.
 3. The lion was recaptured by the trainer before anyone was mauled or bitten.
 4. Swimming isn't a good idea if the water is polluted.
 5. Joseph found his dog gnawing on a bone.
 6. Employees who are often late are dismissed without notice. (*Or*: Employees who are late are often dismissed without notice.)
 7. After we waited for you for more than an hour, the evening was ruined.
 8. As we drove through the desert, our mouths became drier and drier.
 9. Because of her experience, we hired the first designer who applied.
 10. For 20 minutes, the president spoke glowingly of the retiring workers who had worked long and loyally.

Exercise 8.8
 1. Everyone stared as she rode in a bikini through town on a horse.
 2. Though they drink city water daily, many residents distrust it.
 3. Being an introvert who disliked crowds, Paul chose a dog as his chief companion.
 4. Although Jan lives more than 50 km away, he manages to come to nearly every class.
 5. Before you begin to write the exam, prayer is a recommended strategy.
 6. After her Dachshund had given birth to a litter of twelve, my sister had the dog neutered.
 7. I heard on a sports phone-in show about the team's star player being hurt.
 8. Canadians learned in a news flash that a new government had been elected.

9. The police recommend that you check the ownership records before buying a used car.

10. We were almost shot the first time we went into the forest during hunting season.

Answers for Chapter 9: The Parallelism Principle (pages 107 to 113)

Exercise 9.1
1. This is a book to read, enjoy, and remember.
2. The new brochure on career opportunities is attractive and informative.
3. Except that it was too long, too violent, and too expensive, it was a great movie.
4. He ate his supper, did the dishes, watched television, and went to bed.
5. Barking dogs and screaming children keep me from enjoying the park.
6. In this clinic, we care for the sick, the injured, and the disabled.
7. If she wasn't constantly eating chips, playing bingo, and smoking cigarettes, she'd have plenty of money for groceries.
8. Despite the good salary, stimulating environment, and generous benefits, I won't be taking the job.
9. So far, the countries I have most enjoyed visiting are China for its people, France for its food, and Brazil for its beaches.
10. She was discouraged by the low pay, the long hours, and the office politics.

Exercise 9.2
1. During her presentation, she appeared professional, sounded knowledgeable, but felt foolish.
2. They are a good team, hard hitting, fast skating, and quick thinking.
3. I hold a baseball bat right-handed but hold a hockey stick left-handed. (*Or*: I play baseball right-handed but hockey left-handed.)
4. A good student attends all classes and finishes all projects on time.
5. A good teacher motivates with enthusiasm, informs with sensitivity, and counsels with compassion.
6. A good college president has the judgement of Solomon, the wisdom of Plato, and the wit of Rick Mercer.
7. All his life, Churchill was a walking advertisement for Cuban cigars, Portuguese wines, and English hats.
8. Our staff development budget must be increased if we are to provide upgrading, supply training, and encourage personal development for 40 new employees.
9. Canadians must register the cars they drive, the businesses they own, the contracts they make, the houses they buy, and now the guns they possess.
10. Winter for its cozy fires, summer for its outdoor sports, spring for its flowering trees, and autumn for its spectacular colours: each season has its special appeal.

Exercise 9.3
1. sadly
2. taste the wine
3. understand
4. loosen
5. engineering
6. knowledge
7. well educated
8. exploring fully

Exercise 9.5

Photography is a hobby that is educational, **enjoyable**, and practical. Anyone can be successful as a beginning photographer because entry level cameras are **now** well made, almost foolproof, and **quite inexpensive**. The pictures they take, however, are of excellent quality

and encourage the beginner to learn more. The next step might be a 35 mm camera with interchangeable lenses that permit the photographer to enlarge an image and **create special effects**. While these are expensive toys, they provide a great range of possibilities**. T**he "point and press" cameras, no matter how expensive, just don't measure up.

An alternative to 35 mm is digital photography. Compared to 35 mm, digital cameras are less flexible and **more expensive**. These cameras are evolving so rapidly, however, that within a few years, digital will overtake 35 mm in price, quality, and **popularity**. Even now, digital photography has significant advantages. Pictures are loaded on computer disks, so the images can be stored, re-recorded, and **manipulated**. By downloading the pictures into a computer with imaging software, **the photographer can enhance, re-size, and change the images**. Digital photography is the latest stage in the evolution of this intriguing hobby.

Answers for Chapter 10: Refining by Combining (pages 114 to 126)

Exercise 10.1
1. Although the test was difficult, I passed it. (*Or*: The test was difficult, but I passed it.)
2. After eating our lunch, we continued working. (*Or*: We ate our lunch, then we continued working.)
3. correct
4. Since our essay is due tomorrow, we must stay up late tonight. (*Or*: Our essay is due tomorrow, so we must stay up late tonight.)
5. Even though the pictures are good, I hate seeing myself. (*Or*: The pictures are good, yet I hate seeing myself.)
6. correct
7. Though having a car would be convenient, I need the money for other things. (*Or*: Having a car would be convenient, but I need the money for other things.)
8. If this book will help me, I will buy it. (*Or*: This book will help me, so I will buy it.)
9. Where a mistake has been found, it must be corrected. (*Or*: A mistake has been found, so it must be corrected.)
10. correct

Exercise 10.2
1. I have a teacher who always wears a tie.
2. Here is the car that is always breaking down.
3. I am enrolled in an art class that meets Wednesday evenings.
4. That singer whose name I always forget just won a Grammy.
5. The pen that you gave me is broken.
6. My plant, which you never watered, is dead.
7. The cell phone that you always carry is ringing.
8. Lisa babysits for a man whose wife speaks only Japanese.
9. The taxi driver who took me to the airport drove 20 km over the speed limit all the way.
10. My roommate whose snoring keeps me awake is finally moving out.

Exercise 10.3
1. There is bad weather when the wind blows from the east.
2. These shoes fit well, yet they weren't very expensive.
3. Some college students believe that high marks in college are a matter of luck.
4. She has both oars in the water, but they are on the same side of the boat.
5. Rail travel is declining, even though it is economical.
6. Shelagh Rogers, who is an announcer for the CBC, has an unforgettable giggle.
7. Just when they ran out of money, they won the lottery.

8. Newfoundlanders are beginning to realize that their economy cannot rely on unlimited fish stocks.
9. Our department needs an increase in its budget, but the company's accountants want to reduce it.
10. Although it keeps me awake, I love the taste of strong, hot coffee.

Exercise 10.4 (suggested answers)
1. The cursor is blinking, but there is no response.
2. The village that I grew up in is very small.
3. My car is in the repair shop because it needs a new alternator.
4. The textbook contains information that will be on tomorrow's exam.
5. I'm not in favour of apathy, nor am I against it.
6. Banging your head against a wall uses 150 calories an hour.
7. Although the movie was terrible and our car broke down, we had a good time anyway.
8. Many of my friends send me pictures with their e-mail, but my computer doesn't have enough memory to receive them.
9. This restaurant is very expensive, but I don't mind paying the price for good food and excellent service.
10. Some people enjoy hockey while others prefer soccer, the world's most popular spectator sport.

Exercise 10.5 (suggested answers)
1. A good manager must have many skills, but the most important is the ability to delegate.
2. The stapler that was clearly labelled with my name is missing.
3. Weyburn, Saskatchewan, is where I was born, but I have not lived there since I was a baby.
4. Although a sauna provides no proven health benefits, I find one very refreshing when the weather is cold.
5. English muffins were not invented in England nor were French fries invented in France.
6. "Irritainment" is a word used to describe media spectacles that are annoying but strangely addictive.
7. One example of "irritainment" was the Monica Lewinsky scandal, and another was *Survivor*.
8. Our college has a Continuing Education Department that offers both credit and interest courses at night.
9. Tisa is a Canadian citizen who was born in Halifax, but she has American citizenship too because she has lived most of her life in Texas.
10. My roommate, who is not too bright, takes an hour and a half to watch *60 Minutes* on television.

Answers for Chapter 11: Choosing the Right Words (pages 127 to 137)

Exercise 11.2 (suggested answers)
1. Several close friends and I have decided to go to the gym.
2. We were amazed to learn that the painting hanging in our residence was the work of a famous artist.
3. Though small and light, she is the best forward on our team.
4. We can never be free of the violence that surrounds us.
5. The professor then destroyed my concentration by announcing that we had only five minutes left.

Exercise 11.4 (suggested answers)
1. You should be careful when using an axe.
2. We live at the corner of Elm and Trasker Streets.

3. After we looked over the task, we decided to ask for help.
4. His boss is aware of that young man's dislike of work.
5. We are all trying hard to finish this project so that we can submit it by the deadline.

Exercise 11.5 (suggested answers)

1. Prakash is highly talented, so he could have chosen many different careers.
2. Regardless of your opinion, I think the media are fairly reliable.
3. Between you and me, Karol didn't perform very well in this afternoon's practice.
4. The reason I am home now is that I couldn't do anything to help at the hospital. (*Or:* I'm home now because I couldn't do anything to help at the hospital.)
5. The reason you are failing is that you don't do any homework. (*Or:* You are failing because you don't do homework.)
6. We were sure of ourselves going into the race, but once we fell off our bikes, we could hardly hope to win. (*Or . . .* we couldn't hope to win.)
7. Isa's father is not prejudiced; he hates all her boyfriends, regardless of their backgrounds.
8. There have been many investigations into charges that our police department demonstrates prejudice against minority groups.
9. I'm grateful to you for helping me the way you used to so long ago.
10. We drove Karia home because, after the police took her license, she wasn't supposed to be driving anywhere.

Answers for Unit 3 Quick Quiz: Grammar (pages 140 to 142)

(Deleted words are indicated by ***.)

1   "What's in a name?" Shakespeare asked. The answer is, "a lot." For instance, **your name may indicate the decade in which you were born**. Like skirt length and tie width, names **go** in and out of fashion. If your grandparents **were** born in North America, it wouldn't be surprising if their names **were** John and Mary because those names were very popular in the early part of the 20th century. Other favourites of the era **were** William, James, George, Helen, Margaret, and Mildred.

2   If your father and mother were born in the 1940s or 1950s, **he** and **she** might very well be named Robert, Mark, or Richard, and Linda, Barbara, or Patricia. Interestingly, the name Michael first appeared on the top ten list in the 1950s and then **topped** the charts as the most popular male name for the next 40 years. Men's names seem to change fashion more slowly than women's names.

3   In the 1960s, the name Lisa **became** the most popular female name. Other favourites included Kimberley, Donna, and Michelle. If you **were** born in North America in the 1970s, there is a good chance that **your** parents named you Jennifer, Amy, or Jessica; or Christopher, Matthew, or Justin. In the 1980s, baby boys were likely to be named Joshua, Daniel, or Jason. Those little boys probably **went** to kindergarten with a lot of little girls named Amanda, Ashley, and Tiffany. In the 1990s, the most popular names were Jacob, Nicholas, and Tyler for boys; Emily, Brittany, and Megan for girls.

4   What about the future? A Web site called Babyzone.com offers advice for soon-to-be parents. It tells **them** that "power names" for the new century **include** one-syllable names such as Grace, Cole, and Claire. Place names are also high on the list: Dakota, Dallas, Phoenix, and India. For new parents **who** are curious about unusual names celebrities **have given** their children, Babyzone advises that musician Bob Geldof and his wife **named their** three daughters Peaches, Pixie, and Fifi-Trixibelle.

5   If you are interested in tradition, **Babyzone also provides** a list of Shakespearean names. The works of Shakespeare are full of beautiful names (e.g., Miranda, Olivia, Ariel), but if you're tempted to choose a Shakespearean name for your baby, **you should read** the play first. It would be a real burden for a child to go through *** life as Malvolio, Goneril, or Caliban.

IF YOU MISSED . . .	SEE
Paragraph 1:	
the decade in which you were born may be indicated by your name	Chapter 12, Choosing the Correct Verb Form (Active and Passive Voice)
names will go	Chapter 14, Keeping Your Tenses Consistent
If your grandparents was	Chapter 13, Mastering Subject–Verb Agreement
if their names be	Chapter 12, Choosing the Correct Verb Form (Irregular Verbs)
Other favourites . . . was	Chapter 13, Mastering Subject–Verb Agreement
Paragraph 2:	
him and her might	Chapter 15, Choosing the Correct Pronoun Form
then tops the charts	Chapter 14, Keeping Your Tenses Consistent
Paragraph 3:	
the name Lisa become	Chapter 12, Choosing the Correct Verb Form (Irregular Verbs)
If you was born	Chapter 13, Mastering Subject–Verb Agreement
that one's parents	Chapter 17, Maintaining Person Agreement
probably go to kindergarten	Chapter 14, Keeping Your Tenses Consistent
Paragraph 4:	
It tells you	Chapter 17, Maintaining Person Agreement
"power names" for the new century includes	Chapter 13, Mastering Subject–Verb Agreement
For new parents that	Chapter 16, Mastering Pronoun–Antecedent Agreement (Relative Pronouns)
celebrities have gave	Chapter 12, Choosing the Correct Verb Form (Irregular Verbs)
Geldof and his wife names	Chapter 14, Keeping Your Tenses Consistent
his three daughters	Chapter 16, Mastering Pronoun–Antecedent Agreement
Paragraph 5:	
a list of Shakespearean names are also provided	Chapter 12, Choosing the Correct Verb Form (Active and Passive Voice)
the play should be read	Chapter 12, Choosing the Correct Verb Form (Active and Passive Voice)
go through their life	Chapter 16, Mastering Pronoun–Antecedent Agreement

Answers for Chapter 12: Choosing the Correct Verb Form (pages 143 to 158)

Exercise 12.1

1. wear   You **wore** your good hiking boots only once, but after you have **worn** them several times, you won't want to take them off.
2. give   The tourists **gave** Terry a tip after she had **given** them directions to the hotel.
3. begin   After the project had **begun**, the members of the team soon **began** to disagree on how to proceed.
4. eat   I **ate** as though I had not **eaten** in a month.
5. cost   The vacation in Cuba **cost** less than last year's trip to Jamaica had **cost** and was much more fun.
6. bring   If you have **brought** your children with you, I hope you also **brought** a play pen to keep them out of trouble during your stay.
7. grow   The noise from the party next door **grew** louder by the hour, but by midnight I had **grown** used to it, and went to sleep.
8. sit   Marc **sat** in front of the TV all morning; by evening he will have **sat** there for eight hours—a full working day!
9. write   After she had **written** the essay that was due last week, she **wrote** e-mails to all her friends.
10. pay   I **paid** off my credit cards, so I have not **paid** this month's rent.

Exercise 12.2

1. ride   I had never **ridden** in a stretch limo until I **rode** in one at Jerry's wedding.
2. sing   She **sang** a silly little song that her father had **sung** when she was a baby.
3. teach   Harold had been **taught** to play by a loving father, and that was the way he **taught** his daughter.
4. find   He **found** the solution that hundreds of mathematicians over three centuries had not **found**.
5. fly   Suzhu had once **flown** to Whitehorse, so when she **flew** north to Tuktoyaktuk, she knew what to expect.
6. feel   At first, they had **felt** silly in the new uniforms, but after winning three games in a row, they **felt** much better.
7. lie   The cat **lay** right where the dog had **lain** all morning.
8. go   We **went** to our new home to find that the movers had **gone** to the wrong address to deliver our furniture.
9. lose   The reason you **lost** those customers is that you have **lost** confidence in your sales technique.
10. steal   I **stole** two customers away from the sales representative who earlier had **stolen** my best account.

Exercise 12.3

1. think   I had **thought** that you were right, but when I **thought** more about your answer, I realized you were wrong.
2. buy   If we had **bought** this stock 20 years ago, the shares we **bought** would now be worth a fortune.
3. do   They **did** what was asked, but their competitors, who had **done** a better job, got the contract.
4. show   Today our agent **showed** us a house that was much better suited to our needs than anything she had **shown** us previously.
5. hurt   Budget cuts had **hurt** the project, but today's decision to lay off two of our workers **hurt** it even more.
6. throw   The rope had not been **thrown** far enough to reach those in the water, so Mia pulled it in and **threw** it again.

7. lay   Elzbieta **laid** her passport on the official's desk where the other tourists had **laid** theirs.

8. put   I have **put** your notebook in the mail, but your pen and glasses I will **put** away until I see you again.

9. fight   My parents **fought** again today, the way they have **fought** almost every day for the last 20 years.

10. break   She **broke** the Canadian record only six months after she had **broken** her arm in training.

Exercise 12.5

1. _A_   The professor <u>checks</u> our homework every day.
2. _P_   The report <u>is being prepared</u> by the marketing department.
3. _P_   The car <u>was being driven</u> by a chauffeur.
4. _A_   Clyneria <u>will invite</u> Kiefer to the party.
5. _P_   The CN Tower <u>is visited</u> by hundreds of people every day.
6. _A_   My best friend <u>designed</u> this bracelet.
7. _P_   *The English Patient* <u>was written</u> by Canadian author Michael Ondaatje.
8. _A_   Hollywood <u>made</u> the book into a successful movie.
9. _P_   The song <u>was performed</u> by Eminem.
10. _A_   A hurricane <u>is destroying</u> your village!

Exercise 12.6

1. Our homework is checked by the professor every day.
2. The marketing department is preparing the report.
3. A chauffeur was driving the car.
4. Kiefer will be invited to the party by Clyneria.
5. Hundreds of visitors visit the CN Tower every day.
6. This bracelet was designed by my best friend.
7. Canadian author Michael Ondaatje wrote *The English Patient*.
8. The book was made into a successful movie by Hollywood.
9. Eminem performed the song.
10. Your village is being destroyed by a hurricane!

Exercise 12.7

1. Lisa named the puppy.
2. I let out a great sigh of relief.
3. The sales representative gave me his business card.
4. Our computer made an error in your bill.
5. My brother took the short route home.
6. On our first anniversary, we had our portrait taken by a professional photographer.
7. Canadians do not always understand American election practices.
8. Most Americans know very little about Canada.
9. In today's class, all students will work on their research papers.
10. This book contains all the information you need to become a competent writer.

Exercise 12.8

1. Bambi told the professor that she was finding the course too difficult. (Active voice is more effective.)
2. A member of our staff did not type this document. (Passive voice is more effective; the person who did or did not type the document is unknown.)
3. A Ford Explorer running a red light almost ran into a group of pedestrians. (Active voice is more effective.)
4. My new bifocals helped me to read. (Active voice is more effective.)

5. Someone had dragged the body for almost 2 km before hiding it in the underbrush. (Passive voice is more effective because it places the emphasis on the body—the object affected by the action—rather than on the unknown person who performed the action.)

6. At 4:00 each afternoon, the dining room servers lay the linens and set the tables. (Active voice is more effective.)

7. In the parade around the stadium, a biathlete carried the Olympic flag. (Passive voice is more effective because it puts the focus on the Olympic flag, an enduring symbol, rather than on the unknown athlete who happened to carry it in this particular parade.)

8. Poor communication between the members of the team delayed the project. (Active voice is more effective. Projects are often delayed, but we don't always know why they are delayed, so the emphasis on the "actors" gives useful information.)

9. My brother uses his bookcase to hold his bowling trophies and empty fast food containers. (Active voice is more effective.)

10. The provincial government has declared a state of emergency and set up a special fund to aid the flood victims. (Active voice is more effective for two reasons: the doer of the action is known and so should occupy the subject position, and the passive construction is too wordy for easy reading.)

Answers for Chapter 13: Mastering Subject–Verb Agreement (pages 159 to 172)

Exercise 13.1
1. key
2. invoices
3. people
4. Professor Temkin
5. Jupiter, Saturn

Exercise 13.2
1. A <u>girl</u> just <u>wants</u> to have fun.
2. Our <u>dog</u> <u>barks</u> at strangers.
3. The <u>technician</u> <u>has gone</u> to a conference in Vancouver.
4. Under our back porch <u>lives</u> a huge <u>raccoon</u>.
5. <u>Has</u> the lucky <u>winner</u> <u>collected</u> the lottery money?
6. The <u>article</u> in this journal <u>gives</u> you the background information you need.
7. A <u>hotel</u> within walking distance of the arena <u>is</u> a necessity for our team.
8. Only recently <u>has</u> our track <u>coach</u> <u>become</u> interested in chemistry.
9. So far, only <u>one</u> of your answers <u>has been</u> incorrect.
10. The <u>pressure</u> of school work and part-time work <u>has caused</u> many students to drop out.

Exercise 13.3
1. A good <u>example</u> <u>is</u> hockey players.
2. <u>Sardines</u> <u>are</u> a healthy type of oily fish.
3. A <u>necessity</u> in my job <u>is</u> hand held computers.
4. Noisy <u>speedboats</u> <u>are</u> what irritate us on our quiet lake.
5. An important <u>part</u> of a balanced diet <u>is</u> fresh fruits and vegetables.

Exercise 13.4

    A dog seems to understand the **mood** of **its owner. It is** tuned in to any **shift** in emotion or **change** in health of the **human it lives** with. **A doctor** will often suggest adding **a pet** to **a household** where there **is someone** (*or* **a person**) suffering from depression or **an** emotional **problem. A dog is a** sympathetic **companion**. The **mood** of **an elderly person** in **a** retirement **home** or even **a** hospital **ward** can be brightened by **a visit** from **a** pet **owner** and **a dog. A dog** never **tires** of hearing about the "good old days," and **it is** uncritical and unselfish in giving affection. **A doctor** will often encourage **an** epilepsy **sufferer** to adopt **a** specially trained **dog**. Such **a dog is** so attuned to the health of **its owner** that **it** can sense when **a seizure is** about to occur long before **its owner** can. The **dog** then **warns** the **owner** of the coming attack, so the **owner is** able to take safety precautions.

Exercise 13.5

1. live	3. have	5. know
2. reveals	4. fascinates	

Exercise 13.6

1. wants	3. was	5. don't
2. has	4. is	

Exercise 13.7

1. has	3. wants	5. is
2. succeeds	4. makes	

Exercise 13.8

1. is	3. goes	5. takes
2. is	4. was	

Exercise 13.9

1. Not only cat hairs but also ragweed **makes** me sneeze.
2. If either of the twins **wears** blue, the other is sure to wear green.
3. Neither high wind nor heavy rains **were** enough to stop our hike on the Coastal Trail.
4. Every one of the winners **has** accepted an invitation to the awards ceremony.
5. None of the winners **wants** to have her picture taken for publicity.
6. The mother panda, together with her cubs, two handlers, a vet, and three tonnes of food, **is** being shipped on a chartered jet.
7. In every group project, there is one member of the team who always **gets** stuck with most of the work.
8. According to a survey by my fitness club, either weight lifting or aerobic workouts **were** what most members wanted.

Exercise 13.10

1. Each day that passes **brings** us closer to the end of term.
2. A Quetchua Indian living in the Andes Mountains **has** two or three more litres of blood than people living at lower elevations.
3. The sisters as well as their obnoxious brother **plan** to visit us, but each of them **wants** a personal invitation first.
4. Neither your e-mail messages nor your telephone call **was** passed along to me because the office **is** short staffed this week.
5. The original model for the king in a standard deck of playing cards **is** thought to be King Charles I of England.
6. A large planet together with two small stars **is** visible on the eastern horizon.
7. Each of the three heavenly bodies **appears** to be a pale, silvery blue.
8. One faculty member in addition to a group of students **has** volunteered to help us clean out the lab.

Exercise 13.11

The rewards of obtaining a good summer or part-time job **go** well beyond the money you earn from your labour. Contacts that may be valuable in the future and experience in the working world **are** an important part of your employment. Even if the jobs you get while attending school **have** nothing to do with your future **goals**, they offer many benefits. For example, when considering job applicants, an employer always **prefers** someone who can be counted on to arrive at the work site on time, get along with fellow workers, and follow directions. Neither instinct nor instruction **takes** the place of experience in teaching the basic facts of working life. These long-term considerations, in addition to the money that is the immediate reward, **are** what **make** part-time work so valuable. Everyone who **has** worked part time while going to school **is** able to confirm these observations.

Exercise 13.12

1. singular	5. singular	9. singular
2. singular	6. singular	10. singular
3. plural	7. singular	
4. singular	8. plural	

Answers to Chapter 14: Keeping Your Tenses Consistent (pages 173 to 177)

Exercise 14.1
1. When the Leafs scored a goal, the crowd **applauded** politely.
2. Alain went home and **told** Gulçan what happened.
3. Gil tried to laugh, but he **was** too upset even to speak.
4. After his fiancée broke up with him, she **refused** to return his ring.
5. correct
6. The rebellion failed because the people **did** not support it.
7. I enjoy my work, but I **am** not going to let it take over my life.
8. Prejudice is learned and **is** hard to outgrow.
9. A Canadian is someone who thinks that an income tax refund **is** a gift from the government.
10. Janelle goes to the gym every day, where she **works** out and **has** a sauna.

Exercise 14.2
1. We need proof that the picture **is** genuine.
2. When Madonna came on stage, the crowd **went** crazy.
3. The couple living in the apartment next door had a boa constrictor that **kept** getting loose.
4. correct
5. It was getting dark, but Stanley **was** not afraid.
6. I had about 30 computer games on my hard drive until my brother accidentally **erased** them.
7. My deadline is Friday, and I **have** to submit an outline and a rough draft by then.
8. correct
9. I drank a half litre of milk, then I **ate** two protein- and veggie-stuffed wraps, and I **was** ready for anything.
10. It was great music for dancing, and it **was** being played by a super band.

Exercise 14.3
My most embarrassing moment occurred just last month when I **met** an old friend whom I **hadn't** seen in years. We **greeted** each other and **began** to chat, and I **told** her that I **had** been reading her daughter's columns in the newspaper. I **congratulated** her on her daughter's talent. I **told** her that she must be very proud to see her offspring's name in print. My friend **looked** puzzled for a minute, then she **laughed** and **told** me that the writer I **was** praising so highly **wasn't** her daughter. My friend had divorced long ago; her former husband **had remarried**, and the columnist **was** her ex-husband's new wife.

Answers for Chapter 15: Choosing the Correct Pronoun Form (pages 178 to 184)

Exercise 15.1

1. I	5. They	9. they . . . we
2. me	6. he	10. she . . . I
3. She	7. he	
4. her	8. them	

Exercise 15.2

1. Have you and **she** ever tried sky diving?
2. My boyfriend and **I** have completely different tastes in music.
3. It is not up to you or **me** to discipline your sister's children.
4. She and Xan took the videos back before Tami or **I** had seen them.
5. The rest is up to **him** and his team, because **we** volunteers have done enough.
6. Do you insist on seeing **them**, or could **we** possibly help you?
7. **He** and Marie finished on time; except for **them** and their staff, no one else met the deadline.

Exercise 15.3

1. The prize is sure to go to Omar and [to] **her**.
2. No one likes our cooking class more than **I** [do].
3. In fact, nobody in the class eats as much as **I** [do].
4. It's not surprising that I am much bigger than **they** [are].
5. My mother would rather cook for my brother than [for] **me** because he never complains when dinner is burned or raw.
6. At last I have met someone who loves barbecued eel as much as **I** [do]!
7. More than **I** [do], Yuxiang uses the computer to draft and revise his papers.
8. He doesn't write as well as **I** [do], but he does write faster.
9. Only a few Mexican food fanatics eat as many jalapeño peppers as **he** [does].
10. I think you have as much trouble with English as **I** [do].

Answers for Chapter 16: Mastering Pronoun–Antecedent Agreement (pages 185 to 196)

Exercise 16.1

1. Chi Keung is the technician **who** can fix the problem.
2. Halema plays the violin just like the musician **who** taught her to play.
3. A grouch is a person **who** knows himself and isn't happy about it.
4. The student **who** was asked to read claimed to have laryngitis.
5. I wish I could find someone in the class **who** could help me with my homework.
6. My quilt was bought by a woman **who** was looking for a gift for her grandchild.
7. The faculty **who** were present rejected the union steward's proposal.
8. Anyone **who** says he can see right through women is missing a lot. (Groucho Marx)
9. Is this the dog **that** bit the mail carrier **who** carries a squirt gun?
10. Ann has just started on the term paper, **which** was assigned a month ago, for her political science course.

Exercise 16.2

1. Each of the apartments we looked at was appealing in **its** own way.
2. Would someone kindly lend **a** copy of the text to Mei Yee?
3. Everyone is expected to pay **a** portion of the expenses.
4. No one who cares about **her** children will smoke in the house, or let **her** husband or friends smoke, either.

5. No one on the wrestling team has been able to get **his** parents to donate **their** house for the party.
6. None of our best jokes was enough by **itself** to get us hired by Tom Green.
7. Anyone who wants a high mark for **this** essay should see me after class and write out **a** cheque.

Exercise 16.3 (suggested answers)
1. Anyone **who** invests all **his or her** disposable income hopes to retire rich.
2. Every investor must find a level of risk **that is comfortable**.
3. For someone who can tolerate high risk, the return on **investment** can be huge; however, it is also possible **to lose everything one has invested**.
4. Every investment counsellor in this firm uses a Ouija board to make *** stock predictions.
5. For each person **who risks investing** in the stock market, there is someone **who** would rather keep money in a savings account.

Exercise 16.4 (suggested answers)
1. The frustrated programmer whacked the computer with his hand, breaking **the monitor**.
2. Every time David looked at the dog, **it** barked.
3. When I realized that smoking was the cause of my asthma, I gave up **cigarettes** for good.
4. Jack seems to have lost his scoring touch; he hasn't got **a goal** in six games.
5. Yasmin told her sister that their teacher liked **Yasmin's** essay.
6. Telling time seems to be a challenge for my girlfriend, so I'm getting her **a watch** for her birthday.
7. **Our college strictly enforces** the "no smoking" policy.
8. Ali sat down next to Muhsin and began to eat **Muhsin's** lunch.
9. During the all-candidates debate, Stockwell told Preston that **Preston** was not the man he used to be.
10. He didn't see that she had fallen overboard **because** he was concentrating on landing his fish.

Exercise 16.5

It seems that everyone in North America is keen on playing games involving useless bits of information called trivia. **Trivia players are** expected to have at their fingertips the names of obscure musical groups, statistics for unimportant sports events, details of world geography, and total knowledge of the film industry. Team trivia contests have become important fund raisers for charitable organizations, with **team members** expected to answer questions in their **areas** of expertise while as many as 300 rivals in the room cheer or jeer **the** answers. Television offers a variety of programs in which **contestants** must demonstrate their knowledge of useless information. In some games, the host gives the contestant a selection of answers; he may also give **the contestant** clues or aids to answering the question, **if requested**. In other games, the **contestants have** competitors whom they must challenge in order to take home the prize. Whether **people play** alone, with a group at home, in a team at a fund raiser, or on television, they shouldn't take a trivia game too seriously. After all, it's the only game in which the **winners** must admit that they have **more trivial minds** than the **losers**.

Answers for Chapter 17: Maintaining Person Agreement (pages 197 to 203)

Exercise 17.1
1. You shouldn't annoy the instructor if **you want** to get an A.
2. A person can succeed at almost anything if **he or she has** enough talent and determination.
3. When we came up for air, **we** couldn't see the boat!

4. After you have assembled the unit, **you** should give it a coat of paint.

5. You can save a great deal of time if **you fill** out the forms before going to the passport office.

6. Have you decided on a topic for **your** major project yet?

7. Our opinions will never be heard unless **we make** a serious effort to reach the public.

8. I wish that **we** had a few more options to choose from.

9. Anyone with a telephone can get **his or her** voice heard on the radio.

10. Call-in programs give everyone the opportunity to make sure the whole world knows **one's** ignorance of the issues.

Exercise 17.2 (suggested answers)

1. One is never too old to learn, but **one is** never too young to know everything.

2. One always removes **one's** shoes when entering a mosque.

3. When you wish upon a star, **your** dreams come true.

4. **You** ought to remember to keep a tight reign on your temper.

5. No one can blame you for trying to do your best, even if **you do** not always succeed.

6. Experience is that marvellous thing that enables us to recognize a mistake when **we** make it the second time. (F.P. Jones)

7. If you can't cope with the pressure, **you** must be expected to be replaced by someone who can.

8. We all need some unconditional love when **we're** having a bad day.

9. I find that unconditional love is most reliably offered by **my** dog.

10. **My** colleagues and superiors can make **me** feel stupid and insignificant, but my dog's whole world revolves around me.

Exercise 17.3

Those of us who enjoy baseball find it difficult to explain **our** enthusiasm to non-fans. We baseball enthusiasts can watch a game of three hours or more as **we follow** each play with rapt attention. We true fans get excited by a no-hitter—a game in which, by definition, nothing happens. **We** claim that the game offers more pleasures than mere action, but non-fans must be forgiven if **they** don't get the point. To them, watching a baseball game is about as exciting as watching paint dry.

Exercise 17.4 (suggested answers)
(Words or phrases that have been omitted are indicated by ***.)

When **we are** at the beginning of our careers, it seems impossible that **we** may one day wish to work less. The drive to get ahead leads many of us to sacrifice **our** leisure, **our** community responsibilities, even **our** family life for the sake of **our careers**. Normally, as **we age**, **our** priorities begin to change, and career success becomes less important than quality of life. Not everyone, however, experiences this shift in *** priorities. Indeed, some people work themselves to death, while others are so committed to their work throughout their lives that they die within months of *** retirement—presumably from stress caused by lack of work. The poet Robert Frost *** once observed that "By working faithfully eight hours a day, **you** may eventually get to be a boss. Then you can work twelve hours a day." Those of **us** who are living and working in the early years of the 21st century would be wise to take Frost's words to heart.

Answers for Unit 4 Quick Quiz: Punctuation (pages 206 to 208)

1   When we go to a movie, most of us like to sit back, munch away on a bucket of popcorn, and get lost in a good story filled with great-looking people. We forget that a film is a complex technical construct put together by huge teams of professionals who are responsible for its look, sound, and overall effect. Occasionally a "blooper"—a clumsy technical error—will remind us just what a complicated artifact a movie really is.

2   One kind of blooper is the anachronism: something in the movie that is inconsistent with the time period in which the movie is set. For example, in *Gladiator*, set 2,000 years ago in Roman times, tractor tracks are visible in the field that the hero Maximus walks by on his way home. You'll also see saddles with stirrups, an invention that didn't occur until nearly 800 years later. If you look carefully at the cigarettes that characters in *Titanic* are smoking, you'll see filter-tipped models that weren't invented until the 1940s. The ship sank in 1912. In Francis Coppola's classic film, *The Godfather*, two characters walk past a Volkswagen Beetle in 1945. The Beetle didn't come to the United States until well into the 1950s.

3   Then there is the "continuity" goof. Individual shots and scenes in a movie are filmed one at a time and often out of sequence; therefore, it is important to make sure that if, for instance, a character takes a drink from a glass in one shot, the glass has to be less full rather than more full in the next shot. Characters' hair, beards, and even fingernails have to be consistent over entire sequences. So do props. For example, when Sonny Corleone is blown away in *The Godfather*, the windshield of his car is shattered by a blast of **machine gun** fire. Seconds later in the next scene, his bodyguards arrive. They are too late to save Sonny, but somehow the windshield is miraculously intact: a classic continuity blooper.

4   Close viewers are also alert to geography errors. In the 1980 comedy *Caddyshack*, a character says he lives in Nebraska (a prairie state) as he rides by a palm tree in the opening credits. When the doomed ship first appears in *Titanic*, New York's Statue of Liberty is in the background; the geographical problem is that the ship left Southampton, England, and was bound for New York when the iceberg intervened.

5   Another blooper is visible film equipment or crew, but you have to be alert to catch these lapses. If you look closely at *The Matrix*, you'll see a few inches of wire on either side of Neo's hands when he backflips off the train tracks onto the platform. You can also spot a crew member in **blue jeans** sauntering around the background in a scene of *Gladiator*.

6   There are also factual errors. In *Charlie's Angels*, for example, the door of a commercial airline at cruising speed is opened up. Such a thing could not really occur because of the higher air pressure in the cabin. Even if it could happen, everything inside the cabin—**people and** objects—would be sucked outside the aircraft, ruining all the fun.

7   Perhaps ruining the fun is what's happening here. When we encounter a work of art, we want to achieve what the poet Coleridge called "the willing suspension of disbelief." We need to believe because getting lost in the story is the essence of a great movie. Bloopers can interfere with this belief, but so can looking too hard for mistakes!

IF YOU MISSED . . .	SEE
Paragraph 4:	
Caddyshack	Chapter 21, Quotation Marks, . . .
the background**;** the	Chapter 19, The Semicolon (independent clauses)
Paragraph 5:	
crew**,** but you	Chapter 18, The Comma (Rule 3)
*The Matrix***,** you'll	Chapter 18, The Comma (Rule 4)
blue jeans	Chapter 21, Quotation Marks, . . .
Paragraph 6:	
*Charlie's Angels***,** for example,	Chapter 19, The Semicolon (unnecessary semicolon)
people and objects	Chapter 18, The Comma (Rule 1)
Paragraph 7:	
what Coleridge called "the willing suspension of disbelief"	Chapter 21, Quotation Marks, . . .
mistakes**!**	Chapter 22, . . . Exclamation Marks, . . .

Answers for Chapter 18: The Comma (pages 209 to 218)

Exercise 18.1
1. Hirako held two aces, a King, a Queen, and a Jack in her hand.
2. This food is spicy, colourful, nourishing, and delicious.
3. In Canada, the seasons are spring, summer, fall, winter, winter, and winter.
4. correct
5. Cell phones, hand-held computers, and DVD players are three popular new technologies.
6. You need woolen underwear, showshoes, Arctic boots, but very little money to go winter camping.
7. Sleeping through my alarm, dozing during sociology, napping in the library after lunch, and snoozing in front of the TV all are symptoms of my overactive nightlife.
8. Once you have finished your homework, taken out the garbage, and done the dishes, you can feed the cat, clean your room, and do your laundry.
9. Don't forget to bring the photo album, videotape, and souvenirs of your trip to Australia.
10. Both my doctor and my nutritionist agree that I should eat better, exercise more, and give up smoking.

Exercise 18.2
1. Our family doctor, like our family dog, never comes when we call.
2. This photograph, taken when I was only four, embarrasses me whenever my parents show it.
3. Mira's boyfriend, who looks like an ape, is living proof that love is blind.
4. Isn't it strange that the poor, who are often bitterly critical of the rich, buy lottery tickets?
5. Several premiers and a former political advisor, a man now well into his eighties, accompanied the prime minister on his trade mission to China.
6. My car made it all the way to Saskatoon without anything falling off or breaking down, a piece of good luck that surprised us all.
7. A popular mathematics instructor, Professor Lam won the distinguished teaching award again this year.
8. We're going to the shopping mall, a weekly ritual we all enjoy.

9. correct
10. Classical music, which I call Prozac for the ears, can be very soothing in times of stress.

Exercise 18.3
1. This has been a perfect day, and you have been a perfect host.
2. We have a plan and a budget, yet we still don't have the staff we need.
3. Talk shows ran out of things to say years ago, but they haven't stopped talking yet.
4. We discovered that we both had an interest in art, so we made a date to go to an exhibition at the gallery next Friday.
5. correct
6. Take good notes, for there will be an exam on Tuesday.
7. You won't get any sympathy from us, nor will we help you explain to your parents.
8. correct
9. I have travelled all over the world, yet my luggage has visited many more places than I have.
10. Jet lag makes me look haggard and sick, but at least I resemble my passport picture.

Exercise 18.4
1. Unfortunately, we'll have to begin all over again.
2. Mr. Dillinger, the bank wants to speak with you.
3. In the end, the quality of your performance counts more than the effort you put into it.
4. Treading water, we waited for the boat to return and rescue us.
5. Even though this photograph is out of focus, it does show that Remi did take part in the Polar Bear swim.
6. Finally understanding what she was trying to say, I apologized for being so slow.
7. After an evening of watching television, I have accomplished as much as if I had been unconscious.
8. Since my doctor recommended that I get more exercise and eat less, I have been walking around the block during my lunch break.
9. Having munched our way through a large bag of peanuts while watching the game, we weren't interested in food by supper time.
10. Whenever a police officer pulls over an optimist, the optimist thinks it's to ask for directions.

Exercise 18.5
1. correct
2. correct
3. correct
4. Toronto in the summer is hot, smoggy, and humid.
5. Today's paper has an article about a new car made of lightweight, durable aluminum.
6. Using the new, improved model should increase your productivity.
7. This ergonomic, efficient, full-function keyboard comes in a variety of pastel shades.
8. We ordered a large, nutritious salad for lunch, then indulged ourselves with a whipped cream topped dessert.
9. Danni bought a cute, cuddly, pure-bred puppy.
10. Ten months later that cute puppy turned into a vicious, man-eating monster.

Exercise 18.6
1. I call my salary "take home pay," for home is the only place I can afford to go on what I make.
2. Madalena won my heart by laughing at my jokes, admiring my car, and tolerating my obsession with sports.
3. Though I try to remember my password, I seem to forget it at least once a month.

4. Leo went to the bank to withdraw enough money to pay for his tuition, books, and the student activity fee.
5. At her wedding reception, Luisa had an argument with her new mother-in-law about the guest seating.
6. The happiest years of my life, in my opinion, were the years I spent in college.
7. Sabina spends all day sleeping in bed, so she can spend all night dancing in the clubs.
8. Doing punctuation exercises is not very exciting, but it's cleaner than tuning your car.
9. This year, instead of the traditional gold watch, we will be giving retiring employees a framed photograph of our company's president.
10. Called Frobisher Bay until 1987, Iqaluit is a major centre on Baffin Island in Canada's eastern Arctic.

Exercise 18.7

To his surprise, a newly married man noticed that his wife always cut off both ends of a roast before she cooked it. When he asked her why she did this, she told him that her mother had always cut off both ends of the roast, so trimming the roast must be the proper technique for cooking it. In time, the young man got to know his in-laws well enough that he felt he could ask his mother-in-law why she cut the ends off the roast before putting it in the oven. In answer to his question, the mother-in-law replied that she did it because her own mother had always done it, and her mother was a wonderful cook. The young man made a special trip to Calgary, the city where his wife's grandmother lived, followed the directions to her house, and knocked on the door. He introduced himself, and the plump, grey-haired old woman invited him to join her for tea. After a pleasant conversation over tea with homemade scones and jam, he felt comfortable enough to ask his grandmother-in-law why she cut off the ends of a roast before cooking it. The old lady replied that, when she was a young mother, she had only one cooking pot, and it was too small to hold a roast large enough for the family. So she trimmed the roast to fit the pot. And thus a family tradition was born.

Answers for Chapter 19: The Semicolon (pages 219 to 225)

Exercise 19.1
2. correct
3. correct
4. correct
7. correct
10. correct

Exercise 19.2
1. We'll have to go soon; it's getting late. (*Or*: We'll have to go soon, for it's getting late.)
5. Make good notes on this topic; it could be on the exam. (*Or*: Make good notes on this topic, for it could be on the exam.)
6. If a tree falls in the woods where no one can hear it, does it make a noise?
8. Invented by a Canadian in the late 19th century, basketball is one of the world's most popular sports.
9. My neighbour works for a high-tech company, but he can't program his own VCR.

Exercise 19.3
1. We're late again; this is the third time this week.
2. I'm reading a book on levitation; I can't put it down.
3. correct
4. Catalina enjoys listening to music, but her tastes are much different from mine.
5. If you ever need a loan or a helping hand, just call Michel.
6. Travelling in Italy broadens the mind; eating Italian food broadens the behind.

7. North America's oldest continuously run horse race, the Queen's Plate, pre-dates the Kentucky Derby by 15 years.

8. We can't afford dinner at an expensive restaurant; instead, we'll eat some of my famous pork and beans at home.

9. She spends her days playing solitaire on the computer; watching daytime television whenever there's something interesting on; drinking coffee, which she makes so strong you could float a loonie on it; and talking on the phone to her other stay-at-home friends.

10. I am a marvellous housekeeper; every time I leave a man, I keep his house. (Zsa Zsa Gabor)

Exercise 19.4

1. An apple a day keeps the doctor away; however, an onion a day keeps everyone away.
2. Cash your pay cheque right away; this company might be out of business by morning.
3. The telephone has been ringing all day, but there's no one home to take the call.
4. This note says that we are supposed to be at the interview by 9:00 a.m.; consequently, we'll have to leave home by 7:30.
5. Some people are skilled in many fields; Kumari, for example, is both a good plumber and a great cook.
6. The proposal, which was unanimously accepted at the last meeting of our committee, is now sitting on someone's desk.
7. The school counsellors maintain that to succeed at this level, you need excellent note-taking skills; organized study habits; and, most of all, superior time-management strategies.
8. Canada's history is not a very violent one; however, we've had several rebellions of note.
9. In 1813, Laura Secord trekked 25 km to warn the British and the Canadians of an American attack; her information resulted in victory at the Battle of Beaverdams.
10. Many years later, her name became famous, and a chocolate company was named after her.

Answers for Chapter 20: The Colon (pages 226 to 230)

Exercise 20.1

1. correct	4. correct
3. correct	8. correct

Exercise 20.2

(A deleted punctuation mark is indicated by ***.)

2. I stay fit by *** cycling and swimming.
5. My car is so badly built that, instead of a warranty, it came with *** an apology.
6. There are many species of fish in this lake, including *** pike, bass, and walleye.
7. In the words of H.L. Mencken, "Some people don't recognize opportunity when it knocks because it comes in the form of hard work."
9. This apartment would be perfect if it had more storage; there aren't enough closets, bookshelves, or even drawers.
10. After a day at school, I look forward to *** a cool drink, a tasty snack, and an afternoon nap.

Exercise 20.3

(A deleted punctuation mark is indicated by ***.)

1. If at first you don't succeed, become a consultant and teach someone else how to do it.
2. The trees in this park are all native BC species: Douglas fir, arbutus, and dogwood.
3. Our dog knows only one trick: pretending to be deaf.
4. There is a reason I have always felt my little brother was a mean, spiteful child: he always hit me back.

5. She spends too much time *** shopping at the malls, talking on the phone, and watching TV.
6. Milton Berle might have been talking about our city's team when he said, "Our team lives hockey; it dreams hockey; it eats hockey. Now, if only it could play hockey."
7. This essay lacks three important features: a title page, a Works Cited page, and some content in between.
8. The shortstop on our baseball team caught only one thing all season: mononucleosis.
9. My mother always wanted a successful son, so I did my part: I urged her to have more children.
10. correct

Exercise 20.5

Imagine, if you can, Mario's surprise on being told that he had won a big prize in the lottery: one million dollars. At first, he didn't believe it; it was simply too good to be true. Once the reality had sunk in, however, he began to make plans for his fortune. As he thought about how to spend the money, he kept one goal in mind: "I want to help others as well as myself." He talked to the counsellors at the college, who advised him that setting up a scholarship would be a good use of his funds. Every year, five thousand dollars would go to three students who were doing well in school, but who couldn't afford to continue with their education without assistance. It was a perfect way for Mario to share his good fortune with others. Of course, he also bought himself the car of his dreams: a sleek, silver Porsche.

Answers for Chapter 21: Quotation Marks (pages 231 to 238)

Exercise 21.1
1. The most famous quotation in the history of Canadian sports is Foster Hewitt's "He shoots! He scores!"
2. The beaver, which is Canada's national animal, was once described by Michael Kesterton as "a distant relative of the sewer rat."
3. In the opinion of writer Barry Callaghan, "We Canadians have raised being boring to an art form."
4. "All we want," jokes Yvon Deschamps, "is an independent Quebec within a strong and united Canada."
5. Pierre Berton sums up the difference between Canadians and Americans as follows: "You ask an American how he's feeling, and he cries 'Great!' You ask a Canadian, and he answers 'Not bad,' or 'Pas mal.' "

Exercise 21.2
(The italicized titles are also correct if they are underlined.)
1. For me, the most helpful chapter of *The Bare Essentials Plus* is "Cracking the Sentence Code."
2. Canada's national anthem is derived from a French song, "Chant national," which was first performed in Quebec City in 1880.
3. "O Canada," the English version of "Chant national," was written by R. Stanley Weir, a Montreal judge and poet, and was first performed in 1908.
4. In Shakespeare's play *The Winter's Tale*, there is a peculiar stage direction that has baffled scholars for 400 years: "Exit, pursued by a bear."
5. *Crouching Toad, Hidden Lizard*, a humorous documentary made by our college's television students, was shown on the CBC program *Short Shots*.
6. The video documentary *A War of Their Own* is the story of the Canadian troops in World War II who fought in the long, bloody Italian campaign.
7. The CD *Sparkjiver* features some great blues songs, such as "Harlem Nocturne" and "Try a Little Tenderness," performed by an unusual trio of electric organ, sax, and drums.

8. Go to *The Globe and Mail*'s Web page if you want to follow the links to Steve Galea's article "Thunder in the Snow," which describes the appeal and the dangers of snowmobiling.

9. The Diana Krall album *When I Look in Your Eyes* has three of my favourite jazz vocals: "Devil May Care," "I Can't Give You Anything But Love," and "Do It Again."

10. The Outdoors Channel is playing reruns of old *Survivor* episodes to show viewers, as *TV Guide* puts it, "how to live off the land while surrounded by cameras, microphones, TV technicians, and an obnoxious host."

Answers for Chapter 22: Question Marks, Exclamation Marks, and Punctuation Review (pages 239 to 246)

Exercise 22.1

1. correct	5. incorrect	9. incorrect
2. incorrect	6. correct	10. incorrect
3. incorrect	7. incorrect	
4. correct	8. incorrect	

Exercise 22.2

2. I want to know what's going on.
3. Why do they bother to report power outages on TV?
5. If corn oil comes from corn, I wonder where baby oil comes from.
7. I'm curious about where you are going for your vacation.
8. Theo wanted to know if Maria was going to the concert.
9. Do you know another word for *thesaurus*?
10. As a Canadian, I often wonder if God ever considered having snow fall up.

Exercise 22.3

1. I quit. (*Or, if you want emphasis:* I quit!)
2. Stop**,** thief!
3. Don't you dare!
4. He's on the stairway**,** right behind you! (*Or, if you are describing a nonthreatening scene:* He's on the stairway**,** right behind you.)
5. We won! I can't believe it!
6. Brandishing her new credit card, Tessa marched through the mall shouting, "Charge it!"
7. Take the money and run**.**
8. I can't believe it's over! (*Or:* I can't believe it's over**.**)

Exercise 22.4

1. The question was whether it would be better to stay in bed or to go to the clinic**.**
2. Gregory asked Nell if she had ever been to Nanaimo**.**
3. Hurry, or we'll be late!
4. Did you ever notice that the early bird gets the worm, but the second mouse gets the cheese**?**
5. Just imagine! In only three hours they are going to draw my ticket number in the lottery!
6. Is it true that those who live by the sword get shot by those who don't**?**
7. Don't stop! Do you want the bus behind us to run into our rear end**?**
8. Shoot the puck! Why won't he shoot the puck**?**

Exercise 22.6
(Punctuation that has been omitted is indicated by ***.)

1. Good health, according to my doctor, should be defined as *** "the slowest possible rate at which one can die."
2. The fast pace of life does not concern me at all**.** **It**'s the sudden stop at the end that has me worried.

3. My friend Gordon doesn't think much of a healthy lifestyle. **He** often says, "Eat well, exercise regularly, and die anyway."
4. Did you know that the word "karate" in English means empty hands**?**
5. The prescription for a healthy life is well known**:** eat a balanced diet; get regular exercise, even if it's just a five minute walk each day; get regular checkups; and avoid stress.
6. I wonder how many people know that the first episode of the television series *Star Trek*, broadcast in September, 1966, was called "The Man Trap."
7. If you want to make your living as a comedian, you must *** remember the punch line and deliver it with perfect timing.
8. My computer is so old that I can't use it to play any games developed since 1985; I can't use it to access the Internet; it has a two-colour monitor; and, believe it or not, uses 5-1/4-inch floppy disks.
9. When he saw Charlie Chaplin imitating Hitler in the movie *The Great Dictator*, Douglas Fairbanks said, "This is one of the most fortuitous tricks in the history of civilization, that the greatest living villain in the world and the greatest comedian should look alike."
10. One of my favourite Canadian quotations comes from Charlotte Whitton, the first woman mayor of Ottawa, who said, "To succeed, a woman must be twice as good as a man. Fortunately that isn't difficult."

Answers for Chapter 23: Finding Something to Write About (pages 249 to 263)

Exercise 23.1
1. Not specific, and not supportable without a great deal of research
2. Not significant. Every child knows what they are.
3. Not significant
4. Not single or specific
5. Not significant
6. Not single. Choose one.
7. Not specific. Whole books have been written on this topic.
8. Not supportable. How can we know?
9. Not single
10. Not specific

Exercise 23.2
1. Not significant; it's a commonplace fact.
2. Possible, but too broad. You could make it specific and significant by applying one or more limiting factors to it. For example, "Canadian teenagers' notion of ideal female beauty" or "How the notion of physical attractiveness has changed since my parents' generation."
3. Possible. Make it significant by broadening the topic a little: e.g., "How to increase the efficiency of your dishwasher." (If your dishwasher is a human being, the subject has humorous possibilities.)
4. Not specific and not supportable for most of us without substantial research. To be a suitable subject, it would need limiting: e.g., "Some lessons to be learned from Russia's struggle to develop a market economy."
5. Possible, but the subject needs to be limited if it is to be both significant and specific. You might, for example, discuss one influential Canadian woman or write a profile of one "unknown" Canadian woman—i.e., someone who is not a public figure.
6. Unless you are Martha Stewart or can come up with some unusual and useful ideas, this is not significant.
7. As it stands, this topic is unsupportable. It needs to be limited to be specific and supportable: e.g., "Basic palm-reading techniques" or "How computer miniaturization will change our lives."
8. Possible. Make it specific by identifying two or three typical challenges.

Exercise 23.6

1. Seattle Mariners (unrelated to the subject; they're an American team)
2. Improved looks (overlaps with "improved appearance"); improved social life (not *directly* related to S)
3. Travelling (unrelated; already accomplished by the immigrant to Canada); shovelling snow (overlaps with "adjusting to climate")
4. Alcohol (not a reason)
5. Make travel plans (overlaps with "plan the client's itinerary"); get a passport (client's responsibility)
6. Quiz shows (overlaps with "game shows"); Oprah (unrelated; not a "kind" of show)
7. Earthquakes (unrelated; not a "weather system")
8. White shark; hammerhead shark (species, not characteristics, of sharks)

Exercise 23.8

Subject	Order	Main Points	
1. How to start a gas lawn mower	chronological	2	make sure there is enough gas in tank
		3	turn switch to start
		1	put lawn mower on flat ground
		5	when running, adjust to proper speed
		4	pull cord
		6	mow!
2. Differences between spoken and written language	climactic	3	speech is transitory; writing is permanent
		2	speech is direct and personal; writing isn't
		1	speech can't be revised; writing can
3. How to write a research paper	chronological	3	read and take notes on selected research sources
		4	draft the paper
		2	compile a working bibliography of research sources
		1	define the subject
		7	type and proofread paper
		6	prepare footnotes, if needed, and reference list
		5	revise the paper
4. How colleges benefit society	logical	2	they provide the individual with a higher level of general education
		3	society benefits from increased productivity and commitment of an educated populace
		1	they provide the individual with job skills

Subject	Order	Main Points	
5. Effects of malnutrition	logical	_3_	malnutrition affects the productivity and prosperity of nations as a whole
		_1_	malnutrition impedes the mental and physical development of children
		_2_	undernourished children become sickly adults unable to participate fully in their society
6. Why pornography should be banned	chronological	_1_	it degrades the people involved in making it
		_3_	it brutalizes society as a whole
		_2_	it desensitizes the people who view it

7. and 8. Decide on your own climactic arrangements for these questions. Be sure you can explain your choices.

Answers for Chapter 24: Writing the Thesis Statement (pages 264 to 274)

Exercise 24.1

1. The essential features of a good novel (are) interesting characters, a stimulating plot, and exceptional writing.
2. My boss enjoys two hobbies [:] improving his golf game and tormenting his employees.
3. Well-known stars, stunning technical effects, and a hugely expensive advertising campaign (are) the requirements for a blockbuster movie.
4. A typical computer system (consists of) a CPU, monitor, printer, scanner, and interface devices.
5. If I were you, I would avoid eating in the cafeteria (because) the food is expensive, tasteless, and unhealthy.
6. The original Volkswagen Beetle, the Citröen CV, and the Morris Minor (are) three cars that will be remembered for their endearing oddness.
7. *The Simpsons* amuses and provokes viewers (with its depiction of) a smart-aleck, underachieving son; a talented, high-achieving daughter; and a hopeless, blundering father.
8. (Because) they lack basic skills, study skills, or motivation, some students run the risk of failure in college.
9. Fad diets are not the quick and easy fixes to weight problems that they may seem to be (; in fact,) they are often costly, ineffective, and even dangerous.
10. The Canadian political culture differs from American political culture (in terms of) attitudes to universal health care, gun control, and capital punishment.

Exercise 24.2

1. parallel	3. not parallel	5. not parallel
2. not parallel	4. not parallel	

Exercise 24.3
1. correct
2. Good writing involves applying the principles of organization, sentence structure, spelling, and punctuation.
3. Our company requires employees to be knowledgeable, honest, disciplined, and reliable.
4. Hobbies are important because they provide us with recreation, stimulation, and relaxation.
5. Some of the negative effects of caffeine are nervousness, sleeplessness, and heart palpitations.

Exercise 24.4
1. The four kinds of prose writing are description, narration, exposition, and argumentation. (parallelism)
2. Intramural sports offer students a way to get involved in their school, an opportunity to meet new friends, and a chance to stay fit. (significance and parallelism)
3. Increasingly, scientists are finding links between the weather and diseases such as colds, cancer, and arthritis. (parallelism and relevance—aging isn't a disease)
4. The most prolific producers of pretentious language are politicians, educators, advertising copy writers, and sports writers. (overlap between *teachers and administrators* and *educators*; parallelism)
5. There are three categories of students with whom teachers find it difficult to cope: those who skip class, those who sleep through class, and those who disrupt class. (parallelism—and wordiness!)

Exercise 24.5 (suggested answers)
1. violent video games? No, a different topic
   There are three reasons why watching television is a valuable way to spend time: it teaches us many things, it provides laughter and relaxation, and it supplies us with topics to discuss with others.

2. Vancouver is a wonderful place to live
   - moderate climate: Yes, good point
   - traffic: No, doesn't support the thesis
   - Museum of Anthropology: No, it's an example of cultural attractions—not a main point
   - scenery that is beautiful: Yes, good point (though not parallel)
   - rain: No, doesn't support thesis (also covered in "moderate climate")
   - cultural attractions: Yes
   A. Three reasons why Vancouver is a wonderful place to live (are) its moderate climate, beautiful scenery, and cultural attractions.
   B. Vancouver is a wonderful place to live (because of) its moderate climate, beautiful scenery, and cultural attractions.

3. Immigration is a good policy for Canada
   - immigrants offer new skills: Yes, good point
   - immigrants may find it difficult to adjust to life in Canada: No, doesn't support thesis
   - immigrants may bring investment dollars: Yes
   - immigrants must often learn a new language: No, doesn't support thesis
   - immigrants enrich Canadian culture: Yes, supports thesis
   A. Immigration is a good policy for Canada (because) immigrants offer new skills, often bring investment dollars, and enrich Canadian culture.
   B. Immigration is a good policy for Canada: immigrants offer new skills, investment, and cultural enrichment.

4. People love to take vacations, but the kind of vacation depends on the kind of person.
   - beach resorts: Yes, a kind of vacation
   - Las Vegas: No, an example of a place to gamble
   - gambling trips: Yes, a kind of vacation
   - Cancun, Mexico: No, example of a beach resort
   - Buckingham Palace: No, an example of a cultural attraction in London
   - adventure vacations: Yes, a kind of vacation
   - too much sun: No, doesn't support thesis
   - mountain climbing: No, example of an adventure vacation
   - lose money: No, doesn't support thesis
   - touring cultural attraction vacations: Yes, a kind of vacation
   - can be dangerous: No, doesn't support thesis
   A. Different people like different kinds of vacation (; for example,) some people like to relax at a beach resort, some people like to gamble, some people like to have adventures, and other people like to tour cultural attractions.
   B. Some of the kinds of vacations that different people like to take (are) relaxing at a beach resort, playing games of chance, enjoying adventure travel, or touring cultural attractions.

5. Dressing for success
   - career in sales or public relations: Yes, a career field
   - installing computer networks: No, example of a technical career (not main point)
   - career in high-level corporate environment: Yes
   - career in technical field: Yes, a career field
   - CEO: No
   - software sales representative: No
   A. How one dresses for success depends upon the career one is pursuing (; for instance,) careers in sales, technical, and corporate environments dictate different standards of dress.
   B. Whether you are planning to succeed in a career in public relations, a technical field, or a corporate environment (,) you must pay careful attention to the dress code.

Answers for Chapter 25: Writing the Outline (pages 275 to 279)

Exercise 25.2
Introduction

Attention-getter:	Students who come to Canada from tropical countries may not be prepared for the similarity between Canada's weather and its dominant personality types.
Thesis statement:	Canadian personalities fall into two categories: warm and cool.

I. Warm Canadians
   A. Definition: Warm Canadians are enthusiastic about Canada
   B. Characteristics
      1. Praise the beauty of Canada from coast to coast
      2. Enthusiastic about typical leisure activities
      3. Interested in learning about foreign students' homelands
      4. Understand that Canadians and newcomers share common problems
II. Cool Canadians
   A. Definition: Cool Canadians are unenthusiastic about Canada
   B. Characteristics

1. Wonder why someone from a warm climate would move here
2. Emphasize the negative aspects of Canada's climate
3. Not interested in learning about foreign students' homelands
4. Avoid any challenge to their preconceived ideas about other countries

Conclusion

    Summary: Canadians are not consistently warm or cool. The two personality types are subject to change, just like the weather.

    Memorable statement: Dealing with Canada's unpredictable people provides foreign students with an opportunity to display their understanding, tolerance, and acceptance of others as they are.

Answers for Chapter 26: Writing the Paragraphs (pages 280 to 295)

Exercise 26.1

paragraph 4:

topic sentence — Although I am usually able to decipher the gist of quickspeak, I'm never sure that I have translated the message accurately. In many cases, this failure stems from the fact that the writer didn't provide complete or accurate information. Take the example that introduces this essay. I know there will be a meeting (about what?) on Tuesday (which week?) at 9:00 (a.m. or p.m.?). Where is this meeting? Who will be present? What documents am I expected to bring? Without the answers to these questions, how can I prepare? Far from saving time, quickspeak actually wastes it. Now I have to respond to the e-mail sender to find out the answers to these questions. At least three messages will be needed where one would have done. If only the writer had recognized this basic rule of writing: to be brief takes time!

supporting sentences

conclusion

paragraph 5:

topic sentence — E-mail is no different from any other business correspondence: it must be clear and concise. Achieving clarity and conciseness is not difficult, but it does require planning. Begin with an introduction that briefly explains the purpose of your message. Next, outline how you are going to develop that message. Use numbered or bulleted points to guide the reader from your position statement through your reasoning to your conclusion. Reinforce your message with a conclusion that states any follow-up actions you require and that confirms the time, place, and responsibilities of those who are contributing to the project. Next, re-read your message as if you were reading it for the first time. Revise to be sure that you have included all the necessary details: dates, reference numbers, times and places of meetings, and whatever other information is needed to get the right people together in the right places, on the right days, at the right times, with the right information in their briefcases. Use a spell-checker, but don't rely on it to catch all your errors and typos.

supporting sentences

conclusion — Remember: A clear message, clearly delivered, is the essence of effective communication.

paragraph 6:

topic sentence — People who write in quickspeak ignore the reason that rules for correct writing evolved in the first place. Writing that communicates accurately depends upon precise thinking. A message with a statement of purpose, logically arranged points, and a confirming summary is the work of a writer whose message has been thought through and can be trusted. In contrast, quickspeak, which can be bashed out in no time, reflects no planning, little coherent thought, and no sense of order or priority. The message, the reader, and, ultimately, the writer all suffer as a result.

supporting sentences

conclusion

Exercise 26.7
1. process
2. definition + examples
3. specific details
4. comparison and contrast
5. descriptive details
6. examples
7. specific numerical details
8. descriptive details + examples
9. quotations
10. quotation and contrast

Exercise 26.10 (suggested answers)
(Words that have been omitted are indicated by ***.)

   My friends and family find it hard to believe, **but** I've become a fan of classical music. Recently, I had a serious operation, **and** I was forced to stay in bed for almost three weeks while I recovered. I quickly grew tired of the boring, repetitive programs on daytime television, **so** I began listening to the radio. Soon I discovered CBC 2, which is *** a network of stations across Canada that plays classical music by great composers of the past and the present. I don't yet know very much about the music I'm listening to, **but** I am learning. **For example,** I can now recognize many of the more popular works by composers such as Beethoven, Mozart, and Bach. Now that I have discovered this magnificent music, **however**, I don't enjoy pop songs as much as I used to. **Nevertheless,** I am confident that I've gained much more than I've lost.

Answers for Chapter 27: Revising Your Paper (pages 296 to 307)

Exercise 27.1
Attention-getter: As the recipient of approximately 1,000 business-related e-mail messages every month, I am something of an expert on what is effective and what is not in e-mail correspondence.
Thesis statement: The three areas that need attention in most e-mail messages are the subject line, the content and appearance of the message, and the use of attachments.
Main points

I. Subject line
   A. never leave the subject line blank (*or* always include a subject line)
   B. make sure the subject line states clearly what the message is about

II. Message
   A. Content
      1. be concise and to the point
      2. tell the reader what action is needed, by whom, and when
      3. use plain English, not "cyberspeak"
      4. use an appropriate level of language in your message as well as in your salutation and signature
   B. Appearance
      1. use bullets to identify points you want to emphasize
      2. leave white space between points
      3. avoid sending your message in upper case letters (shouting)
      4. avoid smilies and other "cute" computer shorthand symbols

III. Attachments
   A. use only if necessary
   B. may carry viruses
   C. take time to transfer and to open
   D. attach text-only files, unless a graphic is absolutely necessary

Summary: If you follow my recommendations on these three points whenever you write an e-mail, you will make the recipient of your message very happy.
Memorable statement: Especially if you're writing to me.

Exercise 27.2 (suggested answer)
In the following answer, we have corrected only the errors in paragraph structure, sentence structure, and grammar. The passage still contains errors in spelling, punctuation, and usage. We will correct those errors at Step 3.

1   As the recipient of almost 1,000 business-related e-mail messages every month, I am something of an expert on what is effective and what is not in e-mail correspondence. The three areas that need attention in most e-mail messages are the subject line, the content, and appearance of the message and the use of attachments.

2   Some people leave the subject line blank. **T**his is a mistake. I want to know what the message is about before I open it**,** so I can decide if it needs my immediate attention **or** can wait until later. A message with no subject line, or with a line that **doesn't** tell me **anything** about the content of the e-mail, **gets** sent to the bottom of my "to-do" list. There are lots of readers like me: busy people who receive tons of e-mail, much of it unsolicited advertising that **clutters** up **our** in-boxes. For this reason the subject line should always clearly state the subject of the message and should never be vague or cute, like "hello," or "message," or "are you there?"

3   As for the message itself, it's function should be to tell the reader what action **you want. Y**ou need to be clear about this and be as brief as possible. What is it that you want the recipient to do. Who else needs to be involved. By when does the action need to take place. Communicate your message in plain English, not in "cyberspeak." **N**ot everyone knows Net lingo, and even some who are famliar with it find it irritating, not charming. Use an appropriate level of language (general level Standard English **is** always appropriate) to convey you're message. Use the same level of language in you're salutation and closing or "signature." **Never** sign off a message to you're client or you're boss with "love and kisses."

4   Format you're message so that the recipient **can read it quickly and understand** it easily. Use bullets to identify points you want to emphasize **and** separate the bullets with white space so **that your points** can be read at a glance and reviewed individually if neccessary.

5   There are some important points of e-mail etiquette that you should observe. Don't type you're message in upper case letters. **This is** considered "shouting." Do avoid "smilies" and other "cute" computer shorthand symbols. Some of you're readers won't understand them. **O**thers will have seen them so often they will be turned off.

6   Attachments should be included only if they are really necessary. **One reason is that** they may carry virruses and some people won't open them. Another disadvantage is that **attachments** take time to send download and open. Unless I am sure that an attachment is both urgent and vitally important—the agenda of tomorrow's meeting, for example—I don't bother to open it. **F**or all I know, it might contain not only a virus but also footage of the sender's toddler doing her latest photogenic trick. As a general rule **you should** attach only what you must and attach text-only files. Try to include everything you need to say in the message itself; use attachments only as a last resort. Think of them as equivalent to footnotes: supplementary to the message, not an essential part of it.

7   If you follow my recommendations on these three points whenever you write an e-mail, you will make the recipient of your message very happy, especially if you're writing to me.

Exercise 27.3 (suggested answer)
(Words that have been omitted are indicated by ***.)

1   As the recipient of approximately 1,000 business-related e-mail messages every month, I am something of an expert on what is effective and what is not in e-mail correspondence. The three areas that need attention in most e-mail messages are the subject line, the content *** and appearance of the message, and the use of attachments.

2   Some people leave the subject line blank. This is a mistake. I want to know what the message is about before I open it, so I can decide if it needs my immediate attention or can wait until later.

A message with no subject line, or with a line that doesn't tell me anything about the content of the e-mail, gets sent to the bottom of my "to-do" list. There are lots of readers like me: busy people who receive tons of e-mail, much of which is unsolicited advertising that clutters up our inboxes. For this reason, the subject line should always clearly state the subject of the message and should never be vague or cute. **Some examples of inappropriate subject lines include** "hello," *** "message," **and** "are you there?"

3   As for the message itself, **its** function should be to tell the reader what action you want **taken**. *** Be clear about this, and be as brief as possible. What is it that you want the recipient to do? Who else needs to be involved? By when does the action need to **be completed?** Communicate your message in plain English, not in "cyberspeak." Not everyone knows Net lingo, and even some who are **familiar** with it find it irritating, not charming. Use an appropriate level of language (general level Standard English is always appropriate) to convey **your** message. Use the same level of language in **your** salutation and closing or "signature." Never sign off a message to **your** client or **your** boss with "love and kisses."

4   Format **your** message so that the recipient can read it quickly and understand it easily. Use bullets to identify points you want to emphasize, and separate the bullets with white space so that your points can be read at a glance and reviewed individually, if **necessary**.

5   There are some important points of e-mail etiquette that you should observe. Don't type **your** message in upper case letters. This is considered "shouting." Do avoid "smilies" and other "cute" computer shorthand symbols. Some of **your** readers won't understand them. Others will have seen them so often **that** they will be turned off.

6   Attachments should be included only if they are really necessary. One reason is that they may carry **viruses,** and some people won't open them. Another disadvantage is that attachments take time to send, download, and open. Unless I am sure that an attachment is both urgent and vitally important—the agenda of tomorrow's meeting, for example—I don't bother to open it. For all I know, it might contain not only a virus but also footage of the sender's toddler doing her latest photogenic trick. As a general rule, you should attach only what you must, and attach text-only files. Try to include everything you need to say in the message itself; use attachments only as a last resort. Think of them as equivalent to footnotes: supplementary to the message, not an essential part of it.

7   If you follow my recommendations on these three points whenever you write an e-mail, you will make the recipient of your message very happy, especially if you're writing to me.

Answers for Unit 6 Quick Quiz: A Review of the Basics (pages 312 to 313)

1   Humans learn very early how to use their first language. Most of us understand spoken words and respond to them **by** the time we are two or three years old. It takes another few years for us to learn how to read and write, but we acquire our first language fairly easily. **For** most of us, however, learning a second language is **a** slow and exasperating process. Most people who **study English** as a second language are especially **frustrated** by three of its peculiarities: its unsystematic pronunciation, its inconsistent spelling, and its enormous vocabulary.

2   English **has** sounds that are difficult for speakers of other languages. The *th* sound is one of them. Why is it pronounced differently in words such as *this* and *think*? The consonant sounds *l, r,* and *w* also present problems. Many new English speakers don't hear the differences between *light, right,* and *white,* and so they **do not** pronounce them. There are also more vowel **sounds** in English than in most other **languages**. The *a* sound in the words *bat* and *mat* is peculiar to English, so second-language learners often pronounce *bet, bat,* and *but* identically. To native speakers of English, these words **have** quite distinct sounds that many second-language learners do not hear and so cannot pronounce. Many ESL **speakers** find it difficult to pronounce the unusual vowel sounds that occur **in** the words *bird, word,* and *nurse*. The fact that the same sound occurs in words with three different vowels—*i, o,* and *u*—is **an** example of **the** second major difficulty with English: its inconsistent spelling system.

3   Most native speakers **would agree** that English spelling is challenging. Why do *tough* and *stuff* rhyme when their spelling is so different? Shouldn't *tough* rhyme with *cough?* But *cough* rhymes with *off*. Why does *clamour* rhyme with *hammer* while *worm* and *storm*—which should rhyme—don't? There **is no** single answer, but part of the reason is that English is **a** language that has absorbed many words and sounds from other languages, along with their spellings. Almost 75 % of English words **have** regular spellings, but, unfortunately, the most frequently used words in English are the irregular **ones**. All of us, second-language learners and native speakers alike, simply have to learn to cope.

4   English also has a huge vocabulary, in part because it borrows freely **from** other languages. The roots of English are Germanic, but the Celts, Romans, French, and many **others** have contributed heavily to the language. The gigantic *Oxford English Dictionary* lists about 500,000 words and does not include about another half million technical and scientific **words**.

5   English is **a** difficult language for all of these **reasons**, but it's a rich and **satisfying** one that is well worth the effort to learn.

IF YOU MISSED . . .	SEE
Paragraph 1:	
by the time	Chapter 32, Practising with Prepositions
For most of us	Chapter 32, Practising with Prepositions
a slow and exasperating process	Chapter 31, Using Articles Accurately (The Indefinite Article: *A/An*)
study English	Chapter 31, Using Articles Accurately (No Article [Zero Article])
especially frustrated	Chapter 29, More about Verbs (Participial Adjectives)
Paragraph 2:	
English has sounds	Chapter 28, Choosing the Correct Verb Tense
they do not pronounce	Chapter 29, More about Verbs (Forming Negatives)
more vowel sounds	Chapter 30, Solving Plural Problems
most other languages	Chapter 30, Solving Plural Problems (Quantity Expressions)
these words have	Chapter 28, Choosing the Correct Verb Tense
Many ESL speakers	Chapter 30, Solving Plural Problems (Quantity Expressions)
in the words	Chapter 32, Practising with Prepositions
an example	Chapter 31, Using Articles Accurately (The Indefinite Article: *A/An*)
of the second major difficulty	Chapter 31, Using Articles Accurately (The Definite Article: *The*)
Paragraph 3:	
native speakers would agree	Chapter 29, More about Verbs (Modal Auxiliaries)
is no single answer	Chapter 29, More about Verbs (Forming Negatives)
English is a language	Chapter 31, Using Articles Accurately (The Indefinite Article: *A/An*)
words have regular spellings	Chapter 28, Choosing the Correct Verb Tense

IF YOU MISSED . . .	SEE
the irregular ones	Chapter 30, Solving Plural Problems
Paragraph 4:	
borrows freely from	Chapter 32, Practising with Prepositions
and many others	Chapter 30, Solving Plural Problems
scientific words	Chapter 30, Solving Plural Problems
	(Quantity Expressions)
Paragraph 5:	
a difficult language	Chapter 31, Using Articles Accurately
	(The Indefinite Article: *A/An*)
these reasons	Chapter 30, Solving Plural Problems
satisfying one	Chapter 29, More about Verbs
	(Participial Adjectives)

Answers for Chapter 28: Choosing the Correct Verb Tense (pages 314 to 337)

Exercise 28.1

1. (present perfect)	He **has** been **going**.	He **has** been **seeing**.
2. (past progressive)	I was **going**.	I was **seeing**.
3. (simple present)	He **goes**. They **go**.	He **sees**. They **see**.
4. (present progressive)	You **are going**.	You **are seeing**.
5. (simple past)	We **went**.	We **saw**.
6. (future progressive)	She **will** be **going**.	She **will** be **seeing**.
7. (present perfect progressive)	He **has** been **going**.	He **has** been **seeing**.
8. (past perfect)	We had **gone**.	We had **seen**.
9. (simple future)	You **will go**.	You **will see**.
10. (past perfect progressive)	Someone had **been going**.	Someone had **been seeing**.

Exercise 28.2

1. He will **be going** with us. (future progressive)
2. The new year **starts/begins** on January 1. (simple present)
3. Jerome **has** (*or* **had**) always **been** attractive to women. (*has been* = present perfect; *had been* = past perfect)
4. Linda and Joy **are leaving** for China a week from now. (present progressive expressing future)
5. Wolf **had played** in the band for six years, but he quit a year ago. (past perfect)
6. You **have been working** very hard, so why not take a break? (present perfect progressive)
7. The movie **had been playing** for 30 minutes by the time we got there. (past perfect progressive)
8. I **spoke** (*or* **met**) with my manager yesterday. (simple past)
9. I **am taking** off my running shoes right now because they **are killing** my feet. (present progressive)
10. He **was watching** TV when I **called** (*or* another simple past tense verb) him last night. (past progressive; simple past)

Exercise 28.3

1. It **is snowing** again today. In my country, it often **rains**, but it never **snows**.
2. Marc usually **works** as a lifeguard, but this summer he **is working** in his family's restaurant.

3. Ellistine **wants** to fix her car, but she **needs** someone to help her.
4. A ticket home **costs** so much that I **doubt** that I can afford the trip.
5. We still **believe** we have a good team, and now we **are trying** to develop a winning strategy.
6. My mother usually **phones** me every day at 6:00, but it is now 6:30 and I am **still waiting** for her call. I wonder what she **is doing.**
7. The baby **is crying** again. He always **cries** when his mother **leaves**.
8. What **are you doing** right now? I **am learning** English verb tenses.
9. The little girl **looks** tired, but right now she **is looking** at her favourite storybook.
10. Jamala **studies** in the library almost every evening. Tonight she **is having** difficulty concentrating because the student who **is sitting** at the next table **is talking** on his cell phone.

Exercise 28.4
1. Do you like to travel?
   Yes, I do. I **have gone** to many different places during my life. I **have visited** both Central America and South America **since** 1999.
2. Are you taking an ESL course this semester?
   No, I **have already taken** it. I **have studied** English **for** 11 years.
3. Do you love me?
   Yes, I **have always loved** you. I **have known** you **since** I was a little girl, and I **have never loved** anyone but you.
4. Do you get much e-mail?
   Yes, my old computer crashed, and I **have recently bought** a new computer with a high speed connection. Lots of people write to me. For example, I **have already gotten** (*or* **got**) 47 e-mail messages **so far** this morning.
5. When did you move here?
   I moved here in _____. I **have been** here **for** _____ years.

Exercise 28.5
1. It **has been snowing** all day.
2. They **have been studying** physics for three days straight.
3. Desi **has been thinking** about taking a trip to Belize.
4. I **have been talking** to my professors about dropping a course.
5. The phone **has been ringing** all morning.

Exercise 28.6
1. It **has been raining** all night, and the basement is flooded.
2. There **have been** four big rainstorms already this week.
3. I **have sent** several e-mails but got no reply. I **have also phoned** them every day.
4. The children **have been** to the beach. They are covered with sand because they **have been building** sandcastles.
5. How long **have you lived** (*or* **have you been living**) in Canada?

Exercise 28.7
1. Three of us **were smoking** in the upstairs washroom when the boss **walked** in.
2. The cat **was hiding** behind the fish tank when I **saw** his tail twitch and **caught** him.
3. While their sister **was preparing** their lunch, the children **ran** into the house and **turned** on the television.
4. When the movie *Crouching Tiger, Hidden Dragon* **was playing** in the theatre, I **saw** it four times. Later I **bought** the DVD.
5. Marco **was trying** to park his new SUV in the narrow driveway when he **hit** the neighbour's hedge. The branches **made** deep scratches in the paint.

6. As Julio **was telling** his friends about his new job, one of them **asked** him how he **had found** the position.
7. Wai-Lan **was walking** home when the rain **began**. To stay dry, she **waited** under a tree until a taxi **drove** by and rescued her.
8. I **did not hear** you arrive last night because I **was sleeping**.
9. Miranda **disliked** the play because she **thought** it **was** long and boring.
10. I **was studying** in the library when I **became** ferociously hungry and **knew** that I **had** to eat.

Exercise 28.8

1. Sven was late for class. The professor **had just given** a quiz when he **got** there.
2. Yesterday my friend Ronit **saw** an old friend whom she **had not seen** in years.
3. I almost missed my flight. Everyone **had already boarded** the plane by the time I **rushed** in.
4. After our guests **had left** (*or* **left**), we **cleaned** up the kitchen.
5. Devondra **had hardly swum** a single lap of the pool when the rain **started**.

Exercise 28.9

1. It is 6:00 p.m. I **have been working** for ten hours straight, so it is time to go home.
2. It was 6:00 p.m. I **had been working** for ten hours straight, so it was time to go home.
3. I woke up feeling strange this morning because I **had been dreaming** about dinosaurs all night.
4. The child is sad. She **has been crying** all morning.
5. Barbara **had been selling** real estate for 25 years when she realized that she wanted a new career.

Exercise 28.10

1. By the time I **realized** that I needed an elective to graduate, I **had already dropped** my history course.
2. Aunt Mina **had promised** (*or* **promised**) to leave her fortune to Jacob, but unfortunately she **died** before making a will.
3. Karin's sister **arrived** about ten minutes after Karin **had left** (*or* **left**).
4. Felipe **had been planning** a formal dinner party for his father's fiftieth birthday until his mother **suggested** a backyard barbecue instead.
5. By the time Kim **had been working** (*or* **had worked**) the night shift for three months, she **thought** that she would never have a social life again.
6. We **had been looking** forward to our vacation for months when my wife **got** a promotion, and we **had** to cancel our plans.
7. If I **had known** how difficult this course **was**, I would have signed up for something easier.
8. When he **retired**, Professor Green **had been teaching** creative writing for 30 years.
9. We **had decided** (*or* **decided**) to sell our condominium, but we **changed** our minds when the real estate agent **told** us the low price we would get.
10. I **had never realized** how difficult it would be to work for Ms. Wright. She **was** a very demanding boss.

Exercise 28.11

1. Ky and Shona **met** last September and **have been going** (*or* **have gone**) out together ever since.
2. I **had never seen** any of Monet's paintings until I **went** to the Museum of Modern Art in New York last year.
3. We **have been planning** to renovate our house for a long time, but we **decided** on a contractor only last week.

4. Hockey **has always been** Canadians' favourite sport; we **have been playing** the game for more than 150 years.

5. Although Ali **has lived** (*or* **has been living**) in Toronto since he was ten, he **has never visited** the CN Tower.

6. Maria **has been hoping** to go to Newfoundland for a long time. Her sister **has lived** (*or* **has been living**) there for a year, and she **has convinced** Maria that "the Rock" **is** a place she must visit.

7. For six weeks, I **have been waiting** for my transcript to come in the mail. I wonder if the Registrar's Office **has gone** on strike.

8. **Do you know** who **ate** all the pizza last night?

9. Yesterday my father **made** me go to the barber who **has been cutting** (*or* **has cut**) his hair for the past 20 years.

10. While I **was waiting** (*or* **waited**) for my turn, I **noticed** that I **was** the only person in the shop under 50.

Exercise 28.12

1. Elie **is going to work** on his car tomorrow, but I **am not going to help** him.

2. Until Yasmin's grades improve, here parents **won't** (*or* **will not let**) **let** her get a part-time job. But as soon as she can, Yasmin **is going to look** (*or* **will look**) for work in the fashion industry.

3. Since you **are going to take** an elective course next semester, I suggest you sign up for sociology. You **will enjoy** Professor Singh's sense of humour.

4. Our neighbours **are going to build** an addition onto their home next summer. I hope we **will be** on vacation when the construction begins.

5. I **am going to buy** a daytimer schedule because my counsellor says that it **will help** me put some order in my life.

Exercise 28.13

1. I have no idea where I **will be working** next week, but I **will let** you know as soon as I find out.

2. My fiancée insists that I buy her a diamond ring before she **will marry** me, so I **will be buying** a lot of lottery tickets.

3. I **won't** (*or* **will not have**) **have** time to talk on the phone this afternoon because I **will be cooking** a traditional dinner for 14 people.

4. Ranjan is going to Bombay, where she **will be staying** (*or* **will stay**) with her family for two months. They **will be** (*or* **are going to be**) surprised to find how much she has changed in the last year.

5. If Ivo passes this year, he **will go** to school in Vancouver for his final year. He **will be living** (*or* **will live**) with his girlfriend.

Exercise 28.14

1. I **am going to go** (*or* **will go**) to Florida with Josef next spring because by then he **will have earned** (*or* **will earn**) enough money to pay for his share of the trip.

2. We are going to be late because of the terrible traffic. By the time we **reach** the airport, Miryam's plane **will already have arrived**. She **will be worrying** (*or* **will worry**) that something has happened to us.

3. My cat **is going to have** another litter. If she continues to produce litters at her present pace, she **will have given** (*or* **will give**) birth to 68 kittens by the time she is ten years old.

4. You were born in _____. By the year 2050, you **will have lived** (*or* **will have been living**) for _____ years. You **will have seen** (*or* **will see**) many changes!

5. By the time Michelle **will be** ready to leave the party, William **will have been drinking** (*or* **will have drunk**) beer all evening, so she plans to drive home.

Exercise 28.15

1. As soon as Val **graduates**, he **will leave** (*or* **is leaving** *or* **will be leaving**) for Africa.
2. If Ms. Drecho **has** twins, she **will name** (*or* **is going to name**) them Fay and May or Bob and Rob.
3. Sophie **will answer** the phones while Ravi **is** on vacation next week.
4. If it **rains** on the weekend, we **will cancel** (*or* **are going to cancel**) our plans for a beach party.
5. Pierre **will be** here in Canada for at least another year before he **returns** home to Haiti and **gets** a job.

Exercise 28.16

Many of us are studying computers as part of our college programs. In fact, computer skills have become essential for success in almost all of the jobs we **will be doing** in the next decade. Most Canadians take the presence of a computer in the home, at work, and at school for granted. It is astonishing, therefore, to reflect that not so long ago, many people **were treating** computers as a mere fad. During the 1940s, for example, engineers **were predicting** that computers in the future would weigh over a tonne. In the same decade, the chairman of IBM told his company, "We **are not losing** (*or* **aren't going to lose**) sleep over these machines." He thought there would be a world market for "maybe five computers." A decade later, book publishers **were assuring** their employees that data processing was a fad that wouldn't last a year. In 1977, the president of Digital Equipment Corporation **was telling** the company's shareholders that there was no reason for anyone to want a computer in the home.

Today, all of us who **are using** computers know about Bill Gates, the president of Microsoft. In the years to come, his company **will be producing** many of the programs and applications that will become the standard of the future. These programs will use gigabytes of memory. It is hard to believe that in 1981 Bill Gates **was telling** anyone who would listen, "640K ought to be enough for anybody."

Exercise 28.17

Many of us **study** computers as part of our college programs. In fact, computer skills have become essential for success in almost all of the jobs we **will do** (*or* **are going to do**) in the next decade. Most Canadians take the presence of a computer in the home, at work, and at school for granted. It is astonishing, therefore, to reflect that not so long ago, many people **treated** computers as a mere fad. During the 1940s, for example, engineers **predicted** that computers in the future would weigh over a tonne. In the same decade, the chairman of IBM told his company, "We **won't lose** (*or* **will not lose** *or* **are not going to lose**) sleep over these machines." He thought there would be a world market for "maybe five computers." A decade later, book publishers **assured** their employees that data processing was a fad that wouldn't last a year. In 1977, the president of Digital Equipment Corporation **told** the company's shareholders that there was no reason for anyone to want a computer in the home.

Today, all of us who **use** computers know about Bill Gates, the president of Microsoft. In the years to come, his company **will produce** (*or* **is going to produce**) many of the programs and applications that will become the standard of the future. These programs will use gigabytes of memory. It is hard to believe that in 1981 Bill Gates **told** anyone who would listen, "640K ought to be enough for anybody."

The second set of paragraphs, using simple tenses, is a better description of the events described in this passage. Most of the events occurred once, not over a period of time. Simple tenses depict an action; progressive tenses emphasize the duration of an action.

Answers for Chapter 29: More about Verbs (pages 338 to 350)

Exercise 29.1

2. I **do not** (**don't**) trust the bank.

3. Barbara **does not** (**doesn't**) want to visit Las Vegas.
4. The passengers **do not** (**don't**) have their passports in order.
5. You **should not** (**shouldn't**) have given the students a quiz on negatives.
6. Jabez **does not** (**doesn't**) like to shop for clothes.
7. Ling **did not** (**didn't**) forget to pick us up yesterday.
8. We **never** stop for gas at the Big Apple. *Or:* We **don't ever** stop for gas at the Big Apple.
9. José and Marta **did not** (**didn't**) want to eat before the movie.
10. The class **does not** (**doesn't**) need more exercises on verb forms. *Or:* The class needs **no** more exercises on verb forms.

Exercise 29.2
1. Mohammed and Hassan **have not** enjoyed the winters in Canada.
2. I certainly **do not** want to see you.
3. I certainly **did not** want to see you.
4. We **did not** manage to find our way to the lost-and-found department.
5. Most of the class **did not** attend the reception for international students.
6. The Montreal Canadiens **did not** succeed in winning many new fans last season.
7. Solaya **never** wants to come to the movies with us, even when we **want** her to join us.
8. Ivana **isn't** planning a party for her husband's birthday.
9. Ivana **wasn't** planning a party for her husband's birthday.
10. She **didn't** come to the meeting alone.

Exercise 29.3
1. Ivan *loves* Zeta. He is a **loving** man.
2. Allan *loves* Clara. She is a **loved** woman.
3. The movie *interests* the children. They are **interested** children. They are watching an **interesting** movie.
4. The news *surprised* my brother. He is a **surprised** person. The news was quite **surprising**.
5. The gorilla *frightened* the lady. The gorilla is a **frightening** animal. She is a **frightened** lady.
6. The teacher *irritates* the class. The class is **irritated**. The teacher is **irritating**.
7. The task *exhausted* me. I was **exhausted** by this **exhausting** task.
8. The cold, dreary weather *depresses* Sara. Sara is **depressed**. The weather is **depressing**.
9. The child's tantrum *embarrassed* his father. The father was **embarrassed**. The child's tantrum was **embarrassing**.
10. The test results *shocked* the whole town. The **shocked** people could hardly believe the **shocking** test results.

Exercise 29.4
2. an annoying neighbour; I'm annoyed
3. a horrifying accident; I'm horrified
4. I am disgusted; disgusting garbage
5. a satisfying meal; I am satisfied
6. a worried friend; a worrying problem
7. tiring work; a tired mother
8. I'm pleased; pleasing music
9. an amazing answer; I'm amazed
10. an astonished child; an astonishing story

Exercise 29.5
2. **Would** you please **hand** me the phone?
3. You **must not tell** Rani about the party because we want it to be a surprise for her.

4. The baby is just learning to talk but he **can say** five or six words. A few weeks ago he **couldn't talk** at all.
5. **May** I **take** your arm as we cross the street?
6. **Shall** I **prepare** a room for the guests?
7. I didn't get much sleep last night, so I **should go** to bed early tonight.
8. He makes me angry because he **will answer** his cell phone even in a movie theatre.

Exercise 29.6

1. It **is going to** rain later, so you **ought to** take your umbrella.
2. Sergei **used to** be lazy about his schoolwork, so now he **has to** work very hard to catch up.
3. We **were supposed to** go to the beach yesterday, but it was too cold. We hope that we **are able to** go tomorrow.

Exercise 29.7

1. (see) The doctor **may be able to see** you later this afternoon.
2. (finish) If he works very hard, Paulo **may** (*or* **might** *or* **will**) **finish** the project before the deadline.
3. (complete) He **must** (*or* **has to**) **complete** it on time if he wants to get paid.
4. (visit) You **should** (*or* **ought to**) **visit** your grandmother because she misses you.
5. (run) When Oswaldo was younger, he **could run** very fast.
6. (love) Felix bought his girlfriend a beautiful engagement ring; he **must love** her very much.
7. (drink) Her parents **used to drink** heavily, but they have stopped entirely since joining Alcoholics Anonymous.
8. (collect) You **were supposed to collect** the children at daycare; how could you have forgotten them?
9. (help) It **might** (*or* **may** *or* **should**) **help** you remember to pick them up if you tie this string around your finger.
10. (come, not) Wally is in the shower, so he **can't come** to the phone.

Exercise 29.8

1. I wonder when the boat will arrive. It **was supposed to** be here an hour ago.
2. When we were in high school, my friends and I **would** do anything that sounded like fun.
3. If you have a food processor, you **can** prepare this salad in a few minutes.
4. What did you say? **Will/would** you please repeat it?
5. We **ought to/should** fill up the gas tank or we **may/will/might** run out of fuel.
6. The mayor is not in her office; she **may/might/must** be at a meeting.
7. Their whole house is decorated in red; they **must** really love the colour!
8. After you thaw the chicken, you **should/ought to** cook it right away.
9. Our instructor **used to** give us quizzes every day, but now he gives only three a semester.
10. **Will** you **be able to** come to our party? *Or:* **Are** you **able to** come to our party?

Exercise 29.9

I happened to meet my friend Selva yesterday, and we decided that we **ought to/should** get together soon. We **used to** see each other every day at school, but we haven't **been able to** visit as often since we graduated and started to work. "I'**ll** call you tonight," Selva said as she hurried on her way.

Selva called as she had said she **would**. We planned to go to a show the following evening. We both decided we **must** see the new Keanu Reeves film.

Were we ever disappointed! The show was so boring that I **could** hardly keep my eyes open. "Keanu **may/might** be cute," I said, "but no one **would/could** accuse him of being a good actor." Selva and I left halfway through the film, and we went to a restaurant where we **could/were able to** catch up on each other's news.

Answers for Chapter 30: Solving Plural Problems (pages 351 to 366)

Exercise 30.1

2. Your little **girls love their** new **toys**.
3. **Students learn** to take **tests**.
4. Good **doctors listen** to **their patients**.
5. The **taxis** crashed into the **houses**.
6. The **boys visit their girlfriends** every night.
7. These **rooms are** very large.
8. Angry **dogs are** dangerous **animals**.
9. Would **they** like **new cars**?
10. **Our stores have** the **items** you need.

See Chapter 13, Mastering Subject–Verb Agreement, if you missed any of the verb shifts (e.g., is/are, has/have). See Chapter 14, Keeping Your Tenses Consistent, if you missed any of the pronoun shifts (e.g., her/their, this/these).

Exercise 30.2

2. yourselves
3. categories
4. woman
5. sheep
6. feet
7. eyelash
8. phenomena
9. themselves
10. photos
11. pianos
12. tomato
13. criterion
14. monarchs
15. theses
16. thieves
17. husbands
18. tooth
19. heroes
20. valleys

Exercise 30.3

1. cigarettes, matches
2. mushrooms, berries
3. trees, leaves
4. courses, quizzes
5. libraries, wolves
6. cities, communities
7. inquiries, replies
8. knives, forks
9. nineties, attorneys
10. activities, studies

Exercise 30.4

	NC	NC	NC
1.	milk	sugar	coffee

	NC	C
2.	advice	problems

	NC	NC
3.	knowledge	math

	NC	C
4.	beef	dinner

	C	NC
5.	computers	equipment

	NC	C
6.	soil	vegetables

	C	NC
7.	vitamins	health

Exercise 30.5
1. money, luck
2. luggage, suitcases
3. effort, works
4. advice, homework
5. change, pennies

6. light, lights
7. times, time
8. garbage, work
9. history, music
10. lightning, golf

Exercise 30.6
1. Robert is going bald and wants to know where he can get **information** on **hair** replacement.
2. correct
3. You can have **fun** in sports, but the **enjoyment disappears** if you play too much **hockey** or **football**.
4. correct
5. The **rich** get richer, and the **poor** get poorer.
6. Benicio lives on a beautiful ranch with a large herd of **cattle**.
7. All of my relatives had **advice** for me when I came to Canada.
8. We continue to work in **sunshine** and in darkness; in fact, neither rain nor snow nor sleet nor lightning nor wind can interfere with our determination to get the **work** done.
9. We didn't hear much **laughter** coming from the back of the van as we drove through the rush-hour **traffic**.
10. Why don't you change your dirty **clothing**?

Exercise 30.7
    Canadians who enjoy winter are strange people. With their noses red and their fingers frozen, they actually take pleasure in shovelling the huge **mounds** of snow in **their driveways**. **They don't** mind when **their water pipes freeze** or **their cars don't** start. With *** **smiles** on **their faces, they bundle** up in thermal underwear, flannel **shirts, sweaters, down jackets, scarves,** boots, and woolen **toques**. Then **these peculiar creatures go** out into the bitter cold and howling wind to engage in *** **activities** that **leave** *** normal **people** completely baffled. **They look** for **rinks,** or **trails,** or **hills** on which to skate or ski. While *** sensible **people stay** indoors, **huddle** close to the stove, and **warm themselves** with *** hot **drinks,** the winter-loving **Canadians are** outside behaving like *** **children** with new **toys**. Should **they** be admired or pitied?

Exercise 30.8
1. I will read _____ reports. (four, several, ~~much~~, ~~a great deal of~~, some, few, a lot of, too many, ~~every~~, most, ~~a little~~)
2. I will study _____ information. (~~three~~, ~~each~~, much, a lot of, ~~several~~, a great deal of, plenty of, ~~a few~~, a little, hardly any)
3. Shakira owns _____ beautiful dresses. (~~too much~~, hardly any, eleven, a few, ~~a great deal of~~, no, plenty of, some, ~~every~~)
4. Shakira owns _____ beautiful clothing. (~~a few~~, ~~three~~, ~~one~~, some, ~~several~~, ~~a number of~~, much, a lot of, lots of, ~~a couple of~~)

Exercise 30.9
1. **A little** extra money is good to have.
2. Several of the **restaurants** are hiring waiters.
3. Roberto has **few** friends here in Canada, so he feels very homesick.
4. **Most** of the **students** found the course very boring. Only two or three people found it interesting.
5. After Tom Hanks' plane crashed in the movie *Cast Away*, he had **little** chance of being rescued.

6. My best friend has **several** good-looking brothers, so I like to spend as **much** time at her house as I can.
7. **Every** one of her **brothers** is tall, dark, handsome, and smart.
8. I like my coffee sweet, so I put **a great deal** of **sugar** in it; sometimes I also put **a little** cream in it.
9. It takes **plenty of** practice to learn how to ice skate.
10. **Both** of us got home from the game quickly because there was **hardly any** traffic.

Answers for Chapter 31: Using Articles Accurately (pages 367 to 384)

Exercise 31.1

It was **a** dark day when I walked into **an** old dilapidated house. There I met **a** peculiar old man. He was wearing **a** yellow shirt and **a** frayed pair of overalls. He was holding **a** sword, and **an** evil-looking pistol was stuffed into his pocket. "You look like **a** brave young fellow," he said. "Would you like to see **an** impressive collection of stuffed animals upstairs?" My heart was pounding as I politely declined his offer and made **a** hasty retreat.

Exercise 31.2

1. a regular transfer, (no article) information, a secret agent
2. A child, (no article) parents
3. a last drink, a half bottle
4. a cummerbund, an article, a tuxedo
5. As a rule, a rich person
6. an hour and a half, a counsellor
7. Twice a year, an adventure, a friend
8. A baby, (no article) milk
9. a few items, a favour
10. a headache

Exercise 31.3

When you move to **a** new city, you have to think about your housing needs. If you are going to be there for only **a** short time, you can rent **a** furnished apartment. **The** apartment should be in **a** convenient location. Perhaps you should locate yourself in **the** downtown area near public transportation. **The** furnished apartment you rent needs to have **a** decent kitchen. **The** kitchen should have **a** working stove and refrigerator. **The** place where you live is **an** important factor in your adjustment to your new city.

Exercise 31.4

1. **The** elderly deserve **the** support of society.
2. **(No article)** Lightning can be very dangerous, so people should take cover when **(no article)** electrical storms occur.
3. **Do** we know who invented **the** wheel?
4. **The** Internet will play an increasingly large role in our lives.
5. **The** elephant and **the** whale are both huge animals that give birth to **(no article)** live babies; in other words, they are **(no article)** mammals.
6. I like to play games on **(no article)** computers.
7. **(No article)** Life is very interesting, and **the** life of Thomson Highway has been especially interesting.
8. **(No article)** College students need to spend **(no article)** time studying if they want to be successful.
9. My computer crashed and that is **the** reason I didn't finish **the** assignment.
10. Thank you for **the** bananas; I love to eat **(no article)** fruit.

Exercise 31.5

1. I want to find **an** interesting book to read on **the** next flight, but **the** book that Harvey gave me looks quite dull.
2. **The** phase of **the** moon is one of **the** causes of ocean tides.

3. I bought **a** new CD online yesterday, and **the** CD should be here by tomorrow.
4. What is **the** name of **the** student you were talking to this morning? He is **the** first person I talked to in class, and I would like to know his name.
5. Though I had never seen her before, I spoke to **a** beautiful young woman in **the** supermarket this morning; she is one of **the** loveliest human beings I have ever seen.
6. **The** kind of vacation I enjoy most is **a** long train ride.
7. I don't need **a** special destination when I board **the/a** train; for me **the** important thing is **the** journey.
8. Today it is not difficult for **a** woman to succeed as **a** lawyer; 50 years ago, however, **a** woman who entered law school faced many obstacles.
9. Thinking it would give him an image as **a** super salesperson, Tony longed for **a** big, fancy car. To tell **the** truth, **the** small, plain car his company provided was **a** big disappointment to him.
10. In many parts of Canada, **a** college student who begins school in **the** last part of August finishes **the** school year in April.

Exercise 31.6
1. I like to study **(no article)** history; I have learned that **the** history of Bosnia is tragic.
2. Tom Wolfe always wears **(no article)** spats; **the** spats he wears are white leather coverings for his shoes.
3. Everyone has **(no article)** problems in **(no article)** life. **The** problems may be big or small, but everyone must cope with them.
4. **(No article)** Venison is **(no article)** meat that comes from **(no article)** deer. **The** venison we ate last night was delicious.
5. Some of **the** most important products that Canada buys from India are **(no article)** tea, **(no article)** cotton, and **(no article)** rice.
6. **(No article)** Milk is my baby's favourite drink, but she often spills **the** milk that I put in her cup.
7. **(No article)** Kindness is an attractive quality in people, and **the** kindness of that woman is known to all of us.
8. **(No article)** Jewellery is a popular gift; my boyfriend loved **the** jewellery that I gave him.
9. Paula is studying **(no article)** architecture in university, and she is going to Los Angeles to look at **the** architecture of Frank Gehry.
10. **(No article)** Boots are a necessary item of winter clothing in Canada, but **the** boots I bought last year were not very warm.

Exercise 31.7
1. **(No article)** Earthquakes sometimes happen in **(no article)** British Columbia, but they almost never occur in **the** prairie provinces, **(no article)** central Canada, **(no article)** Quebec, or **the** Maritimes.
2. Many of **the** geographical names in Canada are derived from **the/no article** languages of Aboriginal peoples who lived here for thousands of **(no article)** years before **the** first European settlers arrived.
3. For example, **(no article)** Manitoulin Island, in **(no article)** Lake Huron, got its name from the Algonkian word *Manitou*, which means "spirit."
4. **The** Queen Charlotte Islands (also known as Haida Gwaii) off **the** British Columbia coast consist of about 150 islands, the largest of which are **(no article)** Graham Island and **(no article)** Moresby Island.
5. **(No article)** Saskatchewan, **the** province of Ontario, **the** Magnetawan River, **(no article)** Lake Okanagan, and even **the** name "Canada" itself are all examples of **the** influence of native people's languages on Canada's place names.

6. I enjoyed **the** speech by Ms. Gonzalez last night. She spoke about **(no article)** life in **(no article)** Peru.

7. **The** Mojave Desert is in **the** state of California, not too far from **the** Sierra Nevada Mountains.

8. We had a wonderful holiday in **the** Dominican Republic on our way back from **(no article)** South America.

9. **The** St. Lawrence River forms **the** boundary between **(no article)** Ontario in **(no article)** Canada and **(no article)** New York in **the** United States.

10. **The** Bering Strait is between **the** state of Alaska and **the** former U.S.S.R, now known as **(no article)** Russia.

Exercise 31.8

You can tell all you need to know about **a** person from **the** shoes he or she wears. Our economics teacher, for example, wears **(no article)** worn-out, old brown leather loafers. These shoes tell us that he doesn't care about **(no article)** appearances, that he likes to save **(no article)** money, and that he enjoys **(no article)** comfort more than **(no article)** style. On the other hand, our computer teacher is **a** fashionably dressed woman who wears **a** different pair of shoes almost every day. My favourites are her black patent leather pumps with gold buckles on **the** toes. Such **a** stylish selection of **(no article)** shoes tells me that she is **a** fashion-conscious person who cares what **(no article)** people think of her appearance. She appreciates quality and is willing to spend money to buy it. If my theory about **the** relationship between **(no article)** character and footwear is valid, I would be interested in **an** analysis of my English professor, who wears **(no article)** black army boots for two days, **(no article)** white running shoes **the** next day, then **a** pair of cowboy boots, and ends the week with **a** pair of platform disco shoes.

Exercise 31.9

Ramon was searching **the** supermarket shelves for **a** box of detergent when he noticed sugar spilling from **a** broken bag in his shopping cart. He put **the** broken bag of sugar back on **the** shelf and put **a** new bag in **the** cart. Then, as he went up and down the aisles of **the** supermarket, he added coffee, orange juice, ~~the~~ **a** jar of jam, and ~~a~~ fruit to his cart. After selecting **a** bunch of grapes and **a** basket of peaches, Ramon went to **the** vegetable counter where he picked up broccoli, beans, carrots, and **a** kilogram of tomatoes. Finally, he added **a** package of cookies and made his way to a cash register. Only after he had paid for his purchases and left **the** store did he realize that he had forgotten ~~a~~ **(no article or the)** detergent.

Exercise 31.10

~~The~~ goldfish make ~~the~~ terrific pets. I bought three goldfish at **a** local pet store for five dollars, a price that wouldn't even buy **a** collar for **a** dog. Goldfish are also easy to care for. I change **the** water in their bowl once ~~the~~ **a** week, throw ~~the~~ **a** pinch of food in **the** bowl twice ~~the~~ **a** day, and they seem happy and healthy. Furthermore, goldfish are very interesting to watch. I can spend ~~an~~ hours watching them cruise around their little world, occasionally nuzzling or fighting each other. The goldfish may not bark at intruders or rub against my leg when I come home, but for me they are as close to ~~the~~ perfect as pets can get.

Answers for Chapter 32: Practising with Prepositions (pages 385 to 397)

Sometimes more than one preposition can be used in the context of a sentence. The answers we have provided are those that most native speakers would supply in the context; the alternatives given in parentheses are also common and correct responses. Other answers may also be correct; if your answers differ from ours, check with your instructor.

Exercise 32.1
1. by
2. in, before
3. Since, during (in)
4. from, in
5. in, at, on

Exercise 32.2
1. on, in
2. in, at
3. In (At), between
4. beside, with (among)
5. in, within

Exercise 32.3
1. by (past)
2. down, toward (to)
3. through, around
4. out of, from
5. up, into, through

Exercise 32.4
1. of, with
2. with, from
3. of, from
4. about, with
5. from, without

Exercise 32.5
1. at, around
2. After, to (with)
3. until (before), of
4. in, at, of, in

Exercise 32.6
1. during (in), after
2. of, under (underneath, beneath), to, for
3. out of, into, up (down), by (past)

Exercise 32.7
1. for, at, in (at), in, on
2. behind (under), on, with, of, in
3. between, to, at, by (without)
4. from, in, to (until), at, at (by), of

Exercise 32.8

My friend Jamil goes **to** school **at** the King Edward campus **of** Vancouver Community College. **At** the same time, he works full-time **in** (or **at**) his family's grocery business. The store is **across** the street **from** the college, so Jamil doesn't have to travel very far **between** school and work. He has to leave school **at** (or **by**) 4:00 p.m. every day so that he can work **behind** (or **at**) the counter of the store selling goods **to** customers. **Since** September, Jamil has been studying computer and business courses at the college, and he puts a lot **of** effort **into** his school work. Because he works every night **until** midnight, he sometimes does his homework **during** (or **in**) quiet moments **in** (or **at**) the store. **Without** his hard work, Jamil's family couldn't keep the store going. Jamil is working **toward** two important goals: he is determined to succeed **at** (or **in**) his studies, and he is equally determined to help his family prosper.

Index